SHAKESPEARE AND THE FALL OF THE ROMAN REPUBLIC

SHAKESPEARE AND THE FALL OF THE ROMAN REPUBLIC

SELFHOOD, STOICISM AND CIVIL WAR

◆ ◆ ◆

PATRICK GRAY

EDINBURGH
University Press

Edinburgh University Press is one of the leading university presses in the UK. We publish academic books and journals in our selected subject areas across the humanities and social sciences, combining cutting-edge scholarship with high editorial and production values to produce academic works of lasting importance. For more information visit our website: edinburghuniversitypress.com

Edinburgh University Press Ltd
The Tun – Holyrood Road,
12(2f) Jackson's Entry,
Edinburgh EH8 8PJ

Typeset in 11/13 Adobe Sabon by
IDSUK (DataConnection) Ltd, and
printed and bound in Great Britain.

A CIP record for this book is available from the British Library

ISBN 978 1 4744 2745 6 (hardback)
ISBN 978 1 4744 2747 0 (webready PDF)
ISBN 978 1 4744 2748 7 (epub)

CONTENTS

For Elizabeth

Liebe heißt überhaupt das Bewußtsein meiner Einheit mit
einem anderen, so daß ich für mich nicht isoliert bin, sondern
mein Selbstbewußtsein nur als Aufgebung meines Fürsichseins
gewinne, und durch das Mich-Wissen als der Einheit meiner
mit dem anderen und dem anderen mit mir.

G. W. F. Hegel, *Grundlinien der Philosophie des Rechts*

ACKNOWLEDGEMENTS

I would like to thank my doctoral supervisors at Yale, Larry Manley and David Quint, as well as my postgraduate supervisor at Oxford, the late A. D. Nuttall, for their generosity, intellectual rigour and attention to detail. Their editorial feedback was invaluable. I would like to thank my professors at the University of North Carolina at Chapel Hill, Jessica Wolfe, Reid Barbour, Tom Stumpf, Bill Race and the late John Headley, for their kindness, erudition and inspiring example. I would also like to thank my colleagues past and present at Providence College, Deep Springs College, the United States Military Academy at West Point, and Durham University for their camaraderie and support.

This book is the product of many helpful conversations, some in print and some in person. I am grateful to Gordon Braden, Paul Cantor, Russell Hillier, James Kuzner and Leah Whittington for allowing me to read and respond to early drafts of their work on Shakespeare's Rome. I would also like to thank Ewan Fernie and Peter Holbrook for their insight and encouragement, as well as John Cox and Will Hamlin for their friendship, guidance and reassurance. I am especially grateful to Peter for his hospitality during my visit to Brisbane as an Early Career International Research Fellow at the Australian Research Council Centre of Excellence for the History of Emotions, 1100–1800.

An earlier version of an excerpt from Chapter 1 was published in *Shakespeare Jahrbuch*, and an earlier version of the conclusion to Part I in *Comparative Drama*. An abridged adaptation of part of the conclusion to Part II was published in French as a chapter in *Shakespeare au risque de la philosophie*, edited by Pascale Drouet and Philippe Grosos. I am grateful to Elizabeth Bradburn and the readers at *Comparative Drama*, as well as Sabine Schülting and the readers at *Shakespeare Jahrbuch*, for their invaluable feedback on these sections of the book, and to Pascale Drouet for double-checking my French. I would like to thank Michelle Houston, Adela Rauchova and Ersev Ersoy at Edinburgh University Press for their interest in the project, as well as Kevin Curran and the readers for the Press for their enthusiasm and advice.

Above all, I would like to thank my wife, Elizabeth Baldwin Gray, my parents, Patrick Hampton Gray and Hazel Hartsoe, my brother Oliver, my sister Hazel, my extended family, and my friends both here in England and overseas. Your love, confidence and good cheer have helped to sustain me.

CLASSICAL ABBREVIATIONS

Arist. *De an.*	Aristotle, *De anima*
Arist. *Eth. Nic.*	Aristotle, *Ethica Nicomachea*
Arist. *Mag. mor.*	Aristotle, *Magna moralia*
Arist. *Pol.*	Aristotle, *Politica*
August. *De civ. D.*	Augustine, *De civitate Dei*
Cic. *Amic.*	Cicero, *De amitica*
Cic. *De or.*	Cicero, *De oratore*
Cic. *Fin.*	Cicero, *De finibus*
Cic. *Nat. Deo.*	Cicero, *De natura deorum*
Cic. *Off.*	Cicero, *De officiis*
Cic. *Tusc.*	Cicero, *Tusculanae Disputationes*
Diog. Laert.	Diogenes Laertius
Hom. *Il.*	Homer, *Iliad*
Hor. *Epod.*	Horace, *Epodi*
Hor. *Od.*	Horace, *Odes*
Jer. *Adv. Iovinian.*	Jerome, *Adversus Iovinianum*
Jer. *De vir. ill.*	Jerome, *De viris illustribus*
Lact. *Div. Inst.*	Lactantius, *Divinae institutiones*
Luc.	Lucan
Ov. *Met.*	Ovid, *Metamorphoseon libri*
Pl. *Resp.*	Plato, *Respublica*
Plin. *Ep.*	Pliny, *Epistulae*
Plut. *Brut.*	Plutarch, *Brutus*
Plut. *Caes.*	Plutarch, *Caesar*
Plut. *Cat. Mi.*	Plutarch, *Cato Maior*
Plut. *De Stoic.*	Plutarch, *De Stoicorum repugnantiis*
Plut. *Numa*	Plutarch, *Numa*
Plut. *Pel.*	Plut. *Pelopidas*

Prop.	Propertius
Quint. *Inst.*	Quintilian, *Institutio oratoria*
Sen. *Clem.*	Seneca, *De clementia*
Sen. *Const.*	Seneca, *De constantia sapientis*
Sen. *Dial.*	Seneca, *Dialogi*
Sen. *Ep.*	Seneca, *Epistulae*
Sen. *Her. O.*	Seneca, *Hercules Oetaeus*
Sen. *Prov.*	Seneca, *De providentia*
Sen. *Q. Nat.*	Seneca, *Quaestiones naturales*
Sen. *Tranq.*	Seneca, *De tranquillitate animi*
Sext. Emp. *Math.*	Sextus Empiricus, *Adversus mathematicos*
Suet. *Iul.*	Suetonius, *Divus Iulius*
Tert. *De anim.*	Tertullian, *De testimonio animae*
Verg. *Aen.*	Virgil, *Aeneid*

SERIES EDITOR'S PREFACE

Picture Macbeth alone on stage, staring intently into empty space. 'Is this a dagger which I see before me?' he asks, grasping decisively at the air. On one hand, this is a quintessentially theatrical question. At once an object and a vector, the dagger describes the possibility of knowledge ('Is this a dagger') in specifically visual and spatial terms ('which I see before me'). At the same time, Macbeth is posing a quintessentially *philosophical* question, one that assumes knowledge to be both conditional and experiential, and that probes the relationship between certainty and perception as well as intention and action. It is from this shared ground of art and inquiry, of theater and theory, that this series advances its basic premise: *Shakespeare is philosophical*.

It seems like a simple enough claim. But what does it mean exactly, beyond the parameters of this specific moment in *Macbeth*? Does it mean that Shakespeare had something we could think of as his own philosophy? Does it mean that he was influenced by particular philosophical schools, texts and thinkers? Does it mean, conversely, that modern philosophers have been influenced by *him*, that Shakespeare's plays and poems have been, and continue to be, resources for philosophical thought and speculation?

The answer is yes all around. These are all useful ways of conceiving a philosophical Shakespeare and all point to lines of inquiry that this series welcomes. But Shakespeare is philosophical in a much more fundamental way as well. Shakespeare is philosophical because the plays and poems actively create new worlds of knowledge and new scenes of ethical encounter. They ask big questions, make bold arguments and develop new vocabularies in order to think what might otherwise be unthinkable.

Through both their scenarios and their imagery, the plays and poems engage the qualities of consciousness, the consequences of human action, the phenomenology of motive and attention, the conditions of personhood and the relationship among different orders of reality and experience. This is writing and dramaturgy, moreover, that consistently experiments with a broad range of conceptual crossings, between love and subjectivity, nature and politics, and temporality and form.

Edinburgh Critical Studies in Shakespeare and Philosophy takes seriously these speculative and world-making dimensions of Shakespeare's work. The series proceeds from a core conviction that art's capacity to think – to formulate, not just reflect, ideas – is what makes it urgent and valuable. Art matters because unlike other human activities it establishes its own frame of reference, reminding us that all acts of creation – biological, political, intellectual and amorous – are grounded in imagination. This is a far cry from business-as-usual in Shakespeare studies. Because historicism remains the methodological gold standard of the field, far more energy has been invested in exploring what Shakespeare once meant than in thinking rigorously about what Shakespeare continues to make possible. In response, Edinburgh Critical Studies in Shakespeare and Philosophy pushes back against the critical orthodoxies of historicism and cultural studies to clear a space for scholarship that confronts aspects of literature that can neither be reduced to nor adequately explained by particular historical contexts.

Shakespeare's creations are not just inheritances of a past culture, frozen artifacts whose original settings must be expertly reconstructed in order to be understood. The plays and poems are also living art, vital thought-worlds that struggle, across time, with foundational questions of metaphysics, ethics, politics and aesthetics. With this orientation in mind, Edinburgh Critical Studies in Shakespeare and Philosophy offers a series of scholarly monographs that will reinvigorate Shakespeare studies by opening new interdisciplinary conversations among scholars, artists and students.

Kevin Curran

INTRODUCTION: SHAKESPEARE AND THE VULNERABLE SELF

It would generally be a decisive refutation of a moral philosophy to show that moral agency on its own account of the matter could never be socially embodied; and it also follows that we have not yet fully understood the claims of any moral philosophy until we have spelled out what its social embodiment would be.

Alasdair MacIntyre, *After Virtue*[1]

The central claim of this study is that Shakespeare is deeply sceptical of neoclassical as well as classical glorification of the kind of personal autonomy Seneca describes as 'constancy'. Shakespeare sees this pursuit of individual invulnerability, not only as a defining feature of Roman culture, but also as the most fundamental cause of the fall of the Roman Republic. The tragic protagonists of his Roman plays strive to transcend the limits of their own physical bodies, as well as their susceptibility to passions such as pity, grief and fear, and instead come crashing back down to earth. The 'frailty' that they hope to escape proves instead an intransigent given of the human condition. Unsuccessful efforts to achieve what Hannah Arendt calls 'sovereignty' backfire politically, as well.[2] The untrammelled freedom from dependence on all others that Shakespeare's Romans idealise leaves no room for power-sharing between political rivals or for compromise across social classes, but instead leads them inexorably towards violence and, finally, civil war. As a thought-experiment, Shakespeare's Roman plays provide a prescient critique of the vision of the good that animates present-day political liberalism, the ethical ideal Quentin Skinner calls 'neo-Roman liberty'.[3]

For Peter Holbrook, 'Shakespeare's poetic personality is deeply wedded to one particular value: individual freedom.' 'More than any other pre-Romantic writer,' Holbrook argues, 'Shakespeare is committed to fundamentally modern values: freedom, individuality, self-realization, authenticity.'[4] For Ewan Fernie, as well, 'freedom' is 'a supreme Shakespearean value'. 'But what is freedom,' he asks, 'and what does it mean to invoke it as a surpassing value in Shakespeare?' 'Shakespearean drama doesn't give us a smug and sentimental liberalism.' Fernie sees an analogy between 'the politics of Shakespearean form' and 'the classic statement of liberalism', John Stuart Mill's treatise *On Liberty*, in which Mill speaks of 'a *necessary* tension between individual freedom and social flourishing'. 'The Shakespearean struggle for freedom foretells the great political passion of modernity, amounting to a serial and probing experiment in liberal democracy *avant la lettre*.'[5]

In his 'Idea for a Universal History', Kant introduces the counterintuitive claim that 'the cause of lawful order among men' is not any kind of fellow-feeling, but instead our 'antagonism', arising out of what he calls our 'unsocial sociability'. 'Man has an inclination to associate with others,' Kant observes. 'But he also has a strong propensity to isolate himself from others, because he finds in himself at the same time the unsocial characteristic of wishing to have everything go according to his own wish.' Each of us is 'propelled by vainglory, lust for power, and avarice' to achieve 'a rank among his fellows whom he cannot tolerate but from whom he cannot withdraw'. Such dissatisfaction might seem like a species of damnation. Yet, as Kant sees it, this incessant 'opposition' is salutary. 'Thanks be to Nature', he proclaims, 'for heartless competitive vanity, for the insatiable desire to possess and to rule!' 'Thus are taken the first true steps from barbarism to culture.' If human beings were not so competitive, Kant maintains, 'all talents would remain hidden, unborn in an Arcadian shepherd's life, with all its concord, contentment, and mutual affection'.[6]

Shakespeare's Roman plays very precisely contradict Kant's just-so story here of the development of civilization. As Fernie observes, 'Shakespeare is aware of how readily freedom degenerates into a violent free-for-all: a "universal wolf" that will devour everything, including itself.'[7] In his Roman plays, Shakespeare asks what kind of moral character is necessary in order for a republic or, as Fernie says, 'liberal democracy' to function. And Shakespeare's answer is that the Christian virtue of what he calls 'pity' is what binds civil society together, rather than the pagan virtue of what he calls 'ambition'. To explain Shakespeare's sense of what goes wrong in Rome, I draw here on St Augustine's concept of *libido dominandi*, a precursor of the 'insatiable desire to possess and to rule' that Kant defends as 'unsocial sociability' and that Nietzsche later heralds as 'the will to power'. In Shakespeare's Roman plays, as in St Augustine's *City of God*, this 'drive for dominance' proves what A. C. Bradley might identify as the 'tragic trait' of pagan Rome. Figures such as Caesar and Octavian refuse to rest content with anything less than total dominion, even at the cost of provoking civil war.

Fernie sees Shakespeare's plays as staging a struggle to align 'personal freedom' with 'social flourishing'. 'No-one is simply free, no-one simply his or her own.' Instead, 'there are tensions between subjective, familial, national, and larger political identifications as alternative spheres of freedom, and these are tensions which sometimes tear apart the lives of individuals, families, and nations.' How can such disparate interests be reconciled? For a philosophical analogue of this arbitration, Fernie turns to Hegel. Like Shakespeare, Hegel's 'aim', Fernie argues, is 'to marry personal freedom at its most realized and powerful with a more comprehensive and shareable politics of freedom'. The competition for dominance that Kant sees as the engine of civilisation is for Hegel a form of false consciousness, the so-called 'master–slave dialectic', leading to inequality through competitive coercion. 'Hegel's highest evocation of the life of freedom' is instead, as Fernie says, 'mutual recognition', enabling 'reciprocal flourishing'.[8] 'It is only with the release and liberation of the slave', Hegel writes, 'that the master also becomes fully free.' 'In this condition of universal freedom, in being reflected into myself, I am immediately reflected in the other person, and conversely, in relating myself to the other I am immediately related to myself.'[9]

As Francis Fukuyama helped to clarify in his account of 'the end of history', in the wake of the revolutions of 1989, as well as the dissolution of the Soviet Union, communism in effect passed away as what William James would call a 'live option'.[10] What we see now in its place, Patchen Markell suggests, is increasing interest among social and political theorists in Hegel's concept of 'recognition' (*Anerkennung*): 'a general shift away from a "politics of redistribution," focused on the satisfaction of interests and the distribution of material goods, and toward a "politics of recognition," focused on securing equal respect and esteem for the diverse identities borne by members of pluralistic societies.'[11] One of the first to articulate this change in perspective was Charles Taylor. In an essay, 'The Politics of Recognition', which Markell singles out as 'catalytic', Taylor describes reciprocal recognition as a 'vital human need'. 'A person or group of people can suffer real damage, real distortion, if the people or society around them mirror back to them a confining or demeaning or contemptible picture of themselves.'[12] As Fukuyama observes, 'modern identity politics' now 'revolves around demands for recognition of group identities'.[13]

Is this change necessarily for the better? Peter Holbrook finds it unsettling to see 'group rights trumping the individual ones classical liberals defended'. 'We are enjoined to become ever more guarded and careful about language, images, practices that might offend *groups*, a recent landmark example being the controversy over the Danish Mohammed cartoons, in which the reluctance of many to defend free speech showed how far the West had retreated from liberal values.'[14] In his critique of 'the politics of recognition', Markell argues that the 'pursuit of recognition' characteristic of identity politics 'comes to be bound up with a certain sort of *misrecognition*', 'not the misrecognition of *identity*', but 'an even more fundamental *ontological* misrecognition, a failure to acknowledge the nature and circumstances of our own activity'. As an illustration of this problem, Markell turns to Sophocles' *Antigone*, and what he describes as 'tragedy's critique of the pursuit of sovereignty through recognition'. For Markell, Greek tragedy does not represent 'the tension between oneself as an individual and oneself as belonging to a larger community', but instead a more complex, 'cross-cutting' tension between 'the acknowledgment of the openness and contingency of human interaction on the one hand, and the denial of that openness and contingency on the other hand through the pursuit of recognition – either of oneself *qua* individual or of oneself *qua* community member, or both'.[15]

To help explain the danger he sees latent in 'the pursuit of recognition', Markell distinguishes between 'recognition', as Taylor and others use the term, and what Stanley Cavell describes in contrast as 'acknowledgment'. 'The source of relations of subordination lies not in the failure to recognize the identity of the other, but in the failure to acknowledge one's own basic situation and circumstances.' That is to say, the primary problem with identity politics as it is usually pursued is not so much political resistance as it is the kind of identity that it presumes to exist and that it asks its adherents to demand each other recognise. It continues to invoke the 'sovereign self' that it ostensibly aims to displace. 'What's acknowledged in an act of acknowledgment is not one's own identity – at least, not as the politics of recognition conceives of identity: a coherent self-description that can serve as the ground of agency, guiding or determining what we are to do.' Instead, 'acknowledgment is directed at the basic conditions of one's own existence and activity, including, crucially, the *limits* of "identity" as a ground of action, limits which arise out of our constitutive vulnerability to the unpredictable reactions and responses of others.' Acknowledgment is, in brief, 'an avowal of one's own finitude'.[16]

For Markell, 'the fact of human freedom, which is the condition of possibility of effective agency, also limits our practical capabilities because it is not exclusively ours but is mirrored in others'.[17] Shakespeare's Romans are unwilling to acknowledge their participation in what Hannah Arendt calls 'plurality', however, because they are too desperate to be recognised as conforming to an ideal of absolute, unattainable individual 'freedom': what Arendt calls 'sovereignty'. As Arendt observes, 'sovereignty, the ideal of uncompromising self-sufficiency and mastership, is contradictory to the very condition of plurality. No man can be sovereign because not one man, but men, inhabit the earth.' 'Untouchable integrity' could only be achieved, if it were possible, through 'arbitrary domination of all others' or 'as in Stoicism, the exchange of the real world for an imaginary one where these others would simply not exist'.[18]

In *Julius Caesar* and *Antony and Cleopatra*, Shakespeare shows how Romans' characteristic drive for dominance can turn inwards, especially in defeat. Examples include Brutus' retreat into philosophy, modelled on contemporary Neostoicism, as well as Antony's escape to the more sensuous pleasures of Egypt. Antony's withdrawal into a world of wine, women and 'fancy' evokes a fading, medieval ethos of aristocratic licence, as well as the contemporary world of the theatre. The most iconic instance of such involution, however, is the practice Cleopatra calls 'the high Roman fashion': suicide. Shakespeare's Romans' futile efforts to be recognised as absolute masters of themselves prove equally self-destructive throughout, whether in the public or in the private sphere. In their unwillingness to acknowledge the profound vulnerability of the human condition, including especially what Arendt terms 'plurality', Shakespeare's Romans prefigure what Hegel calls the 'Unhappy Consciousness' of the modern individual, and which he associates with 'the Roman Empire, the seat of Stoic strength of mind', in which 'a man lives unto himself alone'.[19] The would-be solipsist is 'unhappy', Hegel explains, because he finds himself torn between a 'Stoic' sense of himself and himself alone as the source of meaning and experience and a refractory 'Sceptical' countercurrent of awareness that he remains subject, somehow, nonetheless, to forces and powers beyond his control.

The new individualism that emerged over the course of the Reformation, as well as the Renaissance, as Jacob Burckhardt suggests, and that came to the fore in the Enlightenment, epitomised by Kant, is deeply indebted to early modern Neostoicism such as that of Justus Lipsius, which itself is modelled on the thought of Seneca.[20] What Lipsius calls 'constancy', echoing Seneca, Kant appropriates, refines and exalts as 'autonomy'. Selfhood is identified with an immaterial faculty of the mind, independent of the body, the emotions or society at large. Its glory is precisely its 'freedom', understood as what Fernie calls 'self-sovereignty, self-possession'.[21] With Romanticism, this dissociation of the self from the world became even more pronounced. As Holbrook notes, 'The drive toward authenticity is not only a nineteenth-century or post-Romantic phenomenon. It has a classical and Renaissance dimension.'[22] Senecan Stoicism in particular, as Geoffrey Miles explains, carries with it an '"antinomian" implication that self-consistency is all that matters, and that each individual can define virtue itself'.[23] What was once understood as an objective moral order began to be seen instead as a subjective work of art, an opportunity for the expression of each individual will.

Classicist Christopher Gill describes the difference between classical and modern subjectivity in terms of a contrast between 'objective-participant' and 'subjective-individualist' concepts of personhood.[24] Charles Taylor calls the transition from one to the other the 'expressivist turn' and traces it back to the influence of Romanticism, a paradigm shift in the history of ethics which he sees as 'tremendously influential'. Shakespeare foreshadows this pervasive change in his Roman plays and calls it into question, anticipating later criticism of political liberalism. Shakespeare enjoys a critical distance from this now-typical perspective which we today can find it difficult to recapture. 'Expressive individuation has become one of the cornerstones of modern culture,' Taylor notes, 'so much so that we barely notice it, and we find it hard to accept that it is such a recent idea in human history and would have been incomprehensible in earlier times.'[25] As David Bentley Hart observes, 'We live in an age whose chief moral value has been determined, by overwhelming consensus, to be the absolute liberty of personal volition, the power of each of us to choose what he or she believes, wants, needs, or must possess.' The result is an unparalleled sense of licence, at once enticing and vertiginous. 'Each of us who is true to the times stands facing not God, or the gods, or the Good beyond beings, but an abyss, over which presides the empty, inviolable authority of the individual will, whose impulses and decisions are their own moral index.'[26]

In his Roman plays, Shakespeare represents this deracinated concept of selfhood as a dangerous mistake. As Stephen Greenblatt suggests, Shakespeare was 'fascinated by the idea of autonomy'. Nonetheless, he concludes, 'Shakespeare doubted that it was possible for even the most fiercely determined human being to live as if he were the author of himself.' 'Autonomy in the strict sense is not a state available for any sentient creature.' Even the supposed 'aesthetic autonomy' of a work of art, such as Cleopatra aims for in her suicide, turns out to be compromised.[27] In this sense, Shakespeare more closely resembles critics of Romanticism and modernity such as T. S. Eliot, Alasdair MacIntyre and Charles Taylor than he does the German and British Romantics who cemented his fame and who strive to claim him as one of their own.[28] Shakespeare does indeed capture the beginning of the cultural turn Isaiah Berlin describes as 'the apotheosis of the Romantic will'.[29] But he portrays this embrace of solipsism as tragically misguided, rather than as moral progress.[30] The self-absorbed, quintessentially modern form of self-consciousness Charles Taylor calls 'radical reflexivity' and that Eric Langley finds adumbrated in Shakespeare's representation of narcissism and suicide may be dazzling on stage, in the person of characters such as Richard II and Falstaff, as well as Cleopatra, but it is not in the end, all things considered, a perspective on life Shakespeare himself idealises or sees as advisable.[31]

Drawing on Shakespeare's *Coriolanus* as a recurring point of comparison, I argue that Shakespeare presents the fall of the Roman Republic, not as a by-product of economic, social or political dysfunction, but instead as a consequence first and foremost of patrician misconceptions about human nature. Violent oscillation between autocracy and civil war is not the disease itself but a symptom, as Shakespeare sees it, of a deeper malady, an a priori misunderstanding of human selfhood. Since Roman noblemen see absolute, unquestioned command as the *summum bonum*, they approach politics as a zero-sum game. Any concession is a loss; any form of dependency is a dangerous, intolerable weakness. In this Hobbesian war of all against all, they see only two ways to attain the *imperium* they seek: either objective rule over others or a retreat from public affairs altogether, in order to focus instead on subjective self-control over their own experience. Shakespeare sees both of these expressions of *libido dominandi* as doomed to tragic failure. Neither the Stoic *sapiens* nor the emperor can escape the essential vulnerability of the human condition. Instead, human beings should be understood as intrinsically interdependent and intersubjective.

In his sense of the constraints on selfhood, Shakespeare does not go as far as twentieth-century antihumanists such as Foucault, Althusser and Lacan. Instead, his emphasis on human interaction more closely resembles the *via media* of authors such as MacIntyre, Taylor and Habermas. The individual is neither a disembodied, disinterested wisp of pure agency, nor altogether flattened out and overwhelmed by impersonal forces such as 'discourse', 'ideology' or 'language'. Instead, each person should be understood as both grounded in a community and at the same time capable of transformative action within that network. Bakhtin's literary criticism of Dostoyevsky and Rabelais provides a point of comparison. The individual is neither entirely determined, like a cog in a machine, nor wholly autonomous, like a god, but instead both passive and active, like a partner in a conversation.

In order to explain Shakespeare's theory of selfhood, as well as how it differs from that of his Roman characters, I introduce the theological concept of 'passibility', meaning, susceptibility to being acted-upon, as the defining difference between the human and the divine. For Shakespeare, the Roman ideal of impassibility is unattainable, the prerogative of God alone. His perspective in this sense is closer to Christianity or to traditional Roman *pietas* than it is to contemporary Neostoicism. The individual is embedded from birth in a web of obligations and liabilities which can never be escaped altogether, even in death. Cicero's treatise *De officiis* ('On Duties') is the most influential classical articulation of this perspective, emphasizing our individual responsibility for each other. 'We are not born for ourselves alone,' Cicero insists. 'Our country claims for itself one part of our birth, and our friends another.'[32]

What exactly does our country claim from us, however, if anything? Would Shakespeare agree with Cicero that representative democracy, in the absence of a monarch, is the best form of government? In his influential study *Shakespeare and Republicanism*, Andrew Hadfield concedes it is 'unlikely' that Shakespeare was a 'convinced republican'. Nevertheless, republicanism 'set the political agenda in Shakespeare's England'; Shakespeare 'dealt with complex and troubling political – specifically, republican – issues, from the start of his career'. As examples of 'the sorts of issues which characterized political discussion in late sixteenth-century and early seventeen-century England', Hadfield provides a useful list: 'when one could resist a tyrant; whether hereditary monarchy was the best form of government; what were the effects of the rule of queens; who could and who should occupy political offices; how exactly the people at large should be represented by their rulers; and so on.'[33]

In their collection of essays, *Shakespeare and Early Modern Political Thought*, editors David Armitage, Conal Condren and Andrew Fitzmaurice, as well as contributors David Colclough and Eric Nelson, argue in sharp contrast to Hadfield that Shakespeare was surprisingly indifferent to such questions.[34] As the editors observe in their collective introduction, citing Hadfield, among others, 'Much of what has been written on Shakespeare and political thought has been devoted to the vexed issue of what kind of constitution he endorsed. While such questions are legitimate, there is an anachronistic element to the collective emphasis upon Shakespeare's constitutional loyalty.' Shakespeare, they argue, should be situated instead 'amid the fundamental political concerns of his contemporaries: that is, in the milieu of values rather than debates about constitutions'. 'What mattered was not any particular constitution but the patterns of conduct and value that should prevail.'[35]

As Eric Nelson explains, 'political thought in Shakespeare's Europe organized itself to a significant degree around the question of what constituted, in Cicero's words, "the best state of a commonwealth".' Nelson finds it understandable, therefore, that scholars have expected to find in Shakespeare's Roman plays, moving as they do from one form of government to another, an 'intervention' in this 'canonical early modern debate'. 'Surely Shakespeare must have had a view about the best constitution (either the best absolutely, or at least the best for Rome); surely his Roman works must show us a Rome that is virtuous when governed correctly, and corrupt when governed incorrectly? Yet the striking fact about the Roman plays is that this is not so.' Shakespeare is neither 'a nostalgic partisan of the Republic' nor 'a defender of the imperial *pax romana*'. Instead, Shakespeare offers 'a view of Roman history that dissolves the question of "the best state of a commonwealth"', since, Nelson maintains, 'he believes that the choice does not matter'.³⁶ The editors, as well, argue in their introduction that Shakespeare was 'cynical about politics', to the point that he refused 'to commit clearly to republican or monarchical government'. 'Pessimistic to an almost Augustinian extent about humanity generally', Shakespeare 'saw no difference in choosing one constitution over another'.³⁷

I would not go so far as Nelson et al. in this regard. As Maurice Samely and I have argued elsewhere, Shakespeare, like most of his contemporaries, was in favour of a mixed government, one which included a monarch. His sense of an ideal government is very close to the one Hegel describes in his *Elements of the Philosophy of Right*, in which popular participation in government is carefully limited. In fact, Samely and I go so far as to surmise that the parallel may not be coincidental; Hegel was an avid reader of Shakespeare's plays. His theorising about politics seems to be informed by Shakespeare's sense of a need for checks and balances on power, as well as Shakespeare's distrust of what Annabel Patterson calls 'the popular voice'.³⁸ Whatever Hegel's debt to Shakespeare may or may not be, however, Shakespeare himself, we propose, does have a considered and consistent view on what Nelson calls 'the best state of a commonwealth', one that is in keeping with a relatively 'pessimistic' view of human nature. As might be expected of an Englishman of his time, Shakespeare takes a compromise position, limited monarchy, in-between classical republicanism and the imperial rule of, as Cassius says, 'one only man' (1.2.156).

In this book, I turn to a different problem. Both Hadfield and Nelson, for all their differences, read Shakespeare's Roman plays as if he were a political theorist. The question they ask is, in effect, whether Shakespeare sees the Roman Republic or the Roman Empire as having been a better form of government. I want to look at Shakespeare's Roman plays, instead, as if Shakespeare were a historian. Why does Rome change from Republic to Empire? What in fact does Shakespeare think happened? How does he explain what I call here 'the fall of the Roman Republic'? Hadfield brings up this question more than once, although he leaves it unresolved; a question Shakespeare shares with his classical sources. As Hadfield points out, Polybius' *History*, for example, 'is really a lament for the loss of the Roman Republic'. 'The question that Polybius fails to ask, however, is why the Roman Republic decayed if it was such an ideal constitution.' Sallust, too, he notes, is 'studiously ambiguous' and 'deliberately avoids the question of causation so vital in charting the reasons for the decline of the republic'. 'He simply informs the reader that the overarching pride of the Romans and the war against Jugurtha happened at the same time as part of the same process, but does not say which came first.' Reading *Titus Andronicus*, Hadfield finds an analogous lack of resolution. Why does the 'body politic' become a 'bloody mess'? 'Exactly how this structural failure occurs – whether the institutions fail the people or the people the institutions – Shakespeare, like Sallust, does not say.'[39]

At the beginning of his account of the Catilinarian conspiracy, Sallust claims that ambition first entered the world with the Persians, Athenians and Spartans. These empires, he says, were the first 'to subdue cities and nations, and to make the lust for dominion [*libido dominandi*] a pretext for war, [and] to consider the greatest empire the greatest glory'.[40] Citing this passage, St Augustine in his *City of God* seizes on Sallust's concept of *libido dominandi* and recasts it as the defining feature of the Roman character; the quintessence of *Romanitas*.[41] This 'earthly city', he explains, 'was itself ruled by its violent, immoderate desire to rule' (*ipsa ei dominandi libido dominatur*).[42] More broadly speaking, *libido dominandi* distinguishes what St Augustine calls 'the City of Man', meaning not just Rome, but all secular civilisation, from what he calls 'the City of God', meaning the Christian community, which, although scattered now, in the end will be gathered together in the 'New Jerusalem' described in the Book of Revelation.

Elaborating on Sallust's history, St Augustine argues that Rome 'grew with amazing rapidity' on account of its 'desire for glory' and love of 'domination'. Eventually, this 'vice', however, led Rome into interminable civil wars.[43] As the Romans fought and conquered other nations, competition within Rome itself was at first kept in check by a desire to be praised for temperance, as well as service to the state, as in the case of Republican heroes such as Cincinnatus. Over time, however, the nobility began to turn on each other. As historian Ronald Syme points out, among the Roman aristocracy, even well before the fall of the Roman Republic, 'competition was fierce and incessant'. 'The political life of the Roman Republic was stamped and swayed, not by parties and programmes of a modern and parliamentary character, not by the ostensible opposition between Senate and People, *Optimates* and *Populares*, *nobiles* and *novi homines*, but by the strife for power, wealth, and glory. The contestants were the *nobiles* among themselves, as individuals or in groups, open in the elections and in the courts of law, or masked by secret intrigue.'[44] Eventually, inevitably, St Augustine explains, 'desire for dominance' was no longer kept in check by 'desire to preserve a reputation'. Internal rivalry spilled over into open violence and shameless self-seeking, with little effort made even to appear as if concerned for the greater good of the commonwealth. This change culminated in the reign of the Emperor Nero, whom St Augustine describes as 'the summit and, as it were, citadel of this vice'. But it began long before. 'History shows that there were many such.'[45]

For Cicero, the epicentre of the fall of the Republic is Julius Caesar, his contemporary. 'If there is any area in which it is impossible for many to be outstanding,' Cicero observes, 'there will generally be such competition there that it is extremely difficult to maintain "sacred fellowship". The rash behaviour of Gaius [Julius] Caesar has recently made that clear: he overturned all the laws of gods and men for the sake of the pre-eminence that he had imagined for himself in his mistaken fancy.' 'When you desire to surpass all others,' Cicero concludes, 'it is difficult to respect the fairness that is a special mark of justice.' 'Here you have a man who longed to be king of the Roman people and master of every nation; and he achieved it! If anyone says that such a greed is honourable, he is out of his mind; for he is approving the death of laws and liberty.'[46]

Writing *The City of God* not long after Alaric's Sack of Rome, St Augustine's most immediate and express aim is not history per se, but instead, by his analysis of the causes of Rome's rise and fall, to defend Christianity against the charge that it was somehow responsible for the ongoing collapse of the Roman Empire. 'Many escaped who now complain of this Christian era', he explains, 'and hold Christ responsible for the disasters which their city endured.'[47] In his *Discourses on Livy*, Machiavelli revives this ancient complaint:

> The ancient religion did not beatify men if they were not full of worldly glory, as were captains of armies and princes of republics. Our religion has glorified humble and contemplative more than active men. It has then placed the highest good in humility, abjectness, and contempt of things human; the other placed it in greatness of spirit, strength of body, and all other things capable of making men very strong.

'This mode of life', Machiavelli writes, 'seems to have rendered the world weak and given it in prey to criminal men, who can manage it securely, seeing that the collectivity of men, so as to go to paradise, think more of enduring their beatings than of avenging them.'[48]

In the Enlightenment, Edward Gibbon took up the same old pagan charge anew. By discouraging Romans' traditional valour and ruthlessness, Gibbon suggests, Christianity left them unable to resist the onslaught of Germanic tribes such as Alaric's Visigoths. In his *Decline and Fall of the Roman Empire*, as if recalling St Augustine's opponents, Gibbon cites 'the contempt and reproaches of the pagans', who, he imagines, 'very frequently asked, what must be the fate of the empire, attacked on every side by barbarians, if all mankind should adopt the pusillanimous sentiments of this new sect?' He concludes:

> As the happiness of a *future* life is the great object of religion, we may hear without surprise or scandal that the introduction, or at least the abuse, of Christianity had some influence on the decline and fall of the Roman empire. The clergy successfully preached

the doctrines of patience and pusillanimity; the active virtues of society were discouraged, and the last remains of military spirit were buried in the cloister.[49]

St Augustine anticipates such charges. The decline and fall of Rome should be traced back, he maintains, not to the emergence of Christianity, but instead to the ruthless *libido dominandi* that spurred on its internecine civil wars.

> How can our opponents have the effrontery, the audacity, the impudence, the imbecility (or rather the insanity) to refuse to blame their gods for these catastrophes, while they hold Christ responsible for these disasters of modern times? The brutal Civil Wars, more bitter, on the admission of their own authors, than any wars against foreign enemies – those Civil Wars which, in the general judgment, brought on the republic not merely calamity but utter destruction – broke out long before the coming of Christ.[50]

As St Augustine points out, when the Gauls and Goths did invade, they proved more merciful to the Romans, relatively speaking, than the Romans themselves had been to each other, during their infighting. 'What was the foulest and most horrible spectacle ever seen in Rome?' St Augustine asks. 'The invasion of the Gauls, long ago? The recent invasion of the Goths? Or the ferocity vented on those who were parts of their own body, by Marius, by Sulla, and by other men of renown, the leading lights of their factions?'[51] During the sack of Rome, Alaric, himself an Arian Christian, showed mercy to those who took sanctuary in Christian shrines; St Augustine argues that the Romans should be grateful. 'The barbarians spared them for Christ's sake, and now these Romans assail Christ's name.' 'They should give credit to this Christian era', instead, 'for the fact that these savage barbarians showed mercy beyond the custom of war'.[52]

For St Augustine, Christianity is the solution, not the problem. In his English history plays, Shakespeare shows himself keenly aware of the possibility of Christian hypocrisy. He understands, as well, the need for occasional moral compromise, especially during times of war.[53] Nor would St Augustine object; even at his most optimistic, he retains a lively sense of the fallenness of human nature. Taking into account, then, these important qualifications, Shakespeare, I believe, would agree with St Augustine's assessment of 'the City of Man'. At the heart of Rome's catastrophic but inevitable decline is the absence of Christianity. In this study, I look closely at two of Shakespeare's plays, *Julius Caesar* and *Antony and Cleopatra*. Taken together, they present his account of the fall of the Roman Republic. As a touchstone for Shakespeare's sense of Roman culture, I also turn repeatedly to Shakespeare's late play about early Rome, *Coriolanus*. As Russell Hillier suggests, 'the belligerent Martius is a synecdoche for Rome', 'the species for the genus', 'the Roman substance unmasked and in the raw'.[54] Like Cicero, as well as St Augustine, Shakespeare presents the pride that Coriolanus represents as the root cause of Rome's transition from Republic to Empire. In this vision of history, the difference between democracy and autocracy is not as important as the difference between paganism and Christianity. That said, however, forms of government are not irrelevant. In the Republic, the drive that Nietzsche calls 'the will to power' strives for outward, objective conquest. In the Empire, by contrast, it turns inwards, seeking consolation in subjective fantasy.

As Hillier notes, 'Both Menenius and Volumnia identify, rather than liken, Martius with the cornerstone of the Capitol. He is, in their view, hypostatized *Romanitas*.'[55] If Coriolanus is, in some sense, Rome incarnate, what is Shakespeare's sense of Rome's distinctive character? Stephen Greenblatt sees in Shakespeare's depiction of Coriolanus 'three dreams' of an elusive, finally unobtainable 'liberty to live after one's own law':

> There is a dream of physical autonomy, exemption from the mortal vulnerability of the flesh or at least from the fear this vulnerability instinctively arouses. There is a recurrent dream of social autonomy, independence from the dense network of friends, family, and alliances that tie the individual to a carefully ordered world. And there is a dream of mental autonomy, the ability to dwell in a separate psychic world, a heterocosm of one's own making.[56]

For Zvi Jagendorf, 'The emblem of this self-sufficiency is Coriolanus fighting alone in the enemy city with its gates shut behind him and his own army outside.'[57] In the end, however, Coriolanus, the would-be 'lonely dragon' (4.1.30), renounces his doomed *bellum unius contra omnes*. Confronted by his formidable mother, Volumnia, as well as his wife and child, he calls off the siege of Rome. 'Ladies,' he proclaims, 'all the swords / In Italy and her confederate arms / Could not have made this peace' (5.3.206–9).[58] It is as if Shakespeare, in this late Roman play, went back to Rome's early history for a change of tack: the restoration of the Republic, rather than its destruction. By going back in time, he gives his own version of Roman history a happy ending – although, to be fair, one not especially happy for Coriolanus himself.[59]

Although he seems for a time an implacable enemy of the common good, Coriolanus becomes in the end an unlikely, grudging martyr to its survival, like the early heroes of the Republic whom St Augustine, like Livy, praises for their self-sacrifice: Mucius Scaevola, Marcus Curtius and Marcus Atilius Regulus. 'Furius Camillus, who was condemned by those who envied him, notwithstanding that he had thrown off from the necks of his countrymen the yoke of their most bitter enemies, the Veientes, again delivered his ungrateful country from the Gauls.'[60] Seen in this light, as Leah Whittington suggests, Coriolanus is of a piece with other late plays such as *Cymbeline* and *The Tempest* which 'show Shakespeare seeking out new ways to explore the dramatic possibilities of estrangement and forgiveness'.[61] Coriolanus' incomplete rebellion against Rome stands in relation to the collapse of the Republic much as the tragicomedy of *The Winter's Tale* stands in relation to the utter, unrelieved tragedy of *Othello*. As Hillier observes, '*Coriolanus* stands apart from Shakespeare's other Roman plays in that pity and compassion overwhelm wrath and fury.'[62]

In *Coriolanus*, Shakespeare revisits and rewrites, in a figurative sense, the history of Rome's tragic decline into civil war. And, in so doing, he presents a compelling alternative to the characteristic Roman exaltation of 'constancy' over mutability, masculinity over femininity, and violence over 'pity' which he presents with such painful clarity in *Julius Caesar*. The senators praise his mother afterward as 'our patroness, the life of Rome' (5.5.1) and call for flowers to be strewn before her, as well as Coriolanus' wife, Virgilia. Coriolanus tells them, 'You deserve / To have a temple built to you' (5.3.206–7). Femininity, inconstancy, pity, tears, prayer, supplication: aspects of the human condition which Romans in other plays tend to despise and disavow, Shakespeare here rehabilitates and recasts as praiseworthy. The Republic cannot function without some measure of vulnerability to the claims of pity.

In *Julius Caesar* and *Antony and Cleopatra*, the characteristic Roman desire for *imperium* tends to retreat under pressure and become subjective. Shakespeare's Romans shift with surprising facility back and forth from conquering others into solipsistic shadow-boxing: an inward-looking struggle over self-perception. Brutus' Stoicism is an introverted, intellectual variation on Caesar's more obvious pursuit of autonomy and invulnerability.[63] Brutus speaks of his own emotional condition, 'the state of man', as 'like to a little kingdom' (2.2.67–8); in his efforts to control its 'insurrection' (2.2.68), 'poor Brutus, with himself at war' (1.2.46) even in silence or in the privacy of his own study can think of himself as if he, too, like Caesar, were a celebrated military commander, a world-bestriding 'Colossus' (1.2.135). Antony's tendency to escape into wine, women and a world of his own 'fancy' is not altogether different from Octavian's relentless focus on military campaigns. Each of these characters desperately wants to be master of his own domain; only for some of them, the world-historical winners, that domain is external, out in the world at large, whereas for others, the ostensible losers, that domain is internal, confined to a smaller, more manageable arena. 'Here is my space!' (1.1.35) Antony cries, embracing Cleopatra. 'Let Rome in Tiber melt, and the wide arch / Of the ranged empire fall!' (1.1.34–5)

The starting point for my sense of this difference between Republic and Empire in Shakespeare's Roman plays is Paul Cantor's seminal study, *Shakespeare's Rome*. Citing Aristotle, Cantor proposes that 'different regimes work to bring out different sides of human nature in their citizens'.[64] 'With our notion of representative government,' he explains, 'we think that rulers should reflect the values or opinions of those they rule; more generally, that a government should take its character from the society out of which it arises.' 'In the classical understanding of the *polis*,' however, 'the regime (*politeia*) has a formative role, and is itself the primary factor in shaping or giving character to the community it rules.' Applying this approach to the contrast between *Coriolanus* and *Antony and Cleopatra*, Cantor observes that 'the comparative rigidity of political hierarchy in the Empire works to redirect the energies of men from public to private life'.[65] Under the Empire, as historian Ronald Syme explains, once-proud *nobiles* 'lost power and wealth, display, dignity, and honour'. 'No more triumphs after war, no more roads, temples, and towns named after their honour and commemorating the glory of the great houses that were the Republic and Rome.'[66] 'The rewards of public life begin to look hollow,' Cantor suggests, 'whereas private life seems to offer new sources of satisfaction.' Antony therefore drifts away from the objective field of battle into a 'private and subjective world'. 'The Roman world portrayed in *Coriolanus* is one of hard, solid objects, palpable to the touch and thus unquestionably real. In *Antony and Cleopatra* this tangible world begins to dissolve into a realm of shadows that seem to hide the true reality.'[67]

In his more recent book *Shakespeare's Roman Trilogy*, Cantor argues that 'the buried theme of Shakespeare's Roman plays is the way that the dissolution of the Roman republican regime prepared the way for the rise of Christianity in the Roman Empire'.[68] Regarding Roman history, Cantor may well be right. Regarding Shakespeare's plays, however, I am not so sure. As a response to imperial subjugation, Hellenistic schools of thought such as Stoicism and Epicureanism were an important precursor of the more radical ethical revolution Christianity represents. Nevertheless, I would be hard-pressed to see this transition as Shakespeare's focus. Cantor misjudges here at times, as it seems to me, Shakespeare's aims in turning to Roman history, as well as Shakespeare's own distinctive sense of historical causation. As a result, our accounts of Shakespeare's Roman plays end up simultaneously entangled and opposed. For example, Cantor is at pains to emphasise the similarities between Stoicism, Epicureanism and Christianity.[69] I, by contrast, draw attention to their differences.

Like Marx, Cantor tends to represent ideology as a product of physical conditions. More specifically, Cantor argues that 'the corruption of the Roman Empire softened it up and made it possible for Christianity to sweep the ancient world'. And, again, he may be right. With time, Cantor maintains, 'Rome's great captains and even its ordinary people are corrupted by the wealth that flows into the city from conquered lands, and devotion to the common good gradually weakens until the city is ripped apart by private factions.'[70] It is a venerable vision of history, one that Cantor shares with Ibn Khaldun, as well as Livy and Montesquieu. Nevertheless, Shakespeare himself does not see cultural history as a product of impersonal economic change. Instead, like St Augustine, Shakespeare tends to represent what Marx would call the 'base' as a product of what he would call the 'superstructure'. Beliefs are the engine of history, not material resources. As George Bernard Shaw was wont to complain, Shakespeare is also more inclined, like Thomas Carlyle, to the 'great man theory of history'.[71] World-historical events in Shakespeare's plays are represented as the result of individual choices between moral paradigms, rather than those choices as themselves a response to such events. Antony, for instance, is not so much victim as author of his own ignominious demise. Cantor focuses on the differences between the Republic and the Empire.[72] I think Shakespeare, however, saw them as two sides of the same coin; two societies equally obsessed with command and control. The effort to secure individual 'liberty' takes on different guises, depending on what Stanislavski would describe as the 'given circumstances' of each character. But the underlying, tragically misguided goal remains the same.

Both Cantor and I agree with A. D. Nuttall that Shakespeare is attracted to Roman history as an occasion to work through ethical and political thought-experiments, evaluating various competing claims in light of a kind of evidence. As Nuttall writes, 'The cultural separateness of the Roman world, its independence of Christianity, makes it a perfect laboratory for free-ranging political hypothesis.'[73] Cantor for his part sees Shakespeare weighing up the relative merits of life in the Republic as opposed to the Empire. 'The Roman plays taken as a whole pose a Hegelian tragic choice between antithetical ways of life, each of which embodies a distinct and defensible vision of human excellence.'[74] Warren Cherniak comes to a similar conclusion about republicanism in the Roman plays, in keeping with a long tradition within Shakespeare studies:

> Shakespeare's habitual practice is to juxtapose differing perspectives on a character or event without privileging a single voice as clearly preferable. This habit of mind has been associated with the rhetorical tradition of arguing *in utramque partem*, speaking with equal eloquence on either side of a given question, or attributed to a Keatsian 'negative capability'.[75]

As Peter Holbrook observes, 'we are often told Shakespeare did not advance a particular view of life.' 'Emphasizing Shakespeare's intellectual openness can be overdone,' however, he believes, 'with the plays and poems ending up a bland, self-cancelling rendezvous of perspectives'.[76] Holbrook cites Richard Strier: Shakespeare is not 'the less Shakespeare' for 'having had beliefs that he expressed in his plays'. 'When Sidney said that the poet "nothing affirms,"'

Strier notes, 'he had in mind factual claims, not ethical and political ones. Only a peculiar version of post-Romantic poetics could lead to the view that the poet "nothing affirms" in general.'[77] As it happens, I tend to disagree with Strier as well as Holbrook regarding what it is, more precisely, that Shakespeare 'affirms'. To wit, I am much more sympathetic than they are to what Strier calls the 'Burkean' thesis that 'Shakespeare's social and political views were deeply conservative'.[78] Setting that contention to one side, however, I wholeheartedly agree with both Holbrook and Strier that Keats' claim about Shakespeare's '*Negative Capability*' is a misleading and counterproductive myth, needlessly disabling even the possibility of fruitful debate.[79]

In contrast to Cantor, as well as Chernaik, I propose here that Shakespeare uses Rome's transition from Republic to Empire as a case study to evaluate the personal and political implications of a proto-liberal ethos which prizes autonomy above relatedness and which was emerging in his own time as an alternative to Christianity, as well as the ethics of Aristotle and Cicero. Over the course of this thought-experiment, weighing the claims of this resurgent neo-Roman paradigm against his sense of human nature, as well as the evidence of history, Shakespeare comes to a conclusion: a society which adopts this individualistic ethos, whether it be as large as a nation or as small as a marriage, will inevitably oscillate between autocracy and civil war. The self-sufficiency that such a radical pursuit of liberty idealises and seeks in vain to secure precludes the power-sharing necessary for stable, peaceful coexistence. Hegel captures this dilemma in his account of the master–slave dialectic, which I am inclined to believe was in part inspired by his study of Shakespeare's Roman plays. 'The earliest writing of Hegel's we have', Ewan Fernie points out, 'is a free adaptation of Act Four, scene one from *Julius Caesar*, which the philosopher wrote as a fifteen-year-old schoolboy.'[80] As Cantor says of Nietzsche, 'sometimes it seems as if everyone studied *Julius Caesar* in high school'.[81]

Rome as Cantor sees it was undone, not only by its windfall of prosperity, once it defeated Carthage, but also by 'its encounter with alien ways of life in the lands the Republic conquered'. 'Adapting to the ways of life of the very peoples they defeated, the Romans came to embrace an ethos of defeat. That is the ultimate tragedy of the Roman Republic.'[82] All of Shakespeare's pagans, however, including his Greeks and Egyptians, as well as his Romans, chase different forms of radical autonomy that from a Christian perspective are impossible to attain, as well as undesirable even if they were. Roman and Egyptian alike are chasing variations on the same impossible dream. Shakespeare's Romans' problem, moreover, as Cantor himself stresses, elsewhere in the book, is by no means 'an ethos of defeat', but the exact opposite. Roman protagonists such as Coriolanus, Julius Caesar and Mark Antony are profoundly unwilling to make any kind of concession to each other, even at the price of deluding themselves, blundering into disaster and committing suicide. 'Shakespeare's Romans are extraordinarily competitive,' Cantor writes, 'just like Nietzsche's Greeks, to the point of striving to become gods, and they are destroyed in the process.'[83]

Alongside Cantor's account of Shakespeare's Rome, I am deeply indebted to Gordon Braden's study of Seneca's influence on drama in the sixteenth century, *Renaissance Tragedy and the Senecan Tradition*. Like St Augustine, Braden presents Seneca's one-time pupil, the Emperor Nero, as the acme of unchecked Roman *libido dominandi*.[84] Having achieved unparalleled authority, Nero became, as it were, baffled. Frustrated, tetchy and increasingly paranoid, he set up rigged artistic competitions, fake chariot races and show trials of imagined opponents, all to have someone, somehow to defeat. Until the rise of Nero's predecessor, Julius Caesar, opportunities for limited political power had been available to most male patricians through a traditional structure Braden calls 'Republican timocracy': 'a finely graded system of clearly specified *dignitates*, competitively achieved, of which the *cursus honorum* is the central, enduring form'. Under Augustus Caesar, however, the corruption of honours and enfeeblement of public offices which began under the influence of Julius Caesar became fixed and definitive. Augustus 'preserved much of the honorific paraphernalia and rhetoric of the Republic', but 'it could no longer mean what it used to mean'.[85]

Braden suggests that 'the politics of imperial terror' can be best understood as an ad hoc response to the dissolution of this traditional Republican structure for acquiring and validating a sense of personal power. Thus its 'bizarre air of improvisation and make-believe': having conquered Rome itself, as well as the better part of the rest of the world, Roman emperors such as Nero no longer knew how to express their will to power. With the collapse of the 'stylized rivalry' at the core of 'Republican timocracy', other aristocrats also found their will to power stymied; indeed, much more obviously so. Their response, Braden suggests, was to turn inwards. Stoicism projects disengagement, detachment, indifference. In fact, however, Braden argues, Stoicism can be better understood as 'the inner form of imperialism'. 'Imperial aggression and Stoic retreat are both informed by a drive to keep the self's boundaries under its own control.'[86] Cicero makes much the same point in *De officiis*. 'There have been many,' he observes, 'and there still are', who seek 'tranquility' by 'abandoning public business and fleeing to a life of leisure', including 'the noblest and foremost philosophers' as well as 'certain strict and serious men who could not endure the behavior of the populace or its leaders'. 'Their aim', 'common both to those who desire power and to such men of leisure', is 'the aim of kings: that needing nothing, and obeying no one, they might enjoy liberty, the mark of which is to live just as one pleases'.[87]

For Braden, Stoicism is what Freud might term a 'sublimation' of the drive that St Augustine calls *libido dominandi*, and that Braden himself more typically refers to by the Greek terms *thymos* or *thymoeides*: 'the ambitious, competitive part of the soul . . . living for victory and honour'. The idealised wise man may be dispassionate, but the actual, practising Stoic is in fact just as driven by ambition, just as much a slave to passion, as a power-mad emperor. '*Imperium* remains the common value, the desideratum for both sage and emperor.' Suicide in this context, the characteristic death of the 'noble Roman', is not a renunciation of worldly power, but instead a demonstration of its all-encompassing scope. 'Suicide is the natural fulfillment of the wise man's life, the point where his drive for control becomes totally and unsurpassably self-referential in a final triumph over the world outside.'[88]

Braden sees the resurgence of Stoicism in the Renaissance as in part an effect of a social 'dislocation' of the aristocracy in the early modern period, a loss of their former political independence which mirrors that of the Roman patriciate in the first century BC, during the transition from Republic to Empire. Stoicism 'serves the need of an honorific selfhood deprived of its referents'. In particular, 'the military function of the nobility as a class was on the way out'. 'Medieval aristocratic values' proved tenacious, however, 'even under changing social and political conditions'.[89] Braden draws particular attention to what Charles Trinkaus calls *autarkeia*, the ideal of 'psychic and moral self-sufficiency' which Petrarch first identified as a distinctive feature of classical thought.[90] For ancient Greek noblemen such as those described in Homeric epic, *autarkeia* ('self-sufficiency, independence') was political, defended by force of arms. Neostoicism allowed the early modern nobility to continue to lay claim to this ideal, if only in a more subjective sense, even as they lost their traditional martial capacity. It also opened up aristocratic modes of self-regard to poets, playwrights and scholars.[91]

In his emphasis on a broader 'Senecan tradition', Braden says relatively little about Shakespeare's Roman plays. In a later article, however, Wayne Rebhorn singles out Shakespeare's *Julius Caesar*.[92] In this tragedy, he argues, Shakespeare depicts 'the transformation of the English aristocracy between the reign of Henry VIII and the Civil War', a historical process Lawrence Stone describes in his classic study *The Crisis of the Aristocracy, 1558–1641*. Rebhorn argues that Shakespeare finds a historical analogue for this contemporary crisis in the fall of the Roman Republic, a collapse which, like Cicero, he sees as beginning with Julius Caesar. Admittedly, he says, '*Julius Caesar* is set well before the start of the Silver Age and the orgies of destruction associated with Tiberius, Caligula, and Nero.' 'Nevertheless', the tragedy presents 'a Renaissance vision of the imperial self whose drive for mastery during the chaos unleashed by the Civil War in Rome has been turned away from the vast expanse of the empire and inward towards the ruling class itself.'[93]

If *Julius Caesar* evokes the beginning of the decline of the Elizabethan aristocracy, *Antony and Cleopatra* shows its *terminus ad quem*, out on the horizon. David Quint proposes that 'Shakespeare's Roman plays' present 'a schematic treatment of a nobility losing its status before the pressure of new historical forces'. In *Coriolanus*, for example, 'the urban populace ... dictates new conditions to the patricians'. In *Antony and Cleopatra*, Shakespeare shows 'the demise of a feudal aristocratic order and its style of greatness'. The two lovers, Antony and Cleopatra, embody 'outmoded noble values and behaviors', receding before the advance of Octavian, the 'universal landlord' (3.13.72).[94] In his Longman edition of the play, Quint presents Antony and Cleopatra in more detail as representative of a 'magnificent individualism', doomed in their own time, as

well as Shakespeare's, by the 'double advent' of 'political absolutism' and 'Christianity'. With the rise of English Calvinism, as well
as a new urban bourgeoisie, 'the Renaissance culture of individual
aggrandisement' was giving way to 'a narrower, less aristocratic,
more mercenary, and more puritanical culture'. Octavian's Rome
represents the future, 'a new era of calculation and efficiency'.
Egypt, 'a realm of excess', 'older and culturally richer', represents
the past, 'the outmoded ethos of an old aristocracy', 'a world of
greatness that now seems to be a dream of the larger possibilities of
human experience'. This 'dream-world' will now become 'a province of homogenizing Rome'.[95]

What Rebhorn sees in *Julius Caesar*, Quint sees in seventeenth-
century tragedy more broadly considered, including French and
Spanish drama, as well as English plays such as those of Shakespeare.

> A defining strain of seventeenth-century tragedy – something larger
> than a subgenre – dramatizes the loss of a particular, high aristo-
> cratic identity and focuses the genre on the travails of a nobility
> newly imperiled and disempowered by the centralizing projects of
> a newly powerful monarchy.

Quint points out that the English 'crisis' Stone identifies is not without contemporary parallels on the Continent. 'Conflict between
king and noble vassal, between royal court and local grandee, provided a political issue and literary theme throughout the Middle
Ages.' By the seventeenth century, however, 'this conflict was, in
fact, nearing its end, decided in favor of the monarch'. The 'style of
noble independence and self-assertion' which Antony and Cleopatra represent had become 'the object of nostalgia'.[96] Stone's description of bellicose, independent English noblemen abandoning their
warlike ways for a new civility can be understood as an instance of
the larger phenomenon Norbert Elias calls 'the civilizing process'.
The warrior culture of aristocrats in feudal society was giving way
to *courtoisie*.

Stone and Elias provide pervasive and appealing paradigms
for present-day critics' understanding of the economic and political bases of early modern intellectual history, including literary
history. There is some question, however, whether they accurately
describe Shakespeare's understanding, as a kind of historian himself, of the Roman history that he presents in *Julius Caesar* and

Antony and Cleopatra. Consider, for instance, St Augustine's concept of a characteristic Roman *libido dominandi*. Every desire or *libido*, one might say, can be reimagined as a species of fear. The desire to dominate, in this case, is the obverse of a fear of being dominated, of being subject to a *dominus* or 'master', in the manner of a slave. This fear could be interpreted, then, as an effect of the rise of a centralised and increasingly overbearing political authority. Roman aristocrats start to crave power so desperately because they feel it slipping away. Once it has indeed dissipated, dissolved by political and economic forces beyond their command, they then try to retrieve it by withdrawing into the one arena still within their control, their own private, domestic and subjective experience, as apparent both in Brutus' Stoic silence and Antony's tendency to distract himself with romantic idylls in Egypt. Shakespeare's plays, however, do not present so neat an order of cause and effect. Antony's debauchery, wasting time and opportunity in Alexandria, does not occur solely after his defeat, as a kind of consolation, but also precedes and in fact causes his political decline. Brutus' withdrawal from public affairs does not begin with Caesar's rise, but instead could be said to help enable that ascent, by removing one of the traditional, competitive restraints on Caesar's populist demagoguery, a patrician counterweight rivalling in stature Caesar's previous opponent, Cato of Utica.

Writing on Shakespeare's early English histories, John Cox begins by acknowledging that these plays 'reproduce what we now recognize as the central processes of change in sixteenth-century English political life'. To speak of Shakespeare, however, he goes on, 'as if he had read Lawrence Stone' would be 'wilful anachronism'. Shakespeare, like most of his cohort, did not conceive of these processes in 'the conceptual terms of the modern social historian'.[97] Wayne Rebhorn makes much the same point in regard to Shakespeare's *Julius Caesar*. 'Like Stone,' he concedes, 'the play suggests that the aristocracy is undergoing a profound change that will eventuate in its ultimate loss as a class of any real power and influence, in its marginalization by increasingly absolutist monarchs.' Nonetheless, 'the analytical perspective offered by the play is not Stone's'. Stone 'emphasizes economics and social history', whereas Shakespeare 'presents the situation in moral terms'. 'Shakespeare's play is analytical, revealing the self-destruction, the suicide, to which an entire class is being impelled by its essential values and mode of self-definition.'[98]

For Shakespeare, subjective *libido dominandi* such as that apparent in Brutus' Stoicism is a displacement or refinement of the kind of objective *libido dominandi* more obviously manifest in Caesar's political ambition. Both Senecan withdrawal and Neronian aggression are expressions of the same core paradigm, a tragically flawed value-system which idealises absolute power. This exaltation of power creates what Rebhorn calls a 'zero-sum game'. Any increase in anyone else's capacity to dominate is seen as an increase in one's own vulnerability to being dominated. The rise of the other thus comes to seem intolerable; a threat to be countered with desperate, pre-emptive aggression, or else avoided by withdrawing from public life altogether. Rebhorn sees *Julius Caesar*, especially, as depicting 'a struggle among aristocrats – senators – aimed at preventing one of their number from transcending his place and destroying the system in which they all ruled as a class'.[99]

In his literary history of what he calls 'the dramaturgy of power', John Cox argues that English court politics in the 1590s gave rise to a 'contemporary shift in the sense of human self', characterised above all by an effort to secure 'social or political invulnerability':

> The scramble to win individual purposes and good advantages became increasingly frantic and cynical, eventually issuing in Essex's violent bid for power just after the turn of the century. Court striving was therefore increasingly risky, like contemporary voyages to the new world: one could win enormous benefits, but in the process one risked losses that were even more spectacular.[100]

Contemporary interest in Tacitus bespeaks a more pervasive sense of Elizabeth herself, at the end of her reign, as ever more capricious, ruthless and autocratic. 'Because the environment of the court was so insecure, it became increasingly receptive to strategies for achieving apparent invulnerability.' Cox draws attention to two such 'strategies' in particular as characteristic developments. Humanists as well as courtiers could pursue 'the new ideal of the invulnerable self' either through Machiavellian maneuvering, like that of the devil or personified 'Vice' of medieval drama, or else through a Senecan withdrawal into cultivated indifference. 'For humanist and courtier alike, social advancement was highly competitive, heavily dependent on favor at the top, and therefore risky

in the extreme.' Stoicism thus became newly 'attractive', as it once
had been for Seneca. 'The ancient Stoic ideal of *apatheia* had been
cultivated in a very similar atmosphere in imperial Rome – the
Rome of Livy, Suetonius, Seneca, and Tacitus.'[101]

Cox suggests that characters such as Caesar and Brutus may be
understood, not only as counterparts to English aristocrats, but
also as representing members of Shakespeare's own more immediate circle, London's humanist intelligentsia: disgruntled Neostoics
such as George Chapman, as well as rebels against Calvinism such
as Christopher Marlowe. 'Interest in the ideal of the invulnerable self became widespread among a new class . . . the privileged
minority whose literacy alone gave them considerable power and
widened their scope for literary self-perpetuation and display.'[102]
Geoffrey Miles observes that '"Stoicism" and "constancy" became
code words for a certain fashionable pose of cynical and affect-
less "cool."'[103] The characteristic striving for autonomy, even to
the point of antinomianism, which Harry Levin gives the name
'overreaching', and which Anthony Esler links to 'the aspiring
mind' of the Elizabethan 'younger generation', a variation on the
self-sufficient 'pose' of Neostoicism, can be seen as readily in the
literary careers of some of Shakespeare's fellow playwrights as
in the more martial exploits of swashbuckling noblemen such as
Raleigh, Sidney and Devereux.[104]

In his study of early modern English republicanism, *Open Subjects*, James Kuzner argues that early modern idealisation of invulnerability, a reaction to increasingly absolutist, centralised power,
is itself inevitably damaging to efforts to replace that autocracy
with healthy, functioning representative government. As Braden
explains, 'Stoicism is not finally a philosophy of political resistance. The essential Stoic strategy for dealing with a tyrant is not
interference but indifference.'[105] For Kuzner, atomistic *autarkeia*
is not a viable model for republican selfhood: neither Senecan
retreat into the self ('refusing to be moved by others' words')
nor Machiavellian striving to dominate the other, even if only,
as a courtier, through flattery and deceit ('occluding interiority
so as to manipulate others'). Instead, Kuzner turns to the kind
of 'open' political engagement Cicero proposes as an alternative.
'For Cicero,' Kuzner observes, 'as for many Renaissance figures,
shared vulnerability is central to community's existence.' 'As
Cicero understands them, republics both must make peace with,

and even recognize their dependence on, vulnerability of various kinds.'[106] Kuzner cites Cicero's *De amicitia* ('On Friendship'), written the same year as Caesar's assassination: 'Take away the bond of kindly feeling from the world, and no house or city can stand.'[107] Kuzner find Cicero's thought in this respect adumbrating that of Jürgen Habermas.[108]

Kuzner sees Shakespeare as profoundly sympathetic to Cicero's sense that 'the courage required of us to embrace vulnerable being' is 'the most crucial republican virtue'. 'Shakespeare', Kuzner argues, 'advocates an intersubjective openness which resembles that advocated in Cicero and Livy in the classical period and, more recently, in Habermas's later work.' In his Roman plays, especially, Shakespeare illustrates the inevitably tragic end of all attempts 'to withdraw into a well-bounded selfhood'. 'For Shakespeare, bounded selfhood is a pernicious fiction.' Cicero recognises that 'susceptibility – to change, decay, and transformation that one does not will – cannot be eliminated, whatever we might wish.' So, too, Shakespeare illustrates that 'selves are vulnerable in constitution, incapable, on their own, of fully mastering either the passions threatening to undo them from within or the violence threatening from without'.[109] Cox sees Shakespeare in much the same light. 'No other Elizabethan playwright is as sensitive and sympathetic to the vulnerability of even the most admirable of human beings, and none so insistently uses this vulnerability as a way of qualifying the claims of privilege.'[110]

In my analysis of Shakespeare's *Julius Caesar* and *Antony and Cleopatra*, I take up the concept that Cox and Kuzner introduce as 'vulnerability' and subsume it under its more formal, technical name of 'passibility'. When these authors refer variously to 'vulnerability', 'susceptibility' or 'weakness', what they are describing is, in more precise language, the theological concept of 'passibility', meaning 'susceptibility to being acted-upon'. To be passible is to be subject to external causation. To be impassible, by contrast, is to be invulnerable to any kind of action from without. The term itself, 'impassibility', as a description of a characteristic of the divine, is derived from Stoicism, which emphasises an analogous state, *apatheia*, as the sine qua non of the ideal human being, the *sapiens* or 'wise man'. Like most forms of classical philosophy, Stoicism tends to assume that anything divine or ideal is by definition impassible. In Kuzner's language, its selfhood is 'bounded', rather than 'open.' Within Stoicism, for example, the degree of *apatheia* that a philosopher attributes to the *sapiens* or ideal 'sage' is the best index of his place in a spectrum of Stoic thought, ranging from radical to moderate. So also, in speaking of deities, the degree of impassibility that a theologian attributes to God or the gods places him in a spectrum of possibilities ranging from the Unmoved Mover of Aristotle to the figure Jesus, whom Nietzsche often describes simply as 'the Crucified'. The degree to which impassibility is idealised is not only the chief criterion for distinguishing between rival schools of Stoicism, but also for distinguishing between rival concepts of the divine, especially the theology found in classical philosophy as opposed to that of Christianity.

What I aim to show in this study as a whole is that throughout *Julius Caesar* and *Antony and Cleopatra* Shakespeare's Romans strive to achieve what Kuzner calls 'bounded selfhood' and Cox describes as 'the new ideal of the invulnerable self'. That is to say, Shakespeare's Romans are distinguished above all by their persistent efforts to escape their own human passibility. This flight from vulnerability is what drives what St Augustine calls *libido dominandi*, both in its objective expression as absolutist political ambition and in its subjective expression as a retreat from reality itself. Since passibility cannot be escaped, the attempt to do so brings tragedy, however, both to individuals and to ancient Rome more generally, as a society. At the root of this problem, as Shakespeare sees it, is a maladaptive value-system. Like aristocratic contemporaries such as the Earl of Essex, as well as ambitious Neostoic humanists, Shakespeare's Romans idealise impassibility. Their ideal self is transcendent, invulnerable. As human beings, however, they would be better served by an ideal that instead embraces the most basic, inescapable facts of our human condition: embodiment, vulnerability, sympathy, dependence. In the symbolic language of the play, 'the northern star', 'the beast without a heart', needs to yield to 'flesh and blood'. In more abstract terms, the Neostoic ideal of 'constancy' needs to give way to the Christian paradox of 'strength made perfect in weakness' (2 Cor. 12:9). As Kuzner explains, 'The strongest social structures are held together by weakness.' 'To form the bonds of friendship – bonds that sustain community – means to give oneself over to susceptibility and to loss.'[111]

An underlying assumption of my argument is that the ideal self or 'ego ideal' of psychoanalytic theory is susceptible to cultural influence. Even Freud, who for the most part sees human behaviour as biologically determined, grants in his later work that the ego ideal reflects the idiosyncrasies of an individual's social context. The ego ideal represents an intersection of the distinctive, historically contingent value-systems of a society as a whole with the individual experience of a given member of that social group. In the first section of the first chapter, 'Brutus vs. Brutus', I briefly introduce the concept of the ego ideal as it appears in the work of Freud and Adler.[112] I then turn to the particular example of Shakespeare's Rome. The behaviour of Shakespeare's Roman characters, I propose, can be described in terms of the peculiar character of their ego ideals, fantasies of selfhood which, as Freud and Adler suggest, we can see represented most clearly in their concepts of the divine.

Such exemplary ideals can also appear in other forms, however. They can be human heroes, for instance, drawn from legends of antiquity.[113] The hypothetical *sapiens* of the Stoics is a good example, as well as his perceived incarnation in figures such as Socrates, Cato and Brutus' own ancestor, Lucius Junius Brutus. Less obviously, the ideal self can be expressed metaphorically as an animal, a star, a monster or even an inanimate object such as a statue or a sword. When Coriolanus asks for followers to accompany him in his drive against Aufidius and his Antiates, for example, the Roman soldiers cry in unison, 'O me alone! Make you a sword of me!' (1.6.76). Coriolanus himself 'outdares his senseless sword / And when it bows, stand'st up' (1.4.53–4). As Dostoyevsky writes in *The Adolescent*,

> A man cannot live without worshipping something; without worshipping he cannot bear the burden of himself. And that goes for every man. So that if a man rejects God, he will have to worship an idol that may be made of wood, gold, or ideas. Those that think they don't need God are really just idol worshippers.[114]

The aspirations that such symbols both express and shape are not always practicable, however, or even internally coherent. Brutus in particular is torn between two rival schools of thought. In keeping with the precepts of Epicureanism, Seneca advocates a complete withdrawal from politics, since such activity will inevitably impinge upon the *apathia* ('freedom from passion') of the true *sapiens*. Cicero, however, much to the contrary, insists on service to the state as a necessary component of virtue. 'Those who are equipped by nature to administer affairs', he maintains, 'must abandon any hesitation over winning office and engage in public life.'[115] In order to convince Brutus to abandon his initial retirement from public life in favour of this kind of more proactive political engagement, Shakespeare's Cassius makes a symbol of Brutus' ideal self, the statue of his ancestor, Lucius Junius Brutus, seem to come alive and exhort him personally to rejoin the political arena. As a statue, mute, immobile and imperturbable, this statue, as well as others in the play, aptly represents Seneca's ego ideal: the indifferent gods of Epicureanism. As it seems to come alive, however, communicating with Brutus in the form of a letter, urging him to take action, the statue comes to represent more closely instead the ego ideal of Ciceronian Stoicism: the illustrious forebear whom it depicts and whom Brutus decides in the end to imitate.

In the second section, '"A marble statue of a man"', I turn from internecine debates within classical philosophy to the later conflict in the Renaissance between Neostoicism and Christianity. In *Julius Caesar*, Shakespeare uses the history of ancient Rome as a testing-ground to evaluate the claims of contemporary Neostoicism, measuring them against the competing standard of Christianity. I stress that Shakespeare is responding primarily to early modern Neostoicism, rather than to classical Stoicism itself, partly to draw attention to the concept of 'constancy', a buzzword promulgated by Shakespeare's Neostoic contemporary, Justus Lipsius, and partly to forestall over-scrupulous questions of exact chronology. Strictly speaking, Seneca post-dates the fall of the Roman Republic by almost a century. Cicero's *De officiis* was written several months after Caesar's assassination, when Rome had already degenerated into open civil war. Shakespeare uses the tipping point of the transition from Republic to Empire as an opportunity to telescope both of these perspectives backwards in time. In Brutus' divided impulses, Shakespeare is able to illustrate both the patriotism of the Republican citizen and the despair of the Imperial subject.

In the first section of the second chapter, 'Power and Passibility', I introduce the theological concept of passibility in more detail as a useful tool for distinguishing between different ethical ideals, both in general and in Shakespeare's Roman plays in particular. Differences between these ideals, I propose, can be seen most clearly in competing concepts of the divine. In keeping with its admiration for absolute power, classical philosophy describes its deities as impassible, even impersonal: abstract forces such as 'Fate', 'the One' or 'the Form of the Good'. Christianity, by contrast, glorifies empathy and therefore describes its version of the divine, 'Christ crucified', as necessarily passible, as well as personal. God must be vulnerable, sentient, in order to feel compassion for the suffering of man. As objects of what Wayne Rebhorn calls 'emulation', a mixture of admiration, imitation and competition, these divine exempla affect day-to-day decision-making. Citing Rebhorn's concept of 'emulation', Coppélia Kahn represents this 'cultural practice' as a root cause of Shakespeare's Romans' characteristic cruelty. The tragedy of Shakespeare's Romans is not emulation itself, however, but the inhuman character of the ideal self which they choose to emulate: the unfeeling, invulnerable form of the divine Caesar describes metaphorically as 'Olympus' and 'the northern star'. This ideal leaves no room for the susceptibility to empathy, reciprocal respect and openness to compromise which Shakespeare, like Cicero, sees as integral to healthy human interdependence.[116]

In his history of personhood, *The Mirages of the Selfe* (*sic*), Timothy Reiss argues that the modern concept of the self, the Cartesian *ego cogito*, emerges in the early modern period, beginning with Petrarch, as a result of an effort to separate personhood from the most basic given of the human condition: the state of being 'embedded in and acted on by' what he calls 'circles' or 'spheres' of influence. Modern concepts of personhood tend to present relational factors such as social status, kinship, moral duties and religious beliefs as mere contingencies, accidents surrounding but not defining the self. In the pre-modern period, however, these various forms of what Reiss calls 'passibility' were understood as intrinsic to selfhood. The self is not autonomous, but embedded, existing in a state of reactivity. Reiss might easily sound therefore as if he were a fellow traveller with those, like Lacan or Althusser, who argue for what Ricœur calls 'the shattered subject'. For these antihumanists, individual agency is an illusion; the self is in fact altogether at the mercy of impersonal forces such as language or economics. Reiss insists, however, that the susceptibility to external influence he ascribes to the passible self is not the same as mere 'passivity'. 'None of this is to say that persons are wholly determined by context, that personal identities are socially, culturally, and ideologically fashioned as mere semes of an overarching discourse, meanings made by a symbolics of power. Webbed, made and making in multiple contexts, personhood still has real agency (of endlessly varied sorts).'[117] Reiss's metaphor, 'webbed', suggests the kinship between his 'circles' of influences and Taylor's conceit of a 'web of interlocution'. Reiss argues that the attempt to project modern concepts of the self as independent of such 'webs' or 'circles' back into the pre-modern past is anachronistic.

Charles Taylor, however, has a different agenda, as does Reiss's other key source, Alasdair MacIntyre. From their perspective, the pre-modern concept of what Reiss calls the 'passible' self is in fact more accurate, even today, than the isolated, incorporeal phantom Ricœur calls 'the Cartesian subject'. Modern ethics as they see it is led astray by efforts to imagine individuals as capable of radical autonomy, much less to represent that 'liberty' as the highest good. Reiss introduces similar misgivings about the application of 'universal' ethics such as those formulated by the United Nations to nations that may not share Western assumptions as to what it means to be a person. Kant's belief, for instance, in the possibility of disinterested action seems to him especially dubious.

Shakespeare, I propose, sees his Romans much as MacIntyre, Taylor, Ricœur and Reiss see us moderns. He sees his Romans' characteristic Neostoicism, moreover, much as these philosophers see Kantian ethics. The problem is not that individual agency, the defining characteristic of the so-called 'bourgeois subject', is entirely illusory. The problem is rather that its scope is more limited than characters such as Caesar, Antony and Coriolanus would like to believe. Like Icarus, they try to fly too close to the sun, and as a result they plummet back down to their death. Kantian disinterestedness, for example, such as Brutus seems to strive for is not so much good or bad as flat-out impossible. The ideal of the unattached, unencumbered self is not only unattainable, but dangerous to pursue; 'liberty' in the 'neo-Roman' sense proves to be a tragically misleading aim.

In the second section of the second chapter, '"Constancy" and "Frailty"', I look more specifically at feminist interpretations of *Julius Caesar* put forward in the 1980s and 1990s by Janet Adelman, Madelon Sprengnether, Cynthia Marshall, Gail Kern Paster and Coppélia Kahn. The characteristic Roman disdain for femininity that these authors attribute in their earlier work to men's

'pre-Oedipal' desires to detach themselves from their 'suffocating mothers' and establish themselves as masculine, and then in
their later work to the political pressures of patriarchy and male
rivalry, I see instead as an effect of a more fundamental Roman
discomfort with passibility. The two female characters in the play,
Portia and Calpurnia, can themselves be read, not only as individuals, but also as symbols of repressed aspects of Brutus and
Caesar. The women represent their husbands' underdeveloped
capacity for pity.

In the conclusion to my analysis of *Julius Caesar*, 'Shakespeare's
passion play', I explore the possibility that Shakespeare's depiction
of Julius Caesar is indebted to the representation of Augustus Caesar
in medieval English biblical drama. Shakespeare's Julius Caesar's
unabashed description of himself as 'Olympus' and 'the northern
star' strongly resembles Augustus Caesar's opening speech in the
Towneley cycle, as well the same character's opening speech in the
Chester cycle. Both of these speeches, moreover, are themselves
parodies of God's opening speech in each case, the great 'Ego sum'
with which each cycle opens. In further support of this suggestion,
I compare Shakespeare's version of the Caesar legend to that of
other, roughly contemporary authors such as Marc-Antoine Muret
and Sir William Alexander. These authors model their Caesar on
the example of Seneca's Hercules, borrowing repeatedly from his
Hercules furens and *Hercules Oetaeus*. That Shakespeare deviates
from this tradition, and that he also departs in various intriguing
details from his most immediate source, Plutarch's 'Life of Julius
Caesar', suggests that he had in mind a different precedent. Like
the traditional cycle-play 'Caesar', Shakespeare's, too, is a bloviat-
ing, ineffectual parody of Christ.

In my discussion of *Julius Caesar*, I focus on susceptibility to
emotions, especially 'pity', and a very literal, physical kind of passibility. In my analysis of *Antony and Cleopatra*, I turn, by contrast,
to a subtler form of vulnerability. Shakespeare, I argue, sees the
self as profoundly sensitive to moral judgement. Every individual
is perpetually, ineluctably embedded in overlapping matrices of
moral evaluation, judging and being judged in turn. I describe this
process of judgement as 'interpellation', modifying the sense that
it has for Althusser, in order to stress the fact that Shakespeare sees
the perceptions of others as a powerful force, not easily dismissed.
Despite the many different, formidable defence mechanisms that

each individual psyche can potentially bring to bear, other people are at times capable of altering our own self-perception. Denial, disavowal and retreat from 'nature' into an alternative world of 'fancy' allow some measure of escape. If other people are more powerful, however, or more numerous, exposure to their opinion can over time prove impossible to ignore. The most drastic example of this kind of exposure, in Shakespeare's Roman plays, is to be led in triumph as a captive through the streets of Rome, and this prospect represents therefore for characters such as Antony and Cleopatra, as well as Brutus, a kind of *summum malum*. Brutus insists that he will not, under any circumstances, 'go bound to Rome'. And, indeed, he does in the end kill himself, once his defeat is apparent. In the first section of the third chapter, 'Stoic Suicide as "Hobgoblin"', I compare Cleopatra to Brutus and propose that Cleopatra's death is in fact surprisingly consistent with Stoicism, despite her vividly passionate life.[118]

Shakespeare's interest in the Roman triumph is one expression, among others, of a more general fascination on his part with a paradox built into the very nature of honour itself. Characters who are concerned about honour pride themselves, above all, on their self-sufficiency. Their claim to honour, as they see it, is grounded in an autarchy akin to that of a medieval lord. They want to see themselves as masters of their own sphere of influence, including their bodies, their emotions and even their relations. They bristle at the thought of any kind of dependence on anything other than themselves, because that measure of fragility, however slight, would imply that they are somehow vulnerable, somehow less than ideal. Much literary criticism of *Antony and Cleopatra* focuses on the differences between the Egyptians and the Romans; in this respect, however, they are essentially akin. The same mindset can be seen in Shakespeare's ancient Greeks, as well, in *Troilus and Cressida* and *Timon of Athens*. Shakespeare's pagans, or at least, those of his pagans who belong to the upper class, such as Cleopatra, reflect the value-system of the contemporary English nobility, but exaggerated, or perhaps rendered clearer, by the absence of Christianity. The self is all; the other is unnecessary, irrelevant; or so they would like to believe.

What such characters discover, much to their chagrin, is that the other, even if despised, is indispensable. The paradox of honour, as Shakespeare sees it, is that the self needs the other in order to confirm its own self-sufficiency. That very need for the other, moreover, shows that their supposed self-sufficiency is delusional. As Paul Cantor observes, a psychological double bind lies at the heart of Coriolanus' character. 'He seeks honor but dislikes the requirement of having other men to honor him. Thinking he can stand alone on the basis of his honor, he finds instead that his pursuit of honor binds him more closely to the city.'[119] Hegel describes the same problem in more abstract terms in his description of the master–slave dialectic. 'Just where the master has effectively achieved lordship, he really finds that something has come about quite different from an independent consciousness. It is not an independent, but rather a dependent consciousness that he has achieved.'[120]

Coriolanus is able to scoff at the opinion of his fellow Romans, not because he is truly impervious to all opprobrium, but because he is so deeply bound to one person, his mother, that no one else's approval seems important in comparison. In *Antony and Cleopatra*, the two lovers cultivate in like manner what amounts to a *folie à deux*. Cleopatra finds one powerful man whom she can seduce, one pre-eminent enough, like Antony or Caesar, that she can take him as representative of the entire world. Antony in turn is able to tap into the legendary, limitless wealth of Egypt, as well as the glamour of having won, in Cleopatra, a singular prize, a latter-day Helen of Troy. While he is in her company, moreover, Antony is able to enjoy what for Roman would have been an unaccustomed degree of absolute rule. As long as he is with Cleopatra in Egypt, Antony no longer has to go through the motions of being merely one more Roman citizen; he does not have to push away the crown, like Caesar in *Julius Caesar*, or negotiate terms with two other triumvirs. Instead, he can unabashedly behave, even in public, as if he were a god: Osiris to Cleopatra's Isis.

In the second section of the third chapter, '"Fancy" vs. "Nature"', I show that such a compact of mutual admiration is not without its own attendant dangers. For it to work without fail, their *folie à deux* would require a sangfroid that Antony and Cleopatra do not possess, perhaps to their credit: a clearheaded self-awareness that its very terms tend to preclude. Antony would have to remember that he is not, in fact, the god that he can pretend to be, while he is at play in Alexandria; his power in the larger Roman world, unlike the obedience of Cleopatra's slaves, does not answer solely to his passing caprice. Caught up in an enchanting delusion, he comes to see himself as more autonomous than in the end he really is. Cleopatra for her part would have to be careful not to fall too deeply in love; she would have to be willing to move on from Antony, when he falls, just as she did from Caesar, to the next world-bestriding colossus, who in this case turns out to be the rather frosty, off-putting 'boy Caesar', Octavian. And, despite all Antony's fears to the contrary, she cannot. She is in the end too old and too enamoured of Antony in particular to be able to play politics with her affections as she perhaps might once have done, in her 'salad days'.

In order to explain Shakespeare's sense of human selfhood as susceptible to moral judgement, in the first part of the next chapter, '"Eye to eye opposed"', I introduce an explanation of what I take to be Shakespeare's understanding of the intersubjective relationship between self and other. Since at least the 1980s, Shakespeare studies has been decidedly historicist, at times even radically so, emphasising the contingency of aspects of the human subject such as sexuality or madness once thought susceptible to description in terms of universal, abiding and objective norms. Elements of personhood which psychologists might describe as a natural consequence of perennial features of human biology have instead been represented as primarily or even entirely dependent on the shifting contexts of contemporary culture. For a time, the influence of Althusser and Foucault became pervasive, even hegemonic. Relationships of power and subjection were held to produce 'ideology', which through literature, as well as other forms of 'discourse', 'interpellates' the individual and shapes him or her into a compliant 'subject'. Peter Holbrook, among others, laments this effect of what he calls 'the "Theory" explosion'. 'Theory's chastening lesson is that the autonomous self is a will-o'-the-wisp and that character is determined by imperious historical forces.'[121]

As Holbrook says, 'I do not recognize myself in the estranged world of the anti-humanists.'[122] Happily, however, as critics such as Nancy Selleck, Christopher Tilmouth and others have begun to suggest, Shakespeare's own understanding of intersubjectivity provides an appealing alternative.[123] In his representation of interpersonal interaction, Shakespeare complicates false dichotomies between supposedly overwhelming cultural forces such as 'discourse', impersonal, diffuse and vast in scope, and the beleaguered, supposedly powerless 'subject'. Other individuals intervene between culture and the subject, shaping and being shaped in turn, mediating the influence of any kind of Zeitgeist. The particularity of these others should not be elided, but instead recognised as introducing the granular specificity of smaller-scale, intersubjective networks within any larger and more sweeping construct such as Foucault's epistemes. As Tilmouth explains, 'Since 1990 several critics have developed the paradoxical claim that Renaissance selfhood was in some degree vested outside the individual, *imagined* as located in other minds.' What Katharine Maus describes as 'inwardness' has been 'reconceived as an experience situated on the boundary between the person and those to whom he relates, within the dialogic domain of intersubjectivity'.[124]

Shakespeare's interpretation of the relation between self and other is in part derived from Aristotle's theory of friendship. As he articulates that theory, however, he also introduces complications, anticipating in several respects one of the most prominent trends in twentieth-century philosophical anthropology. Like Shakespeare, authors such as Martin Buber, Mikhail Bakhtin, Paul Ricœur and Jürgen Habermas have come to emphasise relations between individuals as the ground of human personhood. The other is what Martin Buber calls a 'thou', a partner in a dialogue. This ceaseless, constitutive interaction, the 'I–thou' relationship, is the most fundamental given of the human condition. Nancy Selleck argues that this sense of selfhood as 'interpersonal', 'part of a reciprocally-constituted social field', 'underpins much of the language of selfhood in the sixteenth and early seventeenth centuries'. Other early modern authors such as John Donne, as well as Shakespeare, 'magnify or harp on' this 'sense of engagement with a *live* other': 'a live, concrete, agentive other that is also not alien but in dialogue with the self.' 'The Renaissance self entails other selves.'[125]

Departing from Aristotle, Shakespeare's first innovation is to expand ancient thought about the role of the other in self-knowledge beyond the confines of friendship between two individuals, so that it approximates instead the relationship between actor or playwright and audience. Shakespeare's second point of revision is to present the other much more explicitly as a necessary part of self-perception: integral, not optional. Shakespeare's third alteration, however, is by far the most interesting, and appears most clearly in *Antony and Cleopatra*. As Selleck says of the narrator in Shakespeare's sonnets, in *Antony and Cleopatra* the self finds itself imbricated in 'other frames of reference *that it cannot control*'.[126] The effect of the other upon the self is not something that the self can easily or entirely dismiss. We cannot help but be affected, in some measure, by what other people think of us. Given sufficient exposure to their perspective, their version of our selves, however troubling, begins to impinge upon our own. The risk of such forced alteration in his own self-image is the reason why Coriolanus refuses to go through the proper motions to become consul and why Brutus and Cleopatra are so horrified at the thought of being led in triumph. To be seen a certain way long enough and by enough people is to have one's self-image, howsoever unwillingly, brought into closer conformity with that collective assessment.

To explain Shakespeare's thought about this phenomenon, in the second section of the fourth chapter, '"I would not see't"', I invoke Althusser's well-known metaphor of interpellation or 'hailing', but apply it in a very different sense than Althusser himself. Althusser sees interpellation as a unilateral process with one kind of agent, an impersonal force that he calls 'ideology', and a different kind of subject, the individual, whom he presents as markedly passive, as if ideology were form, and the individual, matter. As Selleck observes, this putative 'passivity' of the subject is 'both crucial to Althusser's theory and one of its more problematic aspects'. 'In contrast to Bakhtinian theory, there is no sense here of the subject's participation in a process: "ideology" is not affected by its subjects.'[127] Like Bakhtin, Shakespeare sees interpellation instead as multilateral and reciprocal. People continually act upon each other's subjectivities, even without meaning to, so as to bring them into closer conformity with their own. Our diverse individual experiences of reality are not and indeed cannot be made entirely solipsistic; cannot be rendered self-contained, even by dint of great effort. Instead, our individual perspectives are inevitably porous, diffuse, bleeding into each other like contiguous inkblots.

Resistance to being subsumed into a shared subjective space is not altogether impossible, however. One can escape from 'common sense' into wine or 'mandragora'; imaginative fantasies ('dreams') or a romantic relationship. Just how far in practice we can escape subjective entanglement with the rival images of ourselves other people have in mind, especially those that are less than flattering, is in general a question Shakespeare seems to have found fascinating, and which he explores in particular detail in his version of the Cleopatra legend, as well as his earlier history play *Richard II*.[128] In both cases, Shakespeare's sense of the limits of perceptual autonomy seems to be that the process I call here 'interpellation' is to some extent voluntary, but not completely so. The ability of an individual to resist interpellation is susceptible to disparities of power and, especially, number. Characters such as Cleopatra see being shown at length before a hostile, jeering crowd as too much to be able to resist, even given great powers of dissociation; such prolonged and multifaceted exposure would inevitably prove overwhelming. So, as the alternative of last resort, they commit suicide. Even suicide, however, Shakespeare suggests, may not prove in the end the definitive exit that these pagan characters imagine it will be. In keeping with Christian doctrine, for Shakespeare, the afterlife promises, not escape, but if anything, even more extensive exposure to the other. As Sartre says, *huis clos* ('no exit').

In Shakespeare's Roman plays, characters such as Antony and Cleopatra, as well as Brutus, strive to escape the possibility of being judged adversely, and their success is never complete or lasting. Coriolanus is the most obvious example; he cannot even bear to be praised, lest it suggest that his sense of himself depends in any way on the good opinion or 'voices' of other people. Coriolanus' ostensible contempt for others' opinion of him, however, is belied by his exaggerated and finally fatal dependence on his mother's approval. He and Volumnia represent the *folie à deux* broken, much as Antony and Cleopatra represent it sustained, even to the point of death. Out of all of Shakespeare's characters, these two lovers in particular come as close as possible to escaping all external interpellation, finding a kind of refuge from opprobrium in each other's flattering gaze. Subtly, however, throughout the play, Shakespeare reminds us that even personalities as grandiose as Cleopatra's may not be able to escape the Last Judgement: 'doomsday'. Human beings by their very nature as human, rather than divine, are vulnerable to processes of moral judgement that they do not and cannot ever entirely control.

In the conclusion to my analysis of *Antony and Cleopatra*, 'The Last Interpellation', I look closely at the play's recurrent, ironic allusions to Scripture and argue that Shakespeare subtly reminds the audience throughout of a Christian revelation of which the characters on stage are themselves unaware. For Shakespeare's Romans, suicide appears to be an unimpeachable defence against the possibility of any further humiliation. Suicide is a means to remain unseen and therefore unaffected by a hostile audience. This view of suicide depends, however, as Shakespeare recognises, on a rejection or else ignorance of the Christian understanding of the afterlife. Death is only an escape, if there is nothing after death, or if death leads, not to heaven and hell, but to some sort of pagan Elysium; one that corresponds with suspicious congruity to the suicide's own fantasies. Whether or not we see Antony and Cleopatra as ultimately successful in their attempt, through suicide, to preserve their own self-contained subjective space depends, in the end, on whether or not we believe Shakespeare shares their vision of what Hamlet calls 'the undiscover'd country'.

Notes

1. MacIntyre, *After Virtue*, 27.
2. On 'sovereignty' and 'the frailty of human affairs', see Arendt, *The Human Condition*. On Arendt and Roman politics, as well as Roman philosophy, see Connolly, 'The Promise of the Classical Canon'.
3. Skinner, *Liberty before Liberalism* (1998). On liberalism and its discontents, see John Gray, 'The Problem of Hyper-Liberalism', 3–5; Deneen, 'The Ignoble Lie'; Deneen, *Why Liberalism Failed*; and Vermeule, 'Integration from Within'; as well as David Bentley Hart, 'Christ and Nothing', in *First Things* (October 2003), 47–56, reprinted in Hart, *In the Aftermath*, 1–19. Cf. Sandel, *Democracy's Discontent*. My own impression is that in the civil rights era, racism was the centre of political contention, at least within the United States. Once civil rights more or less won the day, Christianity became the new faultline, giving rise to the so-called 'Culture Wars' of the 1980s and 1990s. I am relieved that racism is no longer as pervasive as it once was in American society. I am less sanguine, however, about the dissolution of Christianity, for fear of the 'rough beast' that has shown up to fill the void: identity politics, including the so-called 'alt-right', which I see as in essence a peripheral variation on the same. As Christianity loses its former cultural hegemony, what seems to be emerging in its place, not only in the United States, but also in the United Kingdom and Europe, is an antagonism that is not so much racial as tribal. In its sense of quasi-hereditary caste, as well as its proclivity for Machtpolitik, this increasingly unrestrained enmity between social classes, as well as geographic regions, rich vs. poor, city vs. country, at times eerily resembles the Conflict of the Orders in ancient Rome, patrician vs. plebeian, as well as the analogous tension between Roman citizens and their Italian allies (*socii*), leading up to the so-called Social War (*bellum sociale*). So, like Deneen, as well as Sandel, I wonder what happens next. Can liberalism on its own avoid degenerating into what Hobbes calls *bellum omnium contra omnes*?

See Lind, 'Classless Utopia'; Chua, *Political Tribes*; Wuthnow, *The Left Behind*; Lilla, *The Once and Future Liberal*; Codevilla, 'The Rise of Political Correctness'; Lind, 'The New Class War'; Kotkin, *The New Class Conflict*; Codevilla, 'America's Ruling Class'; and Appiah, *Ethics of Identity*.

4. Holbrook, *Shakespeare's Individualism*.
5. Fernie, *Shakespeare for Freedom*, 6, 2, 74, 72, 173, 66.
6. Kant, 'Idea for a Universal History', 15.
7. Fernie, *Shakespeare for Freedom*, 73.
8. Ibid., 79, 164, 6, 201, 207, 198.
9. Hegel, *Hegel's Logic*, § 436; Williams, *Hegel's Ethics of Recognition*, 79.
10. Fukuyama, *The End of History*.
11. Markell, *Bound by Recognition*, 2.
12. Taylor, 'The Politics of Recognition', 24, 26.
13. Fukuyama, 'Identity, Immigration, and Liberal Democracy', 9, *Journal of Democracy* 17 (2006): 5–20; cited in Holbrook, *Shakespeare's Individualism*, 63.
14. Holbrook, *Shakespeare's Individualism*, 63.
15. Markell, *Bound by Recognition*, 59, 108, 221 n. 9.
16. Ibid., 7, 11, 36.
17. Ibid., 36, 79.
18. Arendt, *Human Condition*, 234.
19. Hegel, *Phenomenology of Spirit*, §§ 750–1.
20. See Brooke, *Philosophic Pride* as well as Schneewind, *Invention of Autonomy*.
21. Fernie, *Shakespeare for Freedom*, 6.
22. Holbrook, *Shakespeare's Individualism*, 140.
23. Geoffrey Miles, *Shakespeare and the Constant Romans* (Oxford: Oxford University Press, 1996), 9 n. 26; cited in Holbrook, *Shakespeare's Individualism*, 140.
24. Gill, *Personality*; cf. Gill, *Structured Self*.
25. Taylor, *Sources of the Self*, 376.
26. Hart, 'Christ and Nothing', 47.
27. Stephen Greenblatt, *Shakespeare's Freedom*, 111, 113.
28. On 'Eliot's rejection of Shakespeare', see Holbrook, *Shakespeare's Individualism*, 154–71.
29. Isaiah Berlin, 'The Apotheosis of the Romantic Will: The Revolt Against the Myth of an Ideal World', in Berlin, *The Proper Study of Mankind: An Anthology of Essays*, ed. Henry Hardy and Roger Hausheer (New York: Farrar, Straus, and Giroux, 1998); cited in Holbrook, *Shakespeare's Individualism*, 5.
30. See Patrick Gray, 'Seduced by Romanticism'.
31. Langley, *Narcissism and Suicide in Shakespeare and His Contemporaries*.

32. Cicero, *On Duties*, 1.22. Cicero cites here Plato's apocryphal ninth epistle to Archytas, 358a.

33. Hadfield, *Shakespeare and Republicanism*, 230, 95, 232, 12.

34. Nelson, 'Shakespeare and the Best State of a Commonwealth'; Colclough, 'Talking to the Animals'.

35. Armitage, Condren and Fitzmaurice, 'Introduction', 15–16.

36. Nelson, 'Shakespeare and the Best State of a Commonwealth', 253, 256.

37. Armitage, Condren and Fitzmaurice, 'Introduction', 16.

38. Patrick Gray and Samely, 'Shakespeare and Henri Lefebvre's "Right to the City"'. Cf. Patterson, *Shakespeare and the Popular Voice*.

39. Hadfield, *Shakespeare and Republicanism*, 2–24, 161, 165.

40. August. *De civ. D.* 2.2.

41. Ibid., 3.14.

42. Ibid., 1.1. Cf. Hor. *Epod.* 16.2: *suis et ipsa Roma viribus ruit* ('Rome herself falls by her own strength'); Prop. 3.13.60: *frangitur ipsa suis Roma superba bonis*; Lucan, 1.81: *in se magna ruunt*. See also Ernst Dutoit, 'Le Thème de "la force qui se détruit elle-même"', *Revue des Études Latines* 14 (1936): 365–73; cited in Braden, *Renaissance*, 14, 226 n. 10.

43. August. *De civ. D.* 5.12.

44. Ronald Syme, *The Roman Revolution*, 11–12.

45. August. *De civ. D.* 5.19.

46. Cic. *Off.* 1.26, 64; 3.83.

47. August. *De civ. D.* 1.1.

48. Machiavelli, *Discourses on Livy*, 131 (2.2).

49. Gibbon, *Decline and Fall*, 260 (1.15), 682 (3.38).

50. August. *De civ. D.* 3.30.

51. Ibid., 3.29.

52. Ibid., 1.1.

53. On Shakespeare and the ethics of war, see Patrick Gray, 'Shakespeare and War', 1–25.

54. Hillier, 'Valour Will Weep', 359.

55. Ibid., 374.

56. Greenblatt, *Shakespeare's Freedom*, 106.

57. Jagendorf, '*Coriolanus*: Body Politic and Private Parts', 462.

58. All references to Shakespeare's plays are taken from *The Arden Shakespeare Complete Works*, ed. Richard Proudfoot, Ann Thompson and David Scott Kastan (London: Cengage Learning, 2002).

59. See Whittington, *Renaissance Suppliants*: 'whereas the non-Plutarchan Coriolanus material in circulation in the sixteenth century focused on Volumnia's supplication as a victory of the softer emotions, a harmonious restoration of relations between mother and son undergirded by the psychology of chivalry, Shakespeare found in Plutarch's "Life" the

suggestion that Coriolanus' reconciliation with Rome precipitated his demise.'

60. August. *De civ. D.* 5.18.
61. Whittington, *Renaissance Suppliants*.
62. Hillier, 'Valour Will Weep', 388.
63. On the parallels between Brutus and Caesar, see Rabkin, *Shakespeare and the Common Understanding*, 106–12; de Gerenday, 'Play, Ritualization, and Ambivalence in *Julius Caesar*'; and Pierre Spriet, 'Amour et politique: le discourse de l'autre dans *Julius Caesar*', in *Coriolan: Théâtre*, ed. Jean-Paul Debax and Yves Peyré, ser. B, 5 (Toulouse: Université de Toulouse–Le Mirail, 1984), 227–9; cited in Rebhorn, 'Crisis of the Aristocracy', 79 n. 11.
64. Arist. *Pol.* 3–4; cf. Pl. *Resp.* 8–9.
65. Cantor, *Shakespeare's Rome*, 40, 57, 45.
66. Syme, *Roman Revolution*, 490–1.
67. Cantor, *Shakespeare's Rome*, 128, 175–6.
68. Cantor, *Shakespeare's Roman Trilogy*, 3.
69. Ibid., 47–50.
70. Ibid., 83
71. In the preface to *Saint Joan*, Shaw complains of what he calls 'a void in Elizabethan drama', 'A novice can read his [Shakespeare's] plays from one end to the other without learning that the world is finally governed by forces expressing themselves in religions and laws which make epochs rather than by vulgarly ambitious individuals who make rows.'
72. Cantor, *Shakespeare's Roman Trilogy*, 12–13.
73. Nuttall, *Shakespeare the Thinker*, 171.
74. Cantor, *Shakespeare's Roman Trilogy*, 16.
75. Chernaik, *The Myth of Rome in Shakespeare and His Contemporaries*, 107; cf. 244–6.
76. Holbrook, *Shakespeare's Individualism*, 22.
77. Richard Strier, *Resistant Structures: Particularity, Radicalism, and Renaissance Texts* (Berkeley, CA: University of California Press, 1997), 167; cited in Holbrook, *Shakespeare's Individualism*, 22.
78. Strier, *Resistant Structures*, 166.
79. John Keats, *Letters of John Keats: A Selection*, ed. R. Gittings (Oxford: Oxford University Press, 1992), 32; cited in Holbrook, *Shakespeare's Individualism*, 22. Cf. Patrick Gray, 'Seduced by Romanticism'.
80. Fernie, *Shakespeare for Freedom*, 194. Cf. Hegel, 'A Conversation of Three'. For original German text, see Hegel, *Documente zu Hegels Entwicklung*, 3–6.
81. Cantor, *Shakespeare's Roman Trilogy*, 100.

82. Ibid., 87.

83. Ibid., 164.

84. Braden cites Flaubert, who himself echoes St Augustine: '*C'est l'homme culminant du monde antique.*' Cf. Gustave Flaubert, *Correspondance,* ed. Jean Bruneau, vol. 1 (Paris: Gallimard, 1973), 209 (to Louis de Cormenin, 1844); cited in Braden, *Renaissance Tragedy,* 15.

85. Braden, *Renaissance Tragedy,* 13–14.

86. Ibid., 15–16.

87. Cic. *Off.* 1.69–70.

88. Braden, *Renaissance Tragedy,* 23, 12, 21, 24.

89. Ibid., 77–8.

90. Charles Trinkaus, *The Poet as Philosopher* (New Haven: Yale University Press, 1979), 22, 25; cited in Braden, *Renaissance Tragedy,* 73.

91. Braden, *Renaissance Tragedy,* 80.

92. Rebhorn, 'The Crisis of the Aristocracy in *Julius Caesar*', 81.

93. Ibid., 86. Cf. John R. Kayser and Ronald J. Lettieri, '"The Last of All the Romans": Shakespeare's Commentary on Classical Republicanism', *Clio* 9 (1979–80): 197–227; cited in Rebhorn, 'Crisis of the Aristocracy', 86 n. 23.

94. Quint, 'Tragedy of Nobility', 14–17.

95. Quint, 'Introduction', in William Shakespeare, *Antony and Cleopatra,* xi–xxvi.

96. Quint, 'Tragedy of Nobility', 9–10.

97. Cox, *Shakespeare and the Dramaturgy of Power,* 87.

98. Rebhorn, 'Crisis of the Aristocracy', 108.

99. Ibid., 78.

100. Cox, *Dramaturgy of Power,* 69–71.

101. Ibid., 172; cf. Cox, *The Devil and the Sacred.*

102. Cox, *Dramaturgy of Power,* 70.

103. Miles, *Shakespeare and the Constant Romans,* 80 n. 37. Miles cites Monsarrat, *Light from the Porch,* ch. 4, as well as Sams, 'Anti-Stoicism'.

104. Levin, *The Overreacher;* Esler, *Aspiring Mind;* cf. also Watson, *Shakespeare and the Hazards of Ambition.*

105. Braden, *Renaissance Tragedy,* 17.

106. Kuzner, *Open Subjects,* 115, 3, 19.

107. *On the Good Life: Selected Writings from Cicero,* trans. Michael Grant (London and New York: Penguin, 1971), 189; cited in Kuzner, *Open Subjects,* 61.

108. Kuzner's insight is corroborated by Joy Connolly's work on Cicero's rhetorical theory. For Cicero, she argues, as for Habermas, 'human society exists through and in the interactions of subjects:

it is a network or web of intersubjectivity.' Connolly, *State of Speech*, 143.

109. Kuzner, *Open Subjects*, 23, 6, 115, 18–19.
110. Cox, *Dramaturgy of Power*, 77.
111. Kuzner, *Open Subjects*, 61, 6.
112. For a more detailed history of the concept of the ego ideal, see Sandler, Holder and Meers, 'The Ego Ideal and the Ideal Self'.
113. For the significance of the *exemplum* in Roman thought, see Bartsch, *Mirror of the Self*, 119–20. For its analogous significance in Renaissance thought, see Hampton, *Writing from History*, Lyons, *Exemplum* and 'The Renaissance Crisis of Exemplarity', special issue of *Journal of the History of Ideas* 59 (1998), ed. François Rigolot.
114. Dostoevsky, *The Adolescent*, 373.
115. Cic. *Off.* 1.72.
116. Cf. the concept of tragedy as a failure of 'acknowledgement' in Cavell, *Disowning Knowledge*, as well as Markell, *Bound by Recognition*.
117. Reiss, *Mirages of the Selfe*, 2, 21.
118. The title alludes to Emerson's 'Self-Reliance': 'A foolish consistency is the hobgoblin of little minds.'
119. Cantor, *Shakespeare's Rome*, 95.
120. Hegel, *Phenomenology of Mind*, 236.
121. Holbrook, *Shakespeare's Individualism*, 57.
122. Ibid., 58.
123. Selleck, *Interpersonal Idiom*; Tilmouth, 'Passion and Intersubjectivity'. See also Anderson, *The Renaissance Extended Mind* and Magnusson, *Shakespeare and Social Dialogue*.
124. Tilmouth, 'Passion and Intersubjectivity', 16; cf. Selleck, *Interpersonal Idiom*, 177 n. 38 and 178 n. 41.
125. Selleck, *Interpersonal Idiom*, 4, 15–16.
126. Ibid., 92.
127. Ibid., 176 n. 38.
128. On *Richard II* as an exploration of the limits of this kind of intersubjective interpellation, see Patrick Gray, 'Shakespeare versus Aristotle'.

Part I

Julius Caesar

CHAPTER 1

'A BEAST WITHOUT A HEART': *PIETAS* AND PITY IN *JULIUS CAESAR*

In *Julius Caesar*, Brutus is a deeply attractive character, not only to his wife, Portia, and his friend, Cassius, but even to his murder victim, Caesar, as well as his chief rival, Antony. What makes Brutus so appealing, however, is a quality which he himself sees as a moral vice, empathy, including in this case a sense of civic duty. Despite his initial misgivings, Brutus backslides into political engagement: Cassius lures him away from Senecan philosophical isolation into an obsolescent Ciceronian enthusiasm for service to the state. Brutus' kind-heartedness is political, as well as ethical, finding expression in a sense of *noblesse oblige*. He tries to withdraw from public affairs and 'live unknown' like an Epicurean philosopher, but he has too keen a sense of his responsibilities or what Cicero might call his *officia* ('roles, obligations') as a husband, friend and patriot; he cannot shake his old-fashioned *pietas* ('duty, reverence').

Even more striking, given his ostensible Stoicism, is Brutus' tendency, like Coriolanus, to give way to compassion. Pity is an emotion which they both see, like Seneca, as an embarrassing and distracting weakness. As Russell Hillier observes, 'The natural pity Martius finds within himself for his family and his people when he capitulates to the claims of "Great Nature" (5.3.33) shames him in the eyes of the Romans and the Volscians.'[1] Like Coriolanus, Brutus finds to his chagrin that his strenuous efforts to maintain a sense of command over his inner life repeatedly break down. When he sees that he has hurt his friend, Cassius, or his wife, Portia, he yields, like a Christian, to a humane and generous desire to comfort them in their distress. This unbidden empathy, like his decision to engage in politics, is incompatible with his chosen 'philosophy' (4.3.143).[2] His own ideal self is not the one which Antony describes, the Republican hero, animated by concern for the 'common good' (5.5.72), but instead the quasi-mythical figure of the Stoic *sapiens*, distinguished by his superhuman detachment from the world at large.

In sum, Shakespeare depicts Brutus as torn between two opposed visions of heroism: Stoic and proto-Christian. He aims to become an exemplary Stoic sage. But he fails to remain indifferent to the imminent collapse of the Roman Republic. He cannot bring himself to alienate his own wife, Portia, or his friend, Cassius. Instead, in his concern for other people, Brutus reveals an aspect of his character which cannot be reconciled to his ambition to be seen as a philosopher: a refractory streak of kindness. For Shakespeare, as well as his audience, shaped by the values of a Christian milieu, Brutus' deep-set sense of empathy is attractive. It fits the Christian model of heroism: Christ's self-sacrifice for love. For Brutus himself, however, acts of pity, including his own, are contemptible. His heroism, in so far as it is analogous to Christian heroism, is inadvertent, 'accidental' (4.3.144), rather than deliberate, emerging despite his own best efforts to restrain himself. Brutus' reaction to his wife's death, especially, stands out as a kind of *felix culpa*, redeeming him as a character from otherwise-insufferable Stoic posturing.

For a Stoic, love such as Christ's is not a form of heroism, but a dangerous weakness. As Francis Bacon explains, 'He that hath wife and children, hath given hostages to fortune.'[3] When Brutus grieves for his wife, it humanises him in the eyes of the audience. To a Christian, tears can be noble; Christ himself weeps at the tomb of Lazarus. What Brutus wants, however, is instead to be what a Christian would call hard-hearted. As he sees himself, his concern for others' well-being is not virtuous, but on the contrary an embarrassing, damning lapse in his effort to maintain, at all times, an appearance of Stoic constancy, if not that constancy in fact. Christian *caritas* has no place in that vision of an ideal self, the remote, self-sufficient philosopher exalted in Senecan Neostoicism. There is no room there for political activism; no room even for more discrete, personal acts of human fellow-feeling. Compassion by its very nature entails a loss of self-control: to empathise with others is to lose the emotional self-sovereignty which Seneca, especially, praises as the highest conceivable moral good.

Shakespeare invokes older, more civic-minded Roman thought through the figure of Lucius Junius Brutus, Brutus' ancestor, famous as the man who drove out the tyrannical Tarquins. This hero is a flesh-and-blood character drawn from history, or at least from quasi-historical legend. Within Stoic philosophy, however, the ideal self is often described in the abstract instead, simply as the *sapiens* ('wise man', 'sage'). In Shakespeare's tragedy, this figure appears as well, in a sense, in the form of a statue of the ancestor in question, Lucius Junius Brutus. Reflecting on Seneca in his *Praise of Folly*, Erasmus condemns his ideal *sapiens* as 'a marble statue of a man, utterly unfeeling and quite impervious to all human emotion'.[4] A statue is a vivid symbol of disinterestedness: a visual incarnation of Stoic *apathia*.

Brutus vs. Brutus: Seneca, Cicero and the Stoic Ideal

In this section, I begin by introducing the psychoanalytic concept of the ego ideal, and I argue in the spirit of Freud and Adler that this ideal tends to be articulated in images of the divine. The ideal self can also be hypostasised, however, as a fellow human being: a hero such a Christian saint. The ego ideal is contingent upon cultural context, as well as personal preference, and as such can be a Christian martyr, for example, or a Buddhist monk, just as easily as a warrior such as Achilles or Beowulf. Within Stoicism, the ego ideal is typically described in the abstract as the *sapiens*, a quasi-mythical 'wise man' or 'sage' who always does as he ought. Seneca sometimes identifies the figure of the *sapiens* with specific historical individuals such as Socrates and Cato the Younger. But that identification is pressurised, temporary and subject to doubt. In his essay 'On Cruelty', Montaigne turns against Seneca; after much thought, he concludes that Socrates and Cato did not in fact conform, as Seneca suggests, to the template of the Stoic *sapiens*. Even at their most heroic moments, the very instant of their suicides, they each felt some touch of exultation. 'Witness the younger Cato,' Montaigne writes. 'I cannot believe that he merely maintained himself in the attitude that the rules of the Stoic sect ordained for him, sedate, without emotion, and impassible.'[5]

Despite himself, Shakespeare's Brutus shows like signs of inner conflict: he describes himself as 'with himself at war' (1.2.46), 'vexed' with 'passions of some difference' (1.2.39–40). Brutus is not only torn, like Montaigne's Cato, between his Stoic 'attitude' and his own emotions, but also between two rival moral imperatives. The tension between competing visions of ethics that Shakespeare's Brutus experiences and that largely defines his character reflects the contrast between Seneca's Epicureanism and Cicero's Stoicism. For Seneca, *apathia* is an end unto itself, requiring disengagement from political obligations. Cicero, much to the contrary, denounces 'philosophers' who retire from the public sphere for 'neglecting to defend others' and 'deserting' their 'duty'. 'Hindered by their devotion to learning, they abandon those whom they ought to protect.'[6]

The Greek philosopher Xenophanes once quipped that, if animals were to describe the gods, they would draw pictures of themselves. 'Horses would paint the forms of the gods like horses, and oxen like oxen.'[7] Centuries later, Feuerbach came to much the same conclusion. 'If God were an object to the bird, he would be a winged being.'[8] In the nineteenth century a wide range of intellectuals, including Marx and Durkheim, as well as Fueurbach, came to see man's gods as merely projections of himself. Man draws his own character upon an inanimate, indifferent cosmos. In *Civilization and Its Discontents*, Freud is sympathetic to this tradition, but also introduces an important revision. Man is not so thoroughly self-satisfied as to imagine that God is simply identical to himself. Instead, concepts of the divine reflect a man's concept of an ideal or perfect self, one to which he himself does not necessarily conform. God represents what Freud calls the 'ego ideal'.

> Long ago he [sc. 'man'] formed an ideal conception of omnipotence and omniscience which he embodied in his gods. To these gods he attributed everything that seemed unattainable to his wishes, or that was forbidden to him. One may say, therefore, that these gods were cultural ideals.

Freud then defines more clearly what he means by 'cultural ideals': 'what might be called man's "ideals"' are 'his ideas of a possible perfection of individuals, or of peoples or of the whole of humanity, and the demands that he sets up on the basis of such ideas'.[9]

This understanding of the divine as an articulation of the character of the ideal self appears more clearly in the work of Freud's contemporary rival Alfred Adler. Adler grants that 'each person imagines his God differently'. Nevertheless, God is 'the best conception gained so far of this ideal elevation of mankind', 'the concrete formulation of the goal of perfection'.[10] For Adler, all of man's activity can be explained in terms of a single master motive, comparable in character and explanatory force to Freud's 'libido': a 'striving for perfection', 'superiority' or 'overcoming' which Adler sees as innate and integral to life itself:

> *Mastery of the environment* appears to be inseparably connected with the concept of evolution. If this striving were not innate to the organism, no form of life could preserve itself. The goal of mastering the environment in a superior way, which one can call the striving for perfection, consequently also characterizes the development of man.

Adler takes some pains, however, to distinguish this urge from its most obvious apparent analogue, Nietzsche's 'will to power'. 'Striving for perfection' is not necessarily the same as 'striving for power'.[11]

Unlike Nietzsche, Adler does not see an irreconcilable conflict between man's 'striving for perfection' and his human feelings of compassion or pity: that *'feeling with the whole'* which he calls 'social interest' (*Gemeinschaftsgefühl*, literally 'community feeling'). Instead, he defines Nietzsche's 'will to power' as a subspecies of this 'striving for perfection', a misdirection of its energy away from man's proper goal: the 'common work' of a *'cooperating community'*. 'Deviations and failures of the human character – neurosis, psychosis, crime, drug addiction, etc. – are nothing but forms of expression and symptoms of the striving for superiority directed against fellowmanship (*Mitmenschlichkeit*, literally 'being a fellow-man', 'co-humanity').' For Nietzsche, pity leads to *décadence*, a self-destructive malaise akin to the world-weariness Romantics called *Weltschmerz* (literally, 'world-pain'). For Adler, however, precisely the reverse is true. To 'concretise' one's 'striving for perfection' or *'mastery of the environment'* as a 'striving *to master one's fellow man*' is 'erroneous, contradicting the concept of evolution'. The ambition 'to dominate over others' is the 'incorrect path', leading to the 'decline and fall of the individual', as well as the 'extinction' of entire 'races, tribes, families'.[12]

What Adler calls 'striving for perfection' is not therefore simply synonymous with what Nietzsche calls 'the will to power', and which Freud defines, in more sexual terms, as a longing for phallic potency. The ego ideal is open to a much wider variety of instantiations. If represented by a deity, that God need not be the wholly transcendent, impersonal God of classical philosophy. If represented by a human hero, the *exemplum* need not be a warrior such as Coriolanus. Depending upon a given individual's or culture's definition of 'perfection', the ideal self can at times be found instead in paragons of martyred passivity. It can be Jesus, for example, broken on the Cross. As Adler explains, 'each person imagines his God differently'.[13] In some cultures, it is not the warrior who inspires the most fervent admiration, but instead the martyr or ascetic. The idealisation of masculinity, physical force and invulnerability that defines Shakespeare's Romans can be understood therefore as peculiar to their culture, rather than any kind of biological necessity or given of human nature. Their ego ideals, although compelling, are not the only such ideals possible. Moreover, in their aspirations, Shakespeare's Romans are themselves not wholly internally consistent, either with each other or even within themselves, as individuals. They all seek power, in one sense or another, but power is subject to varying definitions. Caesar, for example, seeks political sovereignty: the power of a king. Brutus, however, wants to be able to control himself: the power of a philosopher.

Like all ethical systems, Stoicism presupposes a discrepancy between the real and the ideal. We are not what we could and should be, if we only recognised what it is we ought to do. Like all ethical systems, Stoicism then explains its exhortations by means of concrete examples, as well as abstract precepts. For Christians, for instance, the rule is the Golden Rule, and the exemplar is Christ. For Buddhists, the rule is the Eightfold Path, and the exemplar is the Buddha. For Stoics, the rule is Epictetus' maxim 'Bear and forebear', or some variation thereon. The example, however, tends to be anonymous: the unnamed 'wise man' or 'sage' (Latin, *sapiens*). Like Hamlet's Stoic friend, Horatio, the *sapiens* can therefore come across as a curious cipher: a mere blank space, albeit with praise attached.[14] Typically, for instance, the 'wise man' is described apophatically, more notable for what he is not ('passion's slave' [3.2.72]) than for what he is.[15] Even so, the Stoics need him as a convenient shorthand. Even if he remains somewhat notional and indefinite, the 'wise man' as a placeholder crystallises their theorising into a personification. Seneca describes the *sapiens* as 'calm' and 'unshaken'. He has 'attained perfection'; his 'mind' is like 'the superlunary world', 'always serene'.[16]

The figure of the Stoic sage also deflects possible charges of hypocrisy. By directing attention to people such as Cato and Socrates, Seneca need not present himself as a hero of his own moral system. 'I hope someday to be a wise man,' he explains, 'but meanwhile I am not a wise man.'[17] This modesty is a trope which he inherits from his Hellenistic Greek precursors, as he reveals in an anecdote about the Stoic philosopher Panaetius.

> I think Panaetius gave a charming answer to the youth who asked whether the wise man would fall in love: 'As to the wise man, we shall see. What concerns you and me, who are still a great distance from the wise man, is to ensure that we do not fall into a state of affairs which is disturbed, powerless, subservient to another, and worthless to oneself.'[18]

This habit of speech, however, gives rise to an obvious question. Is the 'wise man' wholly notional? In the course of human history, has any flesh-and-blood person ever fit this category? If not, could anyone ever even conceivably come to exist who might someday, somewhere live up to its criteria? A living, breathing hero of *apatheia*? Alexander of Aphrodisias, a Hellenistic opponent of Stoicism, insists that 'the majority of men are bad'. Nevertheless, he is willing to grant that 'there have been just one or two good men, as their fables maintain, like some absurd and unnatural creature rarer than the Ethiopian phoenix'.[19] More typically, Greek Stoic philosophers concede that the *sapiens* might not exist. Chrysippus confesses that 'on account of their extreme magnitude and beauty we [Stoics] seem to be stating things which are like fictions and not in accordance with man and human nature'. And he admits, 'Vice cannot be removed completely.'[20] Epictetus also tries to temper expectation. 'Is it possible to remain quite faultless? That is beyond our power ... We must be content if we avoid [. . .] a few faults.'[21] Cleanthes is the most optimistic of the Hellenistic Stoics, and even he gives little room for hope. 'Man walks in wickedness all his life, or, at any rate, for the greater part of it. If he ever attains to virtue, it is late, and at the very sunset of his days.'[22]

With more confidence than his Greek sources, Seneca insists that it is possible for us to perfect ourselves, that is, to free ourselves from passion. Nevertheless, the feat is extremely unusual. 'A good man', 'one of the first class', 'springs, perhaps, into existence, like the phoenix, only once in five hundred years'.[23] 'Perhaps': even here Seneca hedges his bets. In his essay *De constantia* ('On Constancy'), Seneca rebukes his friend, Serenus, for his doubts, but then trails off into careful qualifications of his claims.

> There is no reason for you to say, Serenus, as your habit is, that this wise man of ours is nowhere to be found. He is not a fiction of us Stoics, a sort of phantom glory of human nature, nor is he a mere conception, the mighty semblance of a thing unreal, but we have shown him in the flesh just as we delineate him, and shall show him – though perchance not often; after a long lapse of years, only one. For greatness which transcends the limit of the ordinary and common type is produced but rarely.[24]

Seneca seizes upon two men above all as paragons of Stoic virtue: Socrates and Cato the Younger. And it is in response to Seneca that Montaigne returns to these two figures repeatedly in his *Essays*, testing the philosopher's claims about their supposed *apathia* against his own more grounded sense of human nature.

Shakespeare casts a different character in the role of the possible *sapiens*: Brutus. Brutus combines, so to speak, the philosopher Socrates with the statesman Cato. Cicero, Seneca and Montaigne, for instance, all mention Brutus' authorship of treatises on ethics, now lost.[25] Cicero even dedicates two of his own philosophical treatises to Brutus, *De finibus* ('On Moral Ends') and *Paradoxa stoicorum* ('On the Paradoxes of the Stoics'), citing him there as a friend, a Stoic, and an interlocutor in an ongoing, lifelong debate.[26] Shakespeare shows his version of Brutus reading late into the night, just before the battle at Philippi, like Cato reading Plato's *Phaedo*, just before his suicide, and gives him in his funeral oration the distinctive, staccato 'Attic' style associated with Stoic philosophy.

Throughout *Julius Caesar*, Shakespeare suggests that, if anyone in the play is Seneca's 'phoenix', a hero of proto-Kantian disinterestedness, it is Brutus. In his eulogy at the end of the play, Antony exalts him as 'the noblest Roman of them all' (5.5.68). The Roman people, too, see him, at least at first, as a paragon of virtue. When Cassius tells Casca that he might join their party, Casca is delighted. 'O he sits high in the people's hearts,' Casca crows. 'That which would appear offence in us / His countenance, like richest alchemy, / Will change to virtue and worthiness' (1.3.157–60). The conspirators trust that the Roman people will see Brutus' intervention as an expression of his sense of civic duty, rather than, as in their own case, an outbreak of spite. As Antony observes,

> All the conspirators save only he
> Did that they did in envy of great Caesar.
> He only, in a general honest thought
> And common good to all, made one of them.

> (5.5.69–72)

Antony admires his fallen enemy's *pietas:* 'a general honest thought'. For Brutus himself, however, this same patriotism is a troubling source of cognitive dissonance. The concern for the 'common good' which Antony praises as the best part of his character is incompatible with the Stoic ideal of indifference.

In his study of the concept of 'constancy' in Shakespeare's Roman plays, Geoffrey Miles presents it as divided between a familiar definition as 'steadfastness', associated with Seneca, and a less familiar definition as 'consistency', connected with Cicero.[27] In *De officiis*, Cicero exhorts private citizens to engage in public life, taking on and fulfilling their proper 'offices' or social roles for the good of the commonwealth, rather than remaining in more tranquil seclusion. Giles Monsarrat describes this sense of duty to the state as 'a far cry from the self-sufficiency of the Stoic sage'.[28] Nonetheless, Miles feels comfortable describing Cicero as a Stoic.[29] Cicero does not simply disagree with Stoicism, he argues, but instead co-opts it, redefining its core ethical ideal of 'constancy-to-oneself' as 'constancy-to-others'. Constancy becomes a 'means to an end' rather than an 'end unto itself'. 'Cicero's ideal is a politician who has the moral qualities of a Stoic *sapiens*, but who uses them for the good of the commonwealth, rather than for his own self-perfection.'[30]

Miles is right to see a contrast between Cicero and Seneca, but their differences in this regard are not best explained, technically speaking, as manifestations of opposing interpretations of Stoicism. Marvin Vawter claims that 'the Stoic Wise Man sees himself as an independent entity unwilling to bind himself to any specific community.'[31] Miles agrees, as does Monsarrat. Cicero's sense, however, that even philosophers should engage in politics is entirely in keeping with the Stoic doctrine known as *oikeiōsis*, a term which is not easy to translate; it means, literally, 'the process of making things home'. Sometimes it is rendered as 'appropriation'. According to this aspect of Stoic thought, which Cicero takes up in *De officiis*, the philosopher should extend his sense of himself outward in concentric circles, first to his family, then to his city, then to his nation; finally, to the entire human race, thinking of them as part of himself, so that his natural sense of individual self-preservation becomes instead a more expansive, impartial concern for every human being.[32]

The problem in this case is Seneca's outsized influence on Neostoicism. Seeing him loom so large in the Renaissance imaginary, critics such as Vawter, Monsarrat and Miles whose focus is primarily Shakespeare and his contemporaries tend to mistake Seneca for a more general philosophical standard. But Seneca is not a reliable touchstone for classical Stoicism. Compared to his sources, Seneca is eclectic and idiosyncratic. His occasional exhortations to his friend, Lucilius, to abandon public affairs are not representative of mainstream Hellenistic or even Roman Stoicism, but instead of a rival school of thought: Epicureanism. Seneca's recurrent praise for a private life of leisure and seclusion reflects the Epicurean precept, *lathe biōsas* ('live unknown').[33] Seneca is not entirely consistent on this point; his essay *De beneficiis* ('On Benefits'), in particular, explaining the importance of reciprocal gift-giving, can be understood, like Cicero's *De officiis*, as an articulation and reimagination of the Hellenistic doctrine of *oikeiōsis*.[34] More typically, however, Seneca advocates Epicurean self-sufficiency.[35] The attraction of abandoning court life, fraught with anxiety and danger, for a more carefree, tranquil life of primitive isolation appears with great force, not only in his philosophical prose, but also in his tragedies, in the fantasies of protagonists such as Thyestes and Hippolytus.[36]

In *Julius Caesar*, Shakespeare illustrates the tension between Senecan Epicureanism and Ciceronian Stoicism in the contrast between the statue of Brutus' ancestor, Lucius Junius Brutus, and the man himself whom that statue represents. Striving to persuade Brutus to join his conspiracy against Caesar, Cassius calls this illustrious forebear to mind.

> O, you and I have heard our fathers say
> There was a Brutus once that would have brooked
> Th'eternal devil to keep his state in Rome
> As easily as a king.
>
> (1.2.157–60)

'You and I have heard our fathers say . . .': Cassius' opening captures the importance to a Roman patrician such as Brutus of his sense of his place in a succession of noble patriarchs. As Sallust writes:

> Quintus Maximus, Publius Scipio, and other eminent men of our country were in the habit of declaring that their hearts were set mightily aflame from the pursuit of virtue whenever they gazed upon the masks of their ancestors . . . It is the memory of great deeds that kindles this flame, which cannot be quelled until they by their own prowess have equalled the fame and glory of their forefathers.[37]

Cassius' final word, 'king', is also well chosen. As 'Brutus once' drove out the last 'king' of Rome, so now, he hopes, Brutus will help him forestall Caesar's imminent coronation.

Up until this point, Brutus has been noticeably silent, still and cold, like a statue. He neglects his usual 'shows of love'; his 'look' is 'veiled'; Cassius complains that his 'hand' has become 'stubborn and strange' (1.2.34–7). Cassius must go to great lengths to spark even the slightest 'show / Of fire' (1.2.175–6). To help draw Brutus out of this retreat into himself, Cassius hits upon an unusual expedient.

> Good Cinna, take this paper
> And look you lay it in the praetor's chair
> Where Brutus may but find it. And throw this
> In at this window. Set this up with wax
> Upon old Brutus' statue.
>
> (1.3.142–6)

Fewer than twenty lines later, Shakespeare introduces a new character, as well, Lucius, a young male attendant. Like Macbeth's valet, Seyton, or Antony's, Eros, this minor character's name is designed to reveal the more central protagonist's inner psychomachia. Most immediately, 'Lucius' is derived from *lux* (Latin, 'light'), and, appropriately enough, when he enters, Brutus asks him to fetch a taper. Lucius is also the praenomen, however, of 'old Brutus': Lucius Junius Brutus. It is significant, therefore, that it is this character, Lucius, who brings Brutus the first of Cassius' letters. Unsigned, the letters are designed to appear like missives from the Roman people at large. In addition, however, they give voice to Brutus' sense of his ancestor's example: his likely exhortation, if he were present. Cassius brings 'old Brutus' statue' back to life. 'Speak, strike, redress!' (2.1.47, 55)

Invoking this older model of heroism proves effective in unmooring Brutus from his Senecan withdrawal. His response echoes Cassius' speeches earlier: 'My ancestors did from the streets of Rome / The Tarquin drive, when he was called king' (2.1.53–4). By luring Brutus into this Ciceronian mode of heroism, however, Cassius sets him at odds with himself. In his eulogy, Antony praises Brutus for his public-spirited engagement in politics, much in the spirit of Cicero's *De officiis*. Brutus himself, however, might well balk at this description; he seems to want to come across, instead, as a model of Senecan disengagement. Even at the cost of alienating his own inner circle, as well as the Roman masses, Brutus aspires to be seen as a philosopher, rather than a statesman: a paragon of rational, unpreturbed detachment.

In their opening conversation, Cassius complains to Brutus that he seems cold and standoffish. 'I am not gamesome' (1.2.28), Brutus replies. 'I do lack some part / Of that quick spirit that is in Antony' (1.2.28–9). He strives to seem unmoved; much in contrast to Antony, he seems to pride himself on his own stillness and dissociation. Portia, too, complains that Brutus seems distant and devoid of affection. 'Dwell I but in the suburbs / Of your good pleasure?' (2.1.284–5). What humanises Brutus and renders him a sympathetic figure, a hero despite himself, is not so much his success at being a Stoic as his failure at his own set task. Unable to stick to his Stoic pride, Brutus gives way to compassion instead, prefiguring the very different moral world of Christianity.[38] As A. D. Nuttall writes, 'His love for his wife and his grief at her death, "affections" Brutus is proud to be able to repress, actually redeem him as a human being.'[39]

Under pressure, Brutus occasionally sets aside his performance of Stoic indifference, revealing emotions such as pity, grief and anger. Unfortunately, however, he is only willing to let down his guard in private. This concern for his public reputation as a philosopher is much of the reason why his funeral oration is not more successful. He is not willing to be passionate in public, as Antony is. Instead, he tries to sway his audience through arid, impersonal argument. 'Censure me in your wisdom' (3.2.16), he says, appealing to his fellow Romans' faculty of reason. 'Be patient till the last' (3.2.12). Conceding nothing to what we now might call optics, pausing at no point for any tug at the proverbial heart-strings, Brutus presses *hoi polloi* with challenging counterfactuals and conditionals, in the manner of a present-day analytic philosopher. 'Had you rather Caesar were living, and die all slaves, then that Caesar were dead, to live all free men?' (3.2.22–4). 'If . . . if then . . . this is my answer': Brutus' brusque, interlocking 'if . . . then' statements call to mind the characteristic sorites of Hellenistic Greek Stoics such as Zeno, Cleanthes and Chrysippus. 'As he was ambitious, I slew him' (3.2.26–7). In his dialogue *De finibus* ('On Moral Ends'), Cicero, master orator, complains about the logic-chopping of the Stoics, gives an example and rejects it out of hand as hopelessly unpersuasive: '"Everything good is praiseworthy; everything praiseworthy is moral; therefore everything good is moral." What a rusty sword! Who would admit your first premise?'[40]

Antony wins the people's hearts because Brutus, hindered by a peculiarly Stoic squeamishness, resolutely fails to pre-empt his rival's more persuasive appeal to pathos. His insistence on his own dry logic baffles his audience, which fails to follow his intricate reasoning. Brutus' carefully cultivated persona of disinterest and scrupulous objectivity comes across as unnatural, even repugnant, rather than reassuring. Antony's tears, provocations and mingling with the crowd; his display of Caesar's mangled, bloody cloak and corpse: these oratorical masterstrokes are left to fill an emotional vacuum. 'I will myself into the pulpit first,' Brutus assures Cassius, 'and show the reason of our Caesar's death' (3.1.236–7). 'The reason': how far Brutus overestimates the power of such an appeal to reason soon becomes painfully clear, as the plebeians begin to respond to Antony's emotional fireworks. 'Methinks there is much reason in his sayings' (3.2.109), one remarks. Brutus gets no such commendation. Setting aside questions of rhetorical technique, to permit Antony to speak at all, even to allow him to remain alive, is a grave tactical error, as Cassius recognises. 'The people may be moved' (3.1.234), he warns Brutus. 'You know not what you do' (3.1.232). Brutus, however, underestimates the power of emotions, including feelings such as loyalty or friendship, as well as romantic love.[41]

Not long after, as the Roman Republic collapses into open civil war, recrimination erupts between Brutus and Cassius. The two generals meet in Sardis after some time apart, and Cassius immediately accuses Brutus of betraying his trust. 'Brutus, this sober form of yours hides wrongs' (4.2.40). Brutus urges Cassius to speak 'softly', however, and retire to his tent, out of sight of their respective armies. 'Before the eyes of both our armies here,' he says, 'let us not wrangle' (4.2.43–5). Once he and Cassius are on their own, Cassius complains that Brutus ignored his request that Lucius Pella be pardoned, and Brutus accuses him in exchange of 'an itching palm' (4.3.10), selling 'offices' to 'undeservers' (4.3.11–12). Cassius responds with indignant protests, and the dispute degenerates into acrimonious grandstanding. Cassius threatens Brutus, and Brutus mocks him in return. 'There is no terror, Cassius, in your threats: / For I am armed so strong in honesty / That they pass me by as the idle wind' (4.3.66–8). He, Brutus, will not 'tremble', 'budge' or 'crouch' under Cassius' 'testy humour' (4.3.44–6).

In *De constantia*, Seneca compares the Stoic *sapiens* to 'certain cliffs', which, 'projecting into the deep, break the force of the sea, and, though lashed for countless ages, show no traces of its wrath'.[42] Like these cliffs, or like Caesar, when he calls himself 'Olympus' (3.1.74), Brutus will not be moved. In his account of the ideal Stoic sage, Seneca explains in some detail how he reacts to others' anger. He is unruffled, disdainful, serene, just as Brutus pretends to be here: 'he either fails to notice them, or counts them worthy of a smile'.[43] Cassius, however, is cut to the quick by this show of casual contempt. 'Have you not love enough to bear with me?' (4.3.118), he asks. Seeing that his friend is hurt, Brutus drops his frosty pretence. 'When I spoke that,' he confesses, 'I was ill-tempered too' (4.3.115). 'Much enforced', he admits he showed 'a hasty spark' (4.3.111). Put to the test, Brutus' 'love' for his friend, Cassius, overrides his Stoicism.

In his essay 'Of Books', Montaigne cites Brutus' private quarrelling with Cassius as a paradigmatic example of the discrepancy between a public persona and a private person. He begins by lamenting the loss of Brutus' treatise on virtue, 'for it is a fine thing to learn the theory from those who well know the practice'. Then he doubles back. 'Theory' does not always correspond to 'practice'. 'But since the preachings are one thing and the preacher another, I am as glad to see Brutus in Plutarch as in a book of his own.' As in Shakespeare's play, one episode in Brutus' life stands out: 'I would rather choose to know truly the conversation he held in his tent with some one of his intimate friends on the eve of a battle than the speech he made the next day to his army.'⁴⁴ Montaigne likely has in mind here what would later serve as the classical source text for Shakespeare's scene, a short passage in Plutarch's biography of Brutus. '[Brutus and Cassius] went into a litle chamber together, and bad every man avoyde, and did shut the dores to them. Then they beganne to powr out their complaints one to another, and grew hot and lowed, earnestly accusing one another, and at length both fell a weeping.'⁴⁵

It may well be the case that Shakespeare was influenced by Montaigne's musing about Brutus in his tent: his quarrel scene seems designed to fulfil Montaigne's wish. In this case, however, Montaigne's spirit echoes Plutarch's own. At the beginning of his biography of Alexander the Great, Plutarch distinguishes himself from more traditional historians. 'My intent is not to write histories, but only lives. For, the noblest deedes doe not always shew mens vertues and vices, but oftentimes a light occasion, a word, or some sporte makes mens natural dispositions and maners appeare more plaine, than the famous battells wonne, wherein are slaine tenne thowsande men.'⁴⁶ Seneca, too, stresses the need to examine philosophers' lives for signs of hypocrisy. 'Deed and word should be in accord.'⁴⁷ Shakespeare departs from Plutarch's simpler narrative, however, by suggesting not only that Brutus fails to maintain his composure in private, but also that he tries to cover up that lapse, in order to preserve a public image of himself as a dispassionate Stoic. In Shakespeare's version, Brutus is much more consciously performing the role of a Stoic *sapiens*. He insists that he and Cassius speak inside his tent, for instance, out of earshot of their men.

Brutus' investment in his own reputation as an exemplary Stoic sage is most obvious, however, after this scene, in his reaction to the message from one of his captains, Messala, that his wife, Portia, is dead. Reconciling with Cassius after their heated exchange, Brutus calls for a bowl of wine: a symbol of self-indulgence and momentary emotional liberty. The wine calls to mind, as well, Cassius' initial accusation, outside Brutus' tent: 'Brutus, this sober form of yours hides wrongs' (4.2.40). Brutus is not as 'sober' as he seems, literally as well as figuratively. 'Wrongs', moreover, takes on in retrospect an intriguing ambivalence. Cassius' own meaning is that Brutus has wronged him as a friend; he has been unkind, unsympathetic. Brutus also 'hides wrongs', however, in a Stoic sense: he is more prone to emotional breakdown than he lets on. His studied persona of indifference is 'form', rather than 'substance'. Cassius' word 'form' aptly suggests at once both a detached and unrealised ideal, like a Platonic form, and a hollow shell: an exterior show or pretence, as opposed to an authentic interior lived experience.

Cassius for his part marvels that Brutus lost his temper; Brutus, a man who prides himself above all on his emotional self-control. 'I did not think you could have been so angry' (4.3.141). Brutus replies, 'O Cassius, I am sick of many griefs' (4.3.142). Cassius is surprised at this answer and chides Brutus gently, mostly in jest, for failing to abide by his Stoic principles. 'Of your philosophy you make no use / If you give place to accidental evils' (4.3.143–4). Brutus' pride is stung by this remark, however, and he responds with a clarification, in the form of a slightly disturbing boast. 'No man bears sorrow better. Portia is dead' (4.3.145). Cassius is shocked: again, Brutus' 'sober form hides wrongs' (4.2.40). From one perspective, that of a Stoic, Brutus is in the wrong to be troubled by Portia's death. As he admits, he is 'sick with many griefs' (4.3.142). From another perspective, however, that of human compassion, Brutus is in the wrong not to let himself mourn for his wife's death more fully and openly.

Brutus asks Cassius twice not to mention Portia's death, as if afraid that if he does, he will not be able to contain his grief. 'Speak no more of her' (4.3.156), he says; and again, 'No more, I pray you' (4.3.164). Meanwhile, however, Messala and Titinius enter, bearing letters. Brutus presses Messala for news about Portia, and Messala tells him at last, reluctantly, that 'she is dead, and by strange manner' (4.3.187). Without giving any indication that this report is not the first time he has heard of her death, Brutus abruptly launches into a brief, startling and, again, self-aggrandising speech. 'Why, farewell, Portia: we must die, Messala: / With meditating that she must die once / I have the patience to endure it now' (4.3.188–90). Messala is awed by this display of Stoic virtue, and he heralds Brutus straightaway as a paragon of heroic indifference. 'Even so great men great losses should endure' (4.3.191). Cassius, however, knows better. 'I have as much of this in art as you,' he tells Brutus, cryptically, 'But yet my nature could not bear it so' (4.3.192–3). Like the audience, Cassius knows that Brutus is adopting a persona here. As T. S. Eliot says of Othello, he is *'cheering himself up.'*[48] He is, in fact, deeply affected by Portia's death; he can barely keep himself from breaking down altogether. In order to impress his officers, however, he keeps up appearances. He wants to be seen as Stoic *sapiens*, not as a loving husband.

Some critics have found the so-called 'double announcement' of Portia's death so puzzling as to suggest some sort of mistake, either in the manuscript itself or in the printer's shop.[49] According to this account, two drafts of the announcement, an early and a late, were somehow both included in the only authoritative source for the play, the 1623 Folio. A detail in the second announcement, however, suggests that it was included in full awareness of the first. Messala tells Brutus that Portia died 'by strange manner', and Brutus does not ask him to explain what he means. It is difficult to believe that Shakespeare meant this passage to stand alone. To mention that Portia died 'by strange manner' but not explain what that manner was would be an uncharacteristic disservice to his audience. Brutus' ostensible lack of curiosity here is not a printer's accident, but forms part of Brutus' own deliberate deception of his officers. It is a ruse, and a revealing one, designed to suggest an incredible, awe-inspiring *apathia*.

In contrast to Messala, the audience is supposed to see through Brutus' set-piece speech. Shakespeare uses the double announcement of Portia's death, apparent on stage only to Cassius, to show that the 'form' of the Stoic sage is at best a fiction: a persona which can be performed, like an actor's role, but which cannot in fact be maintained at all times, in private life as well as in public. Shakespeare takes us backstage, so to speak, in order to allow us to see the incongruity between the performer and the performance. In Cassius' terms, Shakespeare presents Stoicism as an 'art' beyond the scope of human 'nature'. Behind the façade of the superhuman Stoic philosopher, Shakespeare allows us to glimpse a different, more complex, and more plausible character. In his grief for his wife, as well as his kindness towards his friend, Brutus falls short of his own stringent philosophical standard. At the same time, however, he becomes a much more attractive human being: a hero in a different sense. In his failure at his own set task, Shakespeare's would-be paragon of Stoic indifference turns out to be instead an admirable example of Christian compassion.

In his *Praise of Folly*, Erasmus censures Seneca for 'removing all emotion whatsoever from the wise man'.[50] Seneca for his part denies that he is making any such claim: 'I do not withdraw the wise man from the category of man, nor do I deny him the sense of pain as though he were a rock that has no feelings at all.'[51] Some things do 'buffet' the wise man, Seneca admits, even though they do not 'overthrow' him: 'bodily pain and infirmity', 'the loss of friends and children' and 'the ruin that befalls his country amid the flames of war'. 'I do not deny that the wise man feels these things,' he maintains. 'The wise man does receive some wounds.' Erasmus thus might seem to misinterpret Seneca. Seneca himself, however, is inconsistent. At the end of *De constantia*, Seneca insists that the wise man is not altogether impervious to injury. 'We do not claim for him the hardness of stone or of steel.'[52] Yet this claim is in fact precisely the boast that he does make at the beginning of the essay. 'The wise man is not subject to any injury. It does not matter, therefore, how many darts are hurled against him, since none can pierce him. As the hardness of certain stones is impervious to steel, and adamant cannot be cut or hewn or ground [. . .] just so the spirit of the wise man is impregnable.'[53] The inconsistency of Shakespeare's Brutus corresponds to an inconsistency in Seneca's representation of the ideal Stoic sage.

Seneca's reversals regarding the *sapiens* show the need, if only in terms of conceptual clarity, of finding a more absolute representation of the Roman ethical ideal, one uncompromised by the vicissitudes of human nature. And it is just such an ideal that can be readily discerned in the concepts of the divine put forward by classical philosophers, including Seneca himself. For example, I began this section by citing the philosopher Xenophanes of Colophon. Much as Plato does later in his *Republic*, Xenophanes disparages the anthropomorphic deities popular among his contemporaries. Xenophanes is not an atheist, however, in the vein of Feuerbach. His aim, rather, is to replace the gods of the poets with a different figure: 'One God, the greatest among gods and men, neither in form like unto mortals, nor in thought.' God, 'the motionless One', is not subject to change. He 'abides ever in the selfsame place, moving not at all; nor does it befit him to go about now hither, now thither'.[54] Already in the thought of this pre-Socratic figure, it is possible to see an adumbration of Aristotle's Unmoved Mover, as well as the impersonal 'World-Soul' of the Stoics.

The idea that God or the gods are wholly impassible, even impersonal, is not limited to the Stoa, but can be found in all major schools of ancient philosophy, including Platonism, Aristotelianism and Epicureanism. Stoicism is simply the most radical, confident attempt to attain this ideal in its purity, as a human being.[55] Impassibility becomes in Stoicism not merely a characteristic of the divine or of the soul after death but a primary aim in this life, as well as the next. It is a condition, moreover, which the Stoic sage is thought to attain, at least to some degree. Seneca adopts the Epicurean idea of the gods as plural and personal, but indifferent to human affairs, and describes the hypothetical Stoic *sapiens* in their likeness. 'The wise man is next-door neighbor to the gods and like a god in all save his mortality.'[56] Or again, 'a good man differs from God in the element of time only; he is God's pupil, his imitator, and true offspring.' The true wise man can even surpass God. 'In this you may outstrip God; he is exempt from enduring evil, while you are superior to it.'[57]

Shakespeare, however, does not share Seneca's confidence in man's ability to escape his own emotions. In the next chapter, '"The northern star"', I present the ideal of impassibility that I have begun to outline here in more detail, both in its original incarnation in classical philosophy and again in its resurgence in sixteenth-century Neostoicism, where it tends to be presented as the virtue of 'constancy'. Like many of his contemporaries, Shakespeare does not see this kind of 'constancy' as compatible with human nature. Caesar, for example, compares himself to 'the northern star': a symbol of aloof invulnerability, like the various statues scattered throughout the play. Roman attempts to emulate these kinds of ego ideals end in tragedy. Caesar is not in fact the godlike figure that he starts to think he is, just as Brutus proves not to be an unshakeable Stoic sage.

Shakespeare's implicit, concrete criticism of the ideal of impassibility resembles the explicit, abstract concerns of contemporary theologians about the possibility of reconciling Stoicism with Christianity, as well as related disputes about the relative merits of each ethical system. In his emphasis on man's susceptibility to passions, accidents and material wounds, as well as his consistent counter-idealisation of an ethos of compassion, Shakespeare sides with the claims of Christianity against those of Stoicism. In the next section of this chapter, '"A marble statue of a man"', I look more closely at early modern debate about the role of 'pity', in particular, in Stoic ethics. In delineating Shakespeare's place along a spectrum of contemporary opinion, the influential Neostoic humanist Justus Lipsius provides a useful point of contrast. The notoriously severe theologian Jean Calvin proves a surprisingly sympathetic point of comparison. Despite manifest sympathy for misguided characters such as Brutus, Caesar and others, Shakespeare is a partisan of a Christian ethos of compassion, over and against the Neostoicism that he brings to life in his representation of ancient Rome.

'A marble statue of a man': Neostoicism and the Problem of Pity

Over the course of the last several decades, following an early article by John Anson on *Julius Caesar* and Neostoicism, critics have tended to agree that a central project of this Roman play is a critique of Neostoic exaltation of 'constancy'.[58] Marvin Spevack in his Cambridge edition describes it as 'the major dramatic, psychological, social, and political ideal' of the play.[59] Coppélia Kahn describes *Romanitas* in Shakespeare as 'ethically oriented', and directs the reader to G. K. Hunter's longer description of 'a set of virtues . . . thought of as characterizing Roman civilization – soldierly, severe, self-controlled, self-disciplined'.[60] Paul Cantor observes, 'It is difficult to find one English word to cover the complex of austerity, pride, heroic virtue, and public service that constitutes Romanness in Shakespeare.'[61] Nevertheless, certain terms do appear repeatedly, and especially one: 'constancy'. Vivian Thomas writes, 'The fundamental values which permeate the Roman plays are: service to the state, constancy, valor, friendship, love of family, and respect for the gods.'[62] Robert Miola narrows the list to three: 'constancy, honour, and *pietas* (the loving respect owed to family, country, and gods)'.[63] I would collapse these even further: a Roman's sense of 'honour', for Shakespeare, depends on his sense of his own 'constancy'.

Geoffrey Miles, especially, argues convincingly that constancy 'for Shakespeare and his contemporaries' represents 'the quintessential Roman virtue'.[64]

As I explained in the previous section of this chapter, 'Brutus vs. Brutus', the ethical ideal of 'constancy' can conceivably be pressed into the service of *pietas*, as in Cicero's *De officiis*. It can also come into conflict with that sense of duty, however, as in the case of Seneca's revised version of Hellenistic Stoicism. Retirement from city to country, *negotium* ('business') to *otium* ('leisure'), is more typically associated with Epicureanism. Nonetheless, Seneca sees withdrawal from public affairs as the shortest route to Stoic 'constancy', understood in this case as imperviousness to external influence.[65] Cicero, by contrast, like Virgil, subordinates the Stoic ideal of constancy to an older Roman ideal of *pietas*: reverence for gods, ancestors and the Roman state. 'Constancy' for Cicero does not mean complete indifference or *apathia*, but instead self-sacrificing service to others. *Dulce et decorum est pro patria mori*.[66] Such patriotism is familiar from legends such as that of Marcus Curtius in Livy's *History*, as well as Aeneas in Virgil's *Aeneid*.

In this section of the chapter, I outline a second such debate about constancy, one more specific to the Renaissance. Much as Cicero and Seneca tried to promote Hellenistic philosophy, a new and controversial import from Greece, within the very different, largely incompatible context of traditional Roman mores, so also Shakespeare's contemporaries, Neostoics such as Lipsius and Du Vair, tried to introduce Stoicism, a resurgent, contested legacy of ancient Rome, into a pervasively Christian milieu. Can the idea that constancy is a virtue be reconciled to Christianity? If Jesus as he appears in the Gospels is understood as the paradigmatic ethical *exemplum*, and constancy is defined, as it is for Seneca, as primarily *apathia*, freedom from emotion, then any such reconciliation is impossible. Jesus weeps, grows angry, suffers, dies; the details of his life forestall any coherent redefinition of this central Christian figure as a latter-day Stoic sage.

In the next chapter, '"The northern star"', I address a third and final debate about constancy: the extent to which it is synonymous with masculinity. Can women be constant? For Shakespeare's Romans, the answer is, for the most part, no. As Hamlet says, 'Frailty, thy name is woman' (1.2.146). The Latin language itself suggests this perspective: *virtus* literally means 'manliness'. For Shakespeare

himself, however, like Montaigne, the question itself would be misguided. Inconstancy is not limited to women but instead a defining
characteristic of human nature, male as well as female. As Benedick
says at the end of *Much Ado about Nothing*, 'man is a giddy thing,
and this is my conclusion' (5.4.106–7). Every man has in this sense
a kind of 'woman' within: a feminine aspect of himself which is susceptible to emotions such as pity and grief. 'What patch or bit of
one's personality is essential?' Peter Holbrook asks. 'Which of our
many contradictory drives is truest? How can we speak of authenticity if, as Montaigne says, "there is as much difference between us and
ourselves as there is between us and other people"?'[67]

At present, however, I will focus on the opposition between
Christianity and Neostoicism. The figure most immediately responsible for the revival of Stoicism in late sixteenth-century Europe
is Justus Lipsius. His seminal work, *De constantia*, appeared in
English translation in 1595, only a few years before the presumed
composition of Shakespeare's *Julius Caesar* in 1599. A shorter
treatise by Guillaume du Vair, *La Philosophie morale des stoïques*
('The Moral Philosophy of the Stoics'), based on Epictetus' *Manual*, appeared in English only a year before, in 1598. Subsequent
scholars such as Bishop Joseph Hall would build upon their ideas,
and Stoicism would in time become a characteristic subject of later
Jacobean drama.[68] Given the early date of *Julius Caesar*, however,
within the development of early modern English Neostoicism, it
is not necessary at present to look beyond these two authors, into
the seventeenth century. J. H. M. Salmon traces Neostoicism in
England in this early period back to the influence, especially, of
the Sidney circle. The Countess of Pembroke herself, for instance,
translated a Neostoic treatise by Philippe de Mornay, his *Excellent
discours de la vie et de la mort* ('Excellent Discourse of Life and
Death'), and published it in 1592 as part of a single volume with
her translation of Garnier's *Marc-Antoine*.

In his work on the Protestant concept of 'conscience', Geoffrey
Aggeler draws attention to the curious fact that most of the Eng-
lish translators of Continental Neostoic treatises were not only
part of the Sidney circle, but also, like Sidney himself, committed
Calvinists.[69] The conjunction might easily seem counter-intuitive.
Drawing upon the final, most pessimistic writings of St Augustine,
Calvin insists on man's utter incapacity to control his own
depraved nature. As a result of the Fall of Man, virtue is entirely

dependent on God's grace. Stoicism, by contrast, emphasises man's ability to master his own emotions. Man in his strength is able to emulate and even exceed the divine, becoming self-sufficient through unaided, individual human effort. Reviewing the intellectual history of the Renaissance and Reformation, William Bouwsma takes up these two schools of thought as emblems of what he calls 'the two faces of humanism'. 'The two ideological poles between which Renaissance humanism oscillated may be roughly labeled "Stoicism" and "Augustinianism."'[70]

At the end of his *Apology for Raymond Sebond*, in response to a lament of Seneca's which he calls 'absurd', Montaigne draws a similar contrast. He cites Seneca: 'O what a vile and abject thing is man, if he does not raise himself above humanity!' 'Man cannot raise himself above himself,' Montaigne replies, except 'by purely celestial means'. 'It is for our Christian faith, not his [sc. Seneca's] Stoical virtue, to aspire to that divine and miraculous metamorphosis.'[71] Pierre de La Primaudaye, too, at the beginning of his popular *French Academie*, criticises the Stoics for not recognising man's need for the grace. On the one hand, he maintains, we are to avoid the pessimism of ancient figures such as 'Timon the Athenian', who saw life as so miserable that he urged his countrymen to hang themselves. Man's is not such 'a vile and abiect estate'. On the other hand, however:

> We must take heed, that we enter not into that presumptuous opinion of many others, who endeuour to lead man to the consideration of his dignitie and excellencie, as being endewed with infinite graces. For they persuade him, that through the quicknes of his vnderstanding, he may mount vp to the perfect knowledge of the greatest secrets of God and nature, and that by the only studie of philosophie, he may of himselfe, following his own nature become maister of all euill passions and perturbations, and attaine to a rare and supreme kind of vertue, which is void of those affections ... Thus whilest they grant to mans power such an excellent and diuine disposition, they lift him vp in a vain presumption, in pride and trust in himselfe, and in his owne vertue, which in the end cannot be but the cause of his vtter undoing.[72]

At the beginning of Shakespeare's *Love's Labour's Lost*, Berowne protests in like vein against the king's proposal that he and his companions swear to forgo the company of women. 'Necessity will make us all forsworn' (1.1.147), he vows. 'For every man with his affects is born / Not by might mastered, but by special grace' (1.1.149–50).

The 'special grace' that Berowne invokes here, like the 'special providence' that Hamlet sees 'in the fall of a sparrow', is a technical concept borrowed from Calvinist theology. 'Special' in this context means 'specific to an individual' and tends to refer in Calvin's *Institutes* to that 'grace' or 'providence' which God offers to each of the elect. Taken together, the two instances, Berowne's 'special grace' and Hamlet's 'special providence', suggest that in Shakespeare's mind, as in the context Aggeler describes, Neostoicism and Calvinism stand connected. Hamlet's comments about 'special providence' arise from his embrace of a fatalism which resembles that of a Roman Stoic. Alan Sinfield, for example, compares Hamlet's speech to Horatio, 'the readiness is all', to Seneca's essay, *De providentia* ('On Providence') as well as Calvin's *Institutes*, as an example of the manifest difficulty in sorting out the two possible lines of influence.[73]

One explanation Aggeler offers for the connection between Calvinism and Neostoicism in Elizabethan England is that Calvin himself was much exercised to distinguish his interpretation of Christian theology from Senecan Stoicism, precisely because, as in the case of Hamlet's determinism, the two could seem so eerily similar.[74] English Calvinists then naturally took an interest in the pagan antagonist of the master. 'Certainly his frequent references to Seneca and other pagan writers were noticed.' Aggeler cites as an example the translator of Du Vair's treatise on Stoic moral philosophy, Thomas James, who in his introduction defends his use of 'words and sentences of the Heathen' by appeal to Calvin's authority.[75]

In his effort to distinguish between Stoicism and Christianity, Calvin insists in particular on the difference in their attitudes towards compassion for the weak and suffering. For example, Calvin's first published book is a commentary on Seneca's *De clementia* ('On Mercy'), a treatise in which Seneca tries to convince his former pupil, the Emperor Nero, to be more merciful to his subjects. On the face of it, the exhortation might seem readily compatible with Christianity. Calvin, however, objects to the spirit in which it is made. Seneca does not appeal to Nero's sense of sympathy, but instead to his sense of his own superiority. He wants to convince

Nero, like Shakespeare's Brutus, to take pride in seeing himself as an aloof and imperturbable *sapiens*, rather than in imposing sudden, cruel violence. 'Cruel and inexorable anger is not seemly for a king, for thus he does not rise much above the other man, toward whose own level he descends by being angry at him.' To bear a grudge is for 'women' or 'wild beasts', and 'not even the noble sort of these'. 'Elephants and lions pass by what they have stricken down; it is the ignoble beast that is relentless.'

For Christians, pity is the chief virtue. For Stoics, however, it is an inexcusable weakness. As Calvin explains in his commentary on Seneca, 'Although it [pity] conforms, in appearance, to clemency, yet because it carries with it perturbation of mind, it fails to qualify as a virtue (according to the Stoics).' As Calvin recognises, Seneca distinguishes carefully between *misericordia* ('pity'), a vice, and *clementia* ('mercy'), a virtue. Pity involves empathy with another person's suffering, and thus a loss of emotional sovereignty: 'the sorrow of the mind brought about by the distress of others'. Mercy, however, as Seneca describes it is a demonstration of power. The *sapiens* is charitable, pardons, gives alms; he does so, however, 'with unruffled mind and a countenance under control'.[76]

Calvin finds this distinction unconvincing. 'Obviously we ought to be persuaded of the fact that pity is a virtue, and that he who feels no pity cannot be a good man – whatever these idle sages discuss in their shady nooks.'[77] The putative opposite of 'pity', a passionless 'clemency', is in his opinion a fiction, founded on a false notion of human nature. 'To use Pliny's words: "I know not whether they are sages, but they certainly are not men. For it is man's nature to be affected by sorrow, to feel, yet to resist, and to accept comforting, not to go without it."'[78] In his later *Commentary on Romans*, Calvin cites St Augustine to similar effect. 'As he [sc. St Paul] mentions the want of *mercy* as an evidence of human nature being depraved, Augustine, in arguing against the Stoics, concludes, that mercy is a Christian virtue.'[79]

In his *Institutes*, even as early as the 1539 Latin edition, Calvin complains about 'new Stoics' who, he says, 'make patience into insensibility, and a valiant and constant man into a stock'.[80] Calvin echoes here the work of an earlier humanist, Erasmus. In his 1529 edition of Seneca, Erasmus questions the authenticity of a supposed record of a correspondence between Seneca and St Paul, now recognised as a fourth-century forgery.[81] In his 1511 *The Praise of Folly*, Erasmus lambastes Seneca's ideal of the 'wise man' or *sapiens*. Like Calvin after him, Erasmus is put off in particular by Stoic disdain for pity. Folly asks, 'Who would not flee in horror from such a man, as he would from a monster or a ghost – a man who is completely deaf to all human sentiment, who is untouched by emotion, no more moved by love or pity than "a chunk of flint or mountain crag" . . .?'[82]

Whereas Erasmus' Folly speaks directly of Seneca, Calvin speaks somewhat more mysteriously of 'new' Stoics 'among the Christians'. Who are these 'new Stoics' (*novi Stoici*)? Calvin does not identify them. Moreover, they predate standard narratives of the history of Neostoicism. Lipsius' *De constantia* did not appear in Latin until 1584: almost fifty years later. Gilles Monsarrat suggests that Calvin is referring here to unspecified contemporary Christians, influenced by the resurgence of Stoic ideas in the sixteenth century. He has trouble identifying any positive instance of such Neostoicism earlier than 1542, however, some years after Calvin's initial composition of the *Institutes*. Even then, the example that he does give, Gerolamo Cardano's *De consolatione*, is not notably Christian; its author was later put in prison by the Inquisition for casting Jesus' horoscope, as well as for writing a book in praise of the Emperor Nero, tormentor of Christian martyrs.[83]

Departing from Monsarrat, I would suggest that 'new' here may perhaps mean 'new' in relation to Seneca, rather than in relation to Calvin's own early modern Europe. Pagan authors in late antiquity tend to criticise Seneca for infelicities of Latin style, as well as his compromising political entanglement with the reviled Nero. Marcia Colish details a countervailing tradition, however, of 'Christian apologists and Church Fathers', dating as far back as the second century, which 'gave Seneca a new and more positive appreciation'. 'These authors were less concerned with his biography and his literary style than with his moral philosophy, which they found strikingly compatible with Christian ethics at some points. They concentrated their attention on his ethical works, borrowing heavily from them and occasionally mentioning him by name as a sage.'[84] Tertullian, for example, refers to Seneca as *Seneca saepe noster* ('Seneca, often ours'). St Jerome later drops the qualifier: Seneca for him is simply *Seneca noster* ('our Seneca').[85]

Calvin is more sceptical. 'Now, among the Christians there are also new Stoics, who count it depraved not only to groan and weep but also to be sad and care-ridden.' In his *Institutes*, as also in his commentary on Seneca's *De clementia*, Calvin is especially appalled by Stoic disapproval of compassion. Appealing to the example of Christ, Calvin presents Stoic opposition to pity as an insurmountable barrier to any proposed reconciliation of Stoic and Christian ethics. 'We have nothing to do with this iron philosophy which our Lord and Master has condemned not only by his word, but also by his example. For he groaned and wept both over his own and others' misfortunes.'[86] Calvin even provides an Old Testament type of this aspect of Christ in his *Commentary on Genesis*, in the person of Joseph. Having risen to preeminence in service to the Pharaoh, Joseph encounters after many years the brothers who betrayed him and sold him into slavery, and they fail to recognise him. He seizes the youngest, Benjamin, as his prisoner, having first framed him for a crime. Knowing his father's love for the boy, one of the older brothers, Judah, offers to serve as a slave in his place instead. And, at this act of pity, Joseph cannot 'restrain himself'. He orders everyone out of his chambers and begins to weep, then invites his brothers back in, reveals who he is, and provides for them in their poverty.

Calvin seizes upon one clause from this story, 'Joseph could not restrain himself', and expounds upon it with unusual vehemence. 'Joseph had done violence to his feelings,' he imagines, 'as long as he presented to them an austere and harsh countenance.' The image calls to mind Shakespeare's Brutus, unable to hide his anxiety from Portia while the conspiracy is afoot; unable later, as well, to contain his anger at Cassius, once he learns that she has passed away. Influence, direct or indirect, is possible. An English edition of the commentary appeared in 1578.[87] My more general point, however, is that Calvin and Shakespeare, as well as English Calvinists interested in Neostoicism, share a common interest in the tension between passion, especially pity, and a misleading appearance of stern, even cruel, impassivity. 'At length,' Calvin continues, 'the strong fraternal affection, which he had suppressed during the time that he was breathing severe threatening, poured itself forth with more abundant force.' This breakdown, however, is not a vice, as Brutus sees it. Instead, Calvin argues, Joseph's pity is laudable. 'This softness or tenderness is more deserving of praise than if he had maintained an equable temper.' On the whole, Calvin concludes, 'the Stoics speak foolishly when they say, that it is a heroic virtue not to be touched with compassion. Had Joseph stood inflexible, who would not have pronounced him to be a stupid or iron-hearted man?'[88]

In Lipsius' dialogue *De constantia*, 'constancy' is defined explicitly as the absence of any 'passion', including sympathy. '"Constancy" is a right and immovable strength of the mind, neither lifted up nor pressed down with external or casual accidents.' Writing during the Wars of Religion, Lipsius wanted to escape the turmoil around him, even if only subjectively, and thus welcomes Seneca's Epicurean quietism. Patriotism, for him, is especially suspect. Lipsius' interlocutor in the dialogue, 'Langius', complains that the word 'piety', a closer translation than usual, in this case, of the Latin term *pietas*, is sometimes used to mean 'affection to our country', rather than 'honour and love toward God and our parents'. Even in this more limited sense, he maintains, *pietas* is a vice; a variation on 'pity', which he reproves, like Seneca, as by its very nature introducing a blameworthy, undesirable susceptibility to external turbulence. Langius attacks the central Christian virtue of compassion with startling directness. 'Commiseration or pitying . . . must be despised by he who is wise and constant, whom nothing so much suits as steadiness and steadfastness of courage, which he cannot retain if he is cast down not only with his own mishaps, but also at other men's.' Lipsius' persona in the dialogue, 'Lipsius', is shocked at the suggestion. 'What Stoical subtleties are these?' he asks. 'Will you not have me to pity another man's case? Surely it is a virtue among good men, and such as have any religion in them? . . . Are we so unkind and void of humanity that we would have no man to be moved at another's misery?'[89]

The context of early modern Neostoicism is post-classical, Christian. Individual Neostoic authors, however, do not therefore inevitably aim at an explicit reconciliation of Stoic and Christian ethics. Lipsius' degree of interest, in particular, in achieving such a synthesis, as well as Du Vair's, can be easily overstated. As Monsarrat observes, Lipsius mentions God frequently in his *De constantia*, but the words 'Christ', 'Christian' or 'Christianity' do not appear at any point.[90] His descriptions of God are drawn from classical sources such as Seneca, not the Bible.[91] The same is true of Du Vair's treatise, which, Du Vair himself attests, amounts to little more than a paraphrase of Epictetus' *Manual*. 'It is nothing els but the selfe same Manuell of *Epictetus* owne making, which I haue taken in peeces, and transposed according to that method and order which I haue thought most conuenient.'[92] The disparity between Christian and Stoic ethics that Calvin emphasises, a difference of opinion about 'pity', is not addressed directly, but instead left unresolved.

The troubling pitilessness which figures so prominently in Calvin's criticism of Stoicism, as well as Erasmus', appears repeatedly in Shakespeare's *Julius Caesar*. The cold indifference to human fellow-feeling which Erasmus mocks and censures in his portrait of Seneca's ideal *sapiens* Shakespeare sees as a characteristic problem of pagan Rome in general. Towards the end of *Titus Andronicus*, for instance, Lucius finds his father wandering the streets of Rome, pleading to the cobblestones for the life of his sons. 'No man is by,' Lucius protests. 'You recount your sorrows to a stone' (3.1.28–9). 'They are better than the Tribunes,' Titus replies. 'When I do weep, they humbly at my feet / Receive my tears and seem to weep with me' (3.1.38, 40–1). Roman authority, by contrast, is 'more hard than stones' (3.1.44).[93]

The opening scene of *Julius Caesar* proves in this sense a microcosm of what is to come. The problem of a characteristic Roman insensibility to the suffering of others is stated explicitly and almost immediately at the beginning of the play when the tribune Murellus rebukes the plebeians for celebrating Caesar's victory over Pompey, a fellow Roman. 'You blocks, you stones, you worse than senseless things! / You hard hearts, you cruel men of Rome, / Knew you not Pompey?' (1.1.35–6). John Anson sees the callous embrace of cruelty Shakespeare's Murellus describes here as the central problem of the play. 'The body politic suffers a gradual loss of sensibility represented by the separation of hand from heart.' Romans themselves become the victims of 'a loss of compassion, an induration of feeling that gradually hardens their hearts'.[94] The language itself, too, suggests that Neostoicism is in play. Murellus' opening term of reproach, 'blocks', echoes Shakespeare's Grumio's pun about Stoics in his earlier *Taming of the Shrew*: 'Let's be no Stoics nor no stocks, I pray' (1.1.31).[95] Calling the Roman people 'stones' alludes, perhaps, to what Geoffrey Miles identifies as a recurrent conceit in Senecan Stoicism, the image of the *sapiens* as an impervious rock.[96]

Most clearly, however, Shakespeare's language echoes that of Heinrich Bullinger in his third *Decade*. Bullinger took a strong interest in England's conversion to Protestantism, keeping up correspondence with English Reformed clergy throughout his life; ministers fleeing the Marian persecution studied with him personally in Zurich and returned in 1558, after Queen Mary's death, under the Elizabethan Settlement. Several became bishops. Parish preachers were required to read his sermons, and his *Ten Decades* were used at Oxford as a guide to 'orthodox' theology. Monsarrat gives details:

> In 1586 Archbishop Whitgift ordered that 'every minister having cure, and being under the degrees of master of arts, and batchelors of law' should purchase the *Decades*, in Latin or in English, read one sermon every week and make notes; the second edition of 1584 was insufficient to meet the demand and a third appeared in 1587.[97]

Bullinger tends to follow Zwingli more closely than Calvin; in his criticism of what he calls 'idle fellows', however, 'exercising themselves in contemplation rather than in working', Bullinger hews closely to Calvin's original. 'Men must reject the unsavory opinion of the Stoics,' he maintains, 'touching which I will recite unto you, dearly beloved, a most excellent discourse of a doctor in the church of Christ', that is, the passages on Stoic ethics from Calvin's *Institutes*, which he repeats almost verbatim. 'Upstart Stoics', Bullinger laments, make 'patience' into 'a kind of senselessness', and 'a valiant and constant man' into 'a senseless block, or a stone without passions'. The same language of 'blocks' and 'stones' reappears in another sermon from the same *Decade*, as well as Shakespeare's Grumio's 'stocks'. 'The Lord', Bullinger says, would not 'have us to be altogether benumbed, like blocks and stocks and senseless stones'.[98]

Throughout *Julius Caesar*, Shakespeare includes a wide variety of instances of coldness, insensitivity and other failures of human sympathy, ranging from the most extreme (murdering a friend) to the most quotidian (a passing social snub). In their opening conversation, Cassius accuses Brutus of being 'too stubborn and too strange', forgoing his former 'gentleness' and 'show of love' (1.2.34–8). 'Y'have ungently, Brutus, / Stole from my bed' (2.1.236–7), Portia complains. 'And when I asked you what the matter was / You stared upon me with ungentle looks' (2.1.240–1). Brutus kills a man whom he insists he also loves. 'I . . . did love Caesar when I struck him' (3.1.183), he tells Antony. To the crowd in the Forum he protests, as well, with an echo of Caesar's characteristic illeism, 'If there be any in this assembly, any dear friend of Caesar's, to him I say, that Brutus's love to Caesar was no less than his' (3.2.18–20).

Brutus emphasises his love for Caesar in order to stress the supposedly disinterested nature of his political engagement. Ultimately, however, the 'assembly' of baffled plebeians find his emotional discipline alienating, instead. As Cassius and Portia speak of Brutus as 'ungentle', so also Antony censures him as 'unkind'. Pointing out the place in Caesar's cloak where, he says, 'the well-belovèd Brutus stabbed' (3.2.174), Antony describes him as having 'unkindly knocked' (3.2.177). 'This was the most unkindest cut of all,' he proclaims. 'For Brutus, as you know, was Caesar's angel. / Judge, O you gods, how dearly Caesar loved him' (3.2.179–80). Antony then begins to speak of his 'countrymen', the gathered multitude, whom he describes as 'kind souls' (3.2.192). Weeping, like him, they feel 'the dint of pity' (3.2.193). 'Dint' recalls 'knock': Antony aligns the audience with the dead Caesar metaphorically, as if they, too, in their 'pity', had been physically affected by Brutus' 'most unkindest cut'.

In addition to the obvious, central event of the play, Caesar's assassination, Shakespeare includes a number of instances in which Caesar and Brutus both alike refuse to be merciful. Just before he is killed, Caesar roundly refuses to pardon Metellus Cimber's brother, Publius. In the quarrel scene, Brutus likewise dismisses Cassius' pleas on behalf of Lucius Pella. In the Capitol, Brutus kneels before Caesar, interceding on Publius' behalf, but fails even so to soften Caesar's resolve. When the other conspirators press him, as well, for Publius' pardon, Caesar points to this rejection: 'Doth not Brutus bootless kneel?' (3.1.75) Caesar seizes upon his resistance to his own known affection for Brutus as a symbol to the other petitioners of his 'constancy' to his own intentions, as if there could be no more striking proof of his imperviousness to their 'prayers' than his indifference to his 'angel' (3.1.59), Brutus. So, too, Brutus refuses to grant Portia's entreaty, when she kneels before him and begs him, by 'all' his 'vows of love' (2.1.269), to tell her why he is 'heavy' with anxiety (2.1.274). 'Kneel not, gentle

Portia' (2.1.277), Brutus replies. Portia, unsatisfied, strikes back with a play on the word 'gentle'. 'I should not need if you were gentle Brutus' (2.1.278).

Brutus and Portia's disputed term for each other here, 'gentle', appears repeatedly in *Julius Caesar*: 'gentle Romans', 'gentle friends' and so on.[99] When Antony learns that Brutus is dead, he proclaims in his eulogy, 'His life was gentle', where 'gentle' seems to mean 'noble', aristocratic: 'he was the noblest Roman of them all.' Alone with Caesar's corpse, however, Antony uses 'gentle' in a different sense: 'Pardon me, thou bleeding piece of earth / That I am meek and gentle with these butchers!' (3.1.254–5). Referring to a series of examples ranging from 1555 to 1769, the *OED* explains that 'gentle' in Shakespeare's time could mean a passive as well as an active quality; not just 'considerate' or 'kind', but also 'flexible, yielding': '*Gentle* a. 5: not harsh or irritating to the touch; soft, tender; yielding to pressure, pliant, supple. *Obs.*' 'Gentleness' in this sense is the opposite of another key concept in the play, 'constancy', understood in contrast as rock-like intractability.

This concept of 'gentle' as 'meek', however, is under pressure from a competing definition of 'gentle' as 'characteristic of the gentility'. In a world of tame courtiers, these two definitions would not necessarily contradict each other; an aristocrat would of necessity be skilled in the art of yielding. In Shakespeare's Rome, however, these two concepts of what it means to be 'gentle' are irreconcilable, investing the term with pointed, dramatic irony. 'Gentle friends, / Let's kill him boldly, but not wrathfully; / Let's carve him as a dish fit for the gods, / Not hew him as a carcass fit for hounds' (2.1.171–4). The increasingly coarse, concrete language of the sentence, beginning with 'gods' and ending with 'hounds', moving from the elegance of 'carve' to the messiness of 'hew', progressively gives the lie to Brutus' wishful, initial description of his co-conspirators as 'gentle'.

In sum, Shakespeare's Rome seems to be both distinguished and destroyed by a peculiar pitilessness. At one point, the haruspices tell Caesar that 'plucking the entrails of an offering forth, / They could not find a heart within the beast' (2.2.39–40). The most obvious interpretation of this omen is that it represents, as Anson says, 'a state without a leader'. On the other hand, Anson adds, the beast without a heart may also represent Caesar himself.[100] When Calpurnia tries to keep him from the Senate house, he protests,

'Caesar should be a beast without a heart / If he should stay at home today for fear' (2.2.42–3). He misinterprets the omen, however, just as he does her dream. As Cicero warns, early on, 'Men may construe things after their fashion / Clean from the purpose of the things themselves' (1.3.34–5). The missing heart does not indicate 'cowardice' (2.2.41), as Caesar suggests, but instead Caesar's own marked lack of compassion. He dismisses his wife's pleas; once he arrives at the Senate, he also dismisses the conspirators' petitions to pardon Publius Cimber. The play begins with his defeat of his own countryman, Pompey, a former ally, as well as the former husband of his daughter, Julia. Equally well, however, the absent heart could be said to represent the ruthless Republican conspirators, including especially Brutus, who kills Caesar despite his professed 'love' for the man. The same hard-heartedness that the tribune Murellus finds reprehensible in the Roman plebs, cheering the downfall of their countrymen, appears again among the aristocracy. High and low, plebeian and patrician, Rome itself seems to be 'a beast without a heart'.[101] Geoffrey Hughes describes the portent as 'an apt symbol of the Roman body politic'.[102]

It would be too simple, however, to say that Shakespeare's Romans are entirely closed-off and callous. The tradesmen who introduce the play, for example, caught off-guard amid their celebration of Caesar's victory over Pompey, prove not insensible to the tribunes' censure of their 'hard hearts'. 'See where their basest mettle be not moved' (1.1.62), Murellus' fellow tribune Flavius observes. 'They vanish tongue-tied in their guiltiness' (1.1.63). A near-exact antithesis of Murellus' condemnation of the Roman people as 'blocks' or 'stones', lacking all 'sense' of other people's suffering, appears about halfway through the play, as well, in a parallel address to the Roman plebs. In his funeral oration, Antony tells the crowd, 'You are not wood, you are not stones, but men' (3.2.143). 'It is not meet you know how Caesar loved you' (3.2.142), he goes on. 'Being men, hearing the will of Caesar, / It will inflame you, it will make you mad' (3.2.144–5). Cassius predicts this outcome, when he warns Brutus against allowing Antony to speak: 'the people may be moved / By that which he will utter' (3.1.234–5).

Throughout *Julius Caesar*, tears represent the exercise of the emotional faculty of compassion. In the opening scene, Flavius urges his 'good countrymen' to 'weep' for their 'fault' (1.1.52), in encouraging Caesar's triumph 'over Pompey's blood' (1.1.57):

> Assemble all the poor men of your sort;
> Draw them to Tiber banks, and weep your tears
> Into the channel, till the lowest stream
> Do kiss the most exalted shores of all.
>
> (1.1.58–61)

The hyperbole is extreme; the core of the conceit, however, is the coming-together of high and low, patrician and plebeian, in an act of extreme sympathy, a movement Antony adeptly recreates in his funeral oration. Yet he reverses its hierarchy: before he asks the poor to take pity on Caesar, he describes Caesar, the great populist, as having sympathy for them. 'When that the poor have cried, Caesar hath wept' (3.2.92). In Flavius' terms, 'the most exalted shores' come down to 'kiss' the 'lowest stream'. So also Antony himself, unlike Brutus, comes down from the pulpit to mingle more immediately with the crowd. 'If you have tears, prepare to shed them now' (3.2.167), he suggests. Before prompting his audience to weep, he first does so himself. 'Poor soul,' one plebeian observes, 'his eyes are red as fire with weeping' (3.2.116).

The basis for such sympathy is the shared experience of being 'flesh and blood' (3.1.67). Howsoever disparate in social status, patricians and plebeians hold in common the basic human given of embodiment. All alike are physically vulnerable, and this vulnerability becomes by extension a symbol of a more intangible susceptibility to being 'moved' emotionally. For example, Flavius' mention of 'Pompey's blood' affects or 'moves' the tradesmen, in the opening scene. So here, Caesar's blood: 'sweet Caesar's wounds' (3.2.218), his 'sacred blood' (3.2.134), symbolise the great man's shared humanity, eliciting pity. Harping on Caesar's 'blood', Antony finally observes his rhetoric take physical effect. 'O, now you weep, and I perceive you feel / The dint of pity: these are gracious drops' (3.2.191–2). 'O piteous spectacle!' (3.2.196) one plebeian cries, as Antony at last unveils Caesar's corpse. 'O most bloody sight!' (3.2.198).

In the next chapter, '"The northern star"', I discuss critical responses to the leitmotif of blood in *Julius Caesar* in more detail, including especially those of feminist critics Gail Kern Paster and Coppélia Khan. More than just femininity, blood represents the passibility of the 'grotesque' body, the shared 'vulnerability' that, through sympathy, enables the formation of human community.

Here, for example, by appealing to pity, Antony the orator is able 'to stir men's blood' (3.2.216). The heart, too, reappears as symbol: Antony is able to 'steal away' the 'hearts' of the people (3.2.209). His own 'heart', he says, 'is in the coffin there with Caesar' (3.2.107). Murellus rebukes the Roman people by calling them 'stones', 'hard hearts'. Antony, however, is able to 'move' these 'stones of Rome' to 'rise and mutiny' (3.2.222–3), by insisting instead that they are 'men' (3.2.143) and that they share a common humanity with the murdered Caesar.

Nor are the patricians immune to pity. Meeting the conspirators for the first time shortly after Caesar's death, Antony initially maintains what he calls 'cold modesty', shaking their bloody hands and greeting them each by name. 'Looking down on Caesar', however, he is momentarily 'swayed from the point' (3.1.219). He begins to lament Caesar's passing – a dangerous digression:

> Pardon me, Julius! Here wast thou bayed, brave hart.
> Here didst thou fall. And here thy hunters stand
> Signed in thy spoil and crimsoned in thy lethe.
> O world, thou was the forest to this hart,
> And this indeed, O world, the heart of thee.
> How like a deer, strucken by many princes,
> Dost thou here lie?
>
> (3.1.204–10)

Antony's foray here into extravagant rhetoric, a characteristic for which he was known, and which expresses his passionate nature, is presented as a lapse into a series of puns, akin to John of Gaunt's deathbed variations on his own name, 'Gaunt', in *Richard II*. The 'hart' at the centre of the wordplay calls to mind Jaques' 'sobbing deer' in *As You Like It*: in each case, the deer functions, like children in *Macbeth*, as a symbol of the object of pity, much as tears represent its exercise.[103] Once the conspirators leave, recoiling at what he calls 'the cruel issue of these bloody men' (3.1.295), Antony imagines a world without pity, in terms that call to mind Shakespeare's Lady Macbeth: 'Mothers shall but smile when they behold / Their infants quartered with the hands of war: / All pity choked with custom of fell deeds' (3.1.267–9). In this nightmare vision, blood no longer evokes pity, but instead becomes 'lethe', wiping out the memory of past affection.

Antony's later weeping in the Forum is politically expedient, but that does not mean it is not also genuine. As if to corroborate Antony's testimony, Shakespeare includes beforehand a more private display of 'passion'. Just before the funeral orations, when Antony's servant sees Caesar's corpse, he begins to weep, and Antony sends him away, lest his own tears, prompted by his servant's, interfere with his ability to remain composed in front of Caesar's assassins. 'Thy heart is big: get thee apart and weep' (3.1.282), he tells the man. 'Passion, I see is catching, for mine eyes, / Seeing those beads of sorrow stand in thine, / Begin to water' (3.1.283–5). In order to be an effective orator, Antony must first be an actor, acting the part of an orator. In other words, he must seem to possess the 'cold modesty' of a traditionalist Roman patrician, Brutus' 'reason' and 'patience', even if in practice what he plans to unleash is populist pathos.

Shakespeare touches upon a dubious dichotomy here that the Romans themselves recognised and fretted about: the thin line between respectable, manly Roman oratory and disreputable, effeminate Greek drama.[104] To win permission to speak, Antony must seem restrained; to speak effectively, however, he must become passionate. In his *De oratore* ('On the Orator'), Cicero compares public speaking to acting, as well as poetry, and insists that in all of these performances, the performer must be 'on fire with passion' in order to be effective.[105] Specifically, the orator must first himself feel even more strongly than his audience the emotion that he wants them to feel. For, as Cicero explains:

> it is impossible for the listener to feel indignation, hatred, or ill-will, to be terrified of anything, or reduced to tears of compassion, unless all those emotions, which the advocate would inspire in an arbitrator, are visibly stamped or rather branded on the advocate himself.

To that end, Cicero adds, 'I give you my word, I never tried, by means of a speech, to arouse either indignation or compassion, either ill-will or hatred, in the minds of the tribunal, without being really stirred myself.'[106]

In the third chapter of this study, '"The high Roman fashion"', I suggest that Brutus is just as theatrical, just as conscious of himself as performing an unnatural *persona*, as Cleopatra, despite obvious differences in their outward behaviour. He is playing the role of the Stoic *sapiens*, as well as that of his ancestor, 'old Brutus', just as she is that of her former self, meeting Antony at Cydnus, as well as that of the goddess Isis. Brutus' role model, Lucius Junius Brutus, was himself noted for a similar near-lifelong performance. In order to deceive the Tarquins, who had killed a number of the most notable men of Rome, including his own brother, 'old Brutus' feigned slow-wittedness, until the rape of Lucrece gave him at last sufficient *casus belli* to foment a full-scale rebellion against the Tarquins' rule. Hence his cognomen: 'dullard' (Latin, *brutus*). The idea that the Stoic resembles an actor is not new; Gordon Braden, citing J. M. Rist, observes in Senecan Stoicism 'a persistent strain of what has been called theatricality'.[107] Braden draws attention to Seneca's description of Cato's suicide: 'Behold a spectacle worthy for a god, intent on his own work, to look at.'[108] As Braden explains, 'the point of Cato's *spectaculum* is not just that it is well-done, but also that it is being watched.'[109] Brutus himself associates 'constancy' with role-playing when, like Lady Macbeth to Macbeth, he exhorts the conspirators not to let their 'looks' reveal their 'purposes'. 'Look fresh and merrily' (2.1.224), he says. 'Bear it as our Roman actors do, / With untired spirits and formal constancy' (2.1.225–6). 'Formal' here suggests not only stiffness or self-control, but also superficiality: 'form' as opposed to 'substance.'

Even Brutus, however, is susceptible to 'pity'. Antony criticises Brutus in his funeral oration as a man driven by a pitiless concern for his own honour, but praises him, more honestly, perhaps, in a eulogy at the end of the tragedy as 'gentle'. Out of all the conspirators, Antony says, Brutus and Brutus alone was motivated by a 'general honest thought' and hope of 'common good to all', rather than 'envy of great Caesar' (5.5.68–71). Antony's qualifiers 'general' and 'common' are especially significant; they show that he sees Brutus as concerned for the well-being of the masses, sympathising with them, in a manner that earlier, in his funeral oration, he reserves for himself and Caesar, representing Brutus as well as the other conspirators as motivated instead by 'private griefs' (3.2.206).

Immediately after Caesar's death, speaking to Antony and corroborating Antony's later assessment of his motives, Brutus defends himself, as well as, less plausibly, his co-conspirators, as inspired above all by a spirit of 'pity to the general wrong of Rome.' You see 'but our hands,' he protests, still stained with Caesar's blood, and so 'we must appear bloody and cruel.' This appearance of callous cruelty, however, he insists, is misleading.

> Our hearts you see not; they are pitiful;
> And pity to the general wrong of Rome –
> As fire drives out fire, so pity pity –
> Hath done this deed on Caesar.

> (3.1.166–73)

Brutus' apology to Antony here, emphasising 'the general wrong of Rome', echoes his earlier soliloquy, 'It must be by his death.' 'For my part,' Brutus there begins, 'I know no personal cause to spurn at him / But for the general' (2.1.10–12). Psychologically, the key point is that Brutus sees, or claims to see, the decision to assassinate Caesar as primarily a question of 'pity' rather than 'honour', as Antony implies in his later funeral oration. His 'pity' for the people of Rome outweighs his 'pity' for Caesar.

What exactly is the 'wrong', however, of which Brutus speaks? Here, honour reasserts itself. As Brutus' soliloquy progresses, it becomes clear that what he fears is, above all, shame. 'Th'abuse of greatness' which he expects from Caesar is that, having climbed the 'ladder' of apparent 'lowliness', he will then turn upon those below him, such as Brutus himself, and treat them with contempt, 'scorning the base degrees by which he did ascend'. 'So Caesar may' (2.1.27), he concludes. 'Then, lest he may, prevent' (2.1.28). The same root concern with the threat of shame, specifically, of being seen as less than 'noble', less than 'Roman', reappears with great force in Brutus' later funeral oration. 'Who is here so base, that would be a bondman?' he asks. 'Who is here so rude, that would not be a Roman? If any, speak, for him have I offended' (3.2.29–31).

Brutus' desire to maintain his reputation as a 'noble Roman', and, by extension, to preserve the Roman 'liberty' that gives that self-image its value, does not wholly blot out, however, his 'pity' for Caesar. He is not indifferent to his affection for the would-be tyrant, just as he is not indifferent to the charms of conjugal love or the claims of longstanding friendship. He initially resists Portia's pleas to be taken into his counsel, but eventually does open up to her, disclosing 'the secrets of [his] heart' (2.1.305). In the quarrel scene, Brutus mocks Cassius, at first, for his blustering, agitated indignation, but in the end embraces him, forgives him and admits that he, too, was in part at fault. 'Do you confess so much?' Cassius asks, astonished. 'Give me your hand' (4.3.116). 'And my heart too' (4.3.117), Brutus replies.

Without question, the Romans in this tragedy are capable of astonishing cruelty. Antony, Octavius and Lepidus sentence their own relatives to death with hardly a moment's hesitation:

ANTONY
           These many, then, shall die; their names are pricked.
OCTAVIUS
           Your brother, too, must die; consent you, Lepidus?
LEPIDUS   I do consent.
OCTAVIUS   Prick him down, Antony.
LEPIDUS   Upon condition Publius shall not live,
           Who is your sister's son, Mark Antony.
ANTONY
           He shall not live. Look, with a spot I damn him.

                                 (4.1.1–6)

The 'prick' of Antony's ink-pen here recalls the stab of a dagger, like Brutus' 'most unkindest cut'. The 'spot' of ink resembles a bleeding wound, like those left in Caesar's body. The metaphorical diminution of murder to such a small-scale, seemingly trivial event, committed indirectly and from afar, without any apparent internal hesitation or deliberation, reflects another order altogether of callous inhumanity. The victims of their proscription seem no more to the triumvirate than dots on a page, despite family ties that would normally evoke affection.

Even so, the faculty of pity is there, somewhere, even if etiolated. Antony may not hesitate to 'damn' his poor nephew, Publius, but he does weep genuine tears for Caesar. Rome is not wholly driven by fear of shame, but instead can be understood as tempered, if only to a limited degree, by a countervailing strain of guilt. 'Our hearts you see not' (3.1.169), Brutus tells Antony, but nonetheless, he insists, they exist. He feels 'pity' for Caesar, just as he also does for the Roman people. The problem is not that Brutus does not feel sympathy for others, but rather that he does not know what to do with this sense of compassion. He wants to operate instead on the basis of 'reason' alone. Antony, by contrast, like an actor, knows how to make use of pathos. A. D. Nuttall describes 'the Roman world' of *Julius Caesar* as 'a place of malfunctioning emotion'. In this play, especially, 'love is an ill-nourished, undeveloped thing. Either it is crushed by Stoic repression or it is rhetorically manipulated and converted into aggression.'[110] In the Neostoic paradigm Shakespeare's Rome represents, there is no place for pity, and as a result it goes underground, becoming unstable and dangerous, like a cellar full of gunpowder.

In insisting on the persistence of pity, Shakespeare presents a variation on a widespread argument against Stoicism, one which can be found in sources ranging from Cicero and Plutarch to Erasmus and Calvin. The objection common to all is that emotions such as pity cannot be eliminated altogether, even if, contrary to fact, it were somehow in our interest to do so. To become a disinterested creature of pure reason is simply impossible, even if it were advisable; sympathy for other people's suffering, right or wrong, is to some extent an ineradicable component of our human nature. We can repress it, we can deny its force, but in the end the heart cannot be removed from the beast. What can happen, however, is that, in being stifled, the human sense of pity, like any other emotion, can become weak, sluggish, unpredictable, and, like the Roman people in this play, prone to sudden explosions. In his essay 'Of Anger', Montaigne warns that hiding anger may in fact make it worse, like water trapped behind a dam. 'We incorporate anger by hiding it; as Diogenes said to Demosthenes, who, for fear of being seen in a tavern, was drawing back further inside it: "The further back you go, the deeper in you are."'[111] Refusing to acknowledge passionate feelings does not make them disappear. Instead, they may even be exacerbated. Or they may break out in places where they do not properly belong.

'The soul discharges its passions on false objects when the true are wanting,' Montaigne writes.[112] Such psychic displacement occurs repeatedly in *Julius Caesar*. Emotions that Romans deny in one arena reappear with disastrous force in another. A crowd of plebeians tear apart the poet Cinna, for example, ignoring his protests that he is not, in fact, the Cinna that they are looking for. Brutus confesses in retrospect that his anger at Cassius in the quarrel scene was at least in part a reaction to his grief at the loss of his wife. Portia's suicide by swallowing hot coals is a vivid, if horrifying, symbol of this hysterical acting-out of unassimilated, disavowed emotional distress. The 'constant' silence that Brutus asks of her earlier in the play is inhuman, deadly, like 'swallowing fire'.[113] Shakespeare frames Portia's suicide so that it becomes an allegory of what Brutus does to himself by pretending, first to Cassius, then to Messala, that he is less affected by the news of her death than he really is. He keeps his mouth shut about his grief, even though it is, so to speak, killing him; he, too, is in a sense 'swallowing fire', and the pain of it drives him to uncontrolled, uncharacteristic anger at his friend and ally, Cassius. As David Quint explains, 'Montaigne's essay on anger is of a piece with the larger moral teaching of the *Essays*.' Unlike Shakespeare's Brutus, the essayist 'gives up on maintaining a constant inner equanimity and outward composure to the observing world'. 'The toll one exacts upon one's nature to do so is simply not worth it,' Montaigne concludes; 'it is better to let the passions run their course.'[114]

Notes

1. Hillier, 'Valour Will Weep', 382.
2. William Shakespeare, *Julius Caesar*, ed. David Daniell. The Arden Shakespeare. Third Series (London: Thomson Learning, 1998).
3. Bacon, *Works of Francis Bacon*, vol. 4, 472.
4. Erasmus, *Praise of Folly*, 45.
5. Montaigne, *Essays*, 308–9.
6. Cic. *Off.* 1.28.
7. Xenophanes of Colophon, *Fragments*, frag. 15.
8. Fueurbach, *Essence of Christianity*, 17.
9. Freud, *Civilization and Its Discontents*, 38, 41.
10. Adler, 'Striving for Superiority', 33.
11. Ibid., 39. Like Nietzsche, as well as Freud, Adler was influenced by contemporary Darwinism. Unlike Nietzsche and Freud, however, Adler takes the perspective of the species, rather than the individual. Thus, he sees sympathetic altruism, which he calls 'social interest', as a necessary component of 'the survival of the fittest', rather than as a 'sickly', 'diseased', or 'neurotic' impulse. Cf. Huber, 'In Search of Social Interest'.
12. Adler, 'Striving for Superiority', 39–40.
13. Ibid., 33.
14. For Horatio as 'a curiously shadowy and undefined figure', see D. G. James, *The Dream of Learning* (Oxford: Clarendon Press, 1965), 72; cited in Monsarrat, *Light from the Porch*, 137.

15. William Shakespeare, *Hamlet*, ed. by Harold Jenkins. The Arden Shakespeare. Second Series (London: Thomson Learning, 1982).
16. Sen. *Ep.* 59.14–16.
17. Ibid., 117.29.
18. Ibid., 116.5.
19. Cited in Long and Sedley, eds, *Hellenistic Philosophers*, 381.
20. Plut. *De Stoic.* 1041f, 1051a–b; cited in Long and Sedley, eds, *Hellenistic Philosophers*, 423, 328.
21. Cited in Long and Sedley, eds, *Hellenistic Philosophers*, 425.
22. Cited in Sext. Emp. *Math.* 9.90. See Sextus Empiricus, *Adversus Mathematicos*.
23. Sen. *Ep.* 42.1.
24. Sen. *Const.* 7.1. English translation of Seneca's *De constantia* is cited from Seneca, *Moral Essays*.
25. For Brutus' treatises *Peri kathēkontos* ('On Duties') and *De virtute* ('On Virtue'), see Sen. *Ep.* 94.45 and Cic. *Fin.* 1.8.
26. On the possibility of a connection between Shakespeare's depiction of Brutus and Cicero's critique of Stoicism, see Vawter, '"After their fashion"' as well as Vawter, '"Division 'tween our souls"'.
27. Miles, *Shakespeare and the Constant Romans*.
28. Monsarrat, *Light from the Porch*, 28.
29. According to Miles, *Shakespeare and the Constant Romans*, 'it is one of the paradoxes of Cicero's philosophical position [as a sceptical "Academic"] that it is possible to call him both a Stoic and a founder of the "anti-Stoic" tradition [. . .]. The essentially Stoic framework of his most famous works, the *Tusculan Disputations* and *De officiis*, and the almost undiluted Stoicism of passages such as the account of emotions in *Tusculans* 4, justify the custom of referring to him casually as a "Stoic." On the other hand, he is sharply critical of some Stoic doctrines' (19–21).
30. Ibid., 5, vii, 29.
31. Vawter, '*Julius Caesar*: Rupture in the Bond', 316.
32. For Cicero's thought on *oikeiōsis*, see Cic. *Off.* 1.4–259. Secondary literature on Stoicism and *oikeiōsis* is too extensive to cite in full. For a brief overview, see Sellars, *Stoicism*, 129–33. For a more detailed discussion, see Striker, 'The Role of οἰκείωσις'. Comprehensive studies include Radice, *Oikeiosis*, and Reydams-Schils, *The Roman Stoic*.
33. For Shakespeare's perspective on Epicurean ethics, see Patrick Gray, '"HIDE THY SELFE": Hamlet, Montaigne, and Epicurean Ethics', in *Shakespeare and Renaissance Ethics*, ed. Patrick Gray and John D. Cox (Cambridge: Cambridge University Press, 2014), 213–36.
34. Malcolm Schofield explains: 'We know of numerous Stoic treatises entitled *On appropriate action*, although the only survivor is Cicero's

transmutation, expansion, and far-reaching Romanisation of Panaetius' version in his *On duties*. Another subject treated by more than
one Stoic was *On acts of benefaction*: again, we possess only a Latin
version, a massive work by Seneca in seven books devoted to the casu-
istry of a practice which was a major ingredient in the moral and social
glue of Roman society' (Schofield, 'Stoic Ethics', 254). For a detailed
commentary on Seneca's *De beneficiis* and its social and intellectual
context, see Griffin, *Seneca on Society.*

35. See Sen. *Ep.* 6–9, as well as 36.
36. On Epicurean withdrawal in Senecan tragedy, as well as Shakespeare's
    response, see Patrick Gray, 'Shakespeare vs. Seneca', 221–2.
37. Sallust, 'The War with Jugurtha', in *Sallust*, 4–5. For further discus-
    sion of the cultural importance of these lifelike wax masks (*imagines*)
    of the dead, see Bartsch, *Mirror of the Self*, 120–7.
38. Cf. A. D. Nuttall on Aeneas in Nuttall, 'The Stoic in Love,' in Nut-
    tall, *The Stoic in Love*, 56–67.
39. Nuttall, *Shakespeare the Thinker*, 185.
40. Cicero, *On Moral Ends*, 4.48.
41. In his dialogue *De amicitia* ('On friendship'), Cicero warns of the
    possibility of the classical discourse of friendship being misused by
    demagogues such as Caesar and Mark Antony. See, for example, his
    discussion of Tiberius Gracchus, 35–44.
42. Sen., *Const.* 3.5.
43. Ibid., 10.4.
44. Montaigne, *Essays*, 302.
45. Plutarch, 'The Life of Marcus Brutus', trans. by Thomas North,
    in Geoffrey Bullough, ed. *Narrative and Dramatic Sources of
    Shakespeare*, 114.
46. Plutarch, *Plutarch's Lives of the Noble Grecians and Romans*, 298.
47. Sen. *Ep.* 20.3; cf. 29.5–6, 52.9, 108.36–7.
48. Eliot, 'Shakespeare and the Stoicism of Seneca', 129.
49. For more on this controversy, see Cantor, *Shakespeare's Roman
    Trilogy*, 43–5, as well as Clayton, '"Should Brutus never taste of
    Portia's death but once?"', and Smith, 'The Duplicate Revelation
    of Portia's Death'; cf. Bowers, 'The Copy for Shakespeare's *Julius
    Caesar*', and Stirling, '*Julius Caesar* in Revision'.
50. Eramus, *Praise of Folly*, 45.
51. Sen. *Ep.* 71.27.
52. Sen. *Const.* 10.54.
53. Ibid., 3.5.
54. Xenophanes of Colophon, *Fragments*, frags. 23 and 26.
55. See, for example, Russell, 'Virtue as "Likeness to God"'.
56. Sen. *Const.* 8.2.
57. Sen. *Prov.* 1.5, 6.6.

58. See Anson, '*Julius Caesar:* The Politics of the Hardened Heart'; Rackin, 'The Pride of Shakespeare's Brutus'; Levitsky, 'The elements were so mix'd. . .', 24–05; and Kaufmann and Ronan, 'Shakespeare's *Julius Caesar*', 18–51, as well as Vawter, '"After their fashion"', and Vawter, '"Division 'tween our Souls"'.

59. William Shakespeare, *Julius Caesar*, ed. Marvin Spevack (Cambridge: Cambridge University Press, 2003), 24; cited in Miles, *Constant Romans*, 4; q.v. for bibliography and further discussion.

60. G. K. Hunter, 'A Roman Thought: Renaissance Attitudes to History Exemplified in Shakespeare and Jonson', in *An English Miscellany: Presented to W. S. Mackie*, ed. B. S. Lee (Capetown and New York: Oxford University Press, 1977), 94; cited in Kahn, *Roman Shakespeare*, 13.

61. Cantor, *Shakespeare's Rome*, 37.

62. Thomas, *Shakespeare's Roman Worlds*, 13.

63. Miola, *Shakespeare's Rome*, 17.

64. Miles, *Constant Romans*, 1.

65. Cf. Sen. *Ot. Sap.* 3.2; cf. Diog. Laert., 7.121, 123, and Plut. *De Stoic.* 1033b–f; cited in Monsarrat, *Light from the Porch*, 17 n. 8.

66. Hor. *Od.* 3.12.13.

67. Holbrook, *Shakespeare's Individualism*, 17; cf. Montaigne, *Essays*, 2.1.

68. See Salmon, 'Stoicism and Roman Example'.

69. Aggeler, '"Sparkes of holy things"', 237 n. 12.

70. Bouwsma, 'The Two Faces of Humanism', 20.

71. Montaigne, *Essays*, 2:12, p. 457.

72. Pierre de La Primaudaye, *The French Academie*, 15–16, trans. T. Bowes (London: Edmund Bollifant for G. Bishop and Ralph Newbery, 1586; facsimile rpt. New York and Hildesheim: Verlag, 1972); cited in Monsarrat, *Light from the Porch*, 75–6.

73. Sinfield, *Faultlines*, 222 ff.; cf. Sinfield, 'Hamlet's Special Providence'.

74. For a more detailed comparison of Stoic determinism and Calvin's, see Partee, *Calvin and Classical Philosophy*, 121–2, and Partee, 'Calvin and Determinism'. cf. also Monsarrat, *Light from the Porch*, 71.

75. Guillaume du Vair, *The Moral Philosophie of the Stoicks*, trans. Thomas James, ed. Rudolf Kirk (New Brunswick, NJ: Rutgers University Press, 1951), 45; cited in Aggeler, '"Sparkes"', 225.

76. Sen. *Clem.*, 1.5.5–6; 2.4.4; 2.4.1; 2.5.3, in Seneca, *Moral Essays*, 356–449.

77. Calvin, *Calvin's Commentary on Seneca's* De Clementia, 359.

78. Ibid., 361; cf. Plin., *Ep.* 8.16.3.

79. Calvin, *Commentary on the Epistle of Paul*, 1:31. Calvin refers here in particular to St Paul's term *astorgous* ('without affection, fondness, familiarity [Gk., *storgē*]').

80. Calvin, *Institutes*, 3.8.10.

81. Seneca, *Opera omnia*, 679.

82. *Dura silex aut stet Marpesia cautes* (than 'a chunk of flint or mountain crag'); Vir., *Aen.* 6.471; cited in Erasmus, *Praise of Folly*, 45–6.

83. Monsarrat, *Light from the Porch*, 52; cf. 73.

84. Colish, *Stoic Tradition*, 17. For an overview of the connections between Roman Stoicism and early Christianity, emphasising Stoicism's influence on the letters of St Paul, St Peter and St Clement, see also Thorsteinsson, *Roman Stoicism and Roman Christianity.*

85. Tert. *De An.* 20.1; Jer. *Adv. Jov.*1.49; cf. Lact. *Div. Inst.* 6.24 and Jer. *De Vir.* 12; cited in Monsarrat, *Light from the Porch*, 30 n. 5.

86. Calvin, *Institutes*, 3.8.9.

87. Calvin, *A commentarie of Iohn Calvine.*

88. Calvin, *Commentaries of the First Book of Moses*, 45:1.

89. Justus Lipsius, *Of Constancy*, 37, 49, 52–3.

90. Monsarrat, *Light from the Porch*, 56.

91. Ibid., 132 n. 41, 135 n. 124.

92. Du Vair, 'Stoicks', 50–1.

93. For further discussion of Shakespeare's representation of ancient Rome in *Titus Andronicus* as a culture indifferent to human suffering, see Patrick Gray, 'Shakespeare and the Other Virgil'.

94. Anson, 'Hardened Heart', 11.

95. For further background on the 'Stoic' as 'stock', see also Braden, *Anger's Privilege*, 240 n. 69.

96. Miles, *Constant Romans*, 45–50.

97. Monsarrat, *Light from the Porch*, 74; cf. *The Decades of Henry Bullinger*, trans. H. I., ed. Thomas Harding, 4 vols (Cambridge: Parker Society, 1849–52), vol. 1, vii–viii, and vol. 4, xxviii–xxxi; cited in Monsarrat, *Light from the Porch*, 74 n. 1.

98. *Decades*, vol. 3, 83–4, 56; cf. Calvin, *Institutes*, 3.10; cited in Monsarrat, *Light from the Porch*, 74.

99. Cf. *Julius Caesar*, 1.2.73, 1.2.234, 2.1.277–8, 3.1.258, 3.2.72, 3.2.140, 4.2.321, 5.5.72.

100. Anson, 'Hardened Heart', 21.

101. Cf. *Titus Andronicus*: 'Why, foolish Lucius, dost thou not perceive / That Rome is but a wilderness of tigers?' (3.1.53–4).

102. Hughes, '"A World Elsewhere"'.

103. On the infant as a symbol of pity in Macbeth, see Cleanth Brooks' famous essay, 'The Naked Babe and the Cloak of Manliness', in *The Well-Wrought Urn*, 22–49.

104. Roman authors, such as Plautus' and Cicero's self-aware exploration of the uneasy similarity between drama and oratory has received substantial attention in recent years from classicists working on Roman rhetoric and performance. See Connolly, *State of Speech*, 198–236, and Bartsch, *Mirror of the Self*, 152–6, as well as Corbeill, *Controlling Laughter*.
105. Cf. Cic. *De or.* 2.193 ff.
106. Cic. *De or.* 2.189.
107. Braden, *Renaissance Tragedy*, 26; cf. J. M. Rist, *Stoic Philosophy* (Cambridge: Cambridge University Press, 1977), 252; cited in Braden, *Renaissance Tragedy*, 229 n. 34.
108. Sen. *Dial.* 1.2.9; cf. Sen. *Ep.* 104.30; cited in Braden, *Renaissance Tragedy*, 27.
109. Braden, *Renaissance Tragedy*, 27.
110. Nuttall, *Shakespeare the Thinker*, 188.
111. Montaigne, *Essays*, 2:31, 543.
112. Montaigne, *Essays*, 1:4, 14.
113. Cf. Shakespeare, *Julius Caesar*, 4.3.150–4.
114. Quint, '"Letting Oneself Go"', 126.

CHAPTER 2

'THE NORTHERN STAR': CONSTANCY AND PASSIBILITY IN *JULIUS CAESAR*

In the general introduction, 'Shakespeare and the Vulnerable Self', I proposed that Shakespeare's concept of personhood rests somewhere between twentieth-century antihumanism such as that of Althusser and the Kantian dream of autonomy that such 'Theory with a capital T' sets itself against. Both extremes are too reductive. The individual is neither entirely transcendent, like some sort of disembodied deity, nor entirely determined, like a cog in a machine, but instead interdependent, at once agent and object, like a partner in a dance or an interlocutor in a dialogue. For an antihumanist such as Lacan, the other is primarily 'the Other with a capital O', an impersonal force or structure such as 'language' or 'discourse'. For Shakespeare, however, the other is in contrast another consciousness: what Martin Buber calls a 'thou', as opposed to an 'it'.

In this chapter, as well as the final chapter on *Antony and Cleopatra*, I turn for purposes of comparison to the literary criticism of Mikhail Bakhtin. Like Lévinas, Barth, Tillich and many other twentieth-century theologians, Bakhtin is deeply indebted to Martin Buber.[1] These theologians, however, tend to emphasise only one instance of what Buber calls the 'I–thou' relationship, man's relationship with God, and to pass over what for Buber was equally important, man's relationship with his fellow man. By turning to a different disciple of Buber, Bakhtin, I hope to reintroduce the 'horizontal', so to speak, alongside the 'vertical'. Citing Buber's description of himself as 'a man among men', Ewan Fernie finds an analogue in 'the truth, as Hegel as describes it, of "I" that is "We" and "We" that is "I."[2] Christopher Tilmouth turns to Hobbes, and Jane Kingsley-Smith to Aristotle, for a similar pivot or reorientation away from the connection between man and God towards, as Buber says, the relations 'between man and man'.[3] Bakhtin for his part finds in Rabelais's 'grotesque' vision of the human body, as well as Dostoyevsky's gift for characterisation, a literary analogue of Buber's emphasis on human interdependence. Whereas Dostoyevsky focuses on relatively intangible questions of ethics, the intersection of 'multiple consciousnesses', Rabelais is more earthy and physical, emphasising the interrelatedness inherent in embodiment. Bakhtin sees in each author, however, Rabelais as well as Dostoyevsky, a preeminent artist of human passibility. Each communicates in his own distinct manner the same basic truth which I argue Shakespeare also presents here in these Roman plays: the unhealthy, dangerous absurdity of attempting to maintain what Bakhtin calls *'proud solitude'*.

In the final chapter on *Antony and Cleopatra*, 'A spacious mirror,' using Bakhtin's analysis of Dostoyevsky as a parallel, I look closely at Shakespeare's sense of human passibility as it extends to the relatively rarefied sphere of ethics: our susceptibility to moral judgement. To some extent, even if limited, we as human beings cannot help but be affected by what other people think of us. In this chapter on *Julius Caesar*, 'The northern star', drawing on Bakhtin's analysis of Rabelais, I turn instead to a more obvious form of passibility: human materiality. In so far as we are 'flesh and blood', we find ourselves enmeshed in a world of physical objects, one which we do not and cannot entirely control. For Shakespeare's Romans, this vulnerability is deeply distressing.

To explain Shakespeare's Romans' perspective on human embodiment, I also turn to a different strain of thought about the other, Derrida's concept of the other as the opposite of the selfsame. As mediated through postcolonial literary criticism, this concept of the other has come to mean an ostensible foil or point of contrast, usually, one drawn from a despised or 'subaltern' culture, which a hegemonic power uses to distinguish itself as 'self'. Derrida's observations on the traces of the selfsame within the other then serve as a model for a demonstration that the supposed opposition between this particular 'self' and its chosen 'other' is not absolute, but instead a self-serving, inaccurate social construction.[4] The distinction between self and other turns out to be permeable, specious. Disavowal of the supposed other does provide an index, however, of what it is that the self sees as less than ideal. In the case of Shakespearean *Romanitas*, the other seems to be femininity. This opposition itself reflects a deeper tension, however, between what Neostoicism calls 'constancy', a form of godlike transcendence, and the 'frailty' inherent to the human condition. Femininity for Shakespeare's Romans is only one symbol or instance of our ineluctable human 'vulnerability'; other aspects include sickness, old age and ignorance.

Power and Passibility: Two Concepts of the Divine

In this section, I explain the concept of 'passibility' in more detail and compare it to other theoretical categories such as vulnerability and femininity. In his history of personhood, Timothy Reiss introduces passibility as means to distinguish between pre-modern and modern perceptions of the self. Along the same lines as Charles Taylor and Alistair MacIntyre, Reiss describes modernity as distinguished by its emphasis on the autonomous agency of the individual, a tendency which he sees emerging in the early modern period in the introspection characteristic of authors such as Petrarch and Montaigne, as well as Descartes. In antiquity, as well as the Middle Ages, the self was understood in contrast as embedded in 'circles' or 'spheres' of relatedness. The susceptibility or 'passibility' of the self to the moral claims of its relationships with others was not considered accidental or extrinsic to its nature, but instead constitutive of its identity. Reiss derives the term 'passibility' from Aristotle. Oddly, however, he omits any mention of its usual field of signification. The concept of passibility has a long history in Christian discourse as a criterion for distinguishing between the human and the divine. For example, the question whether God is passible only in his humanity as the Son or if he is also passible in his divinity as the Father is one of the most contentious subjects of debate in twentieth-century Christian theology, echoing centuries of earlier Patristic controversy.

Passibility not only distinguishes the human from the divine, but also the God of Christianity, a human being, from the various deities or analogues of the Godhead proposed in classical philosophy. Figures such as Aristotle's Unmoved Mover are essentially impassible, whereas Christ, especially at the moment of his Passion, is obviously in some sense passible. This difference between classical and Christian representations of the ideal self corresponds to a key difference between the ethical paradigm of Shakespeare's Romans and Shakespeare's own. Shakespeare's Romans strive to become impassible, like the wholly transcendent deities of classical philosophy. Shakespeare himself believes they would be better served, however, if they made peace with their own human passibility. The healthy functioning of a republic, a marriage or even a friendship requires an openness or vulnerability to the other that these characters see instead as a threat to their sense of their own *imperium*: Patchen Markell might say, to their efforts to be recognised as 'sovereign'.

Theoretically, at least, Christians aim at an ideal of compassion and concession. God as Trinity serves as a model of unbegrudging interpersonal interdependence. Shakespeare's Romans, by contrast, prove fatally uncomfortable with any such arrangement. As Russell Hillier observes, 'in Roman eyes, empathy for a stranger's misfortune is a weakness or an evil'.[5] Shakespeare's Romans are suspicious of political compromise, since it involves giving up some degree of personal autonomy. Cooperation as they see it is at best a necessary evil, a means to an end, rather than a condition they are willing to accept *ad infinitum*. As a result, in *Antony and Cleopatra*, the triumvirate of Octavian, Antony and Lepidus proves a kind of secular anti-Trinity, doomed from the outset to degenerate into deadly rivalry. By grounding Shakespeare's Romans' transition from one political regime to another in their assumptions about ethics, rather than vice versa, I depart from Paul Cantor's approach to Shakespeare's Roman plays, as well as Fredric Jameson's more general claims about ethics in *The Political Unconscious*. The same kind of reversal of assumptions about cause and effect also informs my response here to most extant feminist criticism of Shakespeare's Roman plays. Rather than explaining the psychology of Roman characters as an effect of Roman patriarchy, I argue that Shakespeare's Romans' patent discomfort with femininity, as well their tendency to exclude women from the public sphere, emerges out of a more fundamental idealisation of impassibility.

The 1980s and 1990s saw a remarkable efflorescence of feminist interest in so-called 'pre-Oedipal' male anxiety about masculinity in Shakespeare's plays, including especially *Julius Caesar* and *Coriolanus*. Drawing upon the object relations theories of psychoanalysts such as Nancy Chodorow and Dorothy Dinnerstein, feminist critics Janet Adelman, Gail Kern Paster, Madelon Sprengnether, Cynthia Marshall and Coppélia Kahn present characters such as Coriolanus as striving to escape what Adelman calls 'suffocating mothers'. According to Adelman, 'contemporary object-relations psychoanalysis locates differentiation from the mother as a special site of anxiety for the boy-child, who must form his specifically masculine selfhood against the matrix of her overwhelming femaleness.'[6] In her early book on masculinity in Shakespeare's plays, *Man's Estate*, Coppélia Kahn adheres to much the same paradigm, citing in addition the work of sympathetic psychoanalysts such as Robert J. Stoller and Ralph Greenson. Kahn quotes Stoller: 'still-to-be-created masculinity is endangered by the primary, profound, primeval oneness with the mother.'[7] In sum, Kahn explains,

> the polarization of social roles and behavior into masculine independence, power, and repression of feeling as opposed to feminine dependence, weakness, and tenderness, and the consequent devaluation of femininity by men (and women as well) may arise as 'a quite nonbiological defensive maneuver against an earlier stage: closeness and primitive identification with mother.'[8]

A decade later, in her book on Shakespeare's Roman plays, *Roman Shakespeare*, Kahn revisits this argument, modifying it in ways that reflect the contemporary rise of New Historicism. Given her abiding interest in what she describes as Shakespeare's 'preoccupation with the masculine subject', it is perhaps only natural that Kahn would in time turn to Shakespeare's Rome. In this setting above all, masculinity seems to enjoy pride of place, albeit at tragic cost. Rome is a symbol and an instance of patriarchy and male dominance: 'Romanness' itself, Kahn argues, 'is virtually identical with an ideology of masculinity'. For example, she points out, 'the very etymology of *virtus* [Latin, 'virtue'] is gender-specific'; it is 'derived from *vir*, Latin for man'. 'Roman virtue' is not a 'moral abstraction' but instead 'a marker of sexual difference crucial to construction of the male subject'.[9] In this analysis of *Romanitas*, Kahn no longer appeals to psychoanalytic theory as she did in *Man's Estate*, as what she calls there 'a hermeneutic cornerstone'. No longer an 'intra-psychic phenomenon', grounded in a universal 'pre-Oedipal' complex, masculinity instead appears reconfigured as 'an ideology discursively maintained'. As an 'ideology' in the Althusserian sense, masculinity 'interpellates' the individual through 'discourse' such as the chivalric revival in the last years of Elizabeth's reign, channelling the energy of that subject into the tragic, aristocratic 'cultural practice' of 'emulation'. The concept of 'emulation' is crucial; Kahn cites the *OED* ('to copy or imitate with the object of equalling or excelling'), then gives her own, more complex account. 'In emulation, the admiration that generates a desire to imitate someone easily turns into rivalry, the desire to excel him, and finally to the desire to defeat or destroy him and take his place.'[10]

Kahn does not altogether abandon her argument in *Man's Estate*, however. What she does, rather, is let go of the belief that character is determined primarily during early childhood, the premise Stephen A. Mitchell calls 'infantilism', in favour of a new emphasis on present, adult interaction. This reorientation towards what Mitchell calls the '*current* interpersonal world' is not in itself incompatible with post-Freudian object relations theory.[11] For example, in *Man's Estate*, Kahn summarises and seconds the conclusions of Ralph Greenson. 'For the boy, the critical threat to masculinity is not, as Freud maintains, castration, but engulfment by the mother, and his critical task in establishing his masculinity is not an oedipal one but a pre-oedipal one of "dis-identifying" from his mother and "counter-identifying" with his father.' In *Roman Shakespeare*, Kahn presents what amounts to a revised version of the same narrative. Just as the 'pre-oedipal' male child strives to 'dis-identify' with the mother and 'counter-identify' with the father, so also the Roman man tries to dissociate himself from the feminine more generally considered and instead engage with a masculine 'rival': 'the mirror image of an ideal self'.

Kahn's account of the root cause, however, of male striving for separation from the female is very different from one book to the next. In *Man's Estate*, male children 'dis-identifying' from their mothers is an expression of an innate human drive. In *Roman Shakespeare*, male rejection of the feminine is a consequence of the male individual being interpellated by an ideology, masculinity, which itself is not, so to speak, natural, but instead propaganda in the service, ultimately, of the ruling monarch. 'Up to a point, faction fueled by emulation served the queen's purposes.' Kahn cites Eric Mallin: 'To prevent challenges to the monarchy, the nobles were encouraged to conceive of one another as the sole obstacles to positions of greater and greater strength.'[12] In both books, however, men to be masculine must 'struggle to differentiate them-selves' from women as well as, especially, the feminine within them-selves, with which they share, nonetheless, a degree of primordial unity, and from which they can never entirely escape.'[13]

In the notes to *Roman Shakespeare*, Kahn notes that her empha-sis on emulation takes its cue from Wayne Rebhorn's article, 'The Crisis of the Aristocracy in *Julius Caesar*'. Here, Rebhorn presents emulation as 'the hallmark of the Elizabethan aristocracy' and argues that it is represented on-stage in *Julius Caesar* by the sym-bolic proxy of the Roman aristocracy. Kahn's description of the key difference between her analysis of emulation and Rebhorn's, how-ever, is somewhat misleading. 'While I share his view of the impor-tance of emulation in *Julius Caesar*,' she writes, 'I see it as a cultural practice that contradicts republican ideology, rather than as a "fun-damental drive" or "character type" (1990: 78).'[14] The parentheti-cal citation makes it seem as if Kahn is citing Rebhorn directly, but the phrases 'fundamental drive' and 'character type' are her own interpolation. The choice of words makes Rebhorn seem more psy-choanalytic, more like Kahn herself in her earlier study *Man's Estate* than he really is. To say that Rebhorn sees emulation as a 'funda-mental drive' suggests, in the context Kahn sets up, that he sees it as an innate, biological impetus, akin to the 'pre-oedipal' motives that Kahn describes in *Man's Estate*, when in fact he presents it as emerg-ing out of a specific historical context, the 'crisis of the aristocracy' in early modern England. Rebhorn even uses Kahn's own key term, 'ideology', albeit not in her more technical, Althusserian sense, citing the work of Anthony Esler on what Esler calls 'the aspiring mind' of 'the Elizabethan younger generation'.[15]

A more accurate way to distinguish between Kahn's account of the origin of the early modern English aristocratic emulation and Rebhorn's would be to say that although both see this 'cul-tural practice' as grounded in contemporary, historically contin-gent social relations, Kahn sees it as emerging top-down, whereas Rebhorn sees it as emerging bottom-up. In the manner associated with New Historicism, and of a piece with her use of terms such as 'ideology' and 'interpellation' derived from Althusser, Kahn presents aristocratic emulation as a product of manipulation by the crown, imposing self-sabotage upon the English nobility as a means to keep them in check. By fostering factionalism, Elizabeth forestalled the possibility of a more republican alternative to her relative absolutism. Kahn cites Eric Mallin: 'The proliferation of emulous factions was a crucial component of Elizabeth's method of rule.'

Rebhorn, by contrast, sees emulation as emerging in a more decentralised, diffuse manner, as a result of 'Elizabethans' concern to define aristocratic identity': what Gordon Braden calls 'a crisis of the aristocratic imagination'.[16] This ambient 'concern with aristocratic self-definition' was 'the result of the dislocations caused by social mobility and the ontological insecurity that mobility produced for Englishmen used to living in a seemingly immutable, intensely hierarchical society.' Not only aristocrats themselves, but also their various hangers-on, including writers such as Spenser and Shakespeare, for whom they served as patrons, found themselves obliged to make sense of the nobility's ongoing transition from warriors to courtiers.[17]

On the basis of his reading of *Julius Caesar*, Rebhorn argues that whereas Stone attributes the crisis of the aristocracy that he identifies chiefly to economic causes, Shakespeare tends to see it 'in moral terms'. His play is 'analytical', but his analysis is grounded in the history of ethics, rather than the history of class conflict. The nobility as a class is being 'impelled' to its own 'suicide', literal as well as figurative, not by material changes in the distribution of wealth, but instead by its own 'essential values and modes of self-definition'. The idea of the 'imperial will' or 'imperial self' which Rebhorn argues Shakespeare sees as the engine of aristocratic self-destruction is a concept that he takes up from Gordon Braden. As Braden explains, the desire to preserve the 'imperial self' transforms human relationships into a 'zero-sum' competition for power, breaking down social relations into atomistic factionalism. It as if the nobility would return, if they could, to the medieval landscape of independent fiefdoms; instead, however, they are divided and conquered. Shakespeare's Roman patricians exemplify this inability to coexist: 'driven by the hunger of emulation to extend endlessly the terrain of the self, they destroy and will keep destroying one another until the stage is bare and only a single imperial will is left.'[18] The monarch does not engineer 'emulous factionalism' in order to preserve his own power, as per Mallin's account; rather, the monarch is the last man (or woman) standing once that factionalism has run its course, like the winner of a medieval melee.

In this chapter, I re-examine this concept of the 'imperial self', looking closely, along the lines of Kahn's inquiry, at the ways in which it intersects with Roman concepts of masculinity. In contrast to Kahn, however, I propose that Roman aversion to femininity in Shakespeare's plays is not primarily an ideological instrument of 'patriarchy', designed to preserve male 'dominance' over women. Its point of origin is neither aristocratic 'emulation' nor the male child's desire to secure a discrete identity, separate from what Adelman describes as the 'suffocating mother'. Instead, Roman misogyny can be better understood as one manifestation among many of Romans' profound distrust of passibility, a characteristic anxiety about the most basic given of the human condition which they share, not only with the aristocracy of early modern England, but also with the ancient Greeks, and indeed with much subsequent Western culture.

Outside relatively rarefied debates about Christian theology, the term 'passibility' is likely to be unfamiliar. Kahn gets at something similar through the concept of 'vulnerability', which she associates with its etymological root *vulnus*, the Latin word for wound. 'Wounds mark a kind of vulnerability readily associated with women: they show the flesh to be penetrable, they show that it can bleed, they make apertures in the body.'[19] Kahn moves quickly to ground Roman fear of physical vulnerability in misogyny; I would prefer to step back one remove still further, however, and ground both in a larger anxiety about all forms of 'vulnerability', including the emotional and moral, as well as the physical and political. James Kuzner introduces an analogous broad use of the same term, 'vulnerability', to denote the emotional availability and openness which, like Cicero, he sees as fundamental to the flourishing of any possible commonwealth.[20]

According to Kuzner, a republic to be viable requires of its citizens the virtue of being 'open' to compassion and concession, which itself requires that they choose to accept being embedded in their own society, like Cicero, rather than, like Seneca, attempting to withdraw into an isolated, wary privacy. This kind of voluntary engagement is risky, entailing 'vulnerability' to other people, but even so absolutely necessary for a functioning republic, or even for a healthy friendship. Kuzner thus redefines 'vulnerability' as a virtue, rather than a weakness, somewhat against the grain of classical liberalism, with its characteristic, contrary emphasis on 'negative

liberty'. For Quentin Skinner, in particular, the core of republicanism is 'freedom as non-domination', an ideal he describes as 'neo-
Roman'. In the contrarian spirit of philosophers such as Charles
Taylor and Alasdair MacIntyre, Kuzner presents a 'communitarian'
critique of this 'neo-Roman' vision. 'Freedom' should be understood as 'freedom to' participate in the exercise of government,
rather than 'freedom from' interference with individual liberties.

Kuzner shows that 'vulnerability' can be given a remarkably
expansive sense. For present purposes, however, I would like to
retain the more technical term, 'passibility'. Its denotation admits
of a larger scope, without resorting to extension via metaphor.
More importantly, it serves to introduce some questions of theology that I think are crucial to understanding the distinctive character of Shakespeare's Romans. I am not the first to apply the
concept of passibility to literary criticism; my use of the term is in
part an invocation of what is for me, as well as Kuzner, an important source, Timothy Reiss's recent history of changing concepts
of personhood, *Mirages of the Selfe*. Here, Reiss draws a convincing picture of changing attitudes towards 'passibility' as the pivot
of an intellectual transition to modernity during the early modern period, beginning with Petrarch's break from antiquity and
culminating in Descartes's new vision of the self, the notorious
Cartesian *ego cogito*: 'The idea that consciousness precedes or is
otherwise apart from public interpersonal exchange, sociopolitical
activity, and all forms of material activity and event.'[21]

To some degree, Reiss's argument can be understood as a
refinement of Burckhardt's familiar description of the Renaissance
as the emergence of modern personhood. In the 'Middle Ages',
Burckhardt argues, 'man was conscious of himself only as a member of a race, people, party, family, or corporation – only through
some general category.' Over the course of the Renaissance, however, 'man became a spiritual *individual*, and recognized himself
as such'.[22] Fleshing out what Burckhardt means by 'general category', Reiss introduces the idea of what he calls 'circles', including, for example, 'material world, society, family, animal being,
rational mind, divine'. 'These *circles* or *spheres* – as Cicero, Seneca, Hierocles and Plutarch called them . . . did not 'surround' a
person who somehow fit into them. They *were* what a person was:
integral to my very substance. . . . They named existential spheres
to which the person enlaced in them was in a *reactive* relation.'[23]

One of Reiss's key sources for this insight is Alasdair MacIntyre's history of changes in ethical presuppositions in his *After Virtue*. According to MacIntyre, in 'many pre-modern, traditional societies, to be a man is to fill a set of roles each which has its own point and purpose: member of a family, citizen, soldier, philosopher, servant of God'. Social roles such as the 'offices' Cicero outlines in his *De officiis* are not 'characteristics that belong to human beings accidentally, to be stripped away in order to discover "the real me." They are part of my substance.'[24] Relationships with other people are integral to personhood itself. Reiss introduces an archaic spelling, 'selfe', in order to distinguish and defamiliarise this pre-modern concept of personhood. 'An embedded, passible "selfe" . . . pervious and tied to divine, social, material spheres and historical community, underlay Western experience from Petrarch until Michel de Montaigne, even as dissonances appeared.'[25]

Within Reiss's narrative, 'passibility' refers to the experience of all that the modern, 'Cartesian' reimagining of personhood tries to strip away, leaving behind, as Reiss sees it, little more than a ghost in the machine: a wisp of reified, implausibly pure agency.

> Passibility names experiences of beings whose common denominator was a sense of being *embedded in and acted on by* these circles [i.e. the '*circles* or *spheres*' mentioned above] – including the material world and immediate biological, familial, and social ambiences, as well as . . . cosmic, spiritual, or divine life.

In his *Sources of the Self*, Charles Taylor introduces a similar metaphor, the idea that the individual subject is inevitably entangled in 'webs of interlocution'. We are 'transcendentally embedded', he maintains, in relationships with other people, despite all effort at 'independence'.[26] Like MacIntyre, Taylor aims to rehabilitate this older sense of personhood, which he sees as more accurate than the 'Cartesian', and therefore a sounder basis for ethical action. Reiss, by contrast, is more value-neutral, seeking simply to present an accurate picture of changing conceptions of what he sometimes calls 'who-ness'.

Moving through an astonishing range of literary sources from antiquity and the Middle Ages, Reiss shows passibility ensconced in concepts of personhood throughout. With Petrarch, however, followed by Montaigne, Reiss begins to discern what he calls 'dissonances': forerunners of the modern effort to conceive of a self independent of all possibility. The term itself, 'possibility', is central to his argument. Nevertheless, Reiss's reviewers seem to have found it baffling. Hassan Melehy describes it as 'to this reader's knowledge . . . Reiss's own innovation'.[27] Stephen Nichols puts it in scare quotes and posits that Reiss uses 'the Latinate term . . . for lack of a satisfactory English equivalent'.[28] Neither of these assessments is correct. 'Passibility' is a well-established technical term in Christian theology; in fact, the key term in one of the most contentious academic theological debates of the twentieth century, as well as earlier debates among the Greek Church Fathers.[29] John Donne, for instance, employs it repeatedly in his sermons. 'Passibility', as he uses the term, is the quality that most clearly and profoundly distinguishes man from God. For example, in a sermon delivered before Charles I at court, April 1629, Donne defines God 'in his essence' as 'not mortall, not passible'. Or again, in a sermon at St Dunstan's, Trinity Sunday, 1627: 'God is that which is not mortall, not passible, not moveable.' Man, by contrast, is by definition 'passible'. In a sermon at Lincoln's Inn, 1618, Donne explains that man was immortal before the Fall, but not 'impassible': impassibility is the prerogative of God alone.[30]

In fairness to Reiss's reviewers, Reiss himself makes no mention of this history of his own key term, 'passibility', within Christian theological debate. The source that he cites is instead the brief passage in Aristotle's *De anima* ('On the Soul') which distinguishes between the 'active intellect' (*nous poiētikos*) and the 'passive intellect' (*nous pathētikos*; Scholastic Latin, *intellectus passibilis*).[31] Reiss's definition of the term, as well, is idiosyncratic. 'Passibility' as it is normally used does not refer to 'experiences of being', even experiences of being 'embedded in and acted on', but instead more precisely to the state or condition of being 'vulnerable' to being 'embedded in and acted on'. In other words, passibility is the capacity for experiencing passivity, not the experience itself. In particular, in the context of Patristic debate, to be passible (Greek, *pathētos*; Latin [Vulg.], *passibilis*) is to be capable of feeling emotion, 'passion' (Greek, *pathos*; translated into Latin as *passio*). Most especially, to be passible is to be capable of suffering.[32] Reiss describes the term simply as 'Latin', and it is; at base, it is derived from *pati*, 'to bear, suffer, endure' (cf. Greek, *paschein*). Its origin, however, is more specifically post-classical Christian Latin, as a translation of a Greek concept, *to pathēton* (literally, 'the ability to feel *pathos*', i.e. 'passibility').[33] In his 'Life of Pelopidas', Plutarch describes Dionysius and Hercules, for example, as gods who began as men, but on account of their *aretē* were able to cast aside *to thnēton kai pathēton* ('mortality and passibility').[34] Or, for example, in his 'Life of Numa', he describes Numa as insisting, like Pythagoras, that the divine is not passible (*pathēton*).[35]

The same root (Latin [Vulg.], *passio*) is behind the Christian practice of referring to Christ's crucifixion as his 'Passion'. *'Hysterica passio,'* King Lear cries. 'O, how this mother swells up toward my heart!' This moment of self-diagnosis inspired Adelman's title, *Suffocating Mothers*. And in keeping with Adelman's interest, the feminist implications of the first part of Lear's exclamation, *'hysterica'*, have attracted a great deal of commentary. The theological and philosophical implications of the second part, *'passio'*, however, have been in comparison neglected. Shakespeare's recourse to Latin here, as well as his striking description of Lear's *'passio'* as 'the mother', allows him to connect several of the overarching themes of this chapter in a single cry: a failed attempt at quasi-Stoic self-control (*passio* as *pathos*), the humiliating frailty of embodiment (Latin as medical jargon), femininity (Greek, *hystera*, 'uterus'), (self-)pity ('the mother') and theology (*passio* as the Passion).

The concept of passibility is especially useful as a means to differentiate between the various assumptions about the nature of the divine characteristic of classical philosophy and the new theology put forward by Christianity. Pagan poets such as Hesiod, Homer and Ovid posit anthropomorphic gods who fall prey to passions such as love and anger, who eat, who sleep; Homer in the *Iliad* includes an episode in which the war-god Ares is literally wounded in battle.[36] In Ovid's *Metamorphoses*, the tendency of gods as well as human beings to change shape provides the poem's most basic structural continuity. Pagan intellectuals reacting against this popular tradition tended to emphasise, by contrast, God's otherness: God as immaterial, impersonal and immutable. In other words, the philosophers of antiquity, when they did turn to theology, tended to emphasise the impassibility of the divine, as opposed to the passibility of man.

The pre-Socratic philosopher Xenophanes of Colophon seems to have been one of the first to make fun of the idea that the Godhead in any sense resembles a human being. 'Ethiopians say their gods are snub-nosed and black; / Thracians say they are pale and red-haired.' On the contrary, he maintains, God is something radically other than human: 'in no way similar to mortals in either body or thought'. He is 'one', Xenophanes says, somewhat enigmatically. He does not move, but instead always 'remains in the same place'. In another fragment, Xenophanes complains about Homer and Hesiod attributing all manner of human excess to the gods, including crimes such as theft and adultery.[37] Socrates in Plato's *Republic* seconds Xenophanes' criticisms of popular theology. God does not engage in immoral activity; God does not in fact ever change in any way at all, even voluntarily. God is so impassible, so devoid of emotion, as well as physical embodiment, that he is not even a person; much less, a human being. Instead, in place of Zeus, Plato posits the Form of the Good. Aristotle in like manner, taking up Xenophanes' insistence that God does not move, proposes an impersonal 'Unmoved Mover'. Hellenistic Stoics closely identified God, fate and reason (*logos*) as a single 'World-Soul': the origin of the Christian concept of God as 'the Word' (*logos*).[38]

Roman philosophers carried on this emphasis on divine transcendence.[39] Like Epicurus before him, Lucretius speaks of multiple gods, and therefore might seem an exception. Lucretius' gods, however, are utterly indifferent to anything that happens on earth, including prayers, as well as even the most outrageous crimes. Such *apathia*, like that of the Stoic *sapiens*, is as a variation on the philosophical ideal of impassibility that animates the theology of Plato and Aristotle; it simply limits its scope to the psychological. At times Seneca speaks of Epicurus' gods as moral exempla. But Seneca's reception of Hellenistic philosophy is eclectic. At other times, he speaks as if there were only one God: the 'World-Soul' of the Stoics. For example, Seneca insists that God never changes his mind. 'His will must ever be the same who can never will aught but that which is best. Nor is he on that account less free or less powerful, for he is himself the source of his own destiny.'[40] Or, again, 'The great author and ruler of all things wrote the decrees of fate indeed, but he also follows them. He decreed them once for all; he continually obeys them.'[41]

In his First Letter to the Corinthians, St Paul describes 'Christ crucified' as 'a stumbling-block to the Jews and foolishness to the Gentiles'. And it is easy to see why. For an educated Greek or Roman, as well as for a knowledgeable Jew, the quintessential characteristic of the divine is power. God is that which acts,

not that which is acted-upon. Even the popular conceptions of the
gods taken up by pagan poets present them as more powerful than
human beings; they stand in relation to mankind, roughly speaking, as aristocrats do to commoners. Crucifixion, by contrast, is
the quintessential symbol of powerlessness; a punishment reserved
for slaves and barbarians, involving immobility, helplessness and
profound physical pain, as well as public exposure and humiliation. To equate this experience of the most extreme passibility
with the Godhead must have seemed in context an utter contradiction in terms. Homer shows Ares wounded; Christianity, however,
proclaims that God was not only wounded, but tortured, like a
slave; even that God died, in some sense.[42]

Delighting as ever in paradox, Donne presents God's assumption of passibility in his Incarnation as itself a kind of power:
the power even to become powerless. As Christ tells St Paul: 'my
strength is made perfect in weakness' (2 Cor. 12:9).

> What could God suffer? God himselfe could not; and therefore
> God hath taken a body that could. *And as he is the Head of that
> body*, he is passible, so he may suffer; And, as he is the first born
> of the dead, he did suffer; so that he was defective in nothing; not
> in Power, as God, not in passibility, as man; for *Complacuit; It
> pleased the Father, that in him, All fulnesse* (a full capacity to all
> purposes) *should dwell.*[43]

As Donne's emphasis suggests, Christianity introduces a concept
of the divine which is very different from those found in classical
philosophy; the very opposite, in fact, of the pagan philosophers'
ideal. 'Christ crucified' is obviously in some sense passible, vulnerable, even if that sense might be debated. Aristotle's Unmoved
Mover, however, or Plotinus' 'One', emphatically is not. Like Epicurus' Olympians, the impersonal deities or equivalents of deities
that Aristotle, Plato, Plotinus and the Stoics posit are essentially,
unequivocally impassible.

The distinction between these two concepts of the divine, God
as impassible agent and God as passible subject, becomes all the
more important in so far as concepts of the divine present ethical
ideals. Theology, like hagiography, articulates moral precepts by
means of exempla. What individuals in a given society treat as a
deity is in part a representation of the kind of behavior that they
honour. Theology is not the only medium for such exemplarity;

people often take other people, as well, as their heroes or role models, as Brutus does, for example, with his ancestor 'old Brutus'. To the extent that people do believe in some sort of Godhead, however, their interpretation of the divine comes to serve as a description of what it is that they see as the ideal self. The perception of the Godhead extant in a given culture both shapes and is shaped by that culture's understanding of ethics.

The two concepts of the divine that I have outlined here, the classical philosophical concept of God as impassible and the Christian concept of God as passible, can be seen in this light to correspond to the contrast between Roman *libido dominandi* and Christian pity. The ideal self for Shakespeare's Romans is powerful, active, invulnerable. As Paul Cantor points out, 'Coriolanus believes the gods look down from their heights and laugh at human fallibility and weakness. Evidently for him a god should be imperturbable, unmoved by any human spectacle and hence unmoved by any appeal from men.'[44] The ideal self for an ethos of compassion such as Christianity is instead merciful; he shares in others' suffering, and so must be capable of some degree of suffering himself. If the others with whom he sympathises are material, then he, too, must be material; if the others feel emotions such as love, anger and grief, then he, too, must in some sense take on those emotions. Aristotle's 'Unmoved Mover' is replaced by Isaiah's 'suffering servant.' 'He has born our griefs, and carried our sorrows' (Is. 53:4).[45]

For Shakespeare, the tragedy of Romans such as Caesar and Brutus is that they are emulating the wrong kind of ideal self, a fantasy of impossible autonomy akin to the various concepts of the divine found in classical philosophy, as opposed to the very different understanding of the divine that appears with Christianity. This ideal self is what Rebhorn, following Braden, calls the 'imperial self'. To call it the 'imperial' self, however, is to ground it in politics, and, like Rebhorn, I am not convinced that Shakespeare himself saw the tragedy of Rome in this light. Instead, Shakespeare seems to see the political problem in *Julius Caesar*, the beginning of Rome's degeneration into civil war, as itself a result of a flawed value-system. In their collection, *Shakespeare and Early Modern Political Thought*, editors David Armitage, Conal Condren and Andrew Fitzmaurice stress the role of individual ethics as the bedrock of mass politics in the early modern understanding of political life. 'From the early modern perspective, it was the character and

spirit of those making up the polity that was crucial to its political health. In relative contrast, modern political analysis has put
more stress on the institutional and constitutional arrangements of
politics.'[46] For those of a Marxist bent, it might seem like a matter
of course that facts on the ground, first economic, then political,
precede and determine the shape of ethical debate. But I doubt that
Shakespeare would agree. To make him a kind of Fredric Jameson
avant la lettre is an attractive but misleading distortion of his own
distinctive understanding of historical causation.

Paul Cantor is a rare and valuable example of a critic interested
in the influence of economics on literature who does not accept
Karl Marx's critique of capitalism but instead draws upon the
Austrian school of economics associated with Ludwig von Mises
and Friedrich Hayek. As Cantor points out, 'Economic discussions
of literature are almost all anti-capitalist in spirit, and are often
avowedly pro-socialist.' Given such an overwhelming, largely
unquestioned consensus, it is intriguing to encounter a different
point of view. Cantor defends the usefulness of the free market as
an arbiter of value over against what he sees as the impracticable
pretentions of central planning. He also questions Marx's account
of the relation between 'base' and 'superstructure'. 'What was new
in Marx', he observes, 'was his claim that economic forces are the
determining factor in all history, including cultural history.' For
Cantor, this determinism is 'too reductive'. Human behaviour is
not simply the result of macroeconomic forces, and these forces
are themselves not susceptible to precise mathematical modelling
and forecasting. Instead, Cantor stresses the free choice of individuals, leading to unpredictability within any social system. In
keeping with the 'Austrian principle of consumer sovereignty' as
opposed to the 'Marxist idea of producer hegemony', Cantor sees
individual economic choices as giving rise to what he calls 'spontaneous order'.[47]

Having drawn such a sharp contrast, Cantor acknowledges,
nonetheless, that literary criticism informed by Austrian economics is not in all respects opposed to the Marxist criticism he disparages. 'As economic approaches, both call into question the
Romantic ideal of the autonomy of art and isolated creative genius.
Both Austrian economics and Marxism lead us to picture the
novelist as involved in a social process, but they understand and
evaluate this process very differently.' 'Austrian economics does

complicate our understanding of intentionality,' Cantor explains, 'because it views the market as a means of mediating among the intentions of the vast number of individuals who participate in it, actors whose interaction often produces results larger and more complex than anything at which an isolated individual can aim.' By way of illustration, Cantor distinguishes his own approach from both New Criticism and Deconstruction. Economic criticism as he represents it, Marxist or Austrian, is the opposite of formal criticism.[48]

But there is another option, one that Cantor leaves out. What is missing from Cantor's survey of possible foundations for literary criticism is a view of history, like St Augustine's (or Nietzsche's), that sees ideas, especially theology, as the most important driver of systematic change, rather than either material consumption (as in the Austrian School) or material production (as in Marxist economics). This interpretation of history is often associated with Hegel. Hegel's mature sense of history, however, is not simply, as Marx puts it, Marxism turned back on its head, but instead more complex and idiosyncratic: the World-Soul coming to consciousness of its own nature. 'History is the process', he maintains, 'whereby the spirit discovers itself and its own concept.'[49] Hegel's narrative is modelled on the Christian concept of Providence, but Hegel sidelines Christianity itself. Cantor for his part draws attention to a very early essay of Hegel's, 'The Positivity of the Christian Religion', published posthumously, in which, as Cantor explains, 'Hegel looks for natural causes to explain why Christianity displaced the pagan religions.' Hegel describes Rome here as 'corrupted' by 'fortunate campaigns, increase of wealth, and acquaintance with luxury', and also argues that Rome's expansion led to the demise of its former fervent patriotism: 'the picture of the state as a product of his own energies disappeared from the citizen's soul.'[50]

In *Shakespeare's Roman Trilogy*, Cantor aligns Shakespeare's representation of Roman history with Hegel's here, as well as Livy's *Ab urbe condita* ('From the Founding of the City') and Montesquieu's *Considérations sur les causes de la grandeur des Romains et de leur décadence* ('Considerations on the Causes of Roman Greatness and Their Decline'). Underlying all of these accounts, Hegel's, Livy's and Montesquieu's, as well as the view Cantor attributes to Shakespeare, is the 'quasi-Marxist' premise that changes in Roman

ideology are an effect, rather than a cause, of changes in material conditions. As Cantor says elsewhere, 'In explaining history, for Marx-
ists and quasi-Marxists, economics trumps culture.'[51] Livy describes
Rome's gradual moral decline as a result of Rome's new wealth
after the end of the Punic Wars. Montesquieu ascribes the collapse
of the Roman Republic to Rome's military expansion, which he
argues was inherently unsustainable. Cantor finds in Shakespeare's
Antony and Cleopatra, in particular, a prescient warning regarding what we now call 'globalisation'. Rome's 'commitment to its
traditional republican way of life' is 'subverted by exposure to the
foreign cultures Rome brings within its orbit'. 'As the capital of a
vast and diverse Empire, Rome becomes increasingly cosmopolitan,
the crossroads for a wide variety of competing visions of life, some
of them antithetical to its republican traditions.'[52]

   Problems arise, however, when Cantor moves to align Nietzsche,
as well as Shakespeare, with the materialist explanation of Rome's
decline that he discerns in Hegel, Livy and Montesquieu. In *Human,
All Too Human*, Nietzsche describes 'the spread of Christianity'
as 'the principal cause' of 'the decline of Roman culture'.[53] With
this claim, Nietzsche stands in a long tradition of antagonists to
St Augustine's defence of Christianity in *The City of God*, including most notably Edward Gibbon, as well as Machiavelli. But he is
very far from Marx, or even the Austrian School. In one of his last
books, *The Antichrist*, written on the brink of insanity, Nietzsche
strenuously denounces what is, in effect, Cantor's thesis. 'It is *not*,
as is supposed, the corruption of antiquity itself, of *noble* antiquity,
that made Christianity possible. The scholarly idiocy which upholds
such ideas even today cannot be contradicted loudly enough.'[54]

   Cantor turns, therefore, to Nietzsche's notebooks. 'Why did
Nietzsche not embrace the idea that Roman corruption prepared
the way for Christianity?' Cantor asks. 'If the Roman Empire
was such a rock-solid organization, if it was on course to last for
thousands of years, how did a rag-tag gang of Christian outcasts
ever bring it down?'[55] In his *Nachlass*, Nietzsche presents a more
complex, incremental account of what he calls 'the slave revolt in
morals'. 'Christianity', he writes, 'could grow only in the soil of
Judaism, i.e. amidst a people that had absolutely renounced politics
and lived a kind of parasitic existence within the Roman order of
things. Christianity is a step further on.'[56] Nor is Judaism, it turns
out, the only precursor of Christianity. Nietzche also condemns the

pagan mystery religions which flourished in late antiquity: 'Isis, Mithras, Dionysius, the "Great Mother".'[57] Nietzsche finds fertile ground for Christianity, as well, in the pervasive influence of Greek philosophy. 'Greek moral philosophy had already done everything to prepare the way for and make palatable moral fanaticism even among Greeks and Romans.' Nietzsche describes Plato, in particular, as 'the great viaduct of corruption', 'already marked by Jewish bigotry', in keeping with legends that he had visited Egypt.[58] Christianity 'could only take root in decayed soil,' he insists. 'Moral fanaticism (in short: Plato) destroyed paganism.'[59]

Looking at the evidence Cantor brings to bear, what remains missing is any sense that Nietzsche sees either geographic expansion or increasing wealth as fundamental causes of the changes in ideology he describes: the emergence of Greek moral philosophy, then Greek mystery religions, then Judaism, then Christianity. Material conditions, for Nietzsche, are not explanatory bedrock. Money and territory are not first-order causes, but instead can be better understood as second-order effects of more primary developments within the history of ideas. Christianity alone is not to blame, in Nietzsche's account of the decline and fall of Rome. But ideology is, in the form of 'slave morality', of which Christianity is one example, alongside Judaism, mystery religions and ancient Greek ethics. In this sense, Nietzsche as historian is much closer to Gibbon or Machiavelli, or even St Augustine, than he is to Montesquieu or Livy. Christianity is not a symptom of the collapse of Roman civilisation. As the culmination of 'slave morality', Christianity is itself the reason, 'the principal cause', as Nietzsche says, why the historical change that Stone calls 'the crisis of the aristocracy', and Elias, 'the civilizing process', has not been reversed.

For Nietzsche, religious conversion is not a reflection of a change in political regime (*politeia*), but instead the engine that drives such political transformation. Changes in the concept of the ideal self, he would say, are the reason why so-called 'masters' still today have not shaken off their subjugation to the interests of 'slaves'. Those gifted souls who might once have styled themselves *optimates* are instead constrained by atavistic *caritas*, a sense of obligation to those less fortunate which Habermas, like Nietzsche, has identified as a legacy of Christianity, even among those who see themselves as secular. Shakespeare shares this sense of Christianity as an ethical revolution, but with Nietzsche's idiosyncratic value-judgements turned back right-side up. In the case of Rome, the problem with the Romans, as Shakespeare sees it, is, to put it simply, that they are not Christians. They are not even Ciceronians. They have the wrong ideal in mind, one that leaves no room for pity or concession. This wrongheadedness is not the effect, but the cause, of the fall of the Roman Republic.

'Constancy' and 'Frailty': Femininity as Roman Other

In the previous section, I argued that the most significant distinguishing characteristic of Shakespeare's Romans is their discomfort with human passibility. They are reluctant to be vulnerable to being acted upon, whether emotionally or physically, and therefore attempt either to dominate others entirely or else to escape their influence altogether. This all-or-nothing dynamic shapes their interpersonal interaction within the private sphere of marriage, just as it does within the public sphere of politics. In this section, I argue that femininity for Shakespeare often serves as a symbol of passibility. The sidelined women in *Julius Caesar*, Portia and Calpurnia, represent in part their own husbands' stunted and repressed faculty of pity. Femininity is not the only symbol of human 'frailty', however. Other forms of perceived weakness include old age, infertility, wounds, bleeding, Caesar's 'falling sickness' and mortality. In order to explain how these aspects of embodiment challenge and undermine putative masculine 'constancy', I introduce Bakhtin's distinction between 'grotesque' and 'classical' representations of the body and apply it to a close reading of Caesar's speeches just before his assassination, in which he compares himself to 'Olympus' and claims to be 'constant as the northern star'.

Women in Shakespeare's Roman plays, especially *Julius Caesar*, serve as the primary symbol of the passibility or 'vulnerability' Shakespeare's Romans strive to escape. In particular, women represent susceptibility to pity. Women are also associated with emotion more generally, however, as well as embodiment. The supposed 'frailty' of their flesh, as well as their reason, makes them an apt symbol of 'inconstancy', even when that inconstancy occurs in men. Coppélia Kahn observes that *Julius Caesar* seems at first glance an odd play to choose for a discussion of Shakespeare's perspective on 'sexual difference *per se*'. In terms of women on stage, 'it has only two characters, Portia and Calpurnia, the wives of Brutus and Caesar, and each of them speaks in only two scenes'. As Kahn suggests, however, 'the sexual difference that really counts in *Julius Caesar* . . . does not depend on the presence or absence of female characters'.⁶⁰ The gendering that Shakespeare examines in this play is not 'male or female', in the strict biological sense, but instead the division of both sexes' shared human experience into separate, more abstract categories, 'masculinity' and 'femininity'.

Seen in this light, the very intensity of the repression of femininity apparent in *Julius Caesar*, extending even to the cast list, only makes it more revealing: a case study *in extremis* of a gender bias that seems characteristic of Roman culture. Citing Barbara Babcock, Kahn describes the feminine in *Julius Caesar* as 'socially peripheral', yet 'symbolically central'.⁶¹ I agree, to some extent, but I would also want to modify what I take to be Kahn's intended sense. Femininity is 'symbolically central' in Shakespeare's Roman plays as a symbol, not as itself what is being symbolised. Femininity represents human passibility. Roman bias against the feminine is not fundamental but instead can be better understood as one variety among many of a pervasive, distinctive Roman fear of weakness; an anxiety about 'vulnerability' which is the obverse of their characteristic *libido dominandi*.

My misgivings about Kahn's explanation of Roman gender bias hinge upon questions of cause and effect. Shakespeare's vision of historical causation, right or wrong, gives greater weight to value-systems as cause rather than effect of social practice than Kahn herself seems inclined to grant. Kahn presents Roman concepts of gender as a symptom of Roman patriarchy, rather than its origin: men as subjects are interpellated by an ideology of masculinity which is itself in the service of patriarchy, as well as the 'cultural practice' of 'emulation' or male rivalry, and one effect of this interpellation is disdain for women. Political structures through ideology determine the activity, as well as the beliefs, of any given individual.

Shakespeare himself, however, does not assign such ontological primacy to politics. From his perspective, individuals choose between competing moral paradigms, and that choice then manifests itself in their ad hoc response to whatever political dilemmas they may happen to encounter. In this case, Roman noblemen such as Brutus and Caesar dissociate themselves from the feminine, seen as private and passive, in order to preserve their sense of themselves as public figures, capable of masculine agency. Individuals (Romans) adopt a value-system (the pursuit of *imperium*) which leads to a political structure (patriarchy). Shakespeare's Romans idealise worldly power: self-sufficient independence, invulnerability, a capacity for overwhelming violence against any opponent. Their admiration for this kind of power leads them to be contemptuous of women and to prevent their full participation in society. Women seem to them to be weak; worse, women make them aware of disconcerting weaknesses in themselves.

Kahn at one point suggests that Shakespeare's understanding of social relations adumbrates that of Althusser. 'Because Rome was a patriarchal society, Romanness *per se* is closely linked to an ideology of masculinity.' Shakespeare 'dramatized precisely this linkage and, in doing so, demystified its power'.[62] Shakespeare's view of history, however, much more closely resembles that of Sallust or Cicero, with their emphasis on moral decline, than it does the Marxist perspective of Althusser's own preferred playwright, Bertolt Brecht.[63] By far the closest analogue, however, is St Augustine.[64] I agree in this sense with J. L. Simmons, who argues that 'the most significant historical factor' in Shakespeare's Roman plays is 'the historically pagan environment out of which each tragedy arises', 'antedating of Christian revelation'. Drawing on St Augustine's *City of God*, Simmons interprets the fall of the Roman Republic in *Julius Caesar* and *Antony and Cleopatra* as in large part Shakespeare's conscious demonstration of the inevitable failure of what St Augustine calls 'the Earthly City'. 'All attempts at idealistic vision by the tragic heroes, all attempts to rise above the restrictions of man and his imperfect society, are tragically affected by the absence of revelation and the real hope of glory.'[65]

John Cox presents the influence of St Augustine's political realism as mediated in a more diffuse manner through the precedent of medieval drama. As he writes,

> My point is not that Shakespeare can be collapsed back into Augustine – much less that he should be – but that the attempt to make Shakespeare look forward is inevitably complicated by a residual tradition that antedates Shakespeare himself by more than a thousand years.[66]

In the conclusion to my analysis of *Julius Caesar*, 'Shakespeare's Passion Play', I take up Cox's suggestion that the representation of powerful figures such as Caesar, Herod and Satan in medieval mystery plays, as well as Shakespeare's histories and tragedies, owes much to St Augustine's account of the reasons for Rome's decline. Shakespeare's Romans represent not only the contemporary English aristocracy, but also and more generally what St Augustine calls 'the City of Man', torn apart by competitive *libido dominandi*. In *Julius Caesar*, as Peter Lake suggests, Shakespeare 'stages and reanimates' a 'neo-Roman' ideology which is 'almost entirely secular', then 'tests it to the breaking point by subjecting it, not merely to a secular historical and political critique, but also to a religious, indeed, a Christian critique'.[67]

In contrast to Kahn, I am inclined to think that Shakespeare in *Julius Caesar* sees not only Roman concepts of gender, but also Roman politics and Roman attitudes towards the body, as alike products of a tragically flawed value-system. His Romans are ill at ease with a basic given of the human condition: our vulnerability to each other's influence. The 'zero-sum game' of Roman politics, the 'socially peripheral' status of Roman women, and the Roman propensity for 'pitiless' physical cruelty are all effects, as well as subsequent, reinforcing causes, of a characteristic Roman tendency to idealise power per se, even at the cost of peaceful coexistence. In the absence of the Christian revelation, impassibility, like that which classical philosophers attribute to the gods, comes to be seen as an end unto itself, the *summum bonum*. This fantasy of absolute power, however, and with that power, absolute security from shame, prevents the healthy functioning, not only of the Roman Republic, but also of Roman friendships, because it leaves no room for compromise or interdependence. In particular, it damages the 'little commonwealth' of marriage, including Caesar's marriage with Calpurnia, as well as Brutus' with Portia.

Seen in this light, the unusually circumscribed role of female characters in *Julius Caesar* is not adequately explained simply as a reflection of a tendency in Roman culture to limit female agency to the *oikos*, in order to reinforce male authority in the *polis*. This 'cultural practice' of 'male dominance' is itself a symptom of a deeper malady. The systematic restriction of women's participation in political decision-making is a manifestation of characteristic Roman fears about the power of the feminine more generally considered, or rather, what it is that femininity is held to symbolise, passibility, a quality shared by both men and women. Femininity represents an aspect of the human condition which Shakespeare's Romans tend to see as humiliating, because it is in conflict with their understanding of the ideal self. In *Julius Caesar*, the Roman patriciate sees the fact that they are susceptible to being acted upon, even if only by virtue of their very nature as human, as so intolerably shameful that male aristocrats like Caesar and Brutus tend not to acknowledge it at all, but instead to take refuge in various psychological mechanisms of denial. Calpurnia and Portia should be interpreted by this light, not only as characters in their own right, but also as representations of disavowed pieces of their husbands' respective psyches. They personify emotions or 'passions' such as pity, grief, anger and fear which Brutus and Caesar both at times feel but are both reluctant to acknowledge as their own.

The idea that Shakespeare's *Julius Caesar* is in part an exercise in projection in the manner of a psychomachia is not entirely new. Feminist critics such as Gail Kern Paster, Madelon Sprengnether and Coppélia Kahn have identified wounds, blood and bleeding in the play as symbols of femininity; more specifically, feminine aspects of the masculine self which the men in the play are anxious to deny. A counter-discourse of consistent foils, however, such as statues, processions and 'the northern star' (3.1.60), reveals a running tension throughout the play between images of 'constancy' and symbols of 'frailty'. It is not so much the feminine as such that Roman men such as Brutus and Caesar are trying to avoid as any kind of passibility whatsoever, of which femininity is one important instance. Other examples include feeling emotions, being defeated in battle and succumbing to physical exhaustion. Even to have a body at all is felt to be an embarrassing weakness: Caesar would rather see himself as a bodiless 'star' than as 'flesh and blood' (3.3.67). Like old age, illness and Caesar's own recurrent epileptic seizures, wounds and bleeding emphasise the vulnerability or 'frailty' of corporeality, an aspect of themselves which characters such as Caesar, Portia and Caius Ligarius go to great lengths to disavow.

The damage done to women in this play, both physically and emotionally, and the disdain apparent for their potential contribution as political advisors should be interpreted as one part of a much larger, tragic pattern. Shakespeare's Rome is a place of relative intolerance for human weakness, and this unforgiving rigour proves in the end self-destructive. Most obviously, a parallel unwillingness to acknowledge that they are vulnerable to forces outside their own control cripples the better judgement of both Caesar and Brutus at key moments of political crisis. Discomfort with passibility, however, is not limited to these two characters. Rather, Roman culture in general, as Shakespeare sees it, is defined in *Julius Caesar* by a distinctive, pervasive tendency to exalt 'constancy' and stigmatize 'frailty'.

One way to understand Shakespeare's Romans' unease with femininity is to compare it to their discomfort with embodiment in general. Both tendencies are grounded in a fundamental fear of passibility. Depending on how it is evoked, ancient Rome can just as easily call to mind the bacchanalian luxury of Petronius' *Satyricon* as the severe, off-putting rigour of Plutarch's 'Cato the Censor'. For Shakespeare, however, Rome is inextricable from, on the one hand, fierce aggression towards others, as in the case of Coriolanus; on the other, an equally fierce repression of the physical and emotional self, as in the case of Brutus. Rome as he presents it is a thought-experiment designed to evaluate the origins, effects and limits of both subjective and objective *libido dominandi*, including the traditional bellicosity of medieval and early modern English nobility, as well as the more inward, psychological conquests at the heart of the new Neostoicism. Shakespeare's Rome, therefore, is that of the warrior or the philosopher, rather than that of the sycophant or oversexed sybarite. In so far as Shakespeare's Romans remain within the psychological confines of this limited concept of Rome, distinguished by its ethos of impassibility, their attitudes towards the body can be aptly described by recourse to Bakhtin's familiar distinction between the 'grotesque' and the 'classical'.

In his work on Rabelais, Bakhtin introduces the concept of the 'grotesque' as part of his description of what he calls the 'carnivalesque': the 'uncrowning', 'degradation' or 'lowering' of 'all that is high, spiritual, ideal, abstract . . . to the sphere of the earth and body'. The 'grotesque' body as it appears in medieval festivals, as well as Rabelais's comic novels, emphasises 'those parts of the body that are open to the outside world, that is, the parts through which the world enters the body or emerges from it', 'apertures or convexities' such as 'the open mouth, the genitals, the breasts, the phallus, the potbelly, the nose'. Just as consciousness is inevitably 'multiple', intertwined with and inseparable from other 'consciousnesses', so also the 'grotesque' body is incessantly, materially engaged with other bodies and other objects out there in the world. Like Kuzner's 'open subjects', the grotesque body is 'open': its dependence, vulnerability and embeddedness are ostentatious and essential. 'The grotesque unfinished and open body (dying, bringing forth, and being born) is not separated from the world by clearly defined boundaries; it is blended with the world.' It is not 'separated from the world', 'a closed complete unit'. It 'discloses its essence' in activities such as 'copulation, pregnancy, childbirth, the throes of death, eating, drinking, and defecation'.[68]

What Bakhtin calls the 'classical' body is the exact opposite: 'a strictly completed, finished product . . . isolated, alone, fenced off from other bodies. It is 'self-sufficient', like a statue.[69] Bakhtin associates the embrace of the 'grotesque' body with the Middle Ages and a new preference for the 'classical', by contrast, with the Renaissance, a change in depictions of the body which he attributes to the revival of 'the literary and artistic canon of antiquity'.[70] The dichotomy proposed is, of course, reductive.[71] What Bakhtin does aptly describe, however, is a characteristic Renaissance misinterpretation: the identification of the 'classical' with the neoclassical.[72] Renaissance artists such as Shakespeare may not always have agreed with this canon or abided by it, but they did recognise it and recognise it as distinctively 'antique'; meaning in their case, for the most part, 'Roman'.

Shakespeare's *Julius Caesar*, for example, begins with two tribunes, Murellus and Flavius, 'pulling scarves off Caesar's images' (1.2.284–5). 'Disrobe the images,' Flavius exhorts his companion, 'if you do find them decked with ceremonies' (1.1.65–6), meaning here by 'images', statues of Caesar, and by 'ceremonies', decorations. 'May we do so?' (1.1.67) Murellus asks. 'You know it is the feast of Lupercal' (1.1.68). 'It is no matter' (1.1.69), Flavius replies. 'Let no images / Be hung with Caesar's trophies' (1.1.70). This opening conversation is rich in symbolic import, but its significance depends in part on two anachronisms. First, the tribunes here do not come across as representatives of the people, as they were historically, and as they are represented in Shakespeare's later Roman play, *Coriolanus*. Instead, they are scornful upper-class antagonists, rebuking the people as 'mechanical'. Casca mentions them with sympathy in his conversation later with his aristocratic co-conspirator, Cassius, aligning them further with the patriciate. Second, Shakespeare conceives of Roman statues here as they appeared initially to later centuries, relatively bare and plain, whereas we know now they were originally painted in garish polychrome.

Shakespeare's slight anachronisms in this case are integral to the symbolic significance of the scene. On-stage, the 'grotesque' body associated with coarse, comical 'mechanicals' and 'trades' such as carpenters and cobblers is literally, physically transformed by force into the 'classical body' favoured by the elites: a bare, silent, static, stripped-down statue. Like Murellus and Flavius themselves, later, the 'images' are, in a metaphorical sense, 'put to silence' (1.2.284). Shakespeare acknowledges the presence of the grotesque even within the classical in his allusion to the Lupercalia, an ancient Roman celebration of fertility Plutarch describes in his 'Life of Caesar', and which featured heavy drinking, nudity and animal sacrifice. Shakespeare then adds a pun: Flavius' remark about the Lupercalia, 'It is no matter.' Ostensibly, Flavius means, 'it does not matter, that is to say, it is not important, that today is the feast of the Lupercal.' The compressed statement, however, placed where it is, suggests a more metaphysical truth. The 'classical' body seeks to escape embodiment itself; to be independent of materiality per se. As Gail Kern Paster observes, with regards to Bakhtin, the 'classical' body is not 'a new form of bodiliness'. Instead, it can be better understood as 'a denial of common bodiliness *tout court*'.[73] The 'classical' body is in this sense, as Flavius says, 'no matter'.

Sometimes Christianity is misperceived as likewise opposed to the body. For example, in his study of shame in Shakespeare, Ewan Fernie claims that 'Christianity explicitly regards the human condition itself as shameful', especially 'the body'.[74] Shame about the body is not intrinsic or integral to Christianity, however. Instead, like kudzu in the American South, it is a pervasive, alien interloper; characteristic, but misperceived if seen as indigenous; a legacy of the persistent but extrinsic influence of pre-Christian, Graeco-Roman thought.[75] Christianity emerged in the context of Roman Stoicism, as well as Greek Neoplatonism; in the case of St Augustine, especially, as well as other Latin Church Fathers such as his contemporary St Jerome, it is a common criticism that they never truly put aside their training as young pagans in classical philosophy. For all his dismay about the misbehavior of the 'flesh', St Paul, by contrast, insists on the resurrection of the body:

a radical departure from his intellectual Zeitgeist. Contemporary Neoplatonists, Manicheans and Gnostics all sought escape from the body, not its return. In the context of its origin, the remarkable thing about Christianity, what St Paul calls 'folly (*moria*) to the Gentiles', is precisely not its rejection of 'the body'. What was shocking about Christianity to ancient Romans was on the contrary its exaltation of 'the human condition' at its most vulnerable, including our embodiment. 'We preach Christ crucified' (1 Cor. 2:10), St Paul insists: a broken, bleeding, mortal human, not as a symbol of shame, but as a symbol of glory. What Bakhtin calls the 'grotesque' body becomes instead divine, ideal.

In their work on Shakespeare's Roman plays, especially *Julius Caesar*, feminist critics have directed particular attention to the symbolism of wounds, blood and bleeding. For them, the wound, with its attendant blood, is most obviously a symbol of femininity, imperiling Roman protagonists' sense of themselves as masculine. Of Antony's botched suicide, for example, Cynthia Marshall writes, 'Wounded, bleeding, and lacking agency, Antony takes on a typically feminine position.' Dying in this fashion, he 'troubles an audience's notions of what it means to be a (masculine) hero.'[76] Gail Paster argues that 'in bleeding the male body resembles the body of a woman', the 'leaky vessel' of contemporary humoral theory, which Paster aligns with Bakhtin's concept of the 'grotesque' body. In the case of Caesar's assassination, 'the conspirators use blood as a signifier that differentiates their bodies from Caesar's', 'marking him discursively with the shameful stigmata of ambiguous gender, especially the sign of womanly blood'.[77]

All of these authors also maintain, however, that wounds, blood and bleeding can be recovered by what Paster calls 'the patriarchal ethos' and transformed through rhetoric into their opposite: symbols of masculinity.[78] This reformulation of the import of the wound, these feminist critics tend to present as relatively artificial or 'constructed', however, in comparison to its more natural, immediate function as a telling revelation of the feminine 'other' within the masculine 'selfsame'. Kahn, for example, describes the 'wounds' of her book's subtitle, 'Warriors, Wounds, and Women', as 'the most problematic, self-cancelling figuration of masculinity in the Roman works'. They are a 'fetish' (Portuguese, *feticheria*; fr. Latin, *facticius*), meaning in this case, something made, not natural, and therefore especially useful indices of the 'artifice' involved in 'representations of cultural difference'.[79] Madelon Sprengnether draws attention to Portia; by deliberately wounding herself, Portia 'reveals the underlying paradox of the play, which equates manliness with injury, so that the sign of masculinity becomes the wound'.[80] Her attempt to prove herself capable of manly 'constancy' by appropriating its symbol, the 'voluntary wound', instead reveals the artificial nature of that 'sign'.

Again, however, the question of causal priority interposes difficulties. What is tenor, and what is vehicle? Feminist critics tend to interpret agency in Shakespeare's Roman plays as a symbol of idealised masculinity. I am more inclined, by contrast, to see masculinity in this context as itself a symbol of idealised agency. What Romans really admire, at base, is power; that the kind of power they respect is associated with masculinity is a secondary construction. So also, that the opposite of such power, passibility, is associated with femininity. What makes a wound like Portia's masculine is its prior, more definitive status as 'voluntary'. What makes a wound like Antony's, by contrast, feminine is its prior, more definitive status as involuntary, or at least, as introducing an unintended, unpleasant outcome. Antony does mean to stab himself, but not to linger on afterwards in considerable pain.

In his discussion of figurative conceits in Shakespeare's Roman plays, Maurice Charney writes of *Julius Caesar* that 'the central issue about the meaning of the play is raised by imagery of blood'.[81] Citing Charney, Paster finds in blood, much as Kahn and Sprengnether do in wounds, an ambiguous metaphor: 'shedding blood signifies self-control or its lack'. Considered in its own right, bleeding is a symbol of femininity: 'in bleeding the male body resembles the body of a woman'. Under pressure from the demands of patriarchal ideology, however, male bleeding can be reconfigured, somewhat speciously, as a symbol of violent activity. Paster cites as an example Adelman's analysis of Volumnia's reaction to Virgilia's horror at the thought of Coriolanus bleeding:

> Away, you fool! It more becomes a man
> Than gilt his trophy. The breasts of Hecuba,
> When she did suckle Hector, look'd not lovelier
> Than Hector's forehead when it spit forth blood
> At Grecian sword, contemning.
>
> (1.3.39–43)

As Adelman explains, in Volumnia's conceit, 'feeding, incorporat-
ing, is transformed into spitting out, an aggressive expelling . . .
the wound spitting blood thus becomes not a sign of vulnerability
but an instrument of attack.'[82] Paster agrees: 'male bleeding is represented as a "spitting forth," the combative verb serving to deny
any causative power to the Grecian swords and to endow the forehead itself with voluntary agency and passion.' The forehead itself
is 'the seat of reason', and it will bleed 'voluntarily from contempt'
rather than 'involuntarily from an enemy's blow'. Like Adelman,
Paster sees in this passage an indication of the origin of Coriolanus' characteristic 'fear of dependency'. To bleed 'contemning',
as Volumnia imagines, is 'to reverse the imputation of wounded-
ness and vulnerability, to deny permeability.'[83] Hector, a proxy for
Coriolanus, moves over the course of the conceit from a dependent child at the breast, embedded in the world of the 'grotesque'
body, to an independent, invulnerable adult, scoffing at attempts
to impair his agency.

In her discussion of bleeding, Paster distinguishes in effect
between what she takes to be its natural or *prima facie* significance and what she describes, by contrast, as a factitious, dubious
sense of its symbolic import. Inherently, bleeding represents femininity. With some Procrustean rhetoric, it can be reconfigured as a
symbol of masculinity; this reframing of its meaning, however, is
suspect and difficult to sustain. Setting aside for the moment this
second-order reinterpretation of bleeding as a sign of masculinity,
I would like to address the first. In *Julius Caesar*, blood, like the
body itself, is a symbol of passibility in general, not just femininity. As Paster herself observes, the crux of the difference between
blood as feminine and blood as masculine is 'self-control, self-possession, voluntarism'.[84]

In keeping with this principle, in *Julius Caesar*, the opposite of
the bleeding body is not the masculine body, but the fixed ('constant'), immutable and bodiless, represented here by the stars,
especially, the pole star, the one star that does not seem to move.
For Caesar to insist that his 'blood' cannot 'rebel' or be 'thawed',
that he is 'constant as the northern star', is a sign that he believes
that he has transcended, not only the imputation of femininity, but
still more radically, his own humanity (3.1.40–1). Geoffrey Miles
points out the similarity in this respect between Caesar and another
character who denies his own passibility, Angelo in *Measure for*

Measure. Shakespeare is 'conscious of the folly of this desire to be "perfect" – an aspiration which drives a series of tragicomic figures from the academicians of *Love's Labour's Lost*, through the would-be angelic Angelo, to the Olympian Caesar and Coriolanus'.[85] The stage Puritan, like the Roman, is introduced as a man 'whose blood / Is very snow-broth', 'one who never feels / The wanton stings and motions of the sense' (1.4.57–9). When he falls for Isabella, however, Angelo finds himself forced to confess a very different, more accurate understanding of his own human nature. 'Blood, thou art blood' (2.4.17). Caesar's comeuppance is bloodier still. As Paster writes, 'the assassination . . . discloses the shameful secret of Caesar's bodiliness'.[86]

Caesar's claims to transcendence are already in doubt, however, even as he makes them. Shakespeare lays groundwork for suspicion in the second scene of the play, in Cassius' anecdotal sketch of Caesar's various physical weaknesses: his 'fever' (1.2.119), his 'fit' (1.2.120), his inability to swim across the Tiber without Cassius' help. 'And this man / Is now become a god' (1.2.115–16), Cassius concludes, disgusted. Cassius' sarcastic description of Caesar refers here, not just to public opinion, but also to Caesar's own opinion of himself. For example, at the high point of a later speech in the Senate, just before the conspirators attack, Caesar insists that although 'men are flesh and blood' (3.1.67), he and he alone is in contrast 'unshaked of motion' (3.1.70). As an epileptic, this boast is indeed a remarkable claim for him to make. It bespeaks a thorough-going, delusional identification on his part with his own ego ideal.

Cassius insists on exactly the opposite word, 'shaked', in his account of Caesar's weaknesses. 'He had a fever when he was in Spain, / And when the fit was on him I did mark / How he did shake' (1.2.119–21). Cassius even repeats the word for emphasis, and again speaks sarcastically of Caesar as a 'god'. ''Tis true, this god did shake' (1.2.121). Later Cassius vows, in similar terms, to take Caesar down a peg. 'Let Caesar seat him sure, / For we will shake him, or worse days endure' (1.2.321–2). As if then to adumbrate Caesar's fate, the very next scene begins with Casca describing the very world itself as less than 'sure' in its 'seat'. 'Are you not moved,' he asks Cicero, 'when all the sway of earth / Shakes like a thing unfirm?' (1.3.3–4).

Caesar insists, however, just before he is killed, that he is an exception to the norms of human nature. Just as the pole star differs from other stars, so too he differs from other men. As the conspirators gather about him in the Senate, ostensibly pleading for a pardon for Metellus Cimber's brother, Publius, but in fact preparing to stab their new *dictator perpetuo*, Caesar dismisses their cries and supplications.[87] When they persist nonetheless, now including Brutus among their number, Caesar is surprised. 'What, Brutus?' (3.1.54) he remarks. Nevertheless, he stays firm ('constant') in his refusal to rescind his previous decree. He seems to think that he does not by nature ever change or need to change his mind, as if he had indeed become divine. As Seneca writes in his essay *De providentia*, 'The great author and ruler of all things wrote the decrees of fate indeed, but he also follows them. He decreed them once for all; he continually obeys them.'[88] As Paul Cantor writes, 'Ultimately the tyrannical desire of the Roman heroes takes the form of a will to apotheosis. Spurning any conventional sense of the limits of humanity, these heroes wish to become gods.'[89]

Caesar's description of himself at this fraught, climactic moment, an epic simile in which he compares himself to 'the northern star', bespeaks a remarkably unbridled megalomania. Throughout, he seems to see no gap, no incongruity, between himself as he is in fact and that impassible, ideal self which Shakespeare's Romans, like classical philosophers, more typically identify with the divine:

> I could be well moved if I were as you:
> If I could pray to move, prayers would move me.
> But I am constant as the northern star,
> Of whose true-fixed and resting quality,
> There is no fellow in the firmament.
> The skies are painted with unnumbered sparks:
> They are all fire, and every one doth shine;
> But there's but one in all doth hold his place.
> So in the world: 'tis furnished well with men,
> And men are flesh and blood, and apprehensive.
> Yet in the number I do know but one
> That unassailable holds on his rank
> Unshaked of motion. And that I am he
> Let me a little show it even in this,
> That I was constant Cimber should be banished
> And constant do remain to keep him so.
>
> (3.1.58–73)

The speech gives several signs of interplay with classical philosophy, capturing the basic gist of its theology. First, the emphasis on the contrast between motion and immobility: 'true-fixed', 'resting', 'unshaked' vs. 'moved', 'move', 'motion'. Caesar presents himself here as the equivalent of Aristotle's Unmoved Mover. In his treatise *De constantia*, Lipsius presents *Non moveri* ('Not to be moved') as the motto of the successful Neostoic. 'Lofty against all accident, and upright, consistent in a single demeanor, as in a balance heading neither up nor down, you will lay claim to that great and virtually divine *Non moveri*.'[90] Second, and on a related note, the emphasis on 'constancy', the signature ideal of contemporary Neostoicism: Caesar describes himself here three times as 'constant'. Third, the indifference to 'prayers': like Lucretius' gods, Caesar is not swayed by the pleas of mere men. When Cinna continues, nonetheless, to press for Cimber's pardon, Caesar rebukes him sharply. 'Hence! Wilt thou lift up Olympus?' (3.1.74). The disdain communicated is truly 'Olympian', in today's sense; men are beneath his notice. The direct, third-person reference to himself as 'Olympus' reveals Caesar's sense of himself as divine, as well as his belief that he is utterly impassible. He can no more be 'moved' than a mountain.

'If I could pray to move, prayers would move me.' The protasis of this conditional is the most interesting part. 'If I could pray to move . . .' What Caesar reveals here is that he sees himself not only as indifferent to the prayers of others, but also as himself incapable of praying. 'Constancy' becomes a kind of constraint: he cannot plead with other people, persuade them, 'pray to move' them, because to do so would require some degree of passibility on his own part, as well as theirs. As I addressed in more detail in the second section of the previous chapter, '"A marble statue of a man"', persuading other people requires first being persuaded oneself. Cicero, especially, argues that the orator can only bring others to feel an emotion if he himself, like an actor, or like Mark Antony in his funeral oration, first feels that emotion himself. Both in Caesar's case here, rejecting petitions, alienating his peers, and in Brutus', in his coldly rational, off-putting funeral oration, the attempt to live out an ideal of absolute 'constancy', neither pleading with others, nor heeding their pleas ('prayers'), proves incompatible with effective political action.

Caesar's diction also invites inquiry, in so far as it reveals his perception of other people. The world is 'furnished well with men': the word 'furnished' here is disturbing. To see other men as furnishings is to see them as passive objects for use, not as independent centers of agency. These men, Caesar also describes as 'sparks'. 'The skies are painted with unnumbered sparks: / They are all fire, and every one doth shine.' The generosity is patronising. To speak of these 'sparks' as 'painted' on the skies suggests that their glory or 'shine' is merely superficial. To describe them as 'unnumbered' suggests that they are not important; the word 'unnumbered' stands in sharp contrast to the same passage from Scripture that Hamlet cites, when he mentions the 'fall of a sparrow': 'the very hairs of your head are all numbered' (Matt. 10:30).[91] Caesar's ideal self is indifferent to *hoi polloi*, not animated, like the Christian God, by concern for the minutiae of each and every man's life.

'Sparks', too, seems to have had in contemporary English a specific, now-obsolete meaning, a slang denotation too informal and too specific to Shakespeare's England for Caesar to intend here, and which introduces, therefore, an element of dramatic irony, akin to that produced by the myriad of allusions to Christian Scripture in *Antony and Cleopatra*. Parolles in *All's Well That Ends Well* calls Bertram a 'spark' (2.1.25), and also addresses other young lords who head off to war as 'good sparks' (2.1.40). The word 'spark' serves in this context as a slang term for a young man who is, as Montaigne says, *bisognosi d'honore*. In an essay on 'Caesar's Methods of Making War', Montaigne writes:

> That is what the Italians say when they want to reprove that foolhardiness that is seen in young men, calling them 'needy of honour', *bisognosi d'honore*; adding that they, being still in such great famine and dearth of reputation, are right to seek it at any price whatsoever, which men who have already acquired enough of it should not do.[92]

When Caesar uses the term 'sparks' to refer to the other Roman citizens whom his ambition has sidelined, his description not only hints at his own danger, surrounded, literally, by men with so little to lose, but also aligns them with the young noblemen in Shakespeare's own time who were likewise 'needy of honour': courtiers and frustrated would-be war heroes such as the Earl of Essex. Less flattering to such malcontents, 'spark' could also have yet another colloquial sense, however, and again one connected to the contemporary crisis of the aristocracy. Specifically, 'spark', with a pejorative connotation, could mean something like 'dandy' or 'popinjay': 'a young man who affects elegance of dress'.[93] This connotation speaks to Caesar's description of the sky as 'painted' with such 'sparks'. 'Painting' suggests femininity, make-up, superficiality: all the hypocritical niceties and obligations of a royal court.

'There is no fellow in the firmament.' Caesar's fantasy of himself here is a paradigmatic example of the characteristic desire of Shakespeare's tragic Roman protagonists somehow to transcend or break free from their own inescapable, vulnerable embeddedness in a world of multiple, fluctuating and interdependent consciousnesses. 'Fellow' in this case is significant in its sense of 'like, match, resemblance', as well as its connotation of 'fellowship', as in 'jolly good fellow'. That kind of camaraderie, a relationship of equals, Caesar here forswears as beneath his dignity. 'Firmament' means most obviously the heavens, but also conveys, in a double, punning sense, the moral quality of 'firmness'. No one, Caesar asserts, is his peer in the possession of the character trait of 'firmness' or 'firmament', a quality akin to constancy. The heavens as 'firmament' are the opposite, especially, of 'flesh and blood'. Blood here is not a symbol of femininity, but instead of fluidity, instability; as a liquid, it cannot be 'true-fixed' or 'constant'. So, too, flesh, unlike a star, can be touched; can be wounded; can decay.

'Men are flesh and blood, and apprehensive.' In the previous section of this chapter, 'Power and Passibility', I mentioned that the inspiration for Timothy Reiss's appropriation of the technical term 'passibility' for literary criticism was Aristotle's discussion of the role of passibility in cognition in his treatise on psychology, *De anima*. To explain the more subtle implications of this line of Caesar's speech, it may be helpful to explain that reference a bit more fully here. In brief, Aristotle recognises that perception by nature requires some degree of passivity. In order to grasp or 'apprehend' the outside world, the mind in its character as 'passive intellect' (Scholastic Latin, *intellectus passibilis*) must somehow internalise impressions that it does not already possess, being altered in the process. The experience of experience itself reveals that the mind is in some sense less than complete, lacking, as well as mutable. Otherwise, how could it ever sense new phenomena? How could it learn? At the beginning of his 'Life of Cato Utican', Plutarch observes that Cato, for example, from his youth was by nature 'inflexible, imperturbable, and altogether steadfast', and that as a result, 'when he came to study, he was sluggish of comprehension and slow'. 'Cato's reluctance to be persuaded made his learning anything more laborious. For, to learn is simply to allow something to be done to you.'[94]

Taking up something like the same philosophical problem, but in more concrete terms, Shakespeare suggests that to be 'constant', like a marble statue, is also to be dangerously oblivious. In this scene, the most obvious symbol of that danger is the dramatic irony of Caesar boasting of his impassibility, even as the conspirators press about him, preparing to kill him. The audience knows what it is about to happen, and it makes Caesar's vaunting here look foolish, rather than impressive, even well before the knives come out. To be 'apprehensive' is to be afraid, which Caesar sees as beneath his dignity; to be 'apprehensive' is also to 'apprehend', however, that is, to understand, to perceive. That Caesar's pride in himself as 'Caesar', invulnerable, impassible, is the source of his obliviousness appears even more clearly earlier, when he explains to Antony that Cassius is 'very dangerous' (1.2.209) but then catches himself. 'I rather tell thee what is to be feared / Than what I fear: for always I am Caesar' (1.2.210–11). Shakespeare then, without historical precedent, introduces a physical symbol of Caesar's wilful impercipience: deafness. 'Come on my right hand,' he tells Antony, 'for this ear is deaf, / And tell me truly what thou think'st of him' (1.2.212–13).

Caesar is not the only one, however, in this tragedy who underestimates human passibility, including especially the symbolic power of blood. The surreal bloodbath which Shakespeare invents and attributes to the conspirators, at Brutus' prompting, is analogous to Caesar's boasting about his superiority to mere 'flesh and blood' in that it represents Brutus' belief that he, too, is somehow capable of transcending the emotional volatility and instability of human nature. Still more remarkably, Brutus seems to believe that he can take the Roman people with him; that at his instruction, they, too, can shed their humanity and become creatures of pure, disinterested reason. Like the pugilistic, counterintuitive claims of Stoic philosophers, Brutus' insistence that he and the other conspirators paint themselves and their swords with Caesar's blood before they appear before the public is a deliberate flouting of reality. What victory is it to convince someone of something that he already believes? To command an empire, for Brutus, is not sufficient. Like many an ambitious intellectual, Brutus wants to conquer something even more powerful: common sense.

Just before Brutus suggests that he and the other conspirators 'bathe' their hands in Caesar's blood, he pauses for a moment to engage with Casca in precisely the kind of eristic dialectic for which Stoic philosophers in antiquity had been notorious, moving by rapid-fire syllogisms to markedly, even ostentatiously implausible conclusions:[95]

> CASCA
> > Why, he that cuts off twenty years of life
> > Cuts off so many years of fearing death.
> BRUTUS
> > Grant that, and then death is a benefit.
> > So are we Caesar's friends, that have abridged
> > His time of fearing death.
> > > (3.1.102–6)

In his *De oratore*, Cicero complains about Stoic philosophers redefining words at will, just as Brutus does here with 'death':

> The Stoics hold a different view of good and bad from all their fellow-citizens . . . and give a different meaning to 'honour', 'disgrace', and 'reward' . . . if we were to adopt their terminology, we would never be able to express our meaning intelligibly about anything.[96]

Nuttall describes Brutus' 'idiom' here as 'donnishly abstract'.[97] The incongruity between his tone, that of a scholar at his leisure, and the pressing political problem of having only moments before assassinated a wildly popular military commander provides a formal parallel to the discrepancy in Brutus' argument between his counter-intuitive description of that assassination as a 'benefit' to Caesar and the way that Caesar himself, one imagines, likely understood the same event.

The same sort of verbal would-be conquest of reality that redefines murder as a friendly favour occurs earlier in the play,

as well, in Brutus' notorious soliloquy, 'It must be by his death.'[98]
'Since the quarrel', Brutus concludes, 'will bear no colour for the
thing he is, / Fashion it thus [etc.]' (2.1.28–30). Vawter says of
this speech, 'Nothing more clearly illustrates the historical Cicero's
charge against the Stoics that they construct false syllogisms and
practice "verbal legerdemain."'[99] Nuttall sees a troubling 'streak
of self-satisfaction' in Brutus' 'rationalising'. It is the sophist's
delight in his own powers of persuasion: the more outrageous the
claim that he can somehow make stick, the greater his sense of his
own accomplishment. Cicero is said to have boasted of his defence
of Cluentis, for example, that he 'threw dust in the eyes of the
jury'.[100] Gorgias boasts at the end of his *Praise of Helen*, 'So I, by
words, have made a bad woman good.'[101]

Quintilian, defending the study of oratory, insists that the orator is not himself deceived by his own rhetoric. Brutus, however,
like Cleopatra, is fairly clearly first and foremost interested in fool-
ing himself. As Nuttall writes, 'The root of our unease is a sense
that Brutus is contriving to forget or erase actuality.'[102] Moreover,
I would add, Brutus takes pride in doing so. Denial serves as yet
another feat of spectacular self-control.

> Stoop, Romans, stoop,
> And let us bathe our hands in Caesar's blood
> Up to the elbows, and besmear our swords;
> Then walk we forth even to the marketplace,
> And, waving our red weapons o'er our heads,
> Let's all cry, 'Peace, freedom, and liberty!'
>
> (3.1.106–11)

Waving bloody swords and crying 'peace': George Orwell captures
the sort of stomach-churning disjunction between truth and propaganda that Shakespeare evokes here in his description of what
he calls 'doublespeak'. Big Brother tells the citizens of his dystopia,
'War is peace', and they are to believe it.

Brutus' leadership of the conspiracy against Caesar is marred
afterwards by an attempt to validate his power as an intellectual
over other people, as well as himself, moulding their value-system
into the shape of his own. He turns Hamlet's fantasy of life in the
'nutshell' of his own thoughts outwards, as if it could encompass
the world. 'There is nothing good or bad but thinking makes it so'
(2.2.249–50). What Brutus and the other conspirators discover,

however, is they cannot simply redefine instinctive moral value-judgments arbitrarily. As Michael O'Connell observes, 'blood itself has a power that cannot be controlled by their attempts to assign it meaning.'[103] Roused by Antony's more sympathetic rhetoric, as well as the sight of Caesar's bloody cloak and corpse, the mob of plebeians runs amok. Antony taps into an inescapable susceptibility to pity that Brutus wilfully ignores, the 'heart' that blood here represents, and unleashes it as chaotic rage: anger, aptly enough, at those, like Brutus, who have repressed it, heaped scorn upon it, and denied it the full scope of its force.

The figurative opposition in this play between fixity and fluidity, 'constancy' and 'passibility', of which blood is a part, a dialectic between, on the one hand, blood, tears and the river Tiber, and on the other, statues, stars and the monumental architecture of the Capitol, appears throughout the play, not only as a relatively simple contrast between motion and imperturbable stasis, but also as a more complex opposition between two different kinds of motion, the linear, triumphant march David Quint associates with epic and the erratic wandering that he associates with romance; or, as Quint calls it, 'the loser's epic'.[104] In the speech that immediately precedes Caesar's description of himself as 'Olympus' and 'the northern star', Caesar draws a sharp, if implicit, distinction between his own purposeful action, cleaving to 'pre-ordinance and first decree', and the relatively aimless existence of 'children', free at least in theory from set goals:

> I must prevent thee, Cimber:
> These couchings and these lowly courtesies
> Might fire the blood of ordinary men,
> And turn pre-ordinance and first decree
> Into the lane of children. . . .
> Thy brother by decree is banished.
> If thou dost bend and pray and fawn for him
> I spurn thee like a cur out of my way.
>
> (3.1.35–9, 44–6)

Caesar compares his own progress along a straight line here, like that of an idealised Roman soldier, to the counterfactual indignity of a 'turn' down a 'lane of children': a return, Kahn might say, from the *polis* back to the *oikos*. The shiftless roaming of a 'cur' serves as a foil for the predetermined way, 'my way', Caesar calls it, of the man who 'spurn[s]' that 'cur' aside. Caesar glorifies the advance of the juggernaut, like that of an emperor in triumph, and vilifies, by contrast, the wandering of a meddling stray dog. It is a fine irony, therefore, that Caesar's defeat, which follows not long after this speech, is in part a result of his unwillingness to 'turn' aside from his procession through the streets of Rome, just as he refuses to do here, and read a petition from Artemidorus, warning him of the imminent attempt on his life.

As Shakespeare sees it, the same staunch self-control, proud disdain for self-pity, and resolute determination not to give an inch of ground in a fight that proved tremendous assets to the Romans on the battlefield – in a word, their 'constancy' – also proves their undoing in the end. In the case of Shakespeare's Caesar, fear of acknowledging his own vulnerability manifests itself as a pronounced fear of acknowledging fear itself. To admit that he feels fear, as he obviously does, when he asks Antony for his further thoughts on Cassius, would be to admit that he has some reason to be afraid; in short, that he is vulnerable. Caesar would rather believe that nothing is more powerful than he himself. As he boasts to Calpurnia, 'Danger knows full well / That Caesar is more dangerous than he' (2.3.44–5).

Calpurnia remains unconvinced, however. A reluctance to own up to their anxieties, confessing to themselves the danger that their wives already see, is a large measure of the reason why both Brutus and Caesar alike, at one point or another, push away their wives in defensive scorn. These women, in their femininity, represent that part of themselves which, despite their bravado, remains 'liable to fear' (1.2.200). 'Alas, my lord,' Calpurnia observes, 'Your wisdom is consumed in confidence' (2.2.48–9). Calpurnia for her part is content to serve as scapegoat, as long as it keeps Caesar safe. 'Do not go forth today,' she pleads. 'Call it my fear / That keeps you in the house, and not your own' (2.2.50–1). Caesar is initially open to the stratagem, calling it with contempt her 'humour' (2.2.56), but in the end cannot bear the thought of what Decius calls 'a mock / Apt to be rendered' (2.2.99). 'If Caesar hide himself, shall they not whisper, "Lo, Caesar is afraid"?' (2.2.100–1). 'How foolish do your fears seem now, Calpurnia!' (2.2.105) Caesar blusters. 'I am ashamed I did yield to them. / Give me my robe, for I will go' (2.2.106–7). So, too, Brutus dismisses Portia's concerns about his evident agitation. She complains, 'You answered not / But with an angry wafture of your hand / Gave sign for me to leave you' (2.1.244–6).

In her study of masculinity in Shakespeare's Rome, Kahn argues that 'heroic male subjectivity is, for the most part, configured through the stigmatization or sacrifice of a feminized private realm of emotion, interiority, and dependency.'[105] Turning to *Julius Caesar*, Kahn documents how Caesar and Brutus both alike engage in defensive projection, blaming their wives for feeling what are really their own anxieties, as well.[106] 'Some of Shakespeare's women provide, in effect, an alibi for the heroes with whom they are paired – in that, when impulses inimical to manly virtue are associated with women, such impulses can be disavowed.'[107] I agree; in fact, I think this line of thought can be pursued even further. Projection is also at work here in a different sense, as a component of Shakespeare's characterisation.

In his study of allegory, Angus Fletcher defines 'projection' as a type of allegory in which the nature of a more central protagonist such as Brutus or Caesar is 'revealed, facet by facet', in more minor characters who represent 'aspects of himself'. Spenser's *Faerie Queene* provides Fletcher with the most obvious contemporary examples of this practice: heroes such as Sir Guyon or Sir Calidore 'generate' other, less developed characters through 'splitting' or 'fractionating' their own more complex personality.[108] For example, on a much smaller scale, Shakespeare sometimes represents men's emotions as a personified 'woman' within themselves. 'Frailty, thy name is woman' 1.2.146), Hamlet proclaims. King Lear calls his hysteria a 'mother' (2.2.236) swelling up towards his heart. Laertes breaks down in tears at the news of Ophelia's death, but insists that when his tears are 'gone', 'the woman will be out' (4.8.187–8), meaning, presumably, his grief at the loss. Cassius describes his anger at Brutus as a 'rash humour' which his mother gave him; Brutus then personifies that choler as Cassius' mother herself. 'Henceforth, / When you are overearnest with your Brutus, / He'll think your mother chides, and leave you so' (4.2.175–7).

Kahn sees Portia and Calpurnia as scapegoats for their husbands' disavowed weaknesses. They are also external, symbolic representations, however, of these more central male characters' own quality of passibility. Above all, they represent their husbands' ignored, mutilated faculties of compassion: the pity Neostoicism seeks to suppress. Kahn cites Shoshana Felman: 'The feminine refuses its assigned position "outside the masculine, [as] its reassuring canny *opposite*," and stubbornly remains "inside the masculine, its uncanny *difference from itself*."[109] Portia herself makes something like the same point, if figuratively, when she describes herself to Brutus as 'your self, your half' (2.1.271), and refers to their marriage as 'that great vow / Which did incorporate and make us one' (2.1.272). Calpurnia's sterility, an invention on Shakespeare's part, represents her husband's, Caesar's, barren faculty of mercy, as well as his rejection of the 'grotesque' body. So, too, the relative dearth of female characters in the play represents the way in which empathy in Roman culture as a whole tends to be repressed or, figuratively speaking, kept off-stage.

Female characters in Shakespeare's Roman plays, as well as femininity in a more abstract sense, represent most immediately pity, including self-pity or concern for one's own safety. The chief tension in the Roman psyche, however, is not just between compassion and cruelty, still less between masculinity and femininity, but instead more generally between idealised power and shameful passibility. When Cassius mocks Caesar in absentia for acting like 'a sick girl' (1.2.128), he invokes three different kinds of analogous weakness at once: not just femininity, but also youth and ill health. In another simile from the same speech, Cassius compares himself carrying the 'the tirèd Caesar' out of the Tiber, lest he drown, to Aeneas carrying his father, 'the old Anchises', out of 'the flames of Troy' (1.2.114–17). Here, the vehicles for disparaging Caesar's all-too-human passibility are old age and physical exhaustion. What is shameful in Shakespeare's Rome is not so much to be female or feminine but to lack power of a certain kind in any sense whatsoever: political power, associated here with health, middle age and force of arms, as well as being male. Caesar's epilepsy comes up repeatedly, and Shakespeare attributes a further weakness to him, deafness in one ear, which, unlike Caesar's 'falling sickness', seems to be entirely his own addition.[110] Geoffrey Miles presents a summary list of these and other ways in which Shakespeare insists in this tragedy in particular on the physical limitations of the human condition: 'epilepsy, fever, deafness, shortsightedness, ague, insomnia, fanting, illness real and pretended'.[111]

For Shakespeare's Romans, the ideal self is not the incarnate, suffering, sympathetic Christian God of love, tears, anger and death by crucifixion, but instead classical philosophers' utterly impassible, wholly immaterial Unmoved Mover. Humanity is defined in contrast to the divine by its susceptibility to external influence, physical as well as emotional: a condition that Roman protagonists such as Portia, as well as Caesar and Brutus, strive to transcend. To be human is to bleed, to be vulnerable, to fall sick, to age, to die. As Gail Kern Paster argues, the difference between Bakhtin's two bodily canons can be understood as the difference between man and woman. More fundamentally, however, for Shakespeare's Romans, it is the difference between Godhead and the human condition. The 'grotesque' is the self as it is: embodied, passible, prone to pity. The 'classical', by contrast, is the ideal self: 'the northern star'.

Notes

1. For a sense of Buber's influence, see Friedman, ed. *Martin Buber and the Human Sciences*. Bakhtin in particular once said in an interview that he considered Martin Buber 'the greatest philosopher of the twentieth century, and perhaps in this philosophically puny century, perhaps the sole philosopher on the scene'. Like Lévinas and others, Bakhtin freely acknowledges Buber's central influence on his own thought: 'I am very much indebted to him. In particular for the idea of dialogue. Of course, this is obvious to anyone who reads Buber.' Mariya Kaganskaya, 'Shutovksoi Kohaarovod', *Sintaksis* 12 (1984), 141; cited in Joseph Frank, 'The Voices of Mikhail Bakhtin', *The New York Review of Books*, No. 16 (23 October 1986), 56; cited in Friedman, 'Martin Buber and Mikhail Bakhtin'. Friedman's essay is reprinted as an appendix to the fourth edition (2002) of his *Martin Buber: The Life of Dialogue*, 353–66. For the importance of what he calls 'dialogism' in Bakhtin's thought more generally, see Holquist, *Dialogism*.
2. Fernie, *Shakespeare for Freedom*, 207–8. Cf. Hegel, *Phenomenology*, §177.
3. Jane Kingsley-Smith, 'Aristotelian Shame'; Tilmouth, 'Shakespeare's Open Consciences'.
4. The secondary literature on this topic is too extensive to cite in full. For Derrida's early concept of the other, see Derrida, *Of Grammatology*, trans. Gayatri Chakravorty Spivak (Baltimore: Johns Hopkins University Press, 1976). For Derrida's influence, see Fagan et al., *Derrida*.
5. Hillier, 'Valour Will Weep', 384.
6. Adelman, *Suffocating Mothers*, 7.

7. Robert J. Stoller, 'The "Bedrock" of Masculinity and Femininity: Bisexuality', in Jean Baker Miller, ed., *Psychoanalysis and Women* (New York: Penguin, 1973), 275; cited in Kahn, *Man's Estate*, 11.

8. Kahn, *Man's Estate*, 11–12.

9. Kahn, *Roman Shakespeare*, 2, 14–15.

10. Ibid., 2, 106 n. 3.

11. Mitchell, *Relational Concepts in Psychoanalysis*, 150; cf. 123 ff.

12. Eric Mallin, 'Emulous Factions and the Collapse of Chivalry: *Troilus and Cressida*', 146, *Representations* 29 (1990), 145–79; cited in Kahn, *Roman Shakespeare*, 92.

13. Kahn, *Man's Estate*, 11.

14. Kahn, *Roman Shakespeare*, 106 n. 3.

15. Rebhorn writes, 'As Anthony Esler has demonstrated, the generation growing up in the 1580s and 1590s not only had aspiring minds like Tamburlaine's, but developed an ideology of competition, aspiration, and excelling, in short, of emulation.' Aristocrats such as Essex, Sidney, and their cohort 'possess a shared "character"'. Rebhorn's own scare quotes here indicate that 'character' is not a 'type' in the Platonic or psychoanalytic sense, that is, a reflection of a varietal of a universal human nature. Cf. Rebhorn, 'Crisis of the Aristocracy', 97, 81.

16. Braden, *Renaissance Tragedy*, 9.

17. Rebhorn, 'Crisis of the Aristocracy', 81–2.

18. Ibid., 108–9.

19. Kahn, *Roman Shakespeare*, 17.

20. Kuzner, *Open Subjects*. In its sympathy for Habermas and Cicero, Kuzner's work much resembles that of Joy Connolly in classics; see Connolly, *State of Speech*.

21. Reiss, *Mirages of the Selfe*, 20.

22. Jacob Burckhardt, *Civilization of the Renaissance in Italy*, 98.

23. Reiss, *Mirages of the Selfe*, 2.

24. Alasdair MacIntyre, *After Virtue: A Study in Moral Theory* (Notre Dame, IN: University of Notre Dame Press, 1984), 33; cited in Reiss, *Mirages of the Selfe*, 3.

25. Reiss, *Mirages of the Selfe*, 5.

26. Taylor, *Sources of the Self*, 39–40.

27. Melehy, review of *Mirages of the Selfe*, 723.

28. Nichols, review of *Mirages of the Selfe*, 1356.

29. For Patristic perspectives on divine passibility, see Gavriluyk, *Suffering of the Impassible God*. For more recent discussion, see Keating and White, eds, *Divine Impassibility*.

30. All citations are from *The Sermons of John Donne*, ed. George R. Potter and Evelyn M. Simpson.

31. Arist. *De an.* 3.5 (430a10–25); cited in Reiss, *Mirages of the Selfe*, 92. In fairness to Reiss, Aristotle's understanding of the role of passibility in cognition is indeed intriguing, as well as historically significant; in their efforts to reconcile Aristotle's otherwise incongruent epistemology with Neoplatonism, as well as Islam, medieval Arabic philosophers such as Averroes seized upon it as a launching pad for voluminous commentary. See Davidson, *Alfarabi, Avicenna, and Averroes on the Active Intellect.*

32. For the Greek *pathētos*, see, for example, Acts 26:23.

33. Cicero's neologism *patibilem* in *Nat. Deo.* 3.29 is a notable exception, reflecting Cicero's position as a forerunner in the translation of Greek philosophical concepts.

34. Plut. *Pel.* 16.5.

35. Plut. *Numa* 8.7.

36. Hom. *Il.* 5.850 ff.

37. Xenophanes of Colophon, *Fragments*, frags. 15, 26, 23.

38. Diog. Laert. 7.134–5.

39. My focus here is not so much on Rome per se, in all its historical complexity, as it is on the more limited vision of Rome Shakespeare presents in his Roman plays. On popular Roman religion, see Feeney, *Literature and Religion at Rome.*

40. Sen. *Q. Nat.* 1. prol. 3.

41. Sen. *Prov.* 5.8.

42. In what sense God suffered on the Cross, if at all, has been a subject of much debate within Christianity. Over the course of many centuries, the Church Fathers came to the conclusion that God is indeed impassible, at least in his nature as divine. The Second Person of the Trinity, however, God the Son, is possessed of two natures, one human, one divine. His 'who-ness' is one, but his 'what-ness' is two. Thus, on the Cross, Christ suffered and died in his humanity, but not in his divinity; and so also for any other *pathos*, including most notably his ongoing compassion for the suffering of fallen mankind. Experiences such as the Passion which the Son undergoes by virtue of the passibility inherent in his human nature are accessible to him in his divine nature through a *communicatio idiomatum* (Latin, 'communication of properties') consequent upon the mystical or 'hypostatic' union of his two natures, divine and human, in a single person (Greek, *hypostasis*).

43. John Donne, Sermon at St Paul's, Christmas Day, 1622; from Donne, *Sermons*, ed. Potter and Simpson. In recent decades, the Patristic compromise on passibility that Donne draws upon here has come under renewed and heated pressure. In the wake of the atrocities of the Second World War, many theologians on the more

progressive end of the spectrum have argued that God's compassion extends in some sense to his divinity, as well as his humanity. I will not attempt to address that controversy here; my more basic point is that most Christian theologians would contest the unqualified statement that the Christian God is passible and instead introduce some complex provisos. For an overview of the debate, see Weinandy, 'Does God Suffer?' The seminal text for the modern claim that God is passible in his divinity, as well as his humanity, is Moltmann, *The Crucified God.*

44. Cantor, *Shakespeare's Rome*, 100. Cf. *Coriolanus*, 5.3.183–5: 'Behold, the heavens do ope, / The gods look down and this unnatural scene / They laugh at.' The sentence is an interpolation within a speech which otherwise closely follows North's translation of Plutarch's 'Life of Coriolanus'.

45. Cf. Heb. 2:14–18.

46. Armitage, Condren and Fitzmaurice, 'Introduction', 4.

47. See Cantor, 'The Poetics of Spontaneous Order'.

48. Ibid.

49. Hegel, *Lectures on the Philosophy of World History*, 62.

50. G. W. F. Hegel, 'The Positivity of the Christian Religion,' in Hegel, *Early Theological Writings*, trans. T. M. Knox (Chicago: University of Chicago Press, 1948), 67–181; cited in Cantor, *Shakespeare's Roman Trilogy*, 156–9.

51. Cantor, 'Poetics of Spontaneous Order'.

52. Cantor, *Shakespeare's Roman Trilogy*, 83.

53. Friedrich Nietzsche, *Human, All Too Human: A Book for Free Spirits*, trans. R. J. Hollingdale (Cambridge: Cambridge University Press, 1986), 117 (sec. 247); cited in Cantor, *Shakespeare's Roman Trilogy*, 107.

54. Friedrich Nietzsche, *Portable Nietzsche*, ed. and trans. Walter Kaufmann (New York: Viking: 1954), 634 (*Antichrist*, sec. 54); cited in Cantor, *Shakespeare's Roman Trilogy*, 107.

55. Cantor, *Shakespeare's Roman Trilogy*, 106, 108.

56. Friedrich Nietzsche, *The Will to Power*, trans. Walter Kaufmann and R. J. Hollingdale (New York: Vintage, 1967), 120 (sec. 204; cf. sec. 175); cited in Cantor, *Shakespeare's Roman Trilogy*, 112.

57. Nietzsche, *Will to Power*, 115 (sec. 196); cited in Cantor, *Shakespeare's Roman Trilogy*, 121.

58. Nietzsche, *Will to Power*, 118 (sec. 202); cited in Cantor, *Shakespeare's Roman Trilogy*, 121.

59. Nietzsche, *Will to Power*, 242 (sec. 438); cited in Cantor, *Shakespeare's Roman Trilogy*, 122.

60. Kahn, *Roman Shakespeare*, 77.

61. *The Reversible World: Symbolic Inversion in Art and Society*, ed. Barbara Babcock (Ithaca, NY: Cornell University Press, 1978), 32; cited in Kahn, *Roman Shakespeare*, 78.

62. Kahn, *Roman Shakespeare*, 2.

63. For 'demystification', see Althusser's praise of Brecht in Althusser, 'The "Piccolo Teatro"'. Cf. Greenblatt, *Shakespearean Negotiations*, 126; Wikander, *The Play of Truth and State*; and White, '*Troilus and Cressida* as Brechtian Theatre'. For further discussion of New Historicist efforts to present Shakespeare as a dramatist in the model of Brecht, see also Cox, *Dramaturgy of Power*, 215 ff.

64. On Shakespeare's Augustinianism, see Gillies, 'The Question of Original Sin in *Hamlet*'. On the implications of Shakespeare's Augustinianism for his thought about politics, see Patrick Gray, 'Shakespeare and War', as well as Armitage, Condren and Fitzmaurice, 'Introduction'.

65. Simmons, *Shakespeare's Pagan World*, 3, 7–8.

66. Cox, *Dramaturgy of Power*, xii.

67. Lake, 'Shakespeare's *Julius Caesar* and the Search for a Usable (Christian?) Past', 111. See also Lake, *How Shakespeare Put Politics on the Stage*, 437–510.

68. Bakhtin, *Rabelais and His World*, 19–20, 26.

69. Cf., for example, *Othello*, 'Is this the noble Moor whom our full senate / Call all in all sufficient?' (4.1.265–6). Cf. also Angelo's 'sufficiency' (1.1.10) in *Measure for Measure*, as well as *Much Ado about Nothing*: ''Tis all men's office to speak patience . . . but no man's virtue or sufficiency / To be so moral when he shall endure [etc.]' (5.1.27–30).

70. 'All signs of its [sc. the body's] unfinished character, of its growth and proliferation were eliminated; its protuberances and offshoots were removed, its convexities (signs of new sprouts and buds) smoothed out, its apertures closed. The ever unfinished nature of the body was hidden, kept secret; conception, pregnancy, childbirth, death throes, were almost never shown. The age represented was as far removed from the mother's womb as from the grave, the age most distant from either threshold of individual life. The accent was placed on the completed, self-sufficient individuality of the given body.' Cf. Bakhtin, *Rabelais*, 28–9.

71. Clifford Ronan points out that the concept itself of the 'grotesque' (fr. *grotto*, cave) emerged in the Renaissance, with the discovery of Nero's notorious Domus Aurea underground, and the paintings found on its walls: 'fantastic representations of human, animal, and floral florms, incongruously running into each other'. Cf. Ronan, '*Antike Roman*', 4.

72. Bakhtin to his credit is aware that the ancient world also had its share of the 'grotesque', and cites examples such as Galen's theory of the humors, as well as the satyr plays of ancient Greek dramatists. See Bakhtin, *Rabelais*, 28 n. 10.

73. Paster, *The Body Embarrassed*, 15.

74. Fernie, *Shame in Shakespeare*, 31–3.

75. Kudzu, native to southern Japan and south-east China, is considered an invasive plant in the south-eastern United States, where it has become so pervasive as to be considered iconic. It is notorious for its ability to grow quickly and overshadow indigenous vegetation.

76. Cynthia Marshall, 'Man of Steel Done Got the Blues: Melancholic Subversion of Presence in *Antony and Cleopatra*', *Shakespeare Quarterly* 44 (1993), 403; cited in Kahn, *Roman Shakespeare*, 132.

77. Paster, *Body Embarrassed*, 94–5.

78. Ibid., 95.

79. Kahn, *Roman Shakespeare*, 17–18.

80. Madelon Sprengnether, 'Annihilating Intimacy in *Coriolanus*', in *Women in the Middle Ages and the Renaissance: Literary and Historical Perspectives*, ed. M. B. Rose (Syracuse: Syracuse University Press, 1986), 96; cited in Kahn, *Roman Shakespeare*, 101.

81. Maurice Charney, *Shakespeare's Roman Plays: The Function of Imagery in the Drama* (Cambridge, MA: Harvard University Press, 1961), 48; cited in Paster, *Body Embarrassed*, 94.

82. Adelman, *Suffocating Mothers*, 149; cited in Paster, *Body Embarrassed*, 95.

83. Paster, *Body Embarrassed*, 95–6.

84. Ibid., 95.

85. Miles, *Constant Romans*, 16.

86. Paster, *Body Embarrassed*, 94.

87. On the influence of similar 'scenic structures of kneeling and pleading' in 'late medieval and early Tudor allegorical plays', see Whittington, *Renaissance Suppliants*.

88. Sen. *Prov.* 5.8.

89. Cantor, *Shakespeare's Roman Trilogy*, 169.

90. Lipsius, *De constantia*, 1.6, *Opera omnia*, 4.533; cited in Braden, *Renaissance Tragedy*, 76.

91. Cf. Luke 12:7.

92. Montaigne, *Essays*, 2:34, 561.

93. *OED* Spark *sb*2.2 [*c*.1600].

94. Plutarch, 'Life of Cato Utican', 1.2–4; cited from Plutarch, *Lives*, trans. Bernadotte Perrin, 237–41.

95. Cf. Sen. *Ep.* 45.5, 48.6–7, 82.8–9, 83.9–11. Cf. Cic. *Tusc.* 3.13, 3.22, and Cic. *Fin.* 4.3.

96. Cic. *De or.* 3.18; cited in Vawter, '"Division 'tween our Souls"', 192.
97. Nuttall, *A New Mimesis*, 108.
98. For further analysis of this and other soliloquies as exercises in self-deception, see Patrick Gray, 'Choosing Between Shame and Guilt'.
99. Vawter, '"After their fashion"', 215.
100. Quint. *Inst.* 2.17.21.
101. W. K. C. Guthrie, *The Sophists* (Cambridge: Cambridge University Press, 1971), 180; cited in Nuttall, *Shakespeare the Thinker*, 185.
102. Nuttall, *Shakespeare the Thinker*, 183.
103. O'Connell, 'Blood Begetting Blood', 185.
104. Quint, *Epic and Empire*.
105. Kahn, *Roman Shakespeare*, 18.
106. For more on the concept of 'projection', see, for example, Ornston, 'On Projection', and Novick and Hurry, 'Projection and Externalization'.
107. Kahn, *Roman Shakespeare*, 19.
108. Fletcher, *Allegory*, 35–8; cf. 27–8n. See also Nuttall, *Two Concepts of Allegory*, 151–4.
109. Shoshana Felman, 'Re-reading Femininity', 41, *Yale French Studies* 62 (1981): 19–44; cited in Kahn, *Roman Shakespeare*, 19, 27.
110. See Velz, 'Caesar's Deafness'.
111. Miles, *Constant Romans*, 134.

CONCLUSION TO PART I: SHAKESPEARE'S PASSION PLAY

Shakespeare's representation of Julius Caesar differs notably from that of his contemporaries, as well as from the picture of Caesar that emerges from his most obvious classical source, Plutarch's *Lives*. Plutarch's Caesar is shrewd, resilient and relatively dignified; Shakespeare's, by contrast, is physically weak and surprisingly obtuse; prey to laughable grandiosity. Other early modern authors such as Marc-Antoine Muret and William Alexander model their versions of Caesar on Seneca's Hercules, as well as Plutarch's biography. Shakespeare, however, seems to draw inspiration for his departure from Plutarch from the conventional depiction of Julius Caesar's successor, Augustus, in medieval English mystery plays, as well as other tyrants such as Herod the Great. Over the course of these pageants, depicting Christian salvation history, protagonists such as Moses and Isaac set up a typology of Christ.[1] Meanwhile, however, secular antagonists such as the Pharaoh of Egypt establish a contrary pattern: a typology of Antichrist. Like Lucifer, as well as Antichrist himself, 'Caesar' in the mystery plays is typecast as a blustering, comically inadequate parody of Godhead. Vaunting speeches proclaiming his supreme worldly might echo the language of God the Father. These boasts are then belied, however, by his inability to forestall the coming of Christ, whom he fears as potential political rival. Mystery plays, naturally enough, tend to focus on Augustus Caesar, emperor of Rome at the time of Christ's Nativity.[2] Shakespeare's Julius Caesar, however, stands in the same medieval tradition. As a type of Antichrist, he is a foil for the future Christ. His failure sets the stage for a different and paradoxically more powerful Messiah.

In the nineteenth century, Shakespeare's representation of Caesar as a self-important blowhard met with cries of critical dismay.[3] 'We do not much admire the representation given here of Julius Caesar,' William Hazlitt complains, 'nor do we think it answers to the portrait of him in his commentaries. He makes several vapouring and rather pedantic speeches, and does nothing.'[4] George Bernard Shaw is less restrained. 'It is impossible for even the most judicially-minded critic to look without revulsion of indignant contempt at this travestying of a great man as a silly braggart.'[5] James Boswell, son of the famous biographer, saw the problem as evidence of Shakespeare's proverbial 'small Latin and less Greek'.[6] Citing Caesar's *Gallic Wars*, Boswell writes, 'There cannot be a stronger proof of Shakespeare's deficiency in classical knowledge than the boastful language he has put in the mouth of the most accomplished man of all antiquity, who was not more admirable for his achievements, than for the dignified simplicity with which he recorded them.'[7] By the twentieth century, the problem of the 'two Caesars' was well-established.[8] G. Wilson Knight sums up the dilemma:

> We are, indeed, aware of two Caesars: the ailing and petulant old man, and the giant spirit standing colossal over the Roman Empire to be. There is an insubstantial, mirage-like uncertainty about this Caesar. How are we to see him? He is two incompatibles, shifting, interchanging.[9]

In his commentary on Plutarch's 'Life of Julius Caesar', C. B. Pelling observes that the Greek biographer seems to admire Caesar.[10] Or, at least, Plutarch's portrait of Caesar is more studiously neutral than that of many other classical authors. Suetonius, for instance, praises Caesar for his 'admirable moderation and clemency both in administration and as victor in the civil war', but concludes that 'the balance is tilted by his other actions and words, so that he is thought to have abused his power and to have been justly killed'.[11] Plutarch, by contrast, ends with the remarkable claim that 'nothing cruel or tyrannical sprang from ["Caesar's rule"]'. On the contrary, he maintains, 'it seemed that the state needed monarchy, and Caesar was Heaven's gift to Rome as the gentlest possible doctor'.[12] Throughout Plutarch's account, Caesar comes across as a man of superlative natural gifts, honed by discipline. He is generous, merciful, physically tough, an expert general, and a politician of uncanny shrewdness and foresight.

Shakespeare's Caesar is considerably less dashing and charismatic; less sympathetic and less extraordinary. Shakespeare is much more disparaging about Caesar's epilepsy, for example, than Plutarch is. Plutarch acknowledges the handicap: 'concerning the constitution of his body, he was lean, white, and soft skinned, and often subject to headache, and otherwhile to the falling sickness.' But he frames Caesar's debility as a cause for wonder rather than reproach. 'That he always continued all labour and hardness, more than his body could bear . . . filled them all [i.e. all the soldiers under his command] with admiration.' Caesar

> yielded not to the disease of his body, to make it a cloak to cherish him withal, but contrarily took the pains of war as a medicine to cure his sick body, fighting always with his disease, travelling continually, living soberly, and commonly lying abroad in the field.[13]

In Shakespeare's play, by contrast, Caesar's 'falling sickness' (1.2.253) is presented as an occasion for derision.[14] 'He fell down in the marketplace, and foamed at mouth, and was speechless' (1.2.251–2). According to Casca's bitter conceit, Caesar's 'swoon' was brought on by the 'stinking breath' of the 'rabblement' (1.2.245–7), cheering for him to become their king. 'I durst not laugh,' he quips, 'for fear of opening my lips and receiving the bad air' (1.2.248–9).

Cassius complains about Caesar's epilepsy, as well, and, like Casca, in notes of disdain. He describes him as a man of 'feeble temper' (1.2.129), compares him to 'a sick girl' (1.2.128), and mocks his plaintive request for a drink, as he lay recovering from a seizure in Spain. The request is an interpolation; Plutarch says simply that 'the falling sickness . . . took him the first time, as it is reported, in Corduba, a city of Spain'.[15] Shakespeare also invents a backstory of a swimming-match between Cassius and Caesar, a race across the river Tiber on 'a raw and gusty day' (1.2.100). Caesar not only loses the contest, but in the end almost drowns; Cassius is obliged to rescue him and carry him bodily ashore. Plutarch, by contrast, describes Caesar as a preternaturally strong swimmer. At one point, fighting in Alexandria near the lighthouse of Pharos, Caesar finds himself surrounded by hostile Egyptians:

But he, leaping into the sea, with great hazard saved himself by swimming. It is said, that then, holding divers books in his hand, he did never let them go, but kept them always upon his head above water, and swam with the other hand, notwithstanding they shot marvellously at him.[16]

The sharpest contrast, however, between Shakespeare's Caesar and Plutarch's lies in their assessment of his political savvy. Plutarch presents Caesar as a politician of consummate skill, laying the groundwork for his ascent to power years in advance through shrewd alliances with other power brokers such as Pompey and Crassus, as well as carefully arranged displays of generosity, clemency and eloquence. To illustrate Caesar's 'craftiness', Plutarch recounts his foresight in anticipating his later rivalry with Pompey:

> Now Caesar had of long time determined to destroy Pompey, and Pompey him also. For Crassus being killed amongst the Parthians, who only did see that one of them two must needs fall . . . Till then Pompey had not long feared him, but always before set light by him, thinking it an easy matter for him to put him down when he would, sith he had brought him to that greatness he had come unto. But Caesar contrarily, having had that drift in his head from the beginning, like a wrestler that studieth for tricks to overthrow his adversary: he went far from Rome to exercise himself in the wars of Gaul, where he did train his army, and presently by his valiant deeds did increase his fame and honour.

In Plutarch's account of Caesar's rise to power, Caesar's initial disingenuousness is so convincing that only the wisest of his contemporaries, Cato and Cicero, suspect his ultimate aim, until it is too late to prevent his success. 'Cicero, like a wise shipmaster that feareth the calmness of the sea, was the first man that, mistrusting his manner of dealing in the commonwealth, found out his craft and malice, which he cunningly cloked under the habit of outward courtesy and familiarity.'[17] North's terms, 'craft and malice', are more pejorative than Plutarch's own diction; the original reads '*tyrannikēn . . . dianoian*', meaning simply 'his intention to become an absolute ruler'.[18] Like Cassandra, or Shakespeare's Calpurnia, Cicero and Cato find that their warnings go unheeded. 'Cato, that then foresaw and prophesied many times what would follow, was taken but for a vain man.'[19]

Shakespeare, by contrast, omits all the political skulduggery, battlefield gambles and feats of personal derring-do by which, as Montaigne says, Caesar was able 'to become Caesar'.[20] Caesar appears straightaway at the height of his power. Given his wilful obliviousness, moreover, it is difficult to understand how he ever could have won it. He comes across more like Plutarch's Pompey than he does like Plutarch's Caesar.[21] Speaking to Antony about Cassius, he shows some vestige of political insight: 'Yond Cassius has a lean and hungry look; / He thinks too much: such men are dangerous' (1.2.193–4). Yet his willingness to act upon that sound intuition is limited by an overwhelming drive to assert his own invincibility instead. 'But I fear him not' (1.2.197), he insists. 'I rather tell thee what it is to be fear'd / Than what I fear; for always I am Caesar' (1.2.210–11). This lack of self-awareness then segues into outright comedy. 'Come on my right hand,' he asks Antony, 'for this ear is deaf, / And tell me truly what thou think'st of him' (1.2.212–13). That Caesar is partially deaf is Shakespeare's own invention; it represents his consistent refusal to heed others' counsel, as well as his own generally sensible misgivings.

Later in the play, on the day itself of his assassination, Caesar's wife, Calpurnia, begs him not to go to the Capitol. There are reports of 'horrid sights' (2.2.15), and she herself has had a dream which suggests he might be murdered. Caesar dismisses her concerns. 'Caesar shall forth' (2.2.10), he maintains. 'The things that threaten'd me / N'er look'd but on my back; when they shall see / The face of Caesar, they are vanished' (2.2.10–12). Caesar casts himself here as an irresistible force. Yet the conceit also shows the limits of his self-awareness, in its suggestion of an attack from behind. As the audience is aware, that very day Caesar will be stabbed in the back. 'Alas, my lord,' Calpurnia laments, 'Your wisdom is consumed in confidence' (2.2.48–9). Caesar finally starts to give in to Calpurnia's pleas when he is interrupted by one of the conspirators, Decius Brutus. He then proves surprisingly susceptible to flattery, as well as fear of being mocked for staying home: Decius Brutus is able to convince him, despite his wife's objections, to come with him to the Capitol. The basic premise throughout that Caesar is the gull, the dupe, the victim of manipulation, rather than its master, runs very much counter to the spirit of Plutarch's biography. Nevertheless, Shakespeare's characterisation is consistent: Caesar can see, but only in one direction; he can hear, but only out of one ear. He has a blind spot, and it is what G. Wilson Knight aptly identifies as a boundless 'egotism', an 'almost superstitious respect for his own importance'. He sees himself as at once both man and god: 'almost divinity'. 'Hence his rapid changes, his admixture of fine phrases resonant of imperial glory with trivialities, platitudes, absurdities.'[22]

In an attempt to solve the problem of the 'two Caesars', Harry Morgan Ayres suggests that Caesar suffered towards the end of his life from what we would now call mania: 'a touch of that obfuscation of the judgment which sometimes attacks the wielders of unlimited power, leading to extravagance in language and to schemes, not wholly impossible in themselves, which come to naught'. Ayres compares this condition to the ancient Greek concept of *atē*: 'the infatuation, the judicial blindness laid by the gods on those whose destruction they are premeditating'. Ayres does not assume, however, that Shakespeare had any degree of familiarity with ancient Greek literature. Instead, he suggests a more immediate precedent: Shakespeare was bound by convention to appease 'the preconceptions of his audience', a mental construct which he calls 'the Elizabethan Stage-Caesar'. 'If we could discover . . . they conceived him as a man that thunders, lightens, and roars', then it is easy enough to understand Shakespeare's departure from Plutarch. 'Shakespeare must of necessity endow him with a little strut, a touch of grandiosity, if his audience is to believe that Caesar stands before them.'[23] For Ayres, the most likely source of this 'pomposity of manner and of language' is Seneca's Hercules. He examines several roughly contemporary plays about Julius Caesar, including the Latin *Julius Caesar* (1544) of Marc-Antoine Muret, the French *César* (1558) of Jacques Grévin and the English *Julius Caesar* (1604) of Sir William Alexander, and he finds that they all draw extensively on Seneca's tragedy *Hercules furens*, as well as the pseudo-Senecan *Hercules Oetaeus*. Shakespeare himself was familiar with Seneca's tragedies, as well, in part due to an influential collection of English translations, *Seneca his tenne tragedies* (1581).

Ayres' analysis of Seneca's Hercules, however, is oddly tone-deaf. To describe the protagonist of *Hercules furens* or *Hercules Oetaeus* as a comic figure is a jarring misreading. In keeping with classical notions of decorum, Seneca's creative work observes a strict separation of the comic and the tragic. In his prose satire, the *Apocolyntosis Claudii* or 'Pumpkinification of Claudius',

Hercules does make an appearance as a blustering simpleton, unsure what to make of the Emperor's wandering spirit. In Seneca's tragedies, however, Hercules is a sublime, exemplary Stoic hero. Having completed all his labours, including very literally bearing the world on his shoulders, like Atlas, as well as bringing Cerberus back from the Underworld, Hercules now faces a different task: to overcome himself. As Seneca writes elsewhere, in his letters to Lucilius, *imperare sibi maximum imperium est* ('To rule oneself is the greatest empire').[24] In *Hercules furens*, Juno afflicts Hercules with madness, leading him first to attempt to conquer heaven itself, like the Titans, then to kill his own wife and children, thinking them instead related to his enemy, Lycus. Once he returns to his senses, he is tempted to lose hope and kill himself, but he chooses instead to remain alive, stronger than his own suffering. In *Hercules Oetaeus*, he endures the excruciating pain caused by the fatal Shirt of Nessus, then kills himself by burning himself alive on Mount Oeta. Throughout the entire process of self-immolation, the playwright emphasises Hercules' indomitable and admirable Stoic composure. As in *Hercules furens*, he is cast as an exemplar of dignity in misfortune, revealing the potential strength of the human spirit even in the worst of circumstances.[25]

To find comedy in such material seems misplaced. To be fair to Ayres, however, his interpretation of Seneca's Hercules does reflect a former critical consensus. According to some early twentieth-century critics, Juno represents an impulse within Hercules himself, a tendency towards proud overreaching.[26] More recently, however, other critics have objected that Hercules shows no sign of inappropriate ambition or troubling impiety, outside a sharply circumscribed episode of insanity. The beginning and end of that psychotic break with reality is clearly defined: it begins with a hallucination of an eclipse and ends with his falling down unconscious. For these critics, the tragedy is not a tale of justice, designed to show the consequences of sacrilegious pride, but instead a study in a more Stoic vein, designed to show Hercules' heroic resistance to overwhelming feelings of grief, guilt and despair.[27]

A comparison between this vision of Seneca's Hercules and Shakespeare's Caesar is still illuminating, but not for the reasons that Ayres proposes. Hercules has no choice but to go mad; he is at the mercy of Juno's anger. He is a pawn; a means for her to exact revenge on her wayward husband, Jupiter. Shakespeare's Caesar, by contrast, seems able to rein in his delusions of grandeur, when the mood strikes him. He may be deaf, but only in one ear. The 'baffling' vacillation that G. Wilson Knight identifies in Caesar's language, oscillating between 'two Caesars', one 'a frail man', the other 'almost divinity', is significant, because it shows that Caesar, for all his occasional, outrageous grandiosity, is also capable of lucid moments, grounded in awareness of his own human weakness. He could come down from the heights of his inflated self-image; he simply does not want to. As a result, he seems more blameworthy, more laughable, than Seneca's Hercules. His mistakes are wilful, human, rather than the result of intractable divine opposition.

Ayres also seems to have been misled by the allusion to Seneca's Hercules in *A Midsummer Night's Dream*, a passage which he cites as an interpretive touchstone.[28] When Peter Quince casts Bottom as a lover, Pyramus, the endearing ham actor is sorely disappointed. 'My humor is for a tyrant' (1.2.24), he explains. 'I could play Ercles rarely, or a part to tear a cat in, to make all split' (1.2.25–6). He then declaims a few lines:

> The raging rocks
> And shivering shocks
> Shall break the locks
> Of prison gates;
> And Phibbus' car
> Shall shine from far
> And make and mar
> The foolish Fates.

> (1.2.27–34)

This spoof conflates two passages from John Studley's translation of *Hercules Oetaeus*.[29] 'Phibbus' car' appears in the opening two lines, *Sator deorum, cuius excussum manu / utraeque Phoebi sentient fulmen domus* ('Sire of the gods, whose hand launches the thunderbolts felt by both homes of Phoebus . . .'), which Studley translates, 'O LORDE of Ghostes whose fyrye flashe (that forth thy hand doth shake) / Doth cause the trembling Lodges twain of Phoebus car to quake . . .'[30] 'Raging rocks' that 'break the locks' appear in Deianira's nurse's boast about the scope of her magic powers, *habuere motum saxa, discussi fores / umbrasque Ditis* ('rocks have started to move; I have shattered the doors and darkness of Dis'), which Studley renders as 'the roring rocks have quaking sturd, and none threat hath pusht. / Hell gloummy gates I have brast oape.'[31] Essentially, Shakespeare combines the first two lines of the play, as if to signal his source, with another two lines from further in, chosen to reflect the speaker, Bottom, and the situation. Like Deianira's nurse, Bottom is a lower-class character, claiming unusual power. He is attempting to help, in this case, Peter Quince with his casting decision, and, as with Deianira and her nurse, his solicitous attention does more harm than good.

Bottom himself, however, is very satisfied with this piece of doggerel. 'This was lofty!' (1.2.35) he concludes. 'This is Ercles' vein, a tyrant's vein' (1.2.36). Bottom's admiration for 'Ercles' seems to have led Ayres to imagine that Shakespeare saw Seneca's Hercules as akin to Bottom himself. But the butt of the joke is more the translation, as well as outmoded methods of acting, than it is Hercules. Bottom mangles his source material, much as he does the two Greek names he attempts: 'Ercles' for Hercules, 'Phibbus' for Phoebus. It is also worth noting that Bottom himself does not intend to be amusing. From his perspective, the material is 'lofty'. The problem is not Hercules, but rather Bottom's own inadequacy and grandiosity. A similar mismatch occurs in another early comedy, as well, *Love's Labour's Lost*, and again in a play-within-a-play, the pageant of the Nine Worthies. Like Bottom, the character playing Hercules is woefully ill-suited for the role, albeit physically, rather than intellectually: the slightly built page, Moth, falls far short of Herculean stature. 'Great Hercules is presented by this imp' (5.2.609), explains Holofernes. 'Quoniam he seemeth in minority / Ergo I come with this apology' (5.2.613–14).[32] The introduction of Hercules here suggests Shakespeare may indeed have seen some sort of connection between Hercules and Caesar: the original set of the Nine Worthies, established by tradition on the Continent in the Middle Ages, did not include Hercules, but instead Julius Caesar.[33]

The analogy to be drawn, however, is not between Caesar and Hercules himself, but instead between Shakespeare's Caesar and Shakespeare's comic actors, Moth and Bottom. Like them, he has set himself a role which exceeds his true capacity. In *Hercules furens*, Hercules describes his accomplishments in terms which could seem like bravado. He recounts his legendary Twelve Labours and maintains that he can defeat any remaining monster which Juno might send against him. In context, however, these statements are not idle boasts. Juno agrees with his self-assessment: the only recourse that remains, as she sees it, is to set Hercules against himself. Some critics such as Denis Henry and Elisabeth Walker see Hercules' assertions as arrogant, even laughable. Others, however, such as Anna Lydia Motto and John R. Clark see this criticism as oddly blind to the assumptions of Seneca's imaginary world. Hercules is not to be measured by the standards of an ordinary human being. He is half-divine, the son of Zeus, capable of slaying monsters, returning alive from the Underworld, and standing in for the Titan Atlas. His life ends with an apotheosis, joining the gods among the stars. Within this mythological context, his claims about his own capabilities are not absurd or overblown; they are simply matter of fact. Shakespeare's Julius Caesar, by contrast, is a very different case. He has no superhuman powers, although he sometimes seems to imagine that he does. He is not the son of a god. When he compares himself to 'the northern star' (3.1.60) or to 'Olympus' (3.1.74), his implicit claim to something like Godhead is unfounded; at odds with his own merely human nature.

To think of Shakespeare's *Julius Caesar* as a Christian narrative, even if only by deliberate contrast, may seem counterintuitive. The play does not include any explicit reference to Christianity. As Steve Sohmer suggests, however, it makes sense that an Elizabethan Englishman, steeped in the stories of the Gospels, required to attend church regularly, and old enough to remember the great spectacle of his youth, the Coventry Corpus Christi plays, would have seen ready analogies to Christ's Passion in Plutarch's account of Caesar's assassination. 'In North's Plutarch,' Sohmer imagines, 'Shakespeare and lettered Elizabethans would have encountered a series of uncanny parallels between the lives of Julius Caesar and Jesus Christ.'[34] Helen Cooper argues that 'audiences of the cycle plays' were 'trained to recognize such theatrical analogy': within a given cycle, 'every individual pageant is a subplot in the greater drama of salvation . . . related to it, not just as a chronological step in the sequence, but by typology, by likeness within difference.'[35]

Seen in light of this analogical habit of mind, the story of Caesar's rise and fall lends itself by nature to an intertextual typology of Christ and Antichrist. Caesar's crossing the Rubicon is like Jesus' entry into Jerusalem on Palm Sunday. Caesar arrives at the head of an army, however, whereas Jesus arrives in deliberate self-abasement, riding on a donkey's colt. Caesar is betrayed by a close friend, Brutus, perhaps even his own son; Jesus is betrayed by a chosen disciple, Judas. Caesar is a military commander and a populist, the beloved political leader of the most powerful nation in the world. Jesus, by contrast, refuses to take up arms. His nation is conquered and weak; he himself spurns violence, and as a result he is rejected by his own people. Caesar is pierced by knives; Christ is pierced by nails and a spear. Both of their deaths are attended by prodigies and omens. Each story can be seen as the polar opposite of the other, at once similar and diametrically opposed.

Caesar is mentioned repeatedly in the Gospels, and always as a foil for true divinity. 'Give therefore to Caesar the things which are Caesar's,' Jesus says, 'and give unto God, those things which are God's' (Matt. 22:21; cf. Mark 12:17 and Luke 20:25). This contrast is invoked again when the Jews insist that Jesus is a rival to Caesar, an accusation which finally forces Pilate's hand. 'Pilate sought to loose him, but the Jews cried, saying, If thou deliver him, thou art not Caesar's friend: *for* whosoever maketh himself a King, speaketh against Caesar' (John 19:12; cf. John 19:15 and Luke 23:2). Not so directly a reference to Caesar, but in the same vein, is Christ's rejection of Satan's offer of worldly political power during his temptation in the wilderness. 'All this power will I give thee, and the glory of those kingdoms,' the devil promises; 'if thou . . . wilt worship me, they shall all be thine' (Luke 4:6–7). 'Hence from me, Satan,' Christ replies, 'for it is written, Thou shalt worship the Lord thy God, and him alone thou shalt serve' (Luke 4:8).

In support of his suggestion that Shakespeare's *Julius Caesar* resembles a Passion play, Sohmer points out that Shakespeare incorporates a number of slight but revealing departures from Plutarch, serving to bring his version of events more closely in line with the Gospel account of the events of Easter week.[36] For instance, in Shakespeare's play, but not in Plutarch's 'Life', Caesar is assassinated at 'about the ninth hour' (2.4.23). In all three Synoptic Gospels, Christ finally dies on the Cross at 'the ninth hour' (Luke 23:44–5; Matt. 27:26; Mark 15:34). In Antony's funeral oration, Naseeb Shaheen identifies an allusion to the events of Palm Sunday.[37] Protesting with false modesty, Antony proclaims that if he only had Brutus' rhetorical skill, he would 'put a tongue / In every wound of Caesar that should move / The stones of Rome to rise and mutiny' (3.2.221–3). In the Gospel of Luke, when Jesus enters Jerusalem, 'the whole multitude of disciples began to rejoice, and to praise God with a loud voice' (19:37). The Pharisees ask Jesus to rebuke the disciples for welcoming him 'in the Name of the Lord' (19:38), and he replies, 'I tell you, that if these should hold their peace, the stones would cry' (19:40). Shakespeare also introduces Brutus' curious drive to conceive of the assassination as 'a controlled and dignified ritual', akin to a Christian liturgy. Instead, David Kaula argues, the conspirators produce 'a disastrous imitation of the true redemptive action'.[38]

More recently, Hannibal Hamlin has identified a remarkable array of anachronistic allusions to the Bible running throughout Shakespeare's Roman plays, ranging from references to the Book of Revelation in *Antony and Cleopatra* to suggestions of the Old Testament in *Coriolanus*.[39] In the case of *Julius Caesar*, 'Shakespeare repeatedly draws Julius Caesar into parallel with Christ, by this means calling into question not only his divinity, but the sacrificial nature of his death, and its meaning for the people of Rome (and, in Shakespeare's own day, England).'[40] Hamlin sees the Icarus-like trajectory of Shakespeare's Brutus, as well, as a representation of a failed, proleptic attempt at a purely political salvation, foreshadowing but not fulfilling Jesus' later role. As he is about to die, Brutus tells Volumnius, 'I know my hour is come.' The formulation recalls the Gospels, when Jesus foresees that his Passion is imminent. 'Jesus knew that his hour was come' (John 13:1). 'Behold, the hour is at hand,' he says (Matt. 26:45).[41] Brutus wants to see himself as a 'sacrificer', a 'purger', rather than a 'butcher': Hamlin sees this language as recalling Hebrews 9–10:

> Brutus and Cassius hope that the blood ritual they enact (or wish to think they are enacting) will be repeated by Romans in years to come, in commemoration of the original act, suggesting the sacrifice of Christ regularly commemorated when the participants in the Eucharist consume the 'saving blood' of Christ.[42]

When they wash their hands in Caesar's blood, when they imagine themselves represented on stage to future generations, Brutus and the other conspirators try and fail to set up what amounts to a secular alternative to Christianity.

Another episode from *Julius Caesar* which both resembles and adumbrates the conspirators' odd preoccupation with Caesar's blood is Calpurnia's dream.[43] As part of the plot, a neglected warning, it resembles the dream of Pilate's wife. The original episode appears in only one line in one Gospel, the Book of Matthew: 'when he was set down upon the judgment seat, his wife sent to him, saying, Have thou nothing to do with that just man: for I have suffered many things this day in a dream by reason of him' (27:19). Pilate's wife also appears in a much-expanded role, however, in the York mystery plays. In the Tapisters' and Couchers' play, the Devil hopes to forestall Christ's crucifixion, lest he lose control of men's souls, so he tells Pilate's wife in the guise of a dream that Jesus is innocent, and that if he is condemned to die, she and Pilate will lose their wealth and station. She sends a message to Pilate, advising him that Jesus is innocent, but Ananias and Caiaphas convince him to ignore it as 'wicchecrafte' (292).[44] Their flatteries, bowing and scraping before Pilate, seem to anticipate Shakespeare's Decius Brutus.

Plutarch presents two different versions of Calpurnia's dream, both relatively simple. 'She dreamed that Caesar was slaine, and that she had him in her armes.' Or perhaps, he goes on:

> as amongst other, Titus Livius writeth . . . it was in this sorte. The Senate having set upon the toppe of Caesars house, for an ornament and setting foorth of the same, a certaine pinnacle: Calpurnia dreamed that she sawe it broken downe, and that she thought she lamented and wept for it.[45]

Shakespeare, by contrast, introduces much more detail. As Caesar explains to Decius Brutus:

> She dreamt tonight she saw my statue
> Which, like a fountain with an hundred spouts,
> Did run pure blood; and many lusty Romans
> Came smiling and did bathe their hands in it.
>
> (2.2.76–9)

Calpurnia herself interprets this dream as a 'warning' and 'portent' of 'evils imminent' (2.2.80–1). Decius Brutus, however, proposes a more favourable spin.

> Your statue spouting blood in many pipes
> In which so many smiling Romans bathed
> Signifies that from you great Rome shall suck
> Reviving blood, and that great men shall press
> For tinctures, stains, relics, and cognizance.
>
> (2.2.85–9)

Kaula stresses the anachronism of the key word 'relics' and introduces as a possible historical precedent 'something members of
Shakespeare's audience could have witnessed in their own city: the
avid quest for relics by the followers of Catholic missionary priests
executed at Tyburn'.[46] As A. O. Meyer explains:

> Great as was the care taken to prevent people showing reverence
> to the relics of the martyrs, or dipping cloths in their blood, all was
> in vain. Relics were secured after every execution, and sometimes
> it was the executioner himself who sold to Catholics the martyrs'
> bloodstained garments.[47]

 Later in the play, Antony tells the gathered crowd that if they heard
Caesar's final 'testament', 'they would go and kiss dead Caesar's
wounds, / And dip their napkins in his sacred blood, / Yea, and beg
a hair of him for memory' (3.2.133–5). 'Evoked in Decius' flattery',
Michael O'Connell suggests,

> is the image of angels receiving the blood of the crucified Christ in
> chalices, an image at once medieval and baroque, as well as a possible
> mystery-cycle episode of Veronica's veil. The cure of Longinus' blind-
> ness comes in the vivifying blood that runs from Christ's wounded
> side into his eyes, which is portrayed in the extant cycles of York,
> Towneley, and Chester.[48]

Crucial here, however, is the fact that Decius Brutus' flattering interpretation of Calpurnia's dream is dangerously false. As O'Connell
notes, 'the sense of saving blood is maintained at several levels of
removal from any possible realization.'[49] Hamlin wonders if 'the
proper response to Antony's speech is to recognize the inappro-
priateness of worshipping Caesar or any other man, since he is no
saint, and saints in the Catholic sense were in any case to be rejected
by Shakespeare's original audience, at least by the Protestant majority.'[50] Antony, too, is not merely venting his grief. He uses the sight
of Caesar's wounds to provoke mob violence, aimed at unseating

the conspirators themselves. Each time the Romans eerily anticipate Christian ritual, treating Caesar as if he were Christ, the result
is not security, 'salvation', but instead violent chaos. Caesar is flat-
tered by Decius Brutus' vision of him as a Christlike redeemer. Put
to the proof, however, he is inadequate in that role. He cannot
serve in the end as the linchpin of Rome's long-term well-being; he
cannot save it from itself. What would be a Passion play is instead
marred by an insufficiency at its centre.

For Shakespeare, the most important difference between
Caesar's assassination and Christ's Passion is the relationship in
each case between divine power and human vulnerability. As it is
presented in the Gospels, Christ's death on the Cross is the story
of the voluntary suffering of the 'one man', 'one only man', who
is in fact divine. The transcendent, awe-inspiring God of Moses
and Job is shown as immanent, human: 'flesh and blood' (3.1.67).
This man, Jesus, seems at first incomprehensibly weak, out of all
proportion to his status as divine. He repeatedly calls himself 'the
Son of Man', rather than the Son of God. He allows himself to
be put to death in the most humiliating fashion, crucifixion, that
the Romans could devise. In the end, however, this mysterious,
non-violent Messiah proves surprisingly powerful: able to conquer
death itself. In the Garden of Gethsemane, St Peter draws a sword,
but Jesus tells him to put it away. 'Do you think that I cannot
now pray to my Father, and he will provide me with more than
twelve legions of angels?' (Matt. 26:53). Jesus' death is a conscious
choice, a temporary setback that he himself is able to overcome.

The tragedy of Caesar's assassination, as Shakespeare sees it,
is a counterpoint to this familiar narrative. Caesar seems all but
omnipotent at first, but he is not in fact divine. His grandiosity
is punctured, disproved. He seems unassailable, like a juggernaut, but turns out to be merely 'flesh and blood' (3.1.67), like
other men. He styles himself the salvation of Rome, but instead
proves the rallying cry for a chaotic civil war. The would-be king
of Rome, the man whom Cassius mocks bitterly and enviously
for setting himself up as 'one man' (1.2.152, 154), 'one only man'
(1.2.56), bestriding all others like a 'Colossus' (1.2.135), ends up
as a 'bleeding piece of earth' (3.1.254).

Shakespeare's sense of Caesar as a wrongheaded, secular pseudo-
Messiah is especially apparent towards the end of Antony's funeral oration, in a sequence which invokes the iconography of the

Resurrected Christ in medieval English mystery plays, as well as English churches before the ravages of Protestant iconoclasm. As Pamela King and Clifford Davidson explain, the conventional depiction of the Resurrected Christ in pre-Reformation England showed him 'with a piece of cloth', that is, a cloak or mantle, 'draped over his shoulders (the wound in his side is visible)' and 'making visible the wound created by the nails in his palm, sometimes extending his arm'. As an example, they draw attention to 'the much damaged fifteenth-century Resurrection presented in sculpture on a door frame in the chancel of the Holy Trinity Church in Stratford-upon Avon': 'here the remains of three soldiers are present in a seated posture before the coffer tomb, and above it the torso of a much mutilated Christ rises.'[51]

In his funeral oration, Antony first shows the crowd Caesar's 'mantle', torn and bloody: 'our Caesar's vesture wounded' (3.2.168, 194). Then he shows them Caesar's body itself, 'marred' (3.2.195). Antony describes this 'corse' at some length in an earlier soliloquy, when he compares Caesar's 'wounds', which 'stream forth . . . blood', to 'eyes . . . weeping' (3.1.199–201). The crowd is outraged: 'O piteous spectacle!' (3.2.196); 'O most bloody sight!' (3.2.198). Antony's presentation of Caesar's wounds closely resembles, in other words, the story of Christ's Resurrection, but undermined; ironised. The play even includes its own secularised version of the ransom theory of the Atonement: Antony goes on to explain that Caesar in his will has left 'to every Roman citizen . . . / To every several man, seventy-five drachmas' (3.2.234–5), as well as 'all his walks, / His private arbours and new-planted orchards, / On this side Tiber' (3.2.238–40).

The success of Antony's speech turns upon the same coup de théâtre which seems to have been at the centre of the Resurrection play in England. As Pamela Sheingorn suggests, the audience 'first . . . may have seen a *Christus triumphans* and heard his victory sung by the angels; then, perhaps with a simple motion of pulling aside his cloak and opening out his hands, he became the *Christus patiens* who suffered and continues to suffer for mankind.'[52] Jesus' entrance in the Towneley play of the Resurrection is an apt example: he appears on-stage to the sound of angels singing '*Christus resurgens*', then draws attention to his wounds. 'Behold how dere I wold the by!' (26.236) he tells the audience. 'My woundys ar weytt and all blody' (26.237); 'From harte and syde the blood out-ran' (26.244).

Behold my body, in ilka place
How it was dight –
All to-rent
And all to-shentt,
Man, for thi plight.

(26.250–4)

Compare Antony describing Caesar's mantle: 'Look, in this place ran Cassius' dagger through: / See what a rent the envious Casca made, [etc.]' (3.2.172–3). The Towneley Jesus continues: 'This depe woundys,' he insists, 'Tholyd I the fore' (26.260–1). 'Behald my shankes and my knees, / Myn armes and my thees, / Behold me well, looke what thou sees' (26.269–71). The speech goes on at great length, with unmistakeable emphasis: 'Four hundredth woundys and v thowsand,' Jesus explains, 'Here may thou se' (26.292–3).

Shakespeare's Coriolanus' unwillingness to show his wounds to the public as part of his bid for consul is in marked contrast, not only to the Jesus of the Corpus Christi plays, but also to the version of Coriolanus' life Shakespeare found in Plutarch, where Coriolanus, by contrast, does not object to the practice. As Hannibal Hamlin notes, 'during the mandatory ritual, Coriolanus is, visually, at his most Christlike.' Despite his 'gown of humility' (2.3.41), however, he refuses to play the part. As Hamlin suggests, Shakespeare's use of 'creative anachronism' may have been modelled on Plutarch's own comparative technique in his *Lives*, juxtaposing Greek and Roman noteworthies. 'By means of anachronistic allusions, Shakespeare spins webs of analogies in which the tragedies of the protagonists are all measured against the tragedy (if it is one) of Christ.'[53] Departing here from his classical source, Shakespeare represents his Coriolanus, unlike Plutarch's, as unwilling to show his wounds, in order to emphasise the disparity between Coriolanus and Jesus, especially, the Jesus of medieval biblical drama. 'In the pageants after the Passion,' Michael O'Connell notes, the resurrected Christ would continue to display 'open and bleeding wounds'.[54]

In *Julius Caesar*, the irony is of a slightly different kind. Caesar does not return from the dead, like the resurrected Christ. The appearance of his wounded body is not reassuring, a sign of hope, but instead a provocation to riot. 'Revenge!' the plebeians cry:

'About! Seek! Burn! Fire! Kill! Slay!' (3.2.198). 'Sweet Caesar's wounds', as Antony calls them, 'move / The stones of Rome to rise and mutiny' (3.2.218). That is to say, the 'piteous spectacle' of Caesar's 'corse' provokes, in the end, the same kind of worldly rebellion against Roman power that his fellow Jews hope for from Jesus in the Gospels, and that he, by contrast, pointedly abjures. Shakespeare's *Julius Caesar* maps the story of Caesar's assassination on to the framework of Christ's Passion in order to emphasise telling points of incongruity. Caesar serves as what David Kaula calls a 'distorted replica' or 'imperfect imitation' of the Jesus of the Gospels: a saviour who proves, as Nietzsche says, 'human, all too human'.[55] As Peter Lake observes, 'For all his world-dominating achievements and well-nigh universal fame, Caesar's efforts to transform the Roman state end not only in his own assassination but also with the descent of the Roman world into chaos and civil war.'[56]

What the influence of Christian Scripture does not explain, however, is the comic aspect of Shakespeare's depiction of Caesar. Caesar in the New Testament is foreboding, distant, frightening; not a figure of fun. The obtuse, incongruous bullheadedness of Shakespeare's Roman emperor, undermining his pretention to this kind of grandeur, is not drawn from the Bible itself; at least, not directly. Instead, Shakespeare's tone in this case can be better understood as a legacy of the distinctive influence of medieval English biblical drama. In his discussion of 'comic relief' in Shakespeare, A. P. Rossiter observes that Shakespeare writes 'in the same spirit' as the anonymous authors of the earlier 'Miracle Plays', 'juxtaposing the religious and the farcical, the moving-pathetic and the brutal-comic'.[57] Mulling over Shakespeare's distinctive style, Erich Auerbach concludes, 'the mixture of the sublime with the low cannot in the last analysis come from any other sources than the medieval Christian theatre.'[58]

In keeping with these critics' intuition, the most likely source for the distinctive strain of foolhardy, comic braggadocio in Shakespeare's characterisation of Julius Caesar, the element which Ayres associates with 'the Elizabethan Stage-Caesar', and which so distressed nineteenth-century figures such as Hazlitt and Shaw, is neither Seneca's Hercules nor the Caesar of the Gospels, but instead the stage tyrants of medieval cycle plays, including figures such as Herod, Lucifer and Antichrist, as well as Augustus

Caesar.[59] Heather Mitchell-Buck singles out this archetype, 'the 'ranting tyrant', as 'the superstar of the early English stage': 'Characters like Herod, Pilate, and Caesar were dressed in the most lavish costumes, assigned the longest and most elaborate speeches, and often supplied the actors who brought them to life with a substantial wage.'[60] These antagonists introduce an element of comedy which Shakespeare appropriates, much against the grain of his classical sources.

Shakespeare's *Julius Caesar* was most likely written and produced in 1599.[61] Performances of mystery plays, especially Passion plays, continued well into the 1570s, despite Puritan opposition. At least some members, therefore, of the original audience for Shakespeare's tragedy, those in their twenties and older, would have been familiar with the conventions of this form of traditional theatre. Shakespeare himself could have easily attended the Coventry cycle, which was staged annually until 1579, when he was in his mid-teens. Coventry is less than a day's walk from Stratford-upon-Avon, and its Corpus Christi plays were famous nationwide as an especially spectacular instance of the genre.[62] John Cox notes that the Coventry Herod comes across as 'the liveliest and most memorable' of the various Herods that appear in extant cycle plays, and cites as an example a stage direction prompting the tyrant to rage 'in the pagond and in the strete also'.[63] In Shakespeare's *Antony and Cleopatra*, the cycle-play Herod proves a precedent for Shakespeare's own histrionic Eastern tyrant, Cleopatra. 'That Herod's head I'll have' (3.3.4–5), she exclaims.[64] Vowing to treat Herod as he himself did St John the Baptist, Cleopatra threatens very literally, as Hamlet says, to 'out-Herod Herod' (3.2.14).[65]

Taken together with his tendency to boast and bluster, Caesar's failed pretensions to Godhead connect him to the depiction of his successor, Augustus Caesar, as a comic tyrant in medieval English Corpus Christi plays, alongside other overweening, over-the-top antagonists such as Pharaoh and Lucifer. Other examples include the Towneley Pilate, as well as the figure of Antichrist himself. In his study of the genre, John Parker identifies a typology of Antichrist, as well as Christ: worldly potentates such as Herod, 'one of Antichrist's finer incarnations', present a 'parodic and false approximation' of a saviour who is still to come.[66] 'Impotent and false in themselves', their limitations presage 'the deferred arrival of yet another, more effective Messiah'.[67] This future figure is Christ at the time of his

Second Coming, when he will be revealed beyond all doubt as the heir of God the Father and sweep aside any and all would-be competitors. Until then, however, deluded claimants to divine power such as Lucifer and Antichrist enjoy some degree of liberty. They strut and posture for a time on the stage, as a comic prelude to their inevitable, long-foreseen defeat.

Shakespeare's Julius Caesar is a braggart in this vein: a Christian variation on the *alazōn* or *miles gloriosus*. From the perspective of Elizabethan England, he and his successor, Augustus, are among the few men in human history who came closest to possessing power like that of God the Father: autocratic rule of ancient Rome. Nevertheless, they fall short of full divinity. Unfortunately, all but two of the original Coventry Corpus Christi plays are no longer extant. Given, not least, their likely influence on Shakespeare, Michael O'Connell describes 'the historical lacuna of the Coventry plays' as 'the most grievous theatrical loss of the period': 'the missing link between the epic religious theatre whose performance extended from the late fourteenth century into the middle of Elizabeth's reign and the professional theatre that followed it'.[68]

'Caesar' does appear prominently, however, in two other pageants, the Towneley plays and the Chester Whitsun cycle, and his character there serves as an apt example of a medieval English stage tyrant, illustrating variations as well as continuities within such characters' role, and perhaps allowing us to triangulate what a Coventry Caesar might have been like. In the Towneley plays, 'Caesar Augustus' is a vain, foolish braggart throughout. He revels in the thought of the unprecedented scope of his political dominion and scoffs at the thought of any possible rival. When his minions cannot find the prophesied Christ Child, he grows frustrated, then frantic, to comic effect. In the Chester cycle, 'Octavian the Emperor' begins with stock boasts about his unassailable worldly might. When he learns about Jesus, however, he becomes more thoughtful and subdued. Some of the Roman senators try to proclaim him a god, but he resists their flattery, instead reminding them of his mortality, weakness and ignorance.

Medieval mystery plays typically begin with God the Father giving a grand speech, explaining his own omnipotence. At the opening of the Chester cycle, God announces, 'Ego sum alpha et oo.'[69] He then grounds this pre-eminence in in the absolute efficacy and unchanging nature of his will: 'It is my will it shoulde be soe; /

hit is, yt was, it shalbe thus' (1.1–4). The beginning of the first of the Towneley plays is very similar. 'Ego sum alpha et o,' God proclaims.⁷⁰ 'I am the first, the last also, / Oone god in mageste' (1.1–3). The Towneley God then goes on to emphasise that he alone is divine, pre-emptively undermining any subsequent claimants. 'I am god alone': 'oone god in mageste', 'on god in trinyte', 'oone god in persons three, / which may neuer twynnyd be' (1.8, 1, 2, 6–7).

Types of Antichrist such as Lucifer and Herod make similar claims throughout both sets of plays. The Chester Lucifer boasts, 'I ame pearlesse' (1.184). The Chester Herod: 'I am the greatest above degree / That is, or was, or ever shalbe' (8.180–1). The Chester Antichrist: 'I am verey God of might. / All thinges I made through my might' (22.221–2). The Towneley Lucifer asks, 'In heuen, therfor, wit I wold, / Above me who shuld won. / ffor I am lord of blis, / ouer all this warld' (1.91–4). The Towneley Pharoah proclaims his worldly sovereignty, and like Lucifer, complains that he is not treated with the degree of respect he believes is his due: 'All Egypt is myne awne / To leede aftyr my law; / I wold my myght were knawne / And honoryd, as hyt awe' (8.9–12). The Towneley Pilate introduces himself as 'leyf leder of lawes', and insists, like Lucifer, as well as Pharaoh, that he deserves his pride of place: 'was neuer kyng with crowne / More wor[thy]' (20.8, 13–14).

Shakespeare's Julius Caesar fits this pattern, alongside the Towneley Augustus and the Chester Octavian. The Towneley Caesar protests himself different in kind from all other men: 'Sych an othere / In all thys warld, is none' (9.35–6). He claims absolute authority: 'I am lord and syr ouer all, / All bowys to me, both grete and small, / As lord of euery land' (9.19–21). And, like God himself, he insists on the omnipotence of his will: 'I am he that mighty is, / And hardely all hatheness / Is redy at my will' (9.25–7). Such rhetoric echoes the Towneley God: 'Withoutten me ther may be noght, / For all is in my sight; / Hit shall be done after my will' (1.14–16).

The Chester God warns against pretenders, emphasising from the outset that he is unique: 'Never shalbe twyninge' (1.10). 'Was never none so like me,' he explains, 'soe full of grace, / nor never shall as my figure' (1.120–1). Thus, when the Chester Caesar advances similar claims, the audience is primed to be suspicious. God describes himself as 'Prince principall' (1.22); Octavian deems himself 'preeved prince most of powere' (6.185). 'Under heaven highest am I here' (6.186). Like these figures from medieval drama, Shakespeare's Julius Caesar insists he is unique: 'but one in all' (3.1.65). Like 'the northern star', he maintains, he has 'no fellow in the firmament' (3.1.60, 62). He compares himself to 'Olympus' (3.1.74) and boasts about his 'unassailable' might (3.1.69).

Maynard Mack points out that Caesar's procession, much akin to a triumph, is Shakespeare's own invention: '"Caesar," says Plutarch, "sat to behold."'[71] In his fateful visit to the Senate on the day of his assassination, Shakespeare's Caesar invokes another characteristic of medieval English stage tyrants: their role in clearing and quieting a crowd. Meg Twycross cites her experience of modern productions of medieval drama: 'a lot has been talked about the folk play "ritual" of clearing the magic circle for the players: it is also a physical necessity, as anyone who has performed with an unstructured audience will tell you.' Twycross speculates that this condition of performance, the audience encroaching on the acting space, led to metatheatrical play upon 'practical necessity'. 'If an actor has to push his way through the audience, he can't just pretend they are not there, so one might as well write pushing into the part.'[72]

For practical purposes, then, it is perhaps no coincidence that the opening speech of various stage tyrants in the Towneley plays tends to be an exhortation laced with threats, urging the audience to sit, kneel, clear the way and/or fall silent. Pharaoh begins: 'Peas, of payn that no man pas; / bot kepe the course that I commaunde' (8.1–2). Herod begins, 'I shall tame thare talkyng' (16.80). 'Sesse all this wonder,' he commands, 'ffor I ryfe you in sonder' (16.86–8). 'Peasse both yong and old at my bydyng, I red, / ffor I haue all in wold, in me standys lyfe and dede; / who that is so bold I brane hym thrugh the hede' (16.91–3).

The Towneley Caesar's opening lines seem designed in like vein not only to establish his character, but also to clear a space for the play itself.

> Be styll, beshers, I commawnd yow,
> That no man speke a word here now
> Bot I my self alon;
> And if ye do, I make a vow,

Thys brand abowte youre nekys shall bow,
ffor thy be styll as ston:
And looke ye grefe me noght,
ffor if ye do it shall be boght,
I swere you by mahowne;
I wote well if ye knew me oght,
To slo you all how lytyll I roght,
Ston styll ye wold syt downe.

(9.1–11)

So, too, in the York cycle, *Moses and Pharaoh* begins with Pharaoh declaring, 'O pees, I bidde þat no man passe, / But kepe þe
cours þat I comaunde' (11.1–2). *The Slaughter of the Innocents*
begins with Herod exclaiming 'Stente of youre steuenes stoute /
And still as stone ȝe stande' (19.3–4), and so on. At the beginning
of *Christ before Pilate*, Pilate threatens violence:

Yhe cursed creatures þat cruelly are cryand,
Restreyne you for stryuyng for strengh of my strakis;
Youre pleyntes in my presences vse plately applyand,
Or ellis þis brande in youre braynes sone brestis and brekis.

(30.1–4)

In his procession through the Capitol, Shakespeare's Julius
Caesar recreates this imperious tendency towards physical imposi-
tion. He airily dismisses Artemidorus' petition, unaware it is a warning about the conspiracy against him. As he walks across the Senate
floor, surrounded by an entourage of pleading Senators, he cuts short
their 'couchings' and brushes past their 'lowly courtesies' (3.1.36).
'Thy brother by decree is banished,' he tells Metellus Cimber. 'If thou
dost bend and pray and fawn for him / I spurn thee like a cur out of
my way' (3.1.44–6). He is unswerving, directorial, right up until the
point he is cut down.

Like the Chester God, the Chester Caesar insists on the unfail-
ing power of his will. 'Wholey all this world, iwys, / is readye at
my owne will' (6.195–6). Or again, 'all the world dose my willing'
(6.230). The Towneley Augustus sees 'both ryche and poore, more
& les / At my lyking for to redress, / Whether I wyll saue or spyll'
(9.28–30). The Chester Octavian scoffs at the very idea of opposition. 'Through vertue of my degree,' he boasts, 'All this world,
withowten were — / kinge, prynce, batchlere — / I may destroy in

great dangere' (6.189–92). The bluster recalls Shakespeare's Julius: 'Danger knows full well / That Caesar is more dangerous than he' (2.2.44–5). Despite such swaggering speeches, both medieval Caesars turn out in the end, however, to be troubled and surprisingly weak. The Towneley Caesar admits early on, 'oone thing doys me full mych care, / I trow my land wyll sone mysfare / Ffor defawte of counsel lele' (9.37–9). When he hears of the coming of Christ, who shall his 'force downe fell' (9.72), he is distraught; he sends ruffians to try to find the boy and kill him, but without success. 'Out, harrow, full wo is me!' (9.74), he cries, agitated and anxious.

The Chester Octavian proves more complex. Over the course of the play, after he hears about Christ, he undergoes a change of heart, making peace with the limits of his own powers. When senators come to honour him as a God, he refuses and instead maintains, despite their objections, that he is merely a man. His mortality undercuts any pretence to divinity. 'Godhead' has 'noe begininge' or 'endinge' (6.329–30), he explains, whereas he himself is already growing old: 'of my life most parte is gone, / age showes him soe in mee' (6.327–8). 'I must dye I wotte not what day' (6.319). To help convince the senators, he visits the Sibyl, whom he asks, 'shall ever be any earthlye kinge / to passe mee of degree?' (6.347–8). He hears her prophesy of the coming Christ Child with interest, but without any sign of envy, and retires peacefully.

The Towneley Caesar entertains an amusing streak of vanity: 'Cesar august I am cald, / A fayrer cors for to behald, / Is not of bloode & bone' (9.31–3). He speaks as if he transcended the very stuff from which he is made, simply by virtue of his own supposed good looks. The Chester Caesar, however, insists, by contrast, on the fragility of his own materiality. 'Neyther of iron, tree, ne stonne / am I not wrought' (6.325–6), he protests. 'For of all flesh, blood, and bonne / made I am, borne of a womane' (6.321–2). Shakespeare's Julius Caesar acknowledges that 'men are flesh and blood' (31.67), but he sees himself as exempt from the vulnerability of that condition: 'one / that unassailable holds on his rank / Unshaked of motion' (3.1.68–70). His 'blood', he suggests, is not like that of 'ordinary men' (3.1.37). The Chester Octavian is wiser. 'Though I bee highest worldly kinge,' he concludes, 'of godhead have I noe knowinge. / Hit were unkynde' (6.333–6). 'Unkynde': unlike Shakespeare's Caesar, the Chester Caesar recognises that he is a human being, different in 'kind' from the divine. The Towneley Augustus is foolish, but the Chester Octavian is surprisingly self-aware.

Shakespeare's Julius Caesar strongly resembles the Towneley Augustus, as well as other medieval English stage tyrants such as Herod and Pharaoh. Like these figures, he is a failed pretender to Godhead, a wilfully oblivious *alazōn*. His power at the beginning of the play seems to resemble that of God himself. By the end, however, he turns out to be limited, as we all are, by the most basic givens of the human condition: embodiment, old age, mortality and, especially, ignorance. He is not God, as Christ is; he is less, not more, than he seems to be at first. Over the course of the play he is deliberately stripped of his initial glamour, because he is designed to serve as a foil of the true Messiah: a comic Antichrist.

Shakespeare's indebtedness to what John Parker calls the typology of Antichrist is not limited to *Julius Caesar*. The same overarching, didactic plot-structure of punctured delusion recurs consistently throughout Shakespeare's plays. John Cox sees a similar pattern in *King Lear*, for example, albeit without the comedy. Although Lear's 'rhetoric is more temperate' than that of the typical medieval stage tyrant, it is still 'terrifying' and 'arrogant'. Like Shakespeare's Caesar, or the Coventry Herod, he 'cannot brook the slightest threat to his authority'. And in the end, like these more bombastic, comic figures, Lear is 'shorn of his power, his dignity, and his seemingly invulnerable self-reliance'. This reversal, Cox argues, 'has potent dramaturgical precedent in centuries of popular drama whose central images involved making the high low and the low high'. Seen in light of medieval English drama, Caesar's assassination and the humbling of Lear's arrogance can be understood as variations on a common theme:

> The defeat of Lucifer, the exile of Cain, the destruction of Pharaoh, the conversion of Octavian, the death of Herod, the tricking of Pilate, the abasement of King Robert, all involve essentially the same movement that we see in *Lear*: the powerful are reminded by the example of their own humiliation that they are no better than fools.[73]

The critical problem of the 'two Caesars' is not an inconsistency to be explained away; still less, a product of ignorance; but, instead, a revealing expression of a choice of allegiance. Shakespeare departs from classical sources such as Plutarch's *Lives* in order to tap into the vernacular tradition of the mystery plays. Like the contrast between Christ and Caesar in the Gospels, or between Christ and a stage tyrant in a Corpus Christi pageant, Shakespeare's characterisation of Julius Caesar is designed to foreground the contrast between divine power and human vulnerability. This gulf between God and man is reconciled and overcome in the person of Christ; for all others, however, human weakness is an insurmountable limit, dangerous to ignore. Differences between the two most developed extant versions of the medieval stage Caesar, the Chester and the Towneley, hinge upon their grasp of this fundamental truth about their own human nature: the fact that human 'flesh and blood' falls short of divine omnipotence. John Cox describes the medieval dramaturgical tradition as keenly interested in what St Augustine calls *potentia humilitatis*: 'the power of humility'.[74] In its typology of Antichrist, however, medieval biblical drama also presents what might be called *humiliatio potentatuum*: 'the humbling of the powerful'. This dynamic is what Shakespeare moves to capture, in his vision of the fall of Julius Caesar.

Notes

1. For a more nuanced sense of variation within medieval English biblical drama, see King, 'The Early English Passion Play'. Citing new evidence from the *Records of Early English Drama* project, King argues that English mystery plays were not limited to 'cycles of short pageants mounted on processional wagons that tell the story of the world from Creation to Doomsday, such as those from York and Chester'. Coventry, for example, seems not to have included any episodes from the Old Testament. King argues for a distinctive subgenre, 'the early English Passion play', akin to those in France.
2. See Luke 2:1. References to Scripture are taken from the 1599 Geneva Bible.
3. Cf. Dowden, *Shakespeare*, 285: 'Shakespeare's rendering of the character of Caesar . . . has considerably bewildered his critics.'
4. Hazlitt, *Characters*, 2: 224: 'As here represented, Caesar is, indeed, little better than a grand, strutting piece of puff-paste; and when he speaks, it is very much in the style of a glorious vapourer and braggart, full of lofty airs and mock-thunder, than which nothing could be further from the truth of the man, whose character, even in his faults, was as compact and solid as adamant, and at the same time as limber and ductile as the finest gold.'

5. George Bernard Shaw, in a review of Beerbohm Tree's 1898 production of *Julius Caesar*; cited from Wilson, ed., *Shaw on Shakespeare*, 104.

6. Cf. Brandes, *William Shakespeare*, 1: 361: 'It was because of Shakespeare's lack of historical and classical culture that the incomparable grandeur of the figure of Caesar left him unmoved.'

7. Boswell, ed., *Plays and Poems of William Shakespeare*, 12: 64.

8. Cf. Zander, 'Introduction', 7: 'It has become a convention in scholarship to discuss the two Caesars in the play, the private man and the political, public institution of "Caesar".'

9. Knight, *Imperial Theme*, 65.

10. Pelling, 'Judging', 3–26. See also Pelling, 'Introduction', 18 ff., 1–76.

11. Suet. *Iul.* 76.1; cited in Pelling, 'Judging', 9–10, and Pelling, 'Introduction', 18.

12. Plut. *Brut.* 55 (2).2; cited in Pelling, 'Introduction', 20.

13. Plutarch, *liues*, 766.

14. References to Shakespeare's *Julius Caesar* are taken from William Shakespeare, *Julius Caesar*, ed. David Daniell (London: Thomas Nelson for the Arden Shakespeare, 1998).

15. Plutarch, *liues*, 766.

16. Ibid., 781–2.

17. Ibid., 760.

18. Plut. *Caes.* 4.4.

19. Plutarch, *liues*, 764.

20. Montaigne, 'That the taste of good and evil depends in large part on the opinion we have of them', in *Essays*, 43.

21. I am indebted for this point to Lars Engle.

22. Knight, *Imperial Theme*, 64–6.

23. Ayres, 'Shakespeare's *Julius Caesar*', 194–5, 201, 202, 225–6.

24. Sen. *Ep.* 113.31.

25. For an overview of scholarship on Shakespeare's reception of Senecan tragedy, see Patrick Gray, 'Shakespeare vs. Seneca'.

26. Henry and Walker, 'Futility of Action', 11–22.

27. Motto and Clark, 'Maxima Virtus', 101–17.

28. Ayres, 'Shakespeare's *Julius Caesar*', 227.

29. Seneca, *Hercules Oetaeus*, trans. Studley. See Koeppel, 'Bottoms "Ercles"', 190–1.

30. Seneca, *Oetaeus*, trans. Studley, 193; cf. Sen. *Her. O.* 1–2.

31. Seneca, *Oetaeus*, trans. Studley, 210; cf. Sen. *Her. O.* 458–9.

32. William Shakespeare, *Love's Labour's Lost*, ed. H. R. Woudhuysen (London: Thomas Nelson for the Arden Shakespeare, 1998).

33. Carroll, *Great Feast of Language*, 229. For a more detailed history of the medieval tradition of the Nine Worthies, see Kuskin, 'Caxton's Worthies Series'.

34. Sohmer, *Shakespeare's Mystery Play*, 28.
35. Cooper, 'Shakespeare and the Mystery Plays', 33.
36. Sohmer, *Shakespeare's Mystery Play*, 130.
37. Shaheen, *Biblical References*, 530.
38. Kaula, '"Let us be sacrificers"', 208–10.
39. Hamlin, *Bible in Shakespeare*, 179–230.
40. Hamlin, *Bible in Shakespeare*, 184.
41. Cf. John 2:4, Luke 22.14; cited in Hamlin, *Bible in Shakespeare*, 197.
42. Hamlin, *Bible in Shakespeare*, 194.
43. Cf. Kaula, '"Let us be sacrificers"', 204 ff. See also Kirschbaum, 'Shakespeare's Stage Blood'; Paster, '"In the spirit of men"'; and Davidson, 'Sacred Blood'.
44. Beadle, ed., *The York Plays*, 30.292.
45. Plutarch, *liues*, 785.
46. Kaula, '"Let us be sacrificers"', 204.
47. Meyer, *England and the Catholic Church*, 213. See also Lake and Questier, 'Appropriation and Rhetoric'.
48. O'Connell, 'Blood Begetting Blood', 185.
49. Ibid.
50. Hamlin, *Bible in Shakespeare*, 193–4.
51. King and Davidson, eds, *Coventry Corpus Christi Plays*, 38; cf. Davidson and Alexander, *The Early Art of Coventry*, viii, 59 ff.
52. Sheingorn, 'The Moment of the Resurrection', 122; cf. O'Connell, 'Blood Begetting Blood', 181.
53. Hamlin, *Bible in Shakespeare*, 204–5, 183.
54. O'Connell, 'Blood Begetting Blood', 181.
55. Kaula, '"Let us be sacrificers"', 203, 211. Cf. Spakowski, 'Deification and Myth-Making'.
56. Lake, *How Shakespeare Put Politics on the Stage*, 437.
57. Rossiter, *Angel with Horns*, 282.
58. Auerbach, *Mimesis*, 323.
59. For further discussion of Shakespeare's appropriation and reimagining of the dramatic conventions of medieval mystery plays, see Schreyer, *Shakespeare's Material Craft*; Cooper, 'Shakespeare and the Mystery Plays'; and Cox, *Shakespeare and the Dramaturgy of Power*. On 'medieval' drama more generally in sixteenth-century England, see also Coletti and McMurray Gibson, 'Tudor Origins of Medieval Drama'.
60. Mitchell-Buck, 'Tyrants, Tudors, and the Digby *Mary Magdalen*', 241. As an example of the tyrant as 'superstar', Mitchell-Buck points out that in the 1478 Coventry Smiths' pageant, the actor playing Herod was paid more than double the amount paid to the actor playing Jesus.

61. Daniell, '*Julius Caesar* in London in 1599', 15.
62. See, for example, Schoenbaum, *Shakespeare: A Documentary Life*, 88, 121; Cox, *Dramaturgy of Power*, 22, 39; and O'Connell, *The Idolatrous Eye*, 20–7.
63. *Two Coventry Corpus Christi Plays*, ed. Hardin Craig (London: Oxford University Press, 1957), 'Shearmen and Taylors Pageant', l. 783 s. d.; cited in Cox, *Dramaturgy of Power*, 22.
64. William Shakespeare, *Antony and Cleopatra*, ed. John Wilders (London: Thomson Learning for the Arden Shakespeare, 2006).
65. William Shakespeare, *Hamlet*, ed. Ann Thompson and Neil Taylor (London: Thomson Learning for the Arden Shakespeare, 2006).
66. Parker, *The Aesthetics of Antichrist*, 96.
67. Ibid., x.
68. O'Connell, 'Blood Begetting Blood', 180.
69. References to the Chester cycle are from Lumiansky and Mills, eds, *The Chester Mystery Cycle*. Quotations are cited by play and line number.
70. References to the Towneley cycle are from Stevens and Cawley, eds, *The Towneley Plays*. Quotations are cited by play and line number.
71. Plutarch, *Shakespeare's Plutarch*, trans. Thomas North, ed. C. F. Tucker Brooke, 2 vols (New York: Haskell, 1966), 1.92; cited in Mack, *Everybody's Shakespeare*, 93.
72. Twycross, 'Theatricality of Medieval English Plays', 71.
73. Cox, *Dramaturgy of Power*, 186–7. Sandra Billington sees a similar pattern in English Renaissance drama, but attributes it to the festive tradition of the 'mock king': 'the rise and fall of kings' as 'lords of misrule'. Theatregoers 'experience disorders under the auspices of a mock king who finally resigns (in comedy) or is otherwise disposed of', leading to 'the restoration of order, the promise of such a restoration, or, in the history trilogies, the continuation of disorder through a further false king coming to power'. Billington, *Mock Kings*, 5.
74. Cox, *Dramaturgy of Power*, 26.

Part II

Antony and Cleopatra

CHAPTER 3

'THE HIGH ROMAN FASHION': SUICIDE AND STOICISM IN *ANTONY AND CLEOPATRA*

In *Julius Caesar*, Shakespeare focuses on the most obvious forms of human passibility: our mortality, our physical weakness, and our susceptibility to passions such as anger, grief and pity. In his later Roman play, *Antony and Cleopatra*, Shakespeare turns to a different and more subtle aspect of human vulnerability: our sensitivity to shame. In the general introduction, I suggested that, whereas *Julius Caesar* shows the end of the dying Republic, *Antony and Cleopatra* shows the beginning of the Roman Empire, and that this transition mirrors the contemporary English 'crisis of the aristocracy'. In this later tragedy, Shakespeare considers the attractions of art itself as an escape, given the deep-set sense of humiliation that this kind of crisis can provoke. English aristocrats who once prided themselves on being warriors found to their chagrin that they were now obliged to become courtiers, instead: the yes-men they had once so heartily despised. Shakespeare mocks such spineless flatterers in the form of characters such as Osric in *Hamlet* and Oswald in *King Lear*. The English nobility did not blithely relinquish their traditional conception of themselves, but instead met the diminution of their power with anxiety, indignation and occasional outbreaks of reactionary violence. Essex's ill-considered rebellion is the most obvious example; others include duelling, privateering, foolhardiness on the battlefield, and an effort to revive medieval chivalric practices such as jousting.

As traditional martial autonomy became ever more circumscribed, the same class of noblemen who sought solace in the late Elizabethan chivalric revival also found consolation in the new philosophy of Neostoicism. As it once had in ancient Rome long before, the characteristic will to power St Augustine calls *libido dominandi* turned inwards towards conquering the self rather than the world at large. In *Antony and Cleopatra*, as in *Julius Caesar*, Shakespeare is keenly interested in the mutability and volatility of this kind of thwarted ambition. Uncertain how best to proceed, Roman protagonists such as Brutus and Antony move back and forth, vexed, between the objective pursuit of political independence and the subjective cultivation of emotional invulnerability. Brutus abandons his initial Stoicism to become a man of action, but too late. Even when he does try his hand at politics, he cannot shake off his tendency to approach oratory as if it were a game within his own mind, a logical puzzle to be solved by pure 'reason' (3.1.237). Antony in *Julius Caesar* proves, by contrast, the master of embracing his own passibility, like an actor. He uses the methods of Ciceronian oratory, but against the Republic, as a demagogue, rather than in the service of the 'common good' (5.5.73).

Antony in *Antony and Cleopatra* is more like his former antagonist in *Julius Caesar*, Brutus, than he might seem *prima facie*. Much as Brutus oscillates between Ciceronian engagement in Roman politics and Senecan retreat into 'philosophy', Antony alternates between Roman 'labor' (4.14.48) and Egyptian 'idleness' (1.3.94). The two other major characters, his rival, Octavian, and his lover, Cleopatra, symbolise these two poles of his own split existence. Octavian represents the objective pursuit of political dominance, an aspect of life Antony finds bothersome and boring, but also, despite his desultory efforts, inescapable. Cleopatra represents, by contrast, a subjective retreat into his own imagination, a world of endless feasts, revelry and games where everything answers to his slightest whim, as if he were a god – or a playwright. Shakespeare seems to see in the opposition between Rome and Alexandria something like the opposition between the world as it is, at times a grim and inhospitable place, and the world as it can be in the mind's eye, the 'dream' that comes to life in poetry, as well as on the stage. In the language of the play, 'fancy' is more enchanting than 'nature.' Like a stage-play, however, or a dream, 'fancy' cannot be sustained *ad infinitum*.

Coriolanus serves here, too, as a useful point of both comparison and contrast. Like Antony, Coriolanus is exquisitely sensitive to shame. He is humiliated by anything that suggests that he depends on anyone other than himself, since it would reveal that he falls short of an idealised self-sufficiency. Much as Coriolanus is reluctant to canvass for votes, Antony is deeply upset at the thought of having to beg for mercy from his rival, Octavian. After his defeat at Actium, he laments, 'Now I must / To the young man send humble treaties; dodge / And palter in the shifts of lowness' (3.11.61–3). This indignity is itself a result, however, of a cause for deeper 'shame' (3.11.52): his 'unnoble swerving' (3.11.49) at Actium. As he confesses, he is bound as if in 'strong Egyptian fetters' (1.2.123) by his love for Cleopatra. Coriolanus, too, proves bound to his mother, Volumnia: 'O mother, mother! / What have you done?' (5.3.183–4) he asks. His question is the opposite of a divine fiat; the agency in the scene is finally hers, not his. Like Antony with Cleopatra, he proves unexpectedly, profoundly passible.

Defeated earlier in the play by 'the beast / With many heads' (4.1.1–2), Coriolanus is banished from Rome. And, humiliated, he then tries to project that banishment back on to his opponent. 'I banish you!' (3.3.123) he replies, indignant. 'There is a world elsewhere' (3.3.135). Similar language appears in *Richard II*. When Bolingbroke is banished, his father exhorts him to consider his exile from the perspective of a 'wise man': a reference, perhaps, to the Stoic *sapiens*. 'All places that the eye of heaven visits / Are to the wise man ports and happy havens' (1.3.275–6). For example, Gaunt suggests, 'Think not the king did banish thee, / But thou the king' (1.3.279–80). Bolingbroke insists that there are sharp limits, however, to the consolation provided by this kind of retreat into subjective fantasy. Introspective dissociation, driving a wedge of sheer will between the mind and the world, is not as easy or sustainable as his father makes it out to be. 'O who can hold a fire in his hand,' he protests, 'by thinking on the frosty Caucasus?' (1.3.294–5). Coriolanus possesses, if anything, even less capacity to retreat into his own counterfactual imagination than Bolingbroke. When he says, 'I banish you!' he does not mean it in the sense that Gaunt does. He is not imagining a different, fictional world. Rather, he means more literally that he banishes the Romans from his protective presence, as former defender of their safety. 'Here remain with your uncertainty!' (3.3.124) he goes on. 'Let every feeble rumor shake your hearts!' (3.3.125). When he says, 'There is a world elsewhere!' he does not mean, like Hamlet, the 'nutshell' (2.2.254) of his own mind; instead, he means more objectively that there are other places where he believes he can live and maintain more autonomy, such as with the Volscians.

Although Antony in some ways represents the same kind of 'Herculean hero' as Coriolanus, he is also markedly different, both in circumstances and in character.[1] Like Coriolanus, once he is defeated objectively, he tries to withdraw objectively: he asks Caesar 'To let him breathe between the heavens and earth, / A private man in Athens' (3.12.14–15).[2] For Antony, however, unlike Coriolanus, there is no such 'world elsewhere'. Octavian is the 'universal landlord' (3.13.72), and he dismisses Antony's request out of hand. What Antony does possess, by contrast, that Coriolanus does not is an imagination. He is able to escape subjectively, into a world of make-believe much akin to that of the theatre. 'Let's have one other gaudy night' (3.13.188), he tells Cleopatra, after his defeat at Actium. 'Call to me / All my sad captains. Fill our bowls once more. / Let's mock the midnight bell' (3.13.188–90). Even in the face of utter ruin, Antony is capable of living instead in a world 'as if', a counterfactual alternate reality much like that of an actor on stage. Cleopatra finds his bravado comforting: 'Since my lord / Is Antony again, I will be Cleopatra' (3.13.190–1).

Coriolanus has no such companion. Much as Portia and Calpurnia in *Julius Caesar* represent their husbands' faculty of pity, which they suppress to a fault, Cleopatra represents Antony's distinctive faculty of imagination or 'fancy', which he indulges to excess. This capacity Coriolanus utterly lacks, even to his own detriment. As A. D. Nuttall says, 'he has no inside'.[3] 'Would you have me / False to my nature?' (3.2.14–15) Coriolanus asks, incredulous. 'Rather say I play / The man I am' (3.2.15–16). He cannot give an oration like Antony's in *Julius Caesar*, not because, like Brutus, he is too intellectual, but because he is not intellectual enough. He cannot dissociate the external world from his own internal self-perception, his 'bosom's truth' (3.2.57). Despite his mother's desperate attempts to coach him to 'dissemble' (3.2.62), Coriolanus cannot bring himself to play the 'mountebank' (3.2.132). As Leah Whittington explains,

> It is not simply a question of being unable to tolerate a disjunction between outer expression and inner being; Coriolanus believes that going through the physical motions of pleading will transform him

into a new, corrupted self. The gestures of supplication – smiling, weeping, pleading, kneeling – threaten to imprint themselves on his character, teaching his mind 'a most inherent baseness' that threatens the integrity of his selfhood.[4]

Hence Coriolanus' restless drive in exile to return to Rome and defeat it decisively; he cannot simply forget Rome or pretend as if it does not exist, but instead feels compelled in this, as in every circumstance, to take objective action in the public sphere. He cannot console himself, as Antony does, with a bowl of wine and the company of a woman. He must validate his sense of himself as invincible on the battlefield or die trying: there is no other option.

Coriolanus thus stands at one end of a spectrum of manifestations of the will to power, the *ne plus ultra* of the objective expression of *libido dominandi*. Shakespeare is also fascinated, however, by the subjective expression of this impulse: the desire to be master of one's own experience, independent of the world at large. Antony's tendency to escape into a dream-world of revelry and drunkenness, like Brutus' Stoicism, is but one example among many of this tendency, one version of a story that Shakespeare tells again and again, in various guises: a retreat from a shared, public reality into a more isolated, private alternative, as a response to the loss of power. Seeking refuge in fantasy or 'fancy' reappears repeatedly as a response to the rise of a hostile, absolutist government. Lear escapes into outright madness; Edgar, like Hamlet, into its semblance. Richard II takes refuge in self-aggrandising storytelling: a theatrical reimagining of himself much akin to Cleopatra's final moments. Achilles sulks by his ship, watching Patroclus imitate his countrymen: a kind of play within a play. Timon of Athens tricks his fellow citizens into attending a satirical feast, a bit like a dumbshow, then abandons the city for a cave in the wilderness. The common thread in these disparate narratives is a flight from the world 'as-is' into another world 'as if', modelled on Shakespeare's experience of the theatre.[5] The mind flees the intransigent givenness of an unaccommodating world in favour of self-generated, solipsistic delusions of grandeur.

In his influential study *Personality in Greek Epic, Tragedy, and Philosophy*, Christopher Gill distinguishes between what he calls 'objective-participant' and 'subjective-individualist' concepts of selfhood, 'a contrast that functions', he insists, 'both *within* modern thinking' and '*between* Greek and (some) modern thinking about the person'. In the subjective-individualist tradition, the self is 'characteristically conceived' as 'a solitary center of consciousness, a unitary "I"'. 'The sense of being the centre of a unique, subjective (first-personal) perspective is seen as constitutive of personal identity.'[6] As Thomas Pfau observes, this 'modern, autonomous self', 'the quintessentially modern, solitary individual confined to his study', is 'familiar from the candle-lit interior of Descartes' *Meditations* all the way up to the cork-lined refuge where Proust would labor on his magnum opus'. Examples include 'Descartes' *cogito*, Locke's "consciousness," and Johann Gottlieb Fichte's "founding act" (*Tathandlung*).'[7]

Modern thinkers such as Alasdair MacIntyre, Bernard Williams and, more recently, Thomas Pfau criticise what Gill describes as the 'subjectivist-individualist' concept of selfhood as deracinated. In particular, they object to 'Kant's thesis that the moral response involves, or implies, an act of "autonomy" or self-legislation, by which the individual agent binds herself to universal principles.' 'For Kant himself,' Gill notes, 'the idea of the autonomy (self-legislation) of the person as (individual) moral agent is coupled with a stress on the universality of the moral principles thus legislated.' 'Some subsequent thinkers', however, such as Nietzsche and Sartre, 'conceive of the autonomy of the individual agent in markedly subjective (and subjectivist) terms. Only the individual herself (the possessor of a uniquely subjective viewpoint) can determine the validity of the rules that she legislates for herself.'[8]

In the 'objective-participant' tradition, by contrast, 'thought and other psychological processes' tend to be presented as an 'inner dialogue', rather than a 'unitary "I"'. 'The ethical life of the human being is, at the most fundamental level, shared rather than private and individuated.' We arrive at ethical conclusions through 'shared debate' rather than 'by adopting an individual stance of autonomy or self-legislation' or 'by embarking on a program of (individual) self-realization'.[9] As Pfau insists, 'in both its genesis and its eventual awareness, the self is essentially bound up with its relation to other persons.' 'There is not an autonomous Cartesian self'; 'rather, there is the reciprocity and acknowledgment of one person by another in a dynamic of ipsëity, alterity, and community that is as profound as it is fragile.'[10]

As an example of this point of view, Pfau enlists a surprising ally: Coleridge. 'His late explorations in Trinitarian theology', Pfau explains, 'complete a reflection about the "self-insufficingness" of the person that had arisen from a critique of modern, autonomous, and self-conscious agency begun in *The Friend* and continued in the *Biographia* and the *Lay Sermons*.'[11] 'No human individual is self-sufficing (αὐτάρκης),' Coleridge observes.[12] Towards the end of his life, reflecting on the Christian doctrine of the Trinity, Coleridge turns against 'the modern Cartesian conflation of "consciousness" with "self-identity"'.[13] 'Consciousness itself has the appearance of another,' he maintains.[14] 'There could be no opposite, and of course no distinct or conscious sense of the term "*I*" as far as the consciousness is concerned, without a "*Thou*".'[15]

In a later study, *The Structured Self in Hellenistic and Roman Thought*, Gill argues that 'Hellenistic–Roman thought on personality, like Classical Greek thinking, is best interpreted as "objective-participant" in approach.' This view, he acknowledges, 'runs counter to the claim sometimes made that the Hellenistic–Roman period sees a shift toward a more subjective and individualistic approach to self'.[16] A. A. Long, for example, sees in Stoicism 'a new focus on consciousness, on the individuality of the perceiving subject, as the fundamental feature of the mental'.[17] In her study of 'vision, sexuality, and self-knowledge in the ancient world', *The Mirror of the Self*, Shadi Bartsch takes her conceptual categories from Gill, but finds that 'developments of Roman Stoicism, and in particular the thought of Seneca, innovate in ways that cannot ultimately be contained within the model he sets out for ancient Greek philosophy.'[18] Like Paul Cantor, Bartsch attributes this emerging new form of subjectivity to the change from Republic to Empire. By way of explanation, she draws an analogy to Jeremy Bentham's Panopticon, the ingenious but disturbing form of confinement Foucault draws upon as a metaphor in *Discipline and Punish*. In this hypothetical circular prison, eerily similar to what we now might recognise as an 'open-plan office', every inmate is housed in a lighted glass cell visible to a single warden in a central tower. 'It is the fact of being constantly seen, of always being able to be seen,' Foucault explains, 'that maintains the disciplined individual in his subjection.'[19]

Bartsch argues that the Panopticon does not make sense as a metaphor for the Rome of the Republic. There is 'no reciprocity of the gaze', whereas 'in republican Rome entire social groups are engaged in reciprocal acts of watching and evaluating'. Bartsch cites Andrew Bell: 'In a true republic no citizen monopolizes the gaze.'[20] As a symbol for the court of the Julio-Claudian emperors, however, the Panopticon is apt. 'One of the most salient aspects of the transition to empire' is the 'breakdown' of 'the reciprocity of the gaze'.[21] As Foucault puts it, 'in the peripheric ring, one is totally seen, without ever seeing; in the central tower, one sees everything without being seen.'[22] 'In Seneca's description of the situation in *De tranquillitate*,' Bartsch observes, 'he seems to catapult us . . . into a kind of Foucauldian scopic regime.' 'Constant observation of oneself is torturous,' Seneca complains. 'It's not a pleasant life, nor one free from anxiety, to live constantly wearing a mask.'[23] As a form of defence, Carlin Barton suggests, 'The Romans donned, as it were, the armor of hypocrisy.' 'The face became a façade.'[24]

For Bartsch, the transition from Republic to Empire brings a 'turn of emphasis from the public eye to the self-generated eye', 'from the mirror of the community to a form of mirroring that relied upon a doubling of the self'. For figures such as Homer's Hector or Achilles, the imagined observer Bernard Williams calls 'the internalized other' is 'an *unconscious* development', 'a part of the self that has so thoroughly adopted the values of the community that it itself acts as an audience to the actions of the individual'. 'Socrates' *daimonion* is not a product of his decision to provide himself with an ethical interlocutor; Cicero's conscience can plague him against his will.' As in the case of the kind of moral self-legislation Gill associates with Kant, however, in Seneca's thought 'the internalized other is a conscious product of the will of the Stoic individual'. 'One *must set up* a Cato or an Epicurus in one's mind and pretend he is watching.' 'Can we still speak in terms of a community-sanctioned ethics,' Bartsch asks, 'when the community has shrunk to a number of idealized (dead) watchers, and when even this tiny community is absent barring an act of will?'[25]

As she makes plans to kill herself, Cleopatra appropriates the language of the 'noble Roman'. Her suicide, she claims, will be in 'the high Roman fashion', that is, in the style of austere statesmen such as Cato and Brutus. The incongruity seems jarring, given her very un-Stoic tendency throughout towards extravagant accesses of emotion. Cleopatra's suicide is consistent with Stoicism, however, because, like Stoicism, it represents a wilful dissociation from reality. 'Can Stoicism, the anti-passion philosophy, be turning into, of all things, Romanticism?' A. D. Nuttall asks. 'That is exactly what is happening.' Cleopatra aims to flee from 'nature' into 'fancy' and sees suicide as a means to that end. 'As Stoicism is subjectivized,' Nuttall explains, 'as the impersonal, rational cosmos fades, a curious internal excitement develops.'[26] Like Shakespeare's Romans, Cleopatra as a pagan queen aims in the end to escape passibility itself. Suicide is the culmination of a progressive involution of the will to power, the final step towards a longed-for subjective *autarkeia*. As Eric Langley suggests, like many other early modern authors, Shakespeare in his Roman plays uses 'Stoic structures of politicized self-ownership and aggressive individualism' to represent and reflect upon the early modern pursuit of neo-Roman liberty. Suicide as 'Stoic assertion of autonomous ownership' prefigures the distinctive character of modern selfhood.[27]

In *The Roots of Romanticism*, Isaiah Berlin acknowledges the difficulty inherent in separating the substance of the movement from its accidents. Nevertheless, he maintains, 'There *was* a Romantic movement; it did have something which was central to it; it did create a great revolution in consciousness; and it is important to discover what this is.' 'The general proposition of the eighteenth century,' Berlin explains, 'indeed of all previous centuries,' is 'that there is a nature of things, there is a *rerum natura*.' For the Romantics, by contrast, 'there is no structure of things. There is no pattern to which you must adapt yourself.' 'You create values, you create goals, you create ends, and in the end you create your own vision of the universe, exactly as artists create works of art.' 'The universe is as you choose to make it, to some degree at any rate.'[28]

In Romantic literature, the result is 'admiration of wild genius, outlaws, heroes, aestheticism, self-destruction'. 'Rules must be blown up as such.'[29] Nietzsche in this respect is in effect a late Romantic. As Paul Cantor observes, 'what really attracted Nietzsche to Shakespeare' was 'larger-than-life characters, transgressive and even law-breaking, living (in Nietzsche's later formulation) "beyond good and evil"'.[30] Probably the best example is Schiller's *Robbers*, a play Nietzsche greatly admired. Centre stage now belongs to the glamorous outlaw, the Byronic antihero. Among philosophers, Berlin finds in Fichte the most thoroughgoing Romantic. At the core of Fichte's thought is an 'important proposition': 'things are as they are, not because they are so independent of me, but because I make them so; things depend upon the way I treat them, what I need them for.' The only teleology that matters, that exists, is the one that we our-selves invent and impose upon the malleable, meaningless, mutable world. 'I am not determined by ends,' Fichte proclaims; 'ends are determined by me.'[31] Rousseau puts it more simply: 'What I feel to be right is right.'[32]

Shakespeare's canonisation was assured in the eighteenth cen-tury, when he became a darling of German precursors of Romanti-cism such as Lessing and Herder, as well as Schiller and the *Sturm und Drang* movement. Goethe calls him *unser Shakespeare* ('our Shakespeare'). Romantic rhapsodising about Shakespeare, how-ever, tends to misinterpret the movement of his mind. Like Blake, placing Milton on the side of Satan, Romantic critics too readily identify Shakespeare himself with characters such as Richard II and Falstaff, as well as Cleopatra, whom he goes out of his way to undermine. To read the second tetralogy of English history plays from the point of view of Falstaff is like reading *Lolita* from the perspective of Humbert Humbert.

At the outset of his neo-Romantic defence of Cleopatra, Richard Strier cites Peter Holbrook: 'Shakespeare anticipates the Romantic revolution in morals.'[33] I agree, but I think that Shakespeare sees this development as a dangerous mistake, rather than an improvement. As I argue elsewhere, the moral error Shakespeare seems to find the most beguiling is a kind of self-absorption: the 'transvaluation of all values' that would eventually develop into what we now know as Romanticism.[34] Shakespeare as an artist anticipates Romanticism because 'the whole movement', as Berlin observes, is 'an attempt to impose an aesthetic model upon reality, to say that everything should obey the rules of art.'[35] It makes sense that the great temptation for a playwright would be the fantasy that the world is like a play; that other people are like characters; that the control that he enjoys in the privacy of his imagination, the 'infinite space' of artistic possibility, might also be available somehow outside what Hamlet calls the 'nutshell' of the mind. Shakespeare's Cleopatra is the purest expression of this fantasy. But she is prefigured by, of all people, Shakespeare's Brutus, and behind him, Seneca. As A. D. Nuttall explains, 'We have seen how the exertion of reason by the Roman Stoics can increasingly become a way of denying rather than truly representing reality.'[36]

Stoic Suicide as 'Hobgoblin': Cleopatra and the Question of Consistency

I begin this section by examining Brutus' apparent inconsistency in committing suicide, both in Shakespeare's *Julius Caesar* and in Plutarch's 'Life of Marcus Brutus'. Shakespeare's Brutus condemns Cato for killing himself; suicide, he maintains, is less consistent with his 'rule of philosophy' than 'patience' to endure whatever may befall him in life. Brutus echoes here a criticism of Stoic suicide that can be found in Montaigne's essay, 'A Custom of the Island of Cea', as well as St Augustine's *City of God*. Nevertheless, Brutus does kill himself in the end, dismayed at the thought of being led in triumph. A mistranslation in North's Plutarch exaggerates Brutus' inconsistency in this respect. In the original Greek, Brutus' change of heart about suicide emerges gradually with age, whereas in North's version it comes across as a startling, spur-of-the-moment decision. Shakespeare uses this textual crux to dramatic effect. Brutus' psychological lability becomes a symbol of the impossibility of Stoic 'patience'.

Shakespeare continues to investigate the tension between Stoic 'constancy', understood as a kind of performance, and suppressed human passibility in his later play, *Antony and Cleopatra*. In the character of Cleopatra, Shakespeare exaggerates the same kind of inconsistency that he finds in Brutus ad absurdum. Cleopatra frames her suicide in language that evokes Stoicism, but herself seems as a character the very opposite of a Stoic *sapiens*. Even so, her suicide is not inconsistent. Egyptian pastimes such as drinking, fishing and billiards represent, like Brutus' Stoicism, Cleopatra's attempts to escape awareness of a world outside her own control, retreating instead to a more private, subjective space in which she can be absolute *domina* ('mistress'). Understood psychologically, rather than in terms of abstract ethical principles, Cleopatra's suicide is not so much a non sequitur as the logical culmination of a lifelong involution of her *libido dominandi*. Like other pagan characters, Cleopatra turns inwards in order to escape the shame of outward weakness.

In *Julius Caesar*, Shakespeare adumbrates the more extended treatment of the horror of being led in triumph that he presents in *Antony and Cleopatra*. As Brutus and Cassius prepare for the Battle of Philippi, Cassius is troubled by inauspicious omens. 'Let's reason with the worst that may befall' (5.1.96), he suggests to Brutus. 'If we do lose this battle,' he asks, 'What are you then determined to do?' (5.1.97–8). Brutus' thoughts turn immediately to suicide, prompted by the memory of another, earlier opponent of Caesar, Cato of Utica.

> Even by that rule of philosophy
> By which I did blame Cato for the death
> Which he did give himself – I know not how,
> But I do find it cowardly and vile,
> For fear of what might fall, so to prevent
> The time of life – arming myself with patience
> To stay the providence of some high powers
> That govern us below.

(5.1.100–7)

In plays such as *Hamlet* which are set in a Christian context, the argument against suicide is one sense relatively simple. 'O God! God!' Hamlet cries. 'O . . . that the Everlasting had not fix'd / His canon 'gainst self-slaughter' (1.2.129–32). Hamlet's notorious reluctance to act extends, of course, beyond simple fear of damnation. Nevertheless, he does see suicide in a very different light than an 'antique Roman' (5.2.346). For a character such as Brutus, the question of the moral rectitude of suicide must be answered, not in terms of service or obedience to the Godhead, but instead in terms of its impact on his reputation. How will he appear in the history books? If he were to commit suicide, would that act be seen by posterity as brave or 'cowardly'? Noble or 'vile'? How he will be remembered is, for Shakespeare's Brutus, the equivalent of what heaven or hell is to a Christian. In this respect, as Gordon Braden points out, Shakespeare brings Brutus closer, in fact, to his historical original than the Brutus that he encountered in his most important source for the play, Sir Thomas North's English translation of Jacques Amyot's French translation of Plutarch's *Lives*.[37]

Once it becomes clear that he has been defeated, Brutus does eventually commit suicide, despite the objections that he presents to Cassius here, and it is some question why he reverses his position.

In North's version of his life, Brutus justifies the decision by saying that his good deed in assassinating Caesar, a kind of martyrdom for the sake of his country, is enough to guarantee him a pleasant afterlife, even if he does subsequently commit suicide. 'I gave up my life for my contry in the Ides of Marche, for the whiche I shall live in another more glorious worlde.'[38] Shakespeare's Brutus, by contrast, makes no such reference to life after death. As Gordon Braden points out, this line in North's Plutarch is a mistranslation, however, introduced not initially by North himself, but rather by Jacques Amyot, whose French translation from the Greek served as his source.[39] In the second edition of his *Lives*, but not the first, Amyot changes the tense of the original verb, 'I have lived' (*ezēsa*; aorist), from the perfect to the future. North amends the sentence still further, introducing the idea of 'another more glorious worlde'. In the original, what Brutus says rather is that since the Ides of March, he has lived 'another life [*bion allon*], free and of good repute [*eleutheron kai endoxon*]'.[40] In the context of his larger argument about suicide, what Plutarch's Brutus seems to be saying, in other words, is that he is more comfortable with the prospect of committing suicide than he might be otherwise, because he has already won so much glory by securing his own freedom. Shakespeare is therefore more correct, perhaps, than he even knew in making Brutus' calculations those of honour in this world, rather than glory in the next. Brutus' chief concern is not divine approval, but the praise of other men (*doxē*; cf. *endoxon*): he wants his peers to admire him, both now and *ad perpetuum*, much as he admires his own most illustrious ancestor, Lucius Junius Brutus, celebrated foe of the tyrannical Tarquins.

What is perhaps most intriguing about Marcus Junius Brutus, however, in comparison to his namesake, is that he is not content to be remembered simply as a courageous patrician. It is not enough for him to be the leader of the *optimates*, fighting like Cassius or Casca for the Good Old Cause (so to speak) of the Roman Republic. He wants to be known as a philosopher, as well. As his late-night reading habits suggest, along with Cassius' teasing him about his 'philosophy', Brutus prides himself, like Cato before him, on being educated in what was at the time a relatively new Greek import, and on his adherence to its theoretical precepts. When he considers suicide, Brutus is concerned about its implications for his legacy in this respect, as well: his understanding of himself as strictly rational. If he killed himself, like Cato, would that act be perceived as an illogical access of emotion, or instead as consistent with the principles of his 'philosophy'?

The observation that the Stoics' glorification of suicide seems to be at odds with their more general ethical theory is not Brutus' alone. 'This does not pass without contradiction,' Montaigne writes. In his essay on the ethics of suicide, 'A Custom of the Island of Cea', Montaigne criticises Cato in much the same terms as Brutus does here. 'There is much more fortitude in wearing out the chain that binds us than in breaking it, and more proof of strength in Regulus than in Cato. It is lack of judgment and of patience that hastens our pace.'[41] In his *City of God*, St Augustine makes the same comparison, and to the same end.[42] Even by the standards of the pagans, St Augustine argues, suicide is, as Brutus says, 'cowardly'.

> If you look at the matter more closely, you will scarcely call it greatness of soul, which prompts a man to kill himself rather than bear up against some hardships of fortune. ... Is it not rather proof of a feeble mind, to be unable to bear either the pains of bodily servitude, or the foolish opinion of the vulgar? And is not that to be pronounced the greater mind, which rather faces than flees the ills of life, and which ... holds in small esteem the judgment of men, and specially of the vulgar, which is frequently involved in a mist of error?[43]

Montaigne makes the same point a bit more vividly. 'It is an act of cowardice, not of virtue, to go and hide in a hole, under a massive tomb, in order to avoid the blows of fortune.'[44] Moreover, he adds, 'there being so many sudden changes in human affairs, it is hard to judge just at what point we are at the end of our hope.' As an example of an admirable tenacity, he cites the story of Josephus, who, he says, 'did well to hang on stubbornly to his hopes', and in contrast censures Brutus, as well as Cassius. 'Cassius and Brutus, on the contrary, demolished the last remnants of Roman liberty, of which they were the protectors, by the rash haste with which they have killed themselves before the proper time and occasion.'[45]

In North's version of Plutarch, what changes Brutus' mind about suicide includes the conviction that he will enjoy a 'glorious' afterlife. In Plutarch's original, that motive turns out to be, instead, a sense of self-satisfaction. Come what may, Brutus concludes, he is still the man who secured Roman liberty; he is the tyrannicide who prevented the return of a would-be Tarquin, and no subsequent stain can entirely blot out that achievement. Another aspect of his openness to suicide, however, in Plutarch's original as well as Amyot's French, is a new spirit of moral pragmatism: a willingness to compromise his ideals, which Brutus associates with growing older. In North's translation, this motive drops out of the picture, due to an error in punctuation. North writes:

> Brutus aunswered him, being yet but a young man, and not overgreatly experienced in the world: I trust, (I know not how) a certaine rule of Philosophie, by the which I did greatly blame and reprove Cato for killing of him selfe ... but being nowe in the middest of the daunger, I am of a contrary mind. For if it be not the will of God, that this battell fall out fortunate for us: I will look no more for hope, neither seeke to make any new supply againe, but will rid me of this miserable world, and content me with my fortune.[46]

Corrected in light of the original, the punctuation here (as it does in Amyot's translation) should run instead: 'Brutus aunswered him: being yet but a young man, and not overgreatly experienced in the world', and so on. 'I trust' should also be emended to something more like 'I let loose, put forward' (*aphēka*), with the sense of 'carelessly expounded': again, the Greek aorist seems to have presented difficulties. Here, it should be translated in the past tense, rather than the present. In modern English, the basic sense of this part of the sentence is: 'When I was young [*neos*, with the suggestion of 'new', 'fresh'], I let slip an opinion [*logon*] about philosophy', and so on. In the Greek, 'daunger' also is more ambiguous: *allois ... tychais* ('different fortunes/ circumstances').

North's version of this speech presented a potential stumbling-block for Shakespeare, because it makes it seem as if Brutus changes his mind about suicide abruptly out of cowardice (fear of 'daunger'), rather than as a result of humbling experience and increasing years. M. W. MacCallum presents Shakespeare here, rather than eliding the incongruity, as turning the textual distortion to his advantage as a dramatist, 'making Brutus's latter sentiment the sudden response of his heart, in defiance of his philosophy, to Cassius' anticipation of what they must expect if defeated'.[47] To do so, Shakespeare fleshes out North's interpolation, 'daunger', giving it more specific form and pressure.

> CASSIUS   Then, if we lose this battle,
>   You are contented to be led in triumph
>   Thorough the streets of Rome?
> BRUTUS
>   No, Cassius, no: think not, thou noble Roman,
>   That ever Brutus will go bound to Rome.
>   He bears too great a mind.
>
> (5.1.107–12)

What in Shakespeare's source had come across as a disruption of psychological mimesis becomes instead a masterstroke. Shakespeare uses this interchange to reveal the dissonance of Brutus' double ambition: his desire to be honoured both as a philosopher and as a public man. The two aims prove incompatible; forced to choose between them, Brutus' instincts as a traditional statesman turn out to run deeper. A reputation for philosophical rigour is a welcome bonus; at the end of the day, however, Brutus is not willing, like Alexander the Great, to trade places with Diogenes. Still less is he willing to be Christ, spat upon and jeered at as a failed Messiah. There is a limit to Brutus' willingness to sacrifice his considerable social and political status, simply for the sake of a 'rule of philosophy'.[48]

Like Hamlet, Brutus is deeply attracted to the idea of an escape from politics into the privacy of his own 'mind': his study, his books, his own subjective experience. There, he believes, he can be more completely in control. What he discovers, however, is that he cannot entirely give up his desire for public approbation. The external world impinges upon his consciousness; he cannot simply scoff at the 'foolish opinion of the vulgar', like St Augustine. To be exposed to the scorn of the masses would be more than he believes that he can endure; to be 'led in triumph' would be to lose that 'greatness of mind', Aristotle's *megalopsychia*, which, like Cleopatra, Brutus sees as integral to his own self-definition. That pride in his own idealised self-image is more precious to him than life itself.

Above all, Brutus cannot bear even to imagine the prospect of being displayed to the public as a captive, or to suppose that Cassius is doing so: 'think not, thou noble Roman', he begins. He is not willing to operate in a world in which such a possibility is conceivable.

The epithet, 'noble Roman', indicates what is at stake: he is reminding Cassius, thereby, of their shared identity. He, like Cassius, is
'noble', not a commoner. He is a 'Roman', not a suppliant. He is not
willing to put these attributes in doubt. They are part of a dichotomy
which for him must remain absolute. He must be, as Antony says,
'the noblest Roman of them all', whether or not the world accepts
that moral judgement.

Much literary-critical energy has been spent trying to identify
what Cassius calls simply Brutus' 'philosophy' with this or that
specific ancient school of thought.[49] Brutus' own book *On Virtue*
is no longer extant; judging from Cicero, however, Brutus seems to
have been relatively sympathetic to Stoicism; more so than Cicero
himself. Historically speaking, Brutus, like Cicero, was a fol-
lower of Antiochus of Ascalon, a Greek-speaking expatriate who
claimed to be reviving what he called the Old Academy, and whose
thought is a complicated synthesis of Platonism, Aristotelianism
and Stoicism. What exactly it means to say that Brutus or Cicero
was a student of Antiochus is unclear, however. Students do not
always agree with every one of their teacher's conclusions. More
importantly, painstaking inquiries into the philosophical opinions
of the historical Brutus are in this case beside the point. Even if his
long-lost works were rediscovered, in all their subtlety, they would
not necessarily provide a master key to the 'philosophy' of Shakespeare's Brutus. Looking back on this debate, Geoffrey Miles sees
'a blind alley'.

> It seems undeniable that to represent the 'Romanity' of Brutus,
> and to a lesser extent of other characters, Shakespeare draws
> upon the Stoic traditions descending from Seneca and Cicero, and
> attributes to them attitudes and actions which his audience would
> clearly have identified as 'stoical'.[50]

Shakespeare's Cleopatra, by contrast, easily seems the furthest
thing from a Roman Stoic. In her rapid oscillation between love
and anger, she evokes Seneca's tragic heroines, not his idealised
Stoic *sapiens*.[51] In her decision to kill herself, nonetheless, Cleopatra imagines herself, as well as her chambermaids, as entering Stoic
hagiography. 'What's brave, what's noble / Let's do't after the high
Roman fashion / And make death proud to take us' (4.5.90–2).
Considered as Stoic rhetoric, the word 'fashion' here is out of place,
with its suggestion of the external and the momentary. In its very

incongruity, the slip in diction does reveal, however, the nature of her relationship with Stoicism: ad hoc, superficial. Cleopatra's new Stoicism is in one sense deadly serious; her description of it as a 'fashion', however, suggests that it is merely another stratagem, like billiards or fishing, to escape from the press of reality. 'Now from head to foot / I am marble-constant,' she proclaims. 'Now the fleeting moon / No planet is of mine' (5.2.238–40). Repeated at the head of both of these sentences is the key word 'now': 'now', at this moment, but not necessarily before or after. Cleopatra's suicide, unlike Cato's, is not the culmination of a lifelong attempt to abide by Stoic principles. Instead, Cleopatra's consistency inheres in her very inconsistency itself. She is so mutable that she can even become, for a time, the apparent opposite of that mutability.

Stoic philosophers tend to emphasise logical consistency, even to a fault. Plutarch in particular mocks them in his *Moralia* for insisting that there can be no degrees in virtue, 'just as in the sea the man a cubit from the surface is drowning no less than the one who has sunk 500 fathoms'.[52] Among Stoics, Seneca is relatively pragmatic; even Seneca, however, applies this rule to Cato, as part of his emphasis on the continuity between the Stoic sage's suicide and his other actions. 'Cato's honourable death was no less a good than his honourable life, since virtue admits of no stretching.' Like a 'carpenter's rule', virtue 'admits of no bending'; like 'truth', it does not 'grow', but instead 'has its due proportions and is complete'.[53] By this inhuman standard, Cleopatra falls short; even her 'marble-constant' suicide, howsoever 'noble' or 'brave', does not represent a lifetime of sustained Stoic virtue. Her behaviour, however, is not simply capricious. As Polonius says of Hamlet: 'Though this be madness, yet there is method in't' (2.2.205–6).

The key here is to see Stoicism as a means, rather than an end. Stoic ethical ideals are not the framing narrative, the standard by which Cleopatra is to be measured. Instead, her adoption of Stoic practice should itself be examined in light of a different criterion of consistency, that of psychological mimesis. How does a Stoic suicide illustrate Cleopatra's character? What common thread ties it to her other behaviour? Stoicism itself, moreover, is not necessarily what it proclaims itself to be. Citing Hannah Arendt, Gordon Braden argues that 'there is considerable justification for taking Stoicism as less a philosophy of its announced themes of reason and virtue than a philosophy of the will – even, as Arendt has it, of "the omnipotence of the will".'⁵⁴ In an essay on Epictetus, Arendt explains that, although he sees man as 'entirely powerless in the real world', he also sees him as able 'to reproduce the outside – complete but deprived of reality – inside his mind, where he is undisputed lord and master'. In practice, however, that mastery is in doubt. 'The constant question is whether your will is strong enough not merely to distract your attention from external, threatening things but to fasten your imagination on different "impressions" in the actual presence of pain and misfortune.'⁵⁵ Hamlet for his part registers this difficulty. Speaking to Rosencrantz and Guildenstern, he proclaims, 'I could be bounded in a nutshell and count myself a king of infinite space – were it not that I have bad dreams' (2.2.254–6). A. D. Nuttall observes that Hamlet here, 'separating dream from reality', 'transposes his "dream" to another place in the system': 'the bad dream is the site not of an illusion but of shocking veracity'.⁵⁶ 'Dreams' in this case mean the world at large, impinging on Hamlet's attempt, like a Stoic, to retain control over his own experience. As it turns out, the mind is not entirely, as Milton's Satan says, 'its own place'.⁵⁷ Instead, it is passible, permeable, 'vulnerable' to the painful impressions Hamlet calls 'bad dreams'.

Looking back to Shakespeare's sources, the interest apparent in *Antony and Cleopatra* in the idea of the mind as a refuge from the world owes perhaps most to the influence of Samuel Daniel's *Cleopatra*.⁵⁸ There, in his opening speech, Caesar explains what is chiefly at stake in this, Daniel's version of the story: Cleopatra's assent to be Caesar's subject. 'Behold, my forces vanquisht have this Land' (269), Octavian says. 'Onely this Queene, that hath lost all this all, / To whom is nothing left except a minde: / Cannot into a thought of yeelding fall' (273–5). Caesar wants to rule 'hearts and minds', not just bodies. As he recognises, however, this winning of the will of the other is beyond his power to force outright. 'I see mens bodies only ours, no more, / The rest, anothers right, that rules the minde' (267–8).

> Kingdoms I see we winne, we conquere Climates,
> Yet we cannot vanquish hearts, nor force obedience.
> Affections kept in close-concealed limits,
> Stand farre without the reach of sword or violence.
> Who forc'd do pay us dutie, pay not love:
> Free is the heart, the temple of the minde[.]
>
> (257–62)

Shakespeare's play upon this premise is to focus on perception, especially self-perception, rather than 'affections' such as 'love'. His Antony and Cleopatra want to see themselves as gods, that is, as incarnations of their own ideal selves, and that perception is under threat from without. A retreat into the mind, enabled by withdrawal into some relatively isolated place, such as Alexandria (in comparison to Rome), or the queen's monument (in comparison to Alexandria, besieged) as well as the selection of a sympathetic audience, helps enable the self to preserve its power of self-flattering, self-aggrandising self-definition.

Seen in this light, Cleopatra's suicide is not at all inconsistent with her character, but instead the continuation of a pattern in place from the very beginning of the play. 'Give me to drink mandragora' (1.5.4), she asks Charmian, 'That I might sleep out this great gap of time / My Antony is away' (1.5.5–6). Any time her power proves less than absolute, Cleopatra longs to dissociate from reality itself, through means as mundane as sleep, wine or fantasising about sex, or as exotic as the supposed soporific power of mandrake root. Suicide is simply the most radical version of this retreat into a world of 'dreams', a creation of the beholder's own imagination or 'fancy'. 'I dreamt there was an emperor Antony. / O such another sleep, that I might see / But such another man!' (5.2.75–7).

Shakespeare draws the connection between suicide and drugged or inebriated dissociation from the world, Cleopatra's and Antony's pursuit both alike of what Pompey calls 'Lethe'd dullness' (2.1.27), by foreshadowing Cleopatra's unusual method of suicide, deliberate exposure to the bite of an asp, in two earlier references to 'poison'. When Caesar rebukes Antony for having denied him 'arms and aid' (2.2.94), Antony excuses himself for having been out of sorts. 'Neglected, rather,' he protests, 'and then when poison'd hours had bound me up / From mine own knowledge' (2.2.95–7). When Cleopatra in Antony's absence amuses herself with fantasies of him, in like manner, musing about her, she imagines him 'murmuring, "Where's my serpent of old Nile?"' (1.5.26). Cleopatra does indeed prove Antony's 'serpent', as fatal to him in the end as the asp is to her. She pauses here, however, and reproaches herself for having let herself become lost in a possibly counterfactual reverie. 'Now I feed myself / With most delicious poison' (1.5.27–8). Imagination becomes in her figurative language an unhealthy narcotic, one that she administers to Antony, and he to her, like a serpent biting its victim. Watching Iras succumb to the asp's poison, Cleopatra compares the 'stroke of death' wistfully to 'a lover's pinch' (5.2.294).

'Fancy' vs. 'Nature': Self-deception as Pleasure and Peril

In the previous section, I argued that Cleopatra's suicide is not inconsistent with her character, but instead the culmination of her characteristic escapism. Under pressure, she flees from unpleasant objective fact into soothing fantasies, and she often encourages Antony to do the same. In this sense, Cleopatra is a symbol of Antony's own imagination, as well as 'fantasy' or 'fancy' more generally considered, the faculty that allows the involution to the subjective characteristic of Brutus, as well as Antony, and that Coriolanus, by contrast, seems to lack altogether. Like Brutus retreating to his study, or Hamlet to the 'nutshell' of his own mind, Antony and Cleopatra repeatedly withdraw from the world 'as-is' into another, more subjective world 'as if'. Two celebrated speeches reveal this preference for 'fancy' over 'nature' in particular detail: Enobarbus' description of Cleopatra's arrival by barge at Antony's camp upon the banks of the river Cydnus, and Cleopatra's description of her 'dream' of Antony to her Roman guard, Dolabella.

In the fantasy of themselves that Antony and Cleopatra construct, they represent themselves as divine, ideal figures: Mars and Venus, Isis and Osiris. Over the course of the play, however, objective reality insistently intrudes upon this subjective transformation. The free play of the imagination turns out to be limited, not only by rivalry with Octavian, but also by more impersonal forces such as time and fortune. Anonymous messengers and soothsayers represent a world of fact which the two lovers tend to dismiss or ignore, with tragic consequences. At once actors and audience, they enable each other, like playgoers, to escape their own awareness of mundane obligations, constraints and humiliations. They imbue each other with glamour and create an alternate, mythic vision of themselves. Shakespeare suggests, however, that this *folie à deux* comes at a cost. An escape into subjective fantasy that begins as a voluntary respite from the burdens and indignities of objective passibility becomes in the end an involuntary exile from objective power.

Cleopatra herself is a symbol of the imagination: Aristotle's *phantasia*.[59] Like this faculty of the mind, Cleopatra is at once alluring and suspect; the natural ally of Antony's irrational and unchecked passion. She is, in one sense, Antony's own imagination, personified and rendered external, even though she is also, at the same time, a fully rounded character, much as Portia represents Brutus' own faculty of pity, even though she, too, has her own internal conflicts. For instance, Cleopatra is repeatedly described in terms of another common symbol of fantasy or 'fancy': magic. Pompey describes her as assailing Antony with 'witchcraft' (2.1.22) and 'charms' (2.1.20). Scarus, too, speaks of Antony as 'the noble ruin of her magic' (3.10.19). Antony himself describes her variously as 'enchanting' (1.2.135), a 'great fairy' (4.8.12), 'my charm' (4.12.16), a 'grave charm' (4.12.25), a 'gypsy' (4.12.30; cf. 1.1.10), a 'spell' (4.12.28) and a 'witch' (4.12.47). Caught up in such a reverie, like a wandering knight in a romance, Antony no longer feels the need to impose his will upon the entire Roman world; instead, he can enjoy a feeling of absolute power, if not its reality, ready at hand. As Cleopatra's favourite, he can feast, drink and enjoy all the pleasures of Egypt's wealth, without the headache of Roman politics. Like 'mandragora', Cleopatra enables Antony to escape into a 'dream' of himself.

Like Cleopatra's suicide, Antony's ignominious flight from the Battle of Actium is not unprecedented, but instead the culmination of a characteristic escapism. His retreat, like his suicide, is a synecdoche. The play itself opens, for example, with Philo complaining that his commander's 'goodly eyes', which once 'glowed' over 'the files and musters of the war', 'now bend, now turn / The office and devotion of their view / Upon a tawny front' (1.1.2–6). In Egypt, in his 'lascivious wassails' (1.4.57), Antony finds an easier way to feel like a god than the hardships of the kinds of military campaigns so vividly described, by contrast, by his rival, Octavian: 'famine' (1.4.60) and lack of water, for example, as Antony and his men fled across the Alps from Modena.

In dying, Antony reflects upon the 'miserable change' (4.15.53) in his fortunes. 'Please your thoughts', he tells Cleopatra, 'In feeding them with those my former fortunes, / Wherein I lived the greatest prince o'th'world, / The noblest' (4.15.54–7). Antony is consoling himself in this moment, as well as his mistress; he returns here, if only in memory, to his former days of glory, much as she does later when she proclaims herself 'again for Cydnus' (5.2.227). Imagination of another world 'as if', in this case, 'as if' the past were the present, provides, like suicide, an alternative to an unpalatable, present reality. So also Othello, just before he kills himself, returns in memory to his former days of glory as a soldier for Venice against the Turk: 'in Aleppo once [etc.]' (5.2.350). As T. S. Eliot says, he is 'cheering himself up'; 'endeavoring to escape reality'. Eliot's tone is cruelly unsympathetic, but his assessment nonetheless contains an element of truth. We see in Othello's last moments, as well as those of Antony and Cleopatra, some degree of what he calls '*bovarysme*': 'the human will to see things as they are not'.[60]

Shakespeare provides two touchstones of the fantastical image of themselves that Antony and Cleopatra aim to preserve, even in death. The first is Cleopatra's first meeting with Antony 'upon the river of Cydnus' (2.2.197), as recounted by Enobarbus. The second is the dream of Antony that Cleopatra describes to the Roman soldier Dolabella.[61] The speeches are familiar; in both, the lover in question appears larger than life, like a deity. Cleopatra is compared to Venus; Antony, to Atlas, or perhaps, the Colossus of Rhodes; grander, even. 'His legs bestrid the ocean; his reared arm / Crested the world' (5.2.81–2), and so on. The lines recall Cassius' description of Julius Caesar: 'he doth bestride the narrow world / Like a colossus' (1.2.135–6). As in that speech, the emphasis is on Antony's seemingly unlimited power, akin to that of the god Jupiter. He is able 'to quail and shake the orb' like 'rattling thunder' (5.2.84–5); to give away 'realms and islands' (5.2.90). 'For his bounty, / There was no winter in't' (5.2.85–6). Cleopatra for her part, in Enobarbus' account, makes 'defect perfection' (2.2.241), so that even 'holy priests / Bless her when she is riggish' (2.2.249–50). 'Age cannot wither her, nor custom stale / Her infinite variety' (2.2.245–6).

These two well-known speeches, Enobarbus' on Cleopatra and Cleopatra's on Antony, are united, moreover, by two other conceits. One is that their subjects are held to exceed even the scope of the most outrageous hyperbole. From Enobarbus' perspective, Cleopatra cannot be adequately depicted, no matter how high the comparison. 'As for her person,' Enobarbus declares, 'It beggared all description' (2.2.207–8). Cleopatra describes her vision of Antony as 'past the size of dreaming' (5.2.96). This repeated turn to apophasis, normally associated with descriptions of the Godhead, flags a reaction against the inherent 'givenness' of language, as well as the 'givenness' more generally of the larger world. The speakers reject their own proffered metaphors in the same way that mystics insist their meagre, thread-bare analogies cannot adequately even begin to approach the actual glory of the divine. To connect the subject of their description to the world by figurative language, as tenor to vehicle, is to introduce a sense of limitation that they see as fundamentally alien to its nature.

The other shared conceit is that of a conflict between 'fancy' and 'nature'. Anne Barton calls it 'an Elizabethan cliché, the conceit of an art more realistic than reality itself'.[62] Realism is not the criterion here, however, so much as idealism. In a speech that otherwise follows its source, Plutarch's 'Life of Marcus Antonius', almost word for word, Enobarbus describes Cleopatra as 'O'erpicturing that Venus where we see / The fancy out-work nature' (2.2.210–11). The contest implied between 'fancy' and 'nature' is a Shakespearean interpolation; Plutarch says only that Cleopatra was 'apparelled and attired like the goddesse Venus, commonly drawen in picture.'[63] Building on this brief description, Shakespeare introduces a much more complex analogy. Cleopatra represents the ideal woman more accurately than an unspecified, but presumably extraordinary, picture of Venus, just as that image of the divine, which is itself a creation of 'fancy', exceeds 'nature' (presumably, human nature); women as they typically tend to be, out in the world at large. The nadir that serves as the counterpoint to this zenith is Cleopatra's own lament immediately after Antony's death, 'No more but e'en a woman [etc.].'. Caught off guard, Cleopatra describes herself here, in a moment of rare lucidity, as 'commanded / By', rather than commanding, 'passion', and compares herself, in her shared susceptibility to grief, to 'the maid that milks / And does the meanest chares' (4.15.77–9).

The same concept of a conflict between 'fancy' and 'nature' reappears in even more complicated guise in Cleopatra's defence of her dream of Antony to Dolabella. 'Think you there was or might be such a man / As this I dreamt of?' (5.2.92–3) she asks. 'Gentle madam, no' (5.2.93), he replies. She rebukes him indignantly. 'You lie up to the hearing of the gods!' (5.2.94). They are alone; Cleopatra in her grandiosity, as well as desperation, aligns her own 'hearing' with that of 'the gods'. After first accusing Dolabella baldly of lying, Cleopatra's reply becomes more nuanced:

> But if there be nor ever were one such,
> It's past the size of dreaming. Nature wants stuff
> To vie strange forms with fancy; yet t'imagine
> An Antony were nature's piece against fancy,
> Condemning shadows quite.
>
> (5.2.95–9)

The first line of the passage cited is confusing, because it suggests that Cleopatra has become infected, if only for a moment, with Dolabella's doubt. She does not say simply 'there is' or 'was' 'one such', namely, such as Antony; instead, she introduces an 'if'. 'But' also implies that she is going to qualify her immediately prior accusation, 'You lie', by granting it some degree of truth. Her doubt, however, is not complete. The use of 'be' as well as 'were' in the protasis, combined with the use of present tense in the apodosis (elided 'is' in 'It's') makes it unclear whether the conditional is counterfactual. 'Nor' implies a negative assertion, but is not confirmed in this case by any negative correlative such as 'nor' or 'neither'.

Cleopatra defends her 'dream' of Antony by arguing that the possibility that the idealised, all-powerful version of Antony that she has just attempted to describe might in fact exist exceeds the scope of the limited human imagination. 'It's past the size of dreaming.' She says, in effect, much as Enobarbus says of her, 'for [his] person, it beggar[s] all description'. Nature lacks ('wants') the wherewithal ('stuff') to compete with 'fancy' in the elaboration of 'strange forms'. 'Yet' if it 'were' possible, then 't'imagine / An Antony' would be 'nature's piece', that is, its '[master]piece', in its competition with 'fancy'. Cleopatra's past subjunctive ('were') implies that the conditional at the core of her dream is counterfactual: if the imagination ('fancy') could produce an image of Antony representative enough of Antony to be called 'an Antony', then imagination itself, as part of 'nature', a faculty of the human mind, would surpass itself, 'condemning quite' its other, more chimerical products, such as 'dreams', in comparison as merely thin, insubstantial imitations ('shadows'). In other words, Cleopatra in her response to Dolabella does not forgo so much as double down on her hyperbole, inserting a wedge of apophasis between her description and its object. Dolabella is right to say that 'such a man' never existed, but for the wrong reasons; Cleopatra's dream of Antony as a kind of 'colossus', considered self-consciously as a speech-act, is not exaggerated, as she sees it, but inadequate. Antony was even grander, she claims, than 'fancy' itself can compass.

Other examples of the two lovers' conception of themselves as larger than life are easier to grasp. Antony repeatedly compares himself to Hercules; Cleopatra compares him to Mars, as well. Caesar reports that Cleopatra appears frequently 'in the public eye' in Alexandria 'in th'habiliments of the goddess Isis' (3.6.17), and that Antony accompanies her in the style of an Eastern magnate, much to the disgust of the people of Rome, whom Caesar describes as 'queasy with his insolence'. 'Here's the manner of't' (3.6.2), Caesar explains. 'I'th' market-place, on a tribunal silvered, / Cleopatra and himself in chairs of gold / Were publicly enthroned' (3.6.3–5). In this guise as king, Antony gave Cleopatra 'the stablishment of Egypt', and also proclaimed her 'Absolute Queen' of 'lower Syria, Cyprus, Lydia' (3.6.9–11). Ironically, Octavian, as the later Augustus Caesar, went on in history to hold almost precisely the same kind of power whose display he disparages here. Like Shakespeare's Julius Caesar, however, pushing away a crown, the historical Augustus was much more careful than Antony is in Egypt to avoid the obvious trappings of authoritarianism. He styled himself *princeps*, for example, rather than *rex*. Antony and Cleopatra are caught up in a 'dream' of themselves as deities in the much more open, Egyptian tradition of the Pharaoh, the God-King.[64]

Several forces recur throughout the play as threats to the protagonists' grandiose sense of themselves. The most obvious such opponent is Octavian. Others, however, are more abstract: time, old age, 'Fortune', 'destiny'. In Virgil's *Aeneid*, the rise of Augustus and the fate of Aeneas seem so inextricably intertwined that it can be difficult at times to distinguish one from the other. So also here, each of these forces, including Octavian, can be understood as an analogue for any other. Collectively, they represent objective reality itself, encroaching upon a cherished, unsustainable subjective alternative: the world 'as if', in which the subject has the power, if only in 'fancy', to dismiss such concerns. What Antony and Cleopatra are trying to escape, in a word, is what Heidegger would call our 'thrownness' (*Geworfenheit*). They rebel against the shared facticity of fact, in favour of the malleability of their own private fantasies.

In Egypt, Antony and Cleopatra enjoy fabled, apparently unlimited wealth: 'eight wild boars roasted whole at a breakfast, and but twelve persons there' (2.2.189–90). It makes sense, therefore, that Shakespeare would turn to time, rather than money, as his example of a limiting factor. Time is a resource of which even the wealthiest and most powerful have only a finite supply. Most obviously, time appears in the lovers' age, as they themselves at times acknowledge: Antony's 'head' is 'grizzled' (3.13.17); Cleopatra is 'wrinkled deep in time' (1.5.30), her 'salad days' behind her (1.5.76). Flush with the thrill of victory, Antony prefers, nonetheless, to minimise their manifest years. Cleopatra, he calls 'girl' (4.8.19), an incongruous form of address. He himself, he boasts, 'is able to get goal for goal of youth', 'Though grey / Do something mingle with our younger brown' (4.8.20–2).

The other sense in which time figures as an antagonist is more subtle. Time, it turns out, is not infinitely tractable.[65] Instead, time appears in *Antony and Cleopatra* as what an economist might call a fixed or illiquid asset, prone to depreciation. The author of Ecclesiastes writes, 'To every thing there is a season, and a time to every purpose under heaven' (3:1). So also in Shakespeare's tragedy, particular moments seem to be designated, as if objectively, to certain set purposes, which the protagonists ignore at their peril. The most obvious instance of such negligence is Antony's flight from the Battle of Actium. Not only did he turn away, Scarus complains, but he fled 'i'th' midst o'th' fight / When vantage like a pair of twins appeared / Both as the same – or, rather, ours the elder' (3.10.11–13). The problem of opportunity or 'vantage' is not limited to Antony and Cleopatra: the pirate Menas abandons Pompey's service, precisely because he is not willing to seize an opportune moment to secure his power. 'For this,' Menas vows, 'I'll never follow thy pall'd fortunes more. / Who seeks, and will not take when once 'tis offer'd, / Shall never find it more' (2.7.82–5).

Arthur Bell sees 'the relentless tempo of time and "the times"' as a 'standard' or 'norm' by which 'Antony's degeneration' can be 'measured and explained', a standard which he argues Shakespeare derives most immediately from his chief source, Plutarch's 'Life of Marcus Antonius'. In North's version, Plutarch writes that

Antony 'spent and lost in childish sports . . . and idle pastimes the most precious thing a man can spend, as Antiphon saith: and that is, time'.[66] Shakespeare, Bell argues, 'preserved the same sense of time's relentless surge as the inexorable condition confronting all his characters'.[67] David Kaula argues that 'the world of the play is generally dominated by a heightened sense of temporal change', and that 'major characters' such as Antony, Cleopatra and Caesar 'may be distinguished' in part by their 'sharply differing responses to this condition'.[68] Later in the play, as their rivalry comes to a head, Antony marvels at Caesar's efficiency in execution. 'Is it not strange,' he says, 'He could so quickly cut the Ionian sea, / And take in Toryne?' (3.7.20–3). Canidius agrees: 'This speed of Caesar's / Carries beyond belief' (3.7.74–5). Cleopatra upbraids Antony for his relative delay: 'Celerity is never more admired / Than by the negligent' (3.7.24–5). What Antony acknowledges as his 'slackness' (3.7.27), however, is as much her fault as his. When she joins Antony on the battlefield, Enobarbus is distraught; her distracting his commander at such a juncture, even though it has already been happening, in a less obvious sense, from the very beginning of the play, seems to him preposterous. 'Your presence needs must puzzle Antony; / Take from his heart, take from his brain, from's time, / What should not then be spared' (3.7.10–12).

For Cleopatra, whom Antony calls 'idleness itself' (1.3.94), time is an enemy: an empty space which she tries, often in vain, to while away with amusements such as fishing, billiards, and listening to Mardian sing, and which she would most prefer to fill with Antony's company. Antony himself, by contrast, is torn between competing impulses. 'Struck' by a 'Roman thought' (1.2.88), he recognises early on that 'the strong necessity of time commands / Our services a while' (1.3.43–4). More often, however, he is unwilling to sacrifice time at play with Cleopatra in order to attend to affairs of state.

> For the love of Love and her soft hours
> Let's not confound the time with conference harsh.
> There's not a minute of our lives should stretch
> Without some pleasure now. What sport tonight?
>
> (1.1.45–9)

These same 'soft hours' Antony will describe as 'poison'd' later, back in Rome, when he is confronted with the consequences of his negligence (2.2.96). In Alexandria, however, pleasure replaces business, just as night replaces day. In Rome, recollecting his time in Egypt, Enobarbus brags, 'we did sleep day out of countenance, and made the night light with drinking' (2.2.187–8). Caesar, however, is not impressed: Antony, he complains, 'wastes / The lamps of the night in revel' (1.4.4–5).

The last and most mysterious force that opposes Antony and Cleopatra is 'Fortune' or 'destiny'. The difference between these two concepts is not stressed; instead, the salient point is that they both represent a world that is to some extent fixed or 'given'. The self is not the only locus of authority and agency; vital outcomes depend, instead, on an unassailable, immutable and external power, akin to that of divine providence. Cleopatra rails against 'the false huswife Fortune' (5.15.26), seeing that she favours 'the full-fortuned Caesar' (5.15.25). Since his success depends on 'Fortune', however, ''Tis paltry to be Caesar' (5.2.2). 'Not being Fortune, he's but Fortune's knave, / A minister of her will' (5.2.3–4). What is glorious is to be autonomous, self-sufficient. In contrast to what she represents as Caesar's passive reliance on chance, her suicide, Cleopatra argues, will be all the more grand. To commit suicide is, as she sees it, to escape all such ignoble dependence.

> And it is great
> To do that thing that ends all other deeds,
> Which shackles accidents and bolts up change,
> Which sleeps and never palates more the dung,
> The beggar's nurse and Caesar.
>
> (5.2.4–8)

Cleopatra's language here recalls that of Hamlet, as well as, especially, Duke Vincentio in *Measure for Measure*. To 'exist', the Duke tells Angelo, is not 'noble', because it means to be dependent on 'many a thousand grains that issue out of dust' (3.1.20–1). Embodiment itself impinges upon a prized *autarkeia*. This understanding of suicide as an escape from what Cassius calls 'accidental evils', and Hamlet, 'the slings and arrows of outrageous fortune', seems to be characteristic of aristocratic culture at its most extreme. The sense of death as annihilation more easily possible in pagan culture allows Cleopatra to imagine, as Hamlet and Claudio find they cannot, death as a 'sleep' untroubled by 'dreams'.[69] To die, for her, seems simply to become immune to all further influence from without: death guarantees invulnerability.

Antony's relationship with 'Fortune' is not so much a full-throated and indignant protest at its humiliations, as in the case of Cleopatra, as it is a self-conscious, uneasy denial of its force. A soothsayer tells Antony that Caesar's 'fortunes' will 'rise higher' (2.3.15) than his, and, after dismissing the man, Antony confesses that he 'hath spoken true' (2.3.32). 'The very dice obey him; / And in our sports my better cunning faints / Under his chance: if we draw lots, he speeds' (2.3.32–4). Caesar has luck on his side: his fighting cocks beat Antony's, as well as his quails. Before the Battle of Actium, swallows build their nests in Cleopatra's sails, a poor omen: 'the augurers / Say they know not, they cannot tell; look grimly, / And dare not speak their knowledge' (4.12.4–6). Antony himself alternates between 'hope' and 'fear' (4.12.8); he knows too well, on account of these signs, that he cannot defeat Caesar, yet he repeatedly convinces himself that somehow, nonetheless, he has a fighting chance.

At Cleopatra's court, the kind of destiny or 'Fortune' that so haunts Antony seems, by contrast, to be scarcely understood. After wine is served, itself a symbol of a flight from objective reality, Charmian gives her hand to a 'soothsayer', evidently a palm-reader, and makes an odd request. 'Good sir, give me a good fortune' (1.2.14–15). The verb 'give' here is a false note. 'I make not,' the soothsayer protests, 'but foresee' (1.2.16). Charmian is undaunted: 'Pray then, foresee me one' (1.2.17). She misunderstands the fortune-teller's art; he himself is not the author of the future he discerns. 'In nature's infinite book of secrecy,' he explains, 'a little I can read' (1.2.10–11). Alexas, a Greek lord, is more respectful: 'Vex not his prescience!' (1.2.22). The word 'prescience' suggests knowledge, certainty (Latin, *scientia*, knowledge); Alexas implies thereby that he accepts the fortune-teller's own understanding of 'fortune' or 'destiny' as an external structure of reality, rather than his own creation. Charmian, however, remains dismissive: 'Hush!' (1.2.23).

The palm-reader's prophecies do in fact all come true, even those which Charmian finds objectionable. The riddling manner in which he presents his predictions is in keeping, however, with the ambiguous nature of reality itself, considered as an object of perception. For example, the soothsayer tells Charmian, 'You have seen and proved a fairer former fortune / Than that which is to approach' (1.2.35–6). These words do indeed prove prophetic: Charmian dies young in a barren monument. Charmian herself, however, takes the enigmatic epigram more lightly, as a suggestion that she will give birth to bastards. 'Then belike my children will have no names' (1.2.37–8). Or, for example, the soothsayer predicts that Charmian will be 'far fairer' (1.2.18) than she already is. He means, with the pallor of death; Charmian, however, takes it as a prognostication of middle-aged embonpoint. 'He means in flesh' (1.2.19). Iras disagrees: 'No, you shall paint when you are old' (1.2.20). Like Charmian, Iras takes the soothsayer's warning in jest. Shakespeare, however, does not. In contrast to Cleopatra's chambermaids, Shakespeare seems to accept here the premise that the future is to some degree fixed without irony or doubt. Even Enobarbus' mocking imitation of an oracular pronouncement proves reliable. When Menas suggests that Antony's marriage to Octavia will lead to peace between him and Octavian, Enobarbus dismisses the notion. 'If I were bound to divine of this unity, I would not prophecy so' (2.6.118–19).

Shakespeare's point in this case seems to be that reality has its own objective, independent existence, including the reality of future events. The world exists outside the mind, following its own separate course. Nevertheless, reality does not command or enforce upon the observer any single, reliable interpretation of its own nature. It can be recognised, but it can also be denied. More specifically, Shakespeare sees individual human recognition of the truth, including especially, the truth about the self, as something that is worked out in the context of relationships with other human beings. We establish what we accept as true through conversations with other people. Conversely, we prevent ourselves from being obliged to acknowledge unpleasant realities by avoiding interaction with other people who bring those facts to our attention: snubbing them, shunning them, banishing them; even at times killing them outright.[70]

To present recognition of the truth as a process grounded in social interaction is not the same, however, as presenting truth itself as a social construct. From Shakespeare's perspective, there is something out there to be discerned, regardless of any given society's or individual's ability or willingness to do so. Objective reality exists, independent even of humanity itself. Truth is not a human invention or fiction; it is what a phenomenologist such as Jean-Luc Marion would call a 'given', literally, a *datum* (Latin, 'given').[71] Given the long shadow of Virgil's *Aeneid*, with its sad sense of inevitability, it is perhaps only fitting that in this particular tragedy, *Antony and Cleopatra*, the Roman play closest to the *Aeneid* in its subject matter, the truth in its nature as 'given' or objective 'data' is represented by a Virgilian sense of impersonal, occasionally cruel 'destiny'. Cleopatra's chambermaids do not understand it; for them, the world is a product of will, and the only question is whose: their own or someone else's. Cleopatra herself tries to escape it by the desperate expedient of suicide, seeing it as a gross indignity to be acted upon, rather than agent. Antony tries to pretend he does not sense its hold over him. Caesar, however, finds it a consolation. When Octavia becomes distraught, hearing of Antony's infidelity, he counsels her simply to accept it as a fact. 'Let determined things to destiny / Hold unbewail'd their way' (3.6.86–7).

In *Antony and Cleopatra*, the role of other people as vehicles of truth is represented by two types of characters: for future events, 'soothsayers' or 'augurers'; for past events or present facts, 'messengers'.[72] For the most part, these characters are not named; in a play about the relationship between character and misperception, their very anonymity serves as an index of their relative reliability. They have no strongly distinct personality, and no proportionate propensity, therefore, towards what Bacon calls the 'Idols of the Cave'. They present instead an idealised one-to-one correspondence with the external world. How Antony, Cleopatra and Octavian respond to these characters reveals much, therefore, about their more general relationship to the world at large: specifically, the extent to which they each choose to live in a state of denial.

In light of Shakespeare's notorious predilection for puns, it is useful to distinguish in this case between two possible interpretations of the term itself, 'soothsayer', which he uses to describe the Egyptian equivalent of a Roman augur or haruspex. To be a 'soothsayer' is to be a kind of prophet, like Tiresias or Cassandra; one might say less grandly, a fortune-teller. To be a soothsayer in this sense, however, is not to be a 'soothsayer' in another. More commonly in Shakespeare, 'to soothe' means 'to flatter'. A 'soother' in this case is a yes-man, a toady, a flattering courtier. For example, in *1 Henry IV*, Hotspur boasts, 'By heaven, I cannot flatter: I defy / The tongues of soothers' (4.1.6–7). In *Richard III*, Margaret warns Buckingham not to 'soothe the devil' (1.3.298), meaning Richard. Richard himself, wooing Anne, protests disingenuously, 'I never could learn sweet soothing words' (1.2.156); one might compare this outrageous self-misrepresentation to his later, equally misleading description of himself as a 'plain man' (1.3.45). 'I cannot flatter and look fair,' he claims: 'Smile in men's faces, smooth, deceive, and cog' (1.3.46–7). In *Richard II*, Richard complains to Aumerle of the humiliation of having to utter 'words of sooth' (3.3.137): the 'gentle words' and 'kind commends' (3.3.127) that he finds himself obliged to convey to the newly victorious Bolingbroke.[73]

The word itself, 'soothe', can be traced back to the Middle English verb *soðien*, 'to confirm, verify, affirm as true', itself derived from the adjective *soth*, 'true'. In the Renaissance, the word comes to mean something more precise, as well as perilously close to the opposite of this older sense. 'To soothe' in Shakespeare's language means not simply 'to affirm' but instead more specifically, 'to flatter or humor with feigned agreement; to placate or propitiate by means of disingenuous assent'. To soothe, in other words, means to tell someone that what he or she is saying is true, even though – and here is the Renaissance addition – one knows full well it is false. Soothing is the opposite of 'giving the lie'. It is this kind of 'soothsaying', a 'truthsaying' which ironically is anything but, that Cleopatra's attendant Charmian seems to hope for from Alexas' 'soothsayer', not, as she receives instead, any kind of earnest prophecy. She wants the same type of flattery that her mistress, Cleopatra, seems to crave from her, and, like Cleopatra, she is only disappointed when she is presented with its opposite.

For instance, Cleopatra asks Charmian at one point if her former love for Caesar was ever the equal of her present love for Antony. Cleopatra expects a certain answer: no, of course not; Antony is the obviously the better man. Charmian, however, seizes the opportunity to make fun of her, instead. 'O that brave Caesar!' (1.5.70) she cries, imitating Cleopatra's characteristic hyperbole, and thereby deflating its present application to a different man. 'Be choked with such another emphasis!' (1.5.71). Cleopatra replies. 'Say, the brave Antony' (1.5.72). But Charmian persists. 'The valiant Caesar!' (1.5.72). 'By Isis,' Cleopatra replies, 'I will give thee bloody teeth, / If thou with Caesar paragon again / My man of men' (1.5.73–5).

Swearing by Isis, Cleopatra evokes her understanding of herself as a goddess; it is this view of herself as an ideal, superhuman entity that Charmian's mockery endangers. Cleopatra's reciprocal threats to silence Charmian are also typical: a comical version of the much more serious threats and even physical violence that she brings to bear against the unfortunate messenger who brings her the news that Antony has married Octavia. As throughout, Cleopatra's characteristic method for dealing with an unpleasant truth is to deny it, either by dissociation, up to and including suicide, or by, as the saying is, 'shooting the messenger'. She prefers an echo-chamber of compliant courtiers to an accurate assessment of the world outside.

As often in Shakespeare's plays, the first scene is a microcosm of what is to come. A messenger arrives with 'news' for Antony 'from Rome' (1.1.18). Cleopatra interrupts the emissary, however, before he can present even 'the sum' of his message, taunting Antony mercilessly (1.1.19). 'Nay, hear them, Antony' (1.1.20), she insists, mocking him. 'Call in the messengers!' (1.1.30). Then again: 'The messengers!' (1.1.33). And again: 'Hear the ambassadors!' (1.1.49). From Cleopatra's perspective, to be concerned enough about the external world to interrupt a moment of pleasure is a shameful sign of dependence; a failure of autonomy, like a pet responding to a tug at a leash. Stung by her sarcasm, Antony finally sends the messenger away unheard. 'Speak not to us' (1.1.56), he says. 'No messenger but thine' (1.1.53), he reassures Cleopatra, will he deign to receive. Caesar rebukes him for such a rebuff later: 'You / Did pocket up my letters, and with taunts / Did gibe my missive out of audience' (2.2.77–9).

Eventually, however, Antony changes course. 'A Roman thought hath struck him' (1.2.88), Cleopatra complains, and true to her description, Antony enters almost immediately afterwards deep in conversation with a second messenger, plying the man with requests for further details. 'Well, what worst?' (1.2.100) he asks. The messenger balks. 'The nature of bad news infects the teller' (1.2.101), he protests, and with reason, given the kind of reaction to such news we see later from Cleopatra. Antony, however, scoffs at the objection. 'When it concerns the fool or coward. On!' (1.2.102). Much in contrast to Cleopatra, Antony claims, at least, that he prefers truth to flattery. 'Things that are past are done with me' (1.2.103), he says. That is to say, he accepts the independent reality of time; past events are a given, over which he grants that he has no sway or mastery.

Antony even actively solicits criticism of his own behavior, as well as Cleopatra's. 'Speak to me home; mince not the general tongue: / Name Cleopatra as she is call'd in Rome' (1.2.111–2). He asks his attendants to call in a second messenger: 'From Sicyon how the news? Speak there!' (1.2.119). 'He stays upon your will' (1.2.121), the attendant replies; to which Antony, 'Let him appear' (1.2.121). Such lines might seem superfluous, but they have a symbolic significance. Shakespeare here as elsewhere is trying to express an observation about human perception: recognition of external fact depends upon the internal assent of the 'will.' Antony's attitude towards messengers goes back and forth; sometimes he welcomes them, sometimes he tosses them out without a hearing. Caesar and Cleopatra, by contrast, present consistent, characteristic, diametrically opposed reactions to the messengers they each receive. In the scene in which Caesar first appears, for instance, a messenger arrives and informs him that his 'biddings' have been done: 'every hour', he reassures him, Caesar will receive 'report / how 'tis abroad' (1.4.34–5). As if in confirmation, another messenger arrives only moments later, bringing him news of Pompey's progress.

Lepidus for his part admires and strives to emulate Octavian's obvious command of information. In the same scene, he reassures Caesar that, the next day, he will be 'furnish'd to inform [him] rightly' (1.4.77) what he can offer in terms of troops, and asks him, moreover, to let him be 'partaker' of anything new that he might learn 'meantime' of what 'stirs abroad' (1.2.82–4). Lepidus is no match for his supposed ally, however, in ruthless engagement with reality. Later, when Octavia comes to Caesar to complain about his falling-out with her new husband, Antony, Caesar explains that her husband has been unfaithful to her and reveals that he maintains spies as well as messengers in his service. 'I have eyes upon him,' he says, meaning, Antony, 'and his affairs come to me on the wind' (3.6.63–4).

The contrast with Cleopatra could scarcely be more clear-cut. She uses messengers almost solely to keep tabs on Antony, and even then is very reluctant to hear anything that does not serve to confirm her hold over him. 'How goes it with my brave Mark Antony?' (1.5.40) she asks Alexas, ignoring all other questions of world affairs. Fortunately for him, he brings back a token of Antony's continuing affection: an 'orient pearl' (1.5.43). Later on, an anonymous Egyptian servant does not fare so well. He brings word that Antony has married Octavia, and this news comes as a sharp blow to Cleopatra's hopes. How she reacts to this shock reveals much about her willingness to acknowledge a reality over which she does not reign as absolute mistress. In a surprisingly long scene, about a hundred lines, in a play where some scenes barely make it to a dozen, Cleopatra oscillates rapidly between promising the man rich rewards such as 'gold' (2.5.28, 31), 'a shower of gold' (2.5.45), 'rich pearls' (2.5.46) and even a 'province' (2.5.68), if he tells her what she wants to hear, that is, if he lies, recanting his tidings of Antony's marriage, and threatening him with horrifying torture if he persists instead in telling the truth, ranging in kind from the relatively straightforward (gouging out his eyes [2.5.63–4], ripping out his hair [2.5.64]), to the more inventive (pouring molten gold down his throat [2.5.32–4], whipping him with wires [2.5.65], stewing him in brine [2.5.65]). She strikes him herself, then draws a knife to stab him, at which point he takes to his heels; Cleopatra's maidservants are only with much ado able at last to bring him back before her. 'Should I lie, madam?' (2.5.93) he asks, bewildered. Her reply is telling: 'Oh, I would thou didst!' (2.5.93).

Such long interchanges between Cleopatra and her messenger are not idle by-play, but instead should be understood as revealing indications of Cleopatra's more general relationship to the world outside herself. She is extremely reluctant to acknowledge any aspect of external reality as a 'given' a priori, independent of her desires, and therefore manipulates those around her, through her considerable powers of reward and punishment, into becoming collaborators, whether they like it or not, in elaborate and mutually sustained processes of denial. She surrounds herself with what psychoanalysts would call 'enablers': 'yes-men' and 'yes-women' such as Mardian, Charmian and Iras. By far Cleopatra's preferred method for fortifying her delusions, however, is to see them reflected and confirmed in the subjectivity of some other, more independent individual, a lover, who in this case serves as a kind of flattering mirror. Even one such man, a Caesar or an Antony grand enough to overtop all others, can seem sufficient to validate her own grandiose self-image. Given her superabundance of personal charms, as well as her relative lack of military might, it is much easier for Cleopatra to cultivate the self-abasement of one such renowned general than to exact tribute more directly from the world at large.

Nor is the deal altogether one-sided. Antony for his part is able to find in Cleopatra a welcome respite from the gruelling hardship involved in securing his part of the Empire: fighting Parthians with his lieutenant Ventidius out in the borderlands to the east, or else eating bark and 'strange flesh' (1.4.68) in Alpine passes, as he flees from his own countrymen. Having won Cleopatra's affections provides Antony an easier, more immediate validation of himself as a world-bestriding conqueror than the toil and slog of such thankless, risky and unpleasant military campaigns. Cleopatra's status as a celebrated prize makes her seem sufficient as a substitute for a larger, more hostile world. 'Fall not a tear,' he says, comforting her: 'one of them rates / All that is won and lost' (3.11.69–70). This tear, worth all, Antony says, that he has lost at Actium, is one of several symbols of what he describes in the first scene of the play as 'new heaven, new earth' (1.1.17): the private world of the two lovers, which they hope to recover in the afterlife. The final representation of this shared, self-enclosed subjective space is the tomb-like 'monument' which serves as the setting for the play's final scenes: a less-solitary version of Hamlet's solipsistic 'nutshell' (2.2.254). The tomb is a symbol of their final, immortal grandeur as figures of the imagination: the kind of 'marble' or 'gilded monument' which Shakespeare emulates and aims to exceed in his sonnets.[74] As a symbol of a retreat into 'fancy', however, the monument is also a kind of prison, cutting them off from the world outside. Withdrawal from the world which began as voluntary becomes in the end involuntary.

Another example of this separate world 'as if' is the 'orient pearl' which Alexas delivers to Cleopatra from Antony as a gift upon his departure. Antony calls it 'the treasure of an oyster' (1.5.46), and bestows upon it, before handing it over, 'many doubled kisses' (1.5.42). To call the pearl that Antony sends to Cleopatra 'orient' casts it most immediately as a symbol of a place, the Orient: 'the East', as Antony also calls it. 'I' th' East my pleasure lies' (2.4.39). Yet this place, the 'orient', is itself a symbol of a more imaginary, immaterial locale: the virtual reality, so to speak, Antony shares with Cleopatra. 'Here is my space' (1.1.35), Antony proclaims, embracing her: the pearl represents the referent of that exuberant, indefinite 'here'. To call it 'the treasure of an oyster' calls to mind Erasmus' 'Silenus box': Antony's and Cleopatra's shared subjective 'space' looks one way from the outside, another from within.[75] The adjective 'doubled', applied here to Antony's kisses, suggests not only the degree of his affection, but also the sense in which he depends upon Cleopatra as a 'double', and she upon him. They 'double' each other like reflections in a mirror, reflecting back in each case the other that the other most wants to see.

Shakespeare's most charming representation of the two lovers' 'space', self-enclosed like that of a pearl in an oyster, is the scene the morning before the second battle outside Alexandria, when Cleopatra helps Antony don his armour. The scene is a Shakespearean interpolation, and rich in a significance that shades over into outright allegory. It may seem strange to speak of this scene as representative of Antony's and Cleopatra's private reality, when technically speaking there is another character there, too, Antony's attendant, Eros. Eros, however, can be understood in this case as an allegorical representation of love itself (Greek, *erōs*, 'romantic love'). Shakespeare finds the character's name in Plutarch, but he also makes the most of his material. 'Eros! Mine armor, Eros!' Antony repeatedly cries (4.4.1, 3). It is the same literary device, a symbolic apostrophe to a personified influence, which Shakespeare uses in *Macbeth*, when he shows Macbeth in like manner crying out repeatedly for his manservant 'Seyton' (sc. the homophone 'Satan') to come help him arm himself for battle.[76]

But to return to the scene: Eros helps Antony arm for battle, with the help of Cleopatra, and both prove inept at their task. This clumsiness foreshadows the more abstract truth that love does not, in the end, prove as apt a defence from external reality as lovers themselves might wish. 'Eros' is Antony's 'armor': the juxtaposition in his apostrophe, repeated for emphasis, confirms the symbolism. Like Eros himself, however, that armour will prove fallible. When Cleopatra comes to help Eros arm Antony, Antony at first tries to prevent her. 'Ah, let be, let be!' he tells her. 'Thou art / The armorer of my heart. False, false!' (4.4.6–7). Antony ostensibly draws a distinction between the two armourers, Eros and Cleopatra, but instead ironically flags a similarity: a complex analogy between the literal, physical stage business, his transformation into what Cleopatra calls 'a man of steel' (4.5.34), and the psychological effects of his overwhelming investment in Cleopatra's approbation, to the exclusion of a more prudent, more general concern for the approval of others. Cleopatra protects his sense of himself as a grand, godlike figure, his 'heart', from being subject to anyone else's opinion but her own; when he gives himself over to his love for her, he feels as if he were invulnerable. He is safe from scorn or defeat within the shelter of their comforting *folie à deux*; each partner protects the other's delusions of grandeur from outside attack, in the manner of a suit of armour. Ultimately, however, this armour proves 'false, false'.

A lover's admiration may be reassuring, may even seem an impenetrable shield, but it is not in the end an adequate defence on its own against what Hamlet calls 'the slings and arrows of outrageous fortune'. Like Coriolanus with his mother or actors with an audience, Antony is vulnerable to unexpected disapproval, even outright betrayal; much more vulnerable than he realises. Exposure to the possibility of shame is not so much eliminated altogether as concentrated in a single, highly fraught relationship. Thus Antony's unmitigated distress at the thought that Cleopatra has betrayed him, as well as hers when she finds out that he has married Octavia. The more that Antony succumbs to the allure of the *folie à deux*, the more insulated he becomes from the workaday humiliations of the outside world. The more at the mercy, however, he becomes, as well, of the other partner in question. His feeling of invincibility comes, paradoxically, at a steep cost in actual emotional sovereignty.

Notes

1. Cf. Waith, *The Herculean Hero*.
2. Plutarch gives more details: 'Antonius, he forsooke the citie and companie of his frendes, and built him a house in the sea, by the Ile of Pharos, upon certaine forced mountes which he caused to be cast into the sea, and dwelt there, as a man that banished him selfe from all mens companie: saying that he would lead Timons life.' Cf. Plutarch, 'Life of Marcus Antonius', 304. Shakespeare takes up the story of this kind of literal, physical retreat from society in his own *Timon of Athens*, instead.
3. Nuttall, *New Mimesis*, 116.
4. Whittington, *Renaissance Suppliants*.
5. For more on the concept of acting 'as if', see Vaihinger, *The Philosophy of 'As If'*. Vaihinger's 'fictionalism', itself in part derived from

Jeremy Bentham's earlier *Theory of Fictions*, strongly influenced Adler's concept of a 'fictional final goal', as well as Frank Kermode's discussion of narrative in his *Sense of an Ending*. A useful overview of Vaihinger and his influence is Fine, 'Fictionalism'. See also Ogden, ed., *Bentham's Theory of Fictions*.

6. Gill, *Personality*, 15, 9.
7. Thomas Pfau, *Minding the Modern: Human Agency, Intellectual Traditions, and Responsible Knowledge* (Notre Dame, IN: University of Notre Dame Press, 2013), 1.
8. Gill, *Personality*, 7, 9.
9. Ibid., 15–16.
10. Pfau, *Minding the Modern*, 14, 575.
11. Ibid., 578.
12. Notebook entry of October 1820; cited in Pfau, *Minding the Modern*, 557.
13. Pfau, *Minding the Modern*, 573.
14. Samuel Taylor Coleridge, *Opus Maximum*, ed. Thomas McFarland and Nick Halmi (Princeton: Princeton University Press, 2002), 127; cited in Pfau, *Minding the Modern*, 573.
15. Coleridge, *Opus Maximum*, 74–5; cited in Pfau, *Minding the Modern*, 602.
16. Gill, *Structured Self*, xxi.
17. A. A. Long, *Stoic Studies* (Cambridge: Cambridge University Press, 1996), 266; cited in Bartsch, *Mirror of the Self*, 250, and Langley, *Narcissism and Suicide*, 148.
18. Bartsch, *Mirror of the Self*, 1, 236.
19. Michel Foucault, *Discipline and Punish: The Birth of the Prison*, trans. Alan Sheridan (New York: Vintage, 1979), 187; cited in Bartsch, *Mirror of the Self*, 137.
20. Andrew J. E. Bell, 'Cicero and the Spectacle of Power', 8, *Journal of Roman Studies* 87 (1997): 1–22; cited in Bartsch, *Mirror of the Self*, 137.
21. Bartsch, *Mirror of the Self*, 138.
22. Foucault, *Discipline and Punish*, 201–2; cited in Bartsch, *Mirror of the Self*, 137.
23. Sen. *Tranq.* 17.1; cited in Bartsch, *Mirror of the Self*, 225, as well as Langley, *Narcissism and Suicide*, 149.
24. Carlin Barton, *Roman Honor: The Fire in the Bones* (Berkeley, CA: University of California Press, 2001), 120; cited in Bartsch, *Mirror of the Self*, 225 n. 115.
25. Bartsch, *Mirror of the Self*, 229, 244–5.
26. Nuttall, *Shakespeare the Thinker*, 193.
27. Langley, *Suicide and Narcissism*, 148.

28. Berlin, *Roots of Romanticism*, 20, 114, 119.
29. Ibid., 14, 117.
30. Cantor, *Shakespeare's Roman Trilogy*, 101.
31. Berlin, *Roots of Romanticism*, 89.
32. Jean-Jacques Rousseau, *Émile*, trans. Barbara Foxley (London: Dent, 1982; 1st edition 1911), 193; cited in Nuttall, *Shakespeare the Thinker*, 193.
33. Peter Holbrook, *Shakespeare's Individualism* (Cambridge: Cambridge University Press, 2010), 12–13; cited in Strier, *The Unrepentant Renaissance*, 98 n. 2.
34. Patrick Gray, 'Seduced by Romanticism'.
35. Berlin, *Roots of Romanticism*, 145.
36. Nuttall, *Shakespeare the Thinker*, 193–4.
37. Braden, 'Plutarch, Shakespeare, and the Alpha Males', 192.
38. Plutarch, 'The Life of Marcus Brutus', 120, in Bullough, *Narrative and Dramatic Sources*, 90–132.
39. Braden, 'Fame, Eternity, and Shakespeare's Romans', 37–55. For Cantor's response to this essay, see Cantor, *Shakespeare's Roman Trilogy*, 46, 77, 184.
40. Plutarch, 'Life of Marcus Brutus', 40.4–5. Cf. Amyot, which except for the tense of the word *vivray* (future) remains truer to the Greek. 'Car je donnay aux Ides de mars ma vie à mon païs, pour laquelle j'en vivray une autre libre et glorieuse.' Plutarch, *Les Vies*, 166–7.
41. Montaigne, 'A Custom of the Island of Cea', 253, in Montaigne, *The Complete Essays of Montaigne*, trans. Frame, 251–61.
42. August. *De civ. D.* 1.24.
43. Ibid., 1.22.
44. Montaigne, 'A Custom of the Island of Cea', 254.
45. Ibid., 255–6.
46. Plutarch, 'The Life of Marcus Brutus', 119–20.
47. M. W. MacCallum, *Shakespeare's Roman Plays and Their Background* (London: St. Martin's, 1967), 185; cited in Braden, 'Alpha Males', 192.
48. Cf. Cantor, *Shakespeare's Roman Trilogy*, 49, on Brutus and Cassius as 'political men who profess apolitical philosophies'.
49. See Monsarrat, *Light from the Porch*, 139–44, in which Monsarrat disagrees most immediately with Vawter, 'Division 'tween our Souls'. Monsarrat also cites J. C. Maxwell, 'Brutus's Philosophy', *Notes and Queries*, n.s., 17 (1970): 128, and M. Sacharoff, 'Suicide and Brutus' Philosophy in *Julius Caesar*', *Journal of the History of Ideas* 33 (1972): 115–22. See also Fleissner, 'That Philosophy in *Julius Caesar* Again'.
50. Miles, *Constant Romans*, 126; cf. 4 n. 8.

51. On Shakespeare's reception of Senecan tragedy, see Patrick Gray, 'Shakespeare vs. Seneca'.

52. Plutarch, 'Against the Stoics on Common Conceptions', 1063a, in Plutarch, *Moralia*, vol. 13, part 2.

53. Seneca, *Ad Lucilium epistulae morales*, 71.16–20.

54. Arendt, *Life of the Mind*, 2:73–84; cited in Braden, *Renaissance Tragedy*, 20.

55. Arendt, *Life of the Mind*, 78–9.

56. Nuttall, *Shakespeare the Thinker*, 195–6.

57. John Milton, *Paradise Lost*, 1.233.

58. All references to Samuel Daniel's *Cleopatra* are taken from Daniel, *The Tragedy of Cleopatra (1599 Edition)*, 406–52, in Bullough, *Narrative and Dramatic Sources*, vol. 9.

59. For a sense of the reputation of this faculty in the Renaissance, as well as its classical sources, see Cocking, *Imagination*, as well as Rossky, 'Imagination in the English Renaissance'.

60. Eliot, 'Shakespeare and the Stoicism of Seneca', 110–11.

61. For a complementary reading of these two speeches, see Sugimura, 'Two Concepts of Reality in *Antony in Cleopatra*', 82 ff. Citing similar readings by Charles Martindale and A. D. Nuttall, Sugimura compares them to St Anselm's argument for the existence of God.

62. Barton, '"Nature's piece 'gainst fancy"', 54.

63. Plutarch, 'The Life of Marcus Antonius', 274, in Bullough, *Narrative and Dramatic Sources*, 254–318.

64. See, for example, Plutarch's interesting essay, 'On Isis and Osiris', in his *Moralia*, as well as the passage in his 'Life of Marcus Antonius' about Antony being greeted as the god Dionysius. 'In the citie of Ephesus, women attyred as they goe in the feastes and sacrifice of Bacchus, came out to meete him with such solemnities and ceremonies, as are then used: with men and children disguised like Fawnes and Satyres. Moreover, the citie was full of Ivey, and . . . in their songes they called him Bacchus', and so on: Plutarch, 'Life of Marcus Antonius', 272; cf. 291. Shakespeare replaces Dionysus with Hercules, but retains the basic conceit of Antony and especially, Cleopatra, styling themselves as gods.

65. Janet Adelman argues, by contrast, that time as a 'measurable and inescapable quantity' is merely 'Roman time', which Antony and Cleopatra are in the end able to escape through suicide. 'In their deaths, the lovers escape from time itself.' See Adelman, *Common Liar*, 151–4. I discuss problems with this conclusion in more detail in the conclusion to this part, 'The Last Interpellation'. Briefly put, the 'gap of time' in which Adelman claims Cleopatra 'exists', 'the

hyperbolical time of which Cleopatra is mistress', may not be as infinite in duration as Cleopatra imagines.

66. *Shakespeare's Plutarch*, ed. T. J. B. Spencer (London: Harmondsworth, 1964), 203; cited in Bell, 'Time and Convention', 255 n. 8.

67. Bell, 'Time and Convention', 255.

68. Kaula, 'Time Sense', 215.

69. See Watson, *The Rest is Silence*.

70. See Patrick Gray, 'Shakespeare versus Aristotle'.

71. See Marion, *Being Given*.

72. For a contrary reading of the messengers as extensions of the play's principal characters, see Heffner, 'The Messengers'. For contrary readings of the messengers as an index of the difficulty of attaining certain knowledge of objective reality, see Macdonald, 'Playing till Doomday: Interpreting *Antony and Cleopatra*', and Adelman, *Common Liar*, 34–9.

73. See also, for example, *Comedy of Errors*, 'Is't good to soothe him in these contraries?' (4.4.82) and *Venus and Adonis*, 'Soothing the humor of fantastic wits' (850).

74. Cf. Sonnet 55: 'Neither marble nor gilded monuments / Of princes', and so on.

75. See Erasmus, 'The Sileni of Alcibiades', in *The Adages of Erasmus*, trans. Margaret Mann Phillips, 245 ff.

76. Shakespeare, *Antony and Cleopatra*, 4.4 *passim*; cf. Shakespeare, *Macbeth*, 5.3 *passim*, but esp. 33: 'Give me mine armour.'

CHAPTER 4

'A SPACIOUS MIRROR': INTERPELLATION AND THE OTHER IN *ANTONY AND CLEOPATRA*

In her influential reading of *Antony and Cleopatra*, Janet Adelman argues that the problem of moral judgement is central to the experience of the tragedy, not just for the characters themselves, but also for the audience.[1] 'The desire to judge and be judged correctly is one of the dominant passions of the play.' 'The dramatic design of *Antony and Cleopatra* forces us to acknowledge the process of judgment at every turn.' In keeping with this focus on ethical evaluation, 'the most characteristic dramatic technique in *Antony and Cleopatra* is the discussion of one group of characters by another.' This recurrent 'framing' of the action, as if it were a play within a play, draws in the audience and forces us to participate, as well, in the act of judging. 'For we are, in a sense, the most minor of the characters who stand aside and comment; or at least we as audience are silent extensions of them.'[2]

Anne Barton sees the position of the audience in *Antony and Cleopatra* in much the same light. 'Our place of vantage is basically that of Charmian or Enobarbus: people sufficiently close to their social superiors to witness informal and often undignified behavior, without participating in its motive and reflection like the confidantes in Garnier and Jodelle.' Antony and Cleopatra have a quality of 'opacity', a 'moral ambiguity', that elicits what Barton calls 'evaluation', and Adelman, 'judgment', from other characters, as well as the audience. 'In this tragedy,' Barton writes, 'other characters are continually trying to describe Cleopatra and Antony, to fix their essential qualities in words.' Like Adelman, however, Barton sees this 'dilemma of judgment' as interminable, insoluble.

And, like Adelman, she cites Cleopatra's description of Antony as akin to a perspective painting, one way a 'Gorgon' (2.5.116), the other way a 'Mars' (2.5.117), as a paradigmatic symbol. Like Antony here, *Antony and Cleopatra*, as Barton and Adelman see the play, simultaneously evokes and frustrates the desire for definitive moral judgement. 'In effect,' Adelman writes, 'we are forced to judge and shown the folly of judging at the same time.'[3]

The concept of interpellation that I introduce in this chapter, modifying Althusser's antihumanist version, further develops Adelman's insights into 'judgment', as well as Barton's thoughts on 'evaluation'. Adelman observes, 'Judgment depends on where one stands.' Each moral judgement 'tells us as much about the judge and his perspective as it does about the accused'.[4] I agree; I use the term 'interpellation', however, rather than 'judgement', because I want to emphasise not only, like Adelman, that judgement is grounded in a subjective relationship with another person, rather than in impersonal, objective fact, but also that such judgements are not merely inert, solipsistic expressions of the judging self. Instead, for Shakespeare, judgements possess a kind of power over the other. To judge other people, if they know about that judgement, is to alter their perception of themselves, unless they are able to muster some sort of psychological resistance. Even that resistance, moreover, may be broken down. By being led in triumph, for example, or defeated in open battle, people can be forced to change the way they see themselves.

Shakespeare sees the fall of the Roman Republic as a tragedy, and the way that he describes it evokes, probably not coincidentally, a contemporary decline in the political power of the English nobility. Like Wayne Rebhorn, John Cox and J. L. Simmons, I would suggest, nonetheless, that Shakespeare himself does not see the crisis he describes in such terms, as an effect of economic forces such as Norbert Elias's 'monopoly mechanism'. The rise of the great demagogue, Julius Caesar, and Rome's transition to Empire is in part, as he sees it, a backlash against the injustices of patrician oligarchy. The generosity which Antony attributes to Caesar in his account of Caesar's will goes far to help him win the support of the Roman plebs. But these promises of material gain are not on their own enough to secure the success of his oration.[5] Without Brutus' cold, standoffish emphasis on disinterested reason and Antony's own contrary ability, like an actor, to weep, rail, gesticulate and walk among the people, to show them Caesar's wounded body and elicit pity, it is some question whether the pledges that he claims to have discovered in Caesar's will would have been enough to sway the crowd. If pity itself, especially, were not so pervasively repressed, Antony would not be able to manipulate it so successfully.

Shakespeare recognises that political structures can shape historical change. Like St Augustine, however, as well as Cicero, he sees the collapse of Rome's traditional political institutions as more immediately a result of a flawed moral paradigm. The impassibility that his Roman characters tend to idealise is incompatible in the long run with a functioning civil society, because it leaves no room for compromise or concession. If everyone aims to be a law unto himself, then the only possible end result is what Hobbes calls 'the war of all against all': civil strife, culminating in the rule of a strongman. The exaltation of individual autonomy that drives this political conflict is articulated in Shakespeare's Roman's images of the ideal self: the Stoic *sapiens*, the marble statue, 'the northern star', Mount Olympus. And it is rooted in a set of characteristic misconceptions about the nature itself of selfhood. Shakespeare's Romans seem to believe, at times, that passibility can be transcended, when in fact it is a given of the human condition. They also tend to assume that the relation between self and other is necessarily antagonistic, a zero-sum game, when in fact it can be peaceful, collaborative and mutually beneficial.

In this chapter on *Antony and Cleopatra*, the vulnerability to shame that I describe in terms of interpersonal 'interpellation' should be understood as one more instance of the same basic human condition of passibility that I described in simpler terms in my analysis of *Julius Caesar*. Human beings by their very nature as human, as opposed to divine, are vulnerable to others' moral judgement of their character, just as they are vulnerable to being physically wounded. Shadi Bartsch notes, for example, that the gaze in ancient Rome was seen as capable of playing a 'sinister role', as well as an admiring one, in 'interpersonal dynamics among both the elite and commoners', a role captured in the superstitious fear of the so-called 'evil eye' evident in apotropaic Roman iconography.

> The individual on display could suffer the debilitating effects of the evil rather than the emulatory eye, of aggression and Schadenfreude rather than admiration. This form of the gaze could be figured as a weapon, and was sometimes imagined as penetrating its human object, or else feeding itself on the sight of suffering.[6]

Coriolanus' crisis, when he is confronted by his mother, illustrates this problem. By leading the Volscians' sack of Rome, Coriolanus imagines that he will be able to blot out the Romans' earlier censure of his behaviour, as well as the humiliation of his banishment. As Volumnia explains to him, however, Coriolanus will not thereby free himself from all opprobrium. The world is larger than Rome, and posterity cares about other things outside and beyond the simple exercise of military might. If Coriolanus succeeds, he will go down in history as a traitor, not as vindicated.

> If thou conquer Rome, the benefit
> Which thou shalt thereby reap is such a name
> Whose repetition will be dogg'd with curses,
> Whose chronicle thus writ: 'The man was noble,
> But with his last attempt he wip'd it out,
> Destroy'd his country, and his name remains
> To th'insuing age abhorr'd.
>
> (5.3.142–8)

Antony and Cleopatra imagine that they will find a refuge from such final judgement in the afterlife, in each other's company. As I explain here, however, in the conclusion to my analysis of *Antony and Cleopatra*, 'The Last Interpellation', Shakespeare introduces some significant cause for doubt that the two lovers' imagined escape to Elysium will turn out in the manner they expect.

Ontologically speaking, Shakespeare recognises that the other is an integral participant in self-definition. The other may be divine or human; unchosen or chosen. What it cannot be, however, is altogether eradicated from self-awareness. Without the other as its ground of self-awareness, the self falls into a tautological abyss: a sense of meaninglessness N. K. Sugimura describes as akin to Sartre's existential 'nausea'.[7] When Antony believes that Cleopatra has betrayed him, he is utterly bewildered. 'I made these wars for Egypt' (4.14.15), he explains. Cleopatra and her soldiers, as well as his, represent for Antony what Timothy Reiss calls 'spheres' or 'circles', the matrix of human relationships which he sees as defining passible, pre-modern selfhood. Cleopatra is part of Antony's understanding of himself, the anchor of a constitutive network: 'the Queen – / Whose heart I thought I had, for she had mine, / Which, whilst it was mine, / Had annexed unto't / A million more, now lost' (4.14.15–18). Deprived of his consort, Antony compares himself to a 'cloud' or 'vapor' which for a time looks like a 'citadel' or a 'mountain', but then abruptly 'dislimns' and becomes 'indistinct' (4.14.1–14).

The impossibility of self-definition without reference to another also appears earlier and in a more humorous light in Antony's drunken description of a crocodile. 'What manner o' thing is your crocodile?' (2.7.41) Lepidus asks. 'It is shaped, sir, like itself,' Antony explains. 'It is as broad as it hath breadth. It is just so high as it is [etc.]' (2.7.42–3). 'What color is it of?' (2.7.46) Lepidus asks. 'Of it own color too' (2.7.48). The point of the joke is that it is impossible to describe anything without some sort of reference to something other than itself. The selfsame without the other is incomprehensible. Antony finds himself in like case later on, when he believes that Cleopatra has abandoned him for his rival. The patent inadequacy of his response to Lepidus is amusing at the time, but also a prefiguration of the fate that awaits him, alone and confused on the Egyptian coast after the battle of Actium.

Much as Shakespeare suggests here, in this bit of drunken banter, in his account of what he calls 'recognition' (*Anerkennung*), Hegel advances a claim which at first might seem paradoxical: our individual self-definition is not and cannot be autonomous, but instead can be better understood as emerging out of interpersonal relations between the self and the other.[8] Sticking strictly to philosophy, rather than theology (Buber) or literary criticism (Bakhtin), the most influential twentieth-century inheritors of this Hegelian sense of the importance of the other are Sartre and Ricœur: that is, the claim that the other plays a constitutive role in self-perception, where the other is understood as other people, rather than as God (Lévinas), language (Lacan), 'ideology' (Althusser) or 'discourse' (Foucault).[9] Sartre for his part is dismayed by the intersubjective relatedness Hegel emphasises; the tangling-up of one self-awareness with another that Arendt, as well, considers part of what she calls 'plurality.' This inextricable connection between one consciousness and the next, as Sartre sees it, introduces painful feelings of shame, undermining the very possibility of peaceful human sociability. The self and the other are doomed to perpetual conflict: each aims to reduce the other to an object, an 'it' rather than a 'thou', in order to preserve an incompatible sense of itself as what Arendt would call 'sovereign'. Enjoying one's own agency, Sartre suggests, is possible only at someone else's expense. Ricœur, by contrast, is more optimistic. Like Hegel, he believes that an alternative to the 'master–slave dialectic' is possible: a state of mutual 'recognition' which he sees exemplified in healthy romantic relationships, practices of ritual gift-exchange, and the legal recognition of individual rights.[10] Sartre's sense of the relationship between self and other as a 'zero-sum game' resembles that of Shakespeare's Romans, doomed to oscillate between autocracy and civil war. Ricœur's, by contrast, like Cicero's, envisages a viable republican alternative.

Much akin to this contrast between Sartre and Ricœur, Shakespeare's *Coriolanus* presents two competing models of the circulation of political and economic power. The first paradigm of distribution, that of the patricians, leads to commoners on the dole, as a result of aristocratic hoarding: 'storehouses cramm'd with grain' (1.1.79–80). The other, that of the plebeians, consists of free trade in an open market. Much of the stage business of the play, for example, consists in Coriolanus going to and from 'the marketplace'.[11] Menenius and Volumnia convince him to visit it, however, only much against his wishes. When what he calls the 'price o' the consulship' (2.3.74) proves too high, Coriolanus leaves in a huff. He is unwilling to negotiate; like Sartre, he assumes that a concession to another is simply a loss, rather than perhaps the basis for a long-term gain. It is significant therefore that the plebeians are described repeatedly, by contrast, as 'trades' (3.2.134, 4.1.13). Theirs is a tacit bargain, like that of a 'marketplace': I will honour you, if you will honour me. What Ricœur identifies as 'recognition' thrives upon collaboration, founded in mutual respect. People greet each other in the street; each 'citizen' or 'neighbour' knows and is known; praises and is praised in return. After Coriolanus is banished, the tribune Sicinius rejoices to see 'tradesmen singing in their shops and going / About their functions friendly' (4.6.8–9). As Annabel Patterson suggests, in *Coriolanus*, 'Shakespeare's audience is invited to contemplate an alternative political system': the early Republic.[12] James Kuzner, as well, sees here an inspiring depiction of 'a limited yet germinal version of participatory government'.[13]

Francis Fukuyama takes up this model of shared 'recognition' in his discussion of what he calls 'the end of history': the emergence of liberal democracies in the modern period. 'The failure to understand the thymotic component of what is normally thought of as economic motivation leads to vast misinterpretations of politics and historical change.' For example, 'virtually the entire civil liberties and civil rights agendas, while having economic components, are essentially thymotic contests over recognition.'[14] Fukuyama's definition of *thymos* connects Braden's take on what St Augustine calls *libido dominandi* with Ricœur's emphasis on 'recognition', as well as Charles Taylor's concept of a 'politics of recognition'. '*Thymos* is something like an innate human sense of justice: people believe that they have a certain worth, and when other people do not *recognize* their worth at its correct value – then they become angry.' *Thymos* becomes disordered and unmanageable when characters such as Coriolanus are unwilling to accept others' assessment of that worth as anything less than infinite, divine. A peaceful 'commonwealth' (4.16.14) requires the interdependent exchange of mutually reinforced self-esteem or 'recognition'. Coriolanus, however, balks at this prospect. Like Sartre, he is unable to see the other as anything other than a threat to his own absolute autonomy. This distrust of his fellow citizens is an effect of what Rebhorn calls the 'imperial self', a vision of himself that leaves no room for their independent agency. As Volumnia says, 'thou hadst rather / Follow thine enemy in a fiery gulf / Than flatter him in a bower' (3.2.90–2). For Coriolanus, as for Sartre, 'hell is other people'.[15]

How did Shakespeare arrive at such a prescient understanding of the relation between the self and the other, anticipating the conclusions of nineteenth- and twentieth-century Continental philosophy? The analogy to Ricœur is revealing, in part because his avowed intellectual indebtedness to Aristotle, in addition to other, more modern thinkers such as Hegel, provides a clue to what may be, with some degree of historical plausibility, Shakespeare's own philosophical source. Part of the inspiration for Ricœur's insistence that self-knowledge requires the other is Aristotle's description of friendship in his *Nicomachean* and *Eudemian Ethics*, in which the philosopher describes the friend as *allos autos*, 'another self'.[16] Aristotle argues that, since friends are by nature similar, to perceive a friend is, in a sense, to perceive oneself. Cicero picks up on the idea in his *De amicitia*, translating it by the now-famous phrase *alter idem* (literally, 'another the same').[17]

Shakespeare, however, may have also encountered Aristotle's thought about friendship in another incarnation, as well, the so-called *Magna moralia*, a treatise once thought to have been written by Aristotle, but whose authorship is now disputed, and which as a result has drifted into relative obscurity. In the *Magna moralia*, the author, whoever he may be, vividly compares the friend to a mirror, and Shakespeare seems to take up this conceit, not without some interesting modification, in two conversations much-noted for their philosophical implications. The first exchange, in *Julius Caesar*, begins when Cassius asks Brutus if he can see his own face. The second, much analogous, appears in a slightly later play, *Troilus and Cressida*, when Achilles asks Ulysses what he is reading. As Christopher Tilmouth suggests, *Troilus and Cressida* is 'necessarily central to any discussion of Renaissance intersubjectivity'.[18] Throughout the play, as Lars Engle observes, crises of evaluation 'turn reflexively on themselves and become debates over the nature of the activity of valuing', bringing on 'an anxiety about assessment amounting almost to vertigo'. 'How may value in men and women be assessed?'[19]

'Eye to eye opposed': Shakespeare's 'strange fellow'

I begin this section by comparing Cassius' conversation with Brutus at the beginning of *Julius Caesar* about Brutus' inability to see his own potential with Ulysses' conversation with Achilles in *Troilus and Cressida* about the impossibility of maintaining honour in isolation. The basic premise of both of these discussions is a commonplace of present-day philosophical anthropology: self-image is constructed through relation with the other. Within his much earlier historical context, however, the degree of sophistication Shakespeare brings to bear upon the subject is unusual. In order to explain Shakespeare's sense of the role of the other in self-perception, I draw upon the example of Bakhtin's analysis of Dostoyevsky. Bakhtin's chief source for his concept of intersubjectivity is Buber, and it is some question whether Shakespeare, too, might have been inspired by some more abstract thinker. Ulysses in *Troilus and Cressida* claims to derive his ideas from a 'strange fellow', whom he never names, but whose book he enters reading, and critics have put forward various hypotheses about this author's possible identity. Several have suggested Plato's *First Alcibiades*. Others propose Cicero's *Tusculan Disputations*.

I propose here that the most likely real-world model for Ulysses' book is a summary of Aristotle's ethics, the *Magna moralia*, once thought to have been written by Aristotle, but now considered of dubious authenticity. The theory of friendship that Aristotle or pseudo-Aristotle articulates in this treatise strongly resembles the idea of the other as a reflection of the self that appears in *Antony and Cleopatra* when Maecenas describes Antony as Octavian's 'spacious mirror', and that seems likely to have inspired similar descriptions of the other as a 'mirror' or 'glass' in *Julius Caesar* and *Troilus and Cressida*. The friend is 'another self' (*allos autos*). Shakespeare greatly complicates Aristotle's original conceit, however. In brief, Shakespeare grants the other a much greater degree of independent agency in shaping self-perception than Aristotle does in his theory of friendship, even though he articulates the relationship between self and other in similar figurative language.

Near the beginning of Shakespeare's *Julius Caesar*, Cassius asks Brutus an odd question. 'Tell me, good Brutus, can you see your face?' (1.2.51). The question comes across in context as an abrupt non sequitur. Brutus, however, being of a philosophical bent, does not seem taken aback. Instead, he replies in kind; apparently, he is ready at any moment, without blinking, to enter into a Socratic dialogue or (a more likely model) a Ciceronian philosophical disputation. 'No, Cassius; for the eye sees not itself / But by reflection, by some other things' (1.2.52–3). Cassius, expecting just such an answer, seizes on the concession as an opportunity to begin to flatter his interlocutor:

> Tis just,
> And it is very much lamented, Brutus,
> That you have no such mirrors as will turn
> Your hidden worthiness into your eye
> That you might see your shadow[.]
>
> (1.2.54–8)

Suspecting what game is afoot, Brutus asks Cassius to clarify his intent. 'Into what dangers would you lead me, Cassius, / That you would have me seek into myself / For that which is not in me?' (1.2.63–5) Cassius replies.

> Since you know you cannot see yourself
> So well as by reflection, I your glass
> Will modestly discover to yourself
> That of yourself which you yet know not of.
>
> (1.2.67–70)

Cassius, of course, wants to convince Brutus that he is capable of recreating the glorious accomplishment of his ancestor, Lucius Junius Brutus, in driving out Tarquin Superbus, by joining him and the other conspirators in overthrowing Caesar. For present purposes, however, what is notable about the exchange is the emphasis on the necessity of the other in self-perception, mediated through a recurrent metaphor of a mirror or 'glass'. The trope is not uncommon in ancient literature; for example, in their essays on anger, both Plutarch and Seneca cite the benefits of looking in a mirror when angry. 'To see oneself looking so unnatural and all confused,' Plutarch writes, 'is no small step toward the discrediting of this ailment.'[20] As Jean-Pierre Vernant explains,

> In seeing your face in a mirror you know yourself as others know you, face-to-face, in an exchange of glances. Access to the self is gained through an external projection of that self, through being objectified, as if one were another.[21]

A very similar exchange occurs in a slightly later play, Shakespeare's *Troilus and Cressida*, where it receives much more substantial elaboration. Like Cassius with Brutus, Ulysses wants to persuade his interlocutor, Achilles, to return to the field of action, and he begins his work of persuasion with an unusual opening stratagem: a markedly contemplative conversation, abstract and seemingly divorced from any topical concern. He enters reading, as if oblivious to Achilles' presence; earlier, he specifically instructs the other Greeks to ignore Achilles, so as to set the stage. His curiosity piqued, Achilles falls for the trap. 'What are you reading?' (3.3.95) he asks.

ULYSSES   A strange fellow here
           Writes me that man, how dearly ever parted,
           How much in having, or without or in,
           Cannot make boast to have that which he hath,
           Nor feels not what he owes but by reflection;
           As when his virtues shining upon others
           Heat them, and they retort that heat again
           To the first giver.
ACHILLES This is not strange, Ulysses.
           The beauty that is borne here in the face
           The bearer knows not, but commends itself

> To others' eyes; nor doth the eye itself,
> That most pure spirit of sense, behold itself,
> Not going from itself; but eye to eye opposed
> Salutes each other with each other's form;
> For speculation turns not to itself
> Till it hath traveled and is married there
> Where it may see itself. This is not strange at all.

ULYSSES   I do not strain at the position –
> It is familiar – but at the author's drift;
> Who in his circumstances expressly proves
> That no man is the lord of anything –
> Though in and of him there be much consisting –
> Till he communicate his parts to others;
> Nor doth he of himself know them for aught
> Till he behold them formed in th'applause
> Where they're extended; who, like an arch,
> > reverb'rate
> The voice again, or, like a gate of steel
> Fronting the sun, receives and renders back
> His figure and his heat.

> > > (3.3.95–123)

The continuity between this conversation and that of Cassius and Brutus has been widely recognised, and the identity of the 'strange fellow' who seems to be at the heart of it all, the author of the supposed book in Ulysses' hand, has for decades been a subject of much speculation. Inevitably, any source that Shakespeare might have had in mind would post-date Homer; one reason why he does not name the author, then, might be because he recognises that to do so would be to introduce a jarring anachronism. On the other hand, he does not hesitate to have Hector mention Aristotle elsewhere in the play. From another perspective, then, what is striking about this conversation is how up-to-date it seems. If the scene had been written yesterday, rather than several centuries ago, the field of possible candidates for the 'strange fellow' would be crowded with contenders, including among the most prominent Hegel, Sartre and Ricœur, as well as Buber on what he calls the 'I–thou' relationship. The analogy between Shakespeare's theory of the other and Buber's, in particular, is remarkable. I will explore one other such analogue, Bakhtin, in more detail here, before turning back to the question of possible sources.

In 1961 Mikhail Bakhtin wrote up a set of notes, 'Toward a Reworking of the Dostoyevsky Book', which were published post-humously. Bakhtin was strongly influenced by Martin Buber, who himself owed much to Hegel and Heidegger, and presents in these notes what seems to be a summary of his understanding of Buber's central claim that relationships with other people, as well as God, are the most fundamental given of human existence.

> *To be* means *to communicate*. Absolute death (non-being) is the state of being unheard, unrecognized, unremembered . . . To be means to be for another, and through the other, for oneself. A person has no internal sovereign territory, he is wholly and always on the boundary; looking inside himself, he looks *into the eyes of another* or *with the eyes of another*.[22]

As a literary critic, Bakhtin's purpose in evoking this line of thought is to harness it to the claim that Dostoyevsky's greatness consists chiefly in his artistic method, which is not simply to put forward aspects of his own self, a tendency Bakhtin calls 'mono-logism', but instead to allow his characters to take on a life of their own. 'Here, a multiplicity of consciousnesses is opened up': the 'polyphony' that Bakhtin sees as the distinctive feature of the novel at its best. Bakhtin is reacting here against an idea which he encountered in German criticism, that Dostoyevsky 'only projected the landscape of his own soul', or, in other words, that the artist at his craft is essentially a microcosm of Hegel's World-Soul, making his own nature manifest to his own consciousness by making it sep-arate from himself.[23] To draw an analogy to Shakespeare studies, this latter interpretation of Dostoyevsky's art, the one that Bakhtin rejects, closely resembles Coleridge's account of Shakespeare's method. Reacting against Dr Johnson, Coleridge mocks the idea of Shakespeare 'going about the world with his Pocket-book, noting what hears and observes'.[24] Instead, like the spider in Swift's *Battle of the Books*, Shakespeare spins out his characters from his own internal cogitation – or so Coleridge maintains. 'Whatever forms they assumed, they were still Shakespeare.' Coleridge insists that Shakespeare created 'a vast multiplicity of characters' by 'simple meditation': 'he had only to imitate such parts of his character, or to exaggerate such as existed in possibility, and they were at once nature and fragments of Shakespeare.'[25]

Bakhtin would be horrified by such solipsism. In contrast to Coleridge, Bakhtin argues that the great artist does not derive his material from within, but from without, in his openness to the subjectivity of the other. Dostoyevsky's subject is not himself, but instead, 'interaction among consciousnesses', 'the interdependence of consciousnesses'. 'He depicts confession and the confessional consciousnesses of others in order to reveal their internally social structure.' Dostoyevsky in particular, as well as the novel more generally in its 'polyphony', reveals a great truth about human nature. 'I cannot manage without another, I cannot become myself without another; I must find myself in another by finding another in myself (in mutual reflection and mutual acceptance). Justification cannot be *self*-justification, recognition cannot be *self*-recognition.'[26] It is not a stretch to apply Bakhtin's praise for Dostoyevsky and the novel to Shakespeare and the drama. Shakespeare, in fact, explicitly acknowledges the intersubjectivity that Bakhtin describes, whereas Dostoyevsky's awareness of this aspect of human existence remains more implicit.

The question remains, however: how much of Shakespeare's remarkable philosophical prescience is his own, and how much does he owe to other sources?[27] In brief, the first major source to have been proposed for Shakespeare's thought about the role of the other in self-perception is Plato's *First Alcibiades*.[28] The authenticity of the dialogue is now disputed, but in antiquity it was considered an ideal introduction to Plato's thought. As Steven Forde notes,

> The neo-Platonist Iamblichus wrote that the *Alcibiades* I contains the whole philosophy of Plato, as in a seed. The Islamic sage and Platonic commentator Alfarabi concurs, saying in effect that in the *Alcibiades* I all the Platonic questions are raised as if for the first time.[29]

In the *First Alcibiades*, Plato's Socrates presents a very early account of a phenomenon that, two millennia later, proves to fascinate John Donne, as well as Shakespeare. There is 'something of the nature of a mirror in our own eyes': 'the eye looking at another eye . . . will there see itself.'[30] Or, as Shakespeare writes, 'eye to eye opposed / Salutes each other with each other's form' (3.3.108–9). Plato's application of this conceit, however, is very different from

Shakespeare's.³¹ As an alternative to the *First Alcibiades*, T. W. Baldwin suggests Cicero's *Tusculan Disputations*, available in English in John Dolman's 1561 translation, as a possible source and highlights this passage: 'The soule is not able in this bodye to see him self. No more is the eye whyche although he seeth all other thinges, yet (that whiche is one of the leaste) can not discern his owne shape.'³² Cicero's application of the metaphor of the eye, however, is again very different from Shakespeare's. Cicero himself probably has in mind Plato's *First Alcibiades*; as in that dialogue, his larger argument here is that the soul exists and is distinct from the body, even though it cannot be seen.

In the *First Alcibiades*, Socrates draws an analogy. 'If the eye is to see itself, it must look at the eye.' He then refines the position further: to see itself, the eye must not only look at the eye, but 'at that part of the eye in which the virtue of the eye resides', namely, 'sight'. So also self-knowledge depends upon the soul looking at that part of itself 'in which virtue resides', that part of the soul 'which has to do with wisdom and knowledge' and which thus 'resembles the divine'. To fulfil the Delphic precept, 'Know thyself', Alcibiades must ignore his own handsome body, popularity and great wealth, and instead focus on his intellect: that part of himself which is able to access 'wisdom'. In sum, Socrates' aim here is not to convince Alcibiades that his honour, like Achilles', requires other people's confirmation. On the contrary, he urges Alcibiades to ignore 'the Athenian people', lest his 'true self' be 'spoiled and deformed'. As Shadi Bartsch explains,

> the kind of mirroring that takes place here might be designated vertical rather than horizontal: what it shows back to the viewer is the godlike quality of his own soul, rather than any social truth about himself or his visual partner.³³

Strictly speaking, it is possible that Shakespeare had access to the *First Alcibiades* in various contemporary editions of Ficino's Latin translation. More immediately, however, Shakespeare may have encountered the conceit of eyes reflecting other eyes in the work of his English contemporaries. Kenneth Deighton points out a brief parallel in Nashe's *Unfortunate Traveller*: 'the eye that sees round about it selfe, sees not into it selfe.'³⁴ Baldwin draws attention to similar passages in Sir John Davies' *Nosce Teipsum*, both of which echo Cicero fairly closely. 'The minde is like the eye . . . Whose rayes reflect not, but spread outwardly, / Not seeing it selfe, when other things it sees.' And again: 'Mine Eyes . . . Looke not into this litle world of mine, / Nor see my face, wherein they fixed are.'[35] The introduction of the 'face' here lends plausibility to the idea that these passages may have inspired Cassius' introductory question, 'Can you see your face?' Nevertheless, much is missing, in particular Shakespeare's emphasis in both conversations on the metaphor of 'reflection'.

In the Library chapter of James Joyce's *Ulysses*, John Eglinton, proud of his learning, complains of Shakespeare that 'he puts Bohemia on the sea-coast and makes Ulysses quote Aristotle'.[36] The first charge is obviously correct, but what about the second? In their studies of allusions in *Ulysses*, Weldon Thornton and Don Gifford both see Eglinton as simply mistaken.[37] In *Troilus and Cressida*, it is Hector, not Ulysses, who name-drops Aristotle. Debating whether or not to return Helen to the Greeks, Hector accuses Paris and Troilus of speaking 'not much / Unlike young men, whom Aristotle thought / Unfit to hear moral philosophy' (2.2.167–8). The reference is to the beginning of Aristotle's *Nicomachean Ethics*, where in discussing his method Aristotle emphasises the importance of empirical evidence, rather the more abstract 'demonstrative proofs' typical of Plato. 'A young man is not a proper hearer of lectures on political science; for he is inexperienced in the actions that occur in life . . . and further, since he tends to follow his passions.'[38] The reference is not isolated, although it is more explicit than usual; W. R. Elton identifies a number of other debates, as well, in *Troilus and Cressida* derived from ideas about virtue presented in Aristotle's *Nicomachean Ethics*.[39]

Joyce, or Joyce's Eglinton, may well be right, however, if not perhaps in the sense that he intended. Shakespeare's Ulysses does, in fact, 'quote Aristotle'; or at least, pseudo-Aristotle. Shakespeare's chief source for his understanding of the role of the other in self-perception seems to be Aristotle's concept of friendship, as mediated in particular by an arresting description of the friend as a 'mirror', needful even for the 'self-sufficing man', in the *Magna moralia*. 'The way of thinking about self-knowledge expressed in these Aristotelian passages', Christopher Gill observes, 'is in sharp contrast to the idea, central to the Cartesian tradition in modern thought, that consciousness or knowledge of oneself is primary and fundamental to other kinds of awareness.'[40] Within Shakespeare studies, the key passage comparing the friend to a mirror has been overlooked as a possible source for *Troilus and Cressida*, most likely because it appears in a treatise whose authorship is now disputed, and which has largely dropped out of the standard Aristotelian canon.[41] In classics, however, the metaphor has sparked renewed interest, figuring as a touchstone in work by Martha Nussbaum and Shadi Bartsch on conceptions of selfhood in antiquity. For Nussbaum, this section of this treatise, which she sees as authentically Aristotelian, presents 'the clearest version' of 'Aristotle's argument' that 'one further benefit of friendly love' is 'the increase in self-knowledge and self-perception that comes of seeing and intuitively responding to a person about whom you care'.[42]

The *Magna moralia* is relatively short, despite its name; scholarly opinion remains divided whether it is Aristotle's own early draft of the more complex thought that appears in his *Nicomachean* and *Eudemian Ethics* or a simplified epitome put together by a later author. For brevity's sake, I will simply refer to its author as 'Aristotle'; 'Aristotle' is who Shakespeare, if he did read the work, most likely would have thought its author to be. The most relevant passage runs as follows:

> As then when we wish to see our own face, we do so by looking into the mirror, in the same way when we wish to know ourselves we can obtain that knowledge by looking at our friend. For the friend is, as we assert, a second self.

The context of the passage is an inquiry about the ability of human beings to be self-sufficient, in the manner of Aristotle's God: 'for if God is self-sufficing and has need of none, it does not follow that we shall need no one.'[43] To be self-sufficient is portrayed as an ideal state, one which the idealised 'self-sufficing man', like the Stoic *sapiens*, can to some degree approximate. Even he, however, cannot do without friendship. 'If, then, it is pleasant to know oneself, and it is not possible to know this without having someone else for a friend, the self-sufficing man will require friendship in order to know himself.'[44]

Several details suggest that this passage is the primary source behind Ulysses' 'strange fellow', as well as Cassius' proffering himself as Brutus' 'glass'. Plato's observations about the eye in the *First Alcibiades* are not irrelevant; Shakespeare may well have been

aware of the conceit through one indirect route or another, perhaps by way of Cicero, perhaps by way of Sir John Davies, and he
does seem to press it into service here. The argument which he uses
it to illustrate, however, is not Plato's, but instead, a variation on
Aristotle's theory of friendship. First, the context: Ulysses is trying
to convince Achilles that he cannot be self-sufficient, specifically,
that his pride cannot sustain itself, but instead depends upon the
approbation of other people. Similarly here, Aristotle introduces
the necessity of friendship for self-knowledge as a limit upon what
he calls the 'self-sufficing man'. Second, the conceit: the emphasis
throughout both of the passages from Shakespeare's plays, both
the one in *Julius Caesar*, and the one in *Troilus and Cressida*, on
'mirrors' and 'reflection', ranging from Cassius as Brutus' 'glass'
to Ulysses' later and more artful variations on this theme: an 'arch'
that returns the echo of a 'voice'; a 'gate of steel' that reflects both
the 'heat' and 'figure' of the 'sun'. Third and last, Cassius' description of himself as an idealised friend: a like-minded member of the
aristocratic elite. 'Be not jealous on me, gentle Brutus' (1.2.71),
Cassius asks.

> Were I a common laughter, or did use
> To stale with ordinary oaths my love
> To every new protestor; if you know
> That I do fawn on men, and hug them hard,
> And after scandal them; or if you know
> That I profess myself in banqueting
> To all the rout, then hold me dangerous.
>
> (1.2.72–8)

This emphasis on one singular, virtuous friend, separate from
the crowd, is very much in the spirit of Aristotle. In the *Magna
moralia*, the friend is only a 'second self' if he is 'very great': 'as
the saying has it, "Here is another Hercules, a dear other self."'
In the *Nicomachean Ethics*, Aristotle says bluntly, 'such men
are rare'. Moreover, 'such friendship requires time and familiarity'. It is only this kind of friendship, however, 'the friendship of
the good', which is 'proof against slander'.[45] That such a friend
would be compared to a mirror makes more sense, perhaps, if
we remember that mirrors were once a luxury good. As Shadi
Bartsch observes:

we moderns tend to take mirrors for granted: a cheap one can be bought for a few cents at any drugstore, and they surround us in our lives from the first bathroom stumbles of the morning. The ancient mirror, by contrast, was an object of comparative rarity and considerable expense.[46]

Shakespeare does not simply rest upon what he receives from Aristotle, however. Instead, he gradually revises Aristotle's theory of the role of the other in self-perception, so that it comes to represent his own, rather different social reality instead. Aristotle's sympathies are aristocratic; his social circle, like Plato's, was *hoi kaloikagathoi* ('the beautiful and the good'): the upper-class men of Athens. The opinion of the *dēmos*, the people at large, was held in relative contempt. The milieu was overwhelmingly homosocial. Wealthy, educated men's primary emotional relationships were, for the most part, with each other, often shading over into homosexual romance. Aristotle's idea of the friend as a 'second self' shares, as a result, many of the qualities that people today might more typically look for in a marriage or other romantic partnership.

Shakespeare, by contrast, was a petit bourgeois, a man from the provinces who came to London to seek his fortune. His world was primarily that of the theatre, and the theatre as marketplace, a freewheeling, entrepreneurial endeavour. For Shakespeare, the sturdy support of a single male friend, like Antonio in *The Merchant of Venice* or Antonio in *Twelfth Night*, is a great boon; akin, one might say, to securing a patron. These characters' relationships with Bassanio and Sebastian, respectively, are portrayed sympathetically, and prove occasions for admirable self-sacrifice. For all their inherent nobility, however, such friendships also prove, in the end, doomed and inadequate. Shakespeare rose to prominence hard-pressed by other concerns, as well: those of the hustling, cash-poor capitalist. In such circumstances, the esteem of one friend is not really enough.

'What's aught but as 'tis valued?' (2.2.53) Shakespeare's Troilus asks, speaking of Helen. As a professional playwright, Shakespeare lived under pressure of much the same question, one with immediate, economic force. For him, unlike Aristotle, the other that determines the 'value' of the self is not one but many, not a 'second self' but *hoi polloi*: the people out there paying to see his plays. As Lars Engle points out,

Shakespeare's theatre, itself subject to varied contemporary evaluations and occasionally threatened with closure by the more
adverse of them, produced plays for money; the plays so produced
were subjected to immediate valuation from audiences; through
them actors strove to please.

As I discussed in the introduction to this chapter, in *Coriolanus*,
especially, Shakespeare uses 'the marketplace' as a metaphor for the
social component of self-esteem regulation. Here, I want to focus
instead on a related metaphor, that of the theatre. Shakespeare lays
the groundwork for this underlying conceit in *Julius Caesar* and
Troilus and Cressida, and it comes to a head in the play that is
the subject of this chapter in particular, *Antony and Cleopatra*. As
Engle observes, 'the contingency of evaluation served as a recurrent
enabling irritant for Shakespeare's creativity. Problems of worth,
price, and value everywhere vex his texts.'[47]

In *Julius Caesar*, Cassius invokes the classical topos of the single, privileged male friend. At the same time, however, he is careful to suggest that he is only one of many. He speaks not just of
himself as Brutus' 'glass', but also of 'mirrors', plural, and 'eyes',
plural. 'Many of the best respect in Rome' (1.2.59), he says, 'have
wished that noble Brutus had his eyes' (1.2.62). He has the conspirators scatter anonymous letters to Brutus, so that it seems as
if an eager audience, the Roman people, is already in place, wait-
ing only for Brutus to act in order to bestow their plaudits. Most
telling, however, is a conversation between Cassius and Brutus,
immediately after they assassinate Caesar.

> CASSIUS   How many ages hence
>   Shall this our lofty scene be acted over
>   In states unborn and accents yet unknown?
> BRUTUS   How many times shall Caesar bleed in sport
>   That now on Pompey's basis lies along,
>   No worthier than the dust?
> CASSIUS   So oft as that shall be,
>   So often shall the knot of us be called
>   The men who gave their country liberty.
>   (3.1.111–18)

No such conversation occurs in Plutarch; it is a Shakespearean
interpolation, of a kind that will return again at more length in
Antony and Cleopatra. It is also deeply anachronistic.

For Roman *optimates* such as the historical Brutus and Cassius, keenly conscious of their aristocratic status, to be associated with the theatre would have been a cause for concern, not celebration. Mark Antony's great love of the theatre, for example, like the Emperor Nero's later on, was seen among the senatorial class as scandalous, especially among those more mindful of traditional class distinctions.[48] Conservative statesmen such as Brutus and Cassius did not aim to be represented on stage. In *Antony and Cleopatra*, a later play, Shakespeare corrects the lapse in his own historicism; Cleopatra is plausibly horrified at the thought of being imitated before the public eye. What we see here, by contrast, in *Julius Caesar*, in addition to some rich irony, is Shakespeare's own concept of success, success as a playwright, bleeding over into his characterisation of these ancient figures. He makes sense of the conspirators' desire for lasting glory as liberators of Rome by comparing it to his own desire for immortality as an author. The same kind of shading over into his own experience occurs in *Troilus and Cressida*, as well, when Ulysses speaks of 'applause'. The 'arch', reverberating with the sound of speech, which Shakespeare substitutes there for Aristotle's 'mirror' is an allusion to another echoing, circular space: the 'wooden O' of the theatre.

Not every play meets with 'applause', however. As Brutus and Cassius soon discover, their 'lofty scene' does not prove the smash hit they had expected it to be. Shakespeare's keen awareness of his own dependence as a playwright on the approval of his audience seems the most likely basis for the most radical revision that he makes to the understanding of the role of the other in self-perception that he found in his primary source, Aristotle's theory of friendship. For Aristotle, the friend who serves as the 'second self' is chiefly an object of contemplation, rather than himself a thinking subject. He is not a physician, giving a diagnosis; that kind of evaluation is reserved for the self alone. Instead, he is more like a portrait of the self, 'warts and all', in which one's moral failings can be discerned at one remove. 'We are not able to see what we are from ourselves,' Aristotle says.

> That we cannot do so is plain from the way in which we blame others without being aware that we do the same things ourselves; and this is the effect of favor or passion, and there are many of us who are blinded by these things so that we judge not aright.[49]

Cicero makes much the same point in *De officiis*: 'Somehow it is the case that we can detect failings better in others than in ourselves. Consequently a very easy way for pupils to be corrected is if their teachers imitate their faults in order to remove them.'⁵⁰

For Aristotle, a 'second self' is valuable, because it allows the self to see itself as if it were disinterested. What that second self thinks of the self, the other's opinion of the self, is not really important. Shakespeare includes an example of this kind of 'mirror' in *Antony and Cleopatra*, when Caesar receives the news that Antony is dead and begins to weep. 'Caesar is touched' (5.1.33), Agrippa observes. Maecenas replies: 'When such a spacious mirror's set before him, / He needs must see himself' (5.1.34–5). In this moment of apparent grief, Caesar invokes Aristotle's concept of the single, extraordinary friend, 'another Hercules', describing Antony in death as 'my brother, my competitor / In top of all design, my mate in empire, / Friend and companion' (5.1.42–4). The comparison flatters the speaker, however, as well as its subject; by praising Antony in these terms, Octavian moves to appropriate his dead rival's residual grandeur for himself.

For Shakespeare, the other is not merely an object, however, like a statue or in Antony's case, a dead body, but an independent subjectivity. The other judges the self, and that judgement has weight. This independence of the other, a freedom either to approve or disapprove of the self, is, in fact, his or her most important quality. Whether or not the other resembles the self in external, objective respects such as social status, wealth or gender is not nearly as important to Shakespeare as it is to Aristotle (or Octavian). Instead, what matters is the other's internal, subjective opinion of the self. This new emphasis on the other as a thinking subject is the reason why Shakespeare complicates Aristotle's relatively simple image of a mirror by introducing an additional, much more complex simile, the self and the other as two eyes reflecting each other: a conceit that he borrows, perhaps, from Plato. Shakespeare wants to stress the idea that the other is not merely an object, like a 'glass', but instead itself sentient, itself a locus of consciousness. The self looks at the other, and the other, of equal dignity, also looks back: 'eye to eye opposed / Salutes each other with each other's form' (3.3.108–9).

In the conversations about intersubjective 'reflection' in *Julius Caesar* and *Troilus and Cressida*, Shakespeare's primary point seems to be that the self requires the approval of the other in order to sustain its own positive self-image. He points out, in other words, the fatal flaw in narcissism. Narcissus starving beside his own reflection is a symbol of the inability of the proud to sustain their pride without Echo, that is, without other people.[51] In *Troilus and Cressida*, Agamemnon complains about Achilles' arrogance in terms that evoke, not only Narcissus, but also Shakespeare's Roman paragon of pride, Coriolanus. 'He that is proud eats up himself. Pride is his own glass, his own trumpet, his own chronicle; and whatever praises itself but in the deed, devours the deed in the praise' (2.3.156–8). The last conceit here is much compressed, and may therefore be obscure; what Agamemnon means is that whoever praises himself in any way other than doing the deed itself for which he would be praised, forestalls whatever praise would have otherwise accrued to him for that deed.

Agamemnon's basic premise, that pride leads to a kind of emotional starvation, appears again as a central motif in *Coriolanus*. As Volumnia says, indignant, 'Anger's my meat: I sup upon myself / And so shall starve with feeding' (4.2.50–1). Bakhtin describes such narcissism as '*proud solitude*': the attempt 'to do without recognition, without others'. This would-be escape from the other, which he sees as the essence of pride, Bakhtin also sees as profoundly impossible. The proud man cannot heal his wounded honour in isolation, because, Bakhtin explains, 'no human events are developed or resolved within the bounds of single consciousness'. 'A single consciousness is *contradiction in adjecto*. Consciousness is in essence multiple. *Pluralia tantum*.' Like Shakespeare, as opposed to Aristotle, Bakhtin insists that the other is not simply an object of perception, but instead itself an independent, thinking subject, collaborating in the very act of perception itself, even as it is being perceived. 'Not another *person* remaining the object of my consciousness, but another autonomous consciousness standing alongside mine, and my own consciousness can only exist in relation to it.'[52]

In *Antony and Cleopatra*, Shakespeare takes the idea that the other is a thinking subject, rather than an object, still one step further. The other is not merely a necessary sounding-board or reflective device, required to sustain a positive self-image. The other is also active, possessed of agency. It need not simply accept whatever self-representation the self puts forward, like wax taking on the impress of a seal. Instead, the other can reject that image and put forward an alternative, a representation of the self that might well be less than flattering. The self, now on the receiving end, is then obliged somehow to metabolise that bitter medicine. Just as the other is surprisingly active, so also the self can be surprisingly passive. The self can be acted-upon, can have its self-image forced into a different shape, whether it wants to accept that revision or not. In a lucid moment early on, Antony presents this process in a surprisingly positive light, as akin to plowing a field or 'earing': a pun on 'hearing'. 'Oh, then we bring forth weeds / When our quick minds lie still, and our ills told us / Is as our earing' (1.2.115–17). Without feedback from others regarding our 'faults', Antony suggests, we are prone to fall prey to delusions about ourselves: 'weeds'. 'Speak to me home,' he says. 'Mince not the general tongue' (1.2.111).

What if the self, however, does not have such 'ears to hear' (Ezek. 12:2; Matt. 11:15, 13:9, 13:43; Mark 4:9, 4:23, 7:16; Luke 8:8, 14:35)? We are not immediately or entirely obliged to change our understanding of ourselves, in response to external feedback; we can deny the validity of criticism, repress our awareness of it, or project it onto someone else; perhaps even the accuser. For other people to be able to introduce humbling changes in our self-perception, the kind of reality check Antony calls 'earing', either we ourselves must be receptive to that change, or the other must be sufficiently powerful, somehow, to be able to overcome our psychological defences: mechanisms such as denial, repression and projection, supported by a combination of intelligence, confidence and charisma. That power of the other over the self can come about through a single, unusually strong cathexis, such as that of Coriolanus with Volumnia or Antony with Cleopatra. It can also be a function of sheer, stupefying number, however, as, for instance, when the other is not a single person, but an entire populace: a massive, hostile crowd lining the streets of Rome. Hence the significance of the Roman triumph in Shakespeare's thought: the triumph is a species of involuntary theatre, the scenario in which the power of the other over the self, a power to revise the self's proffered version of itself, is most keenly evident. To be led in triumph is public exposure of powerlessness at its most extreme: an exaggerated, clear-cut version of life's many other, less overwhelming occasions for embarrassment.

'*I would not see't*': Suicide as Audience Management

In the previous section, I set out Shakespeare's understanding of the relation between self and other in some detail. What are the limits of our ability to deceive ourselves, in the interests of preserving an internal sense of control? Through the power of the imagination, the grandiose self can often persevere, at least temporarily, as if sceptical, nay-saying critics were powerless, or did not exist, and could not therefore redefine its self-image, through their power of 'reflection', as less than ideal. This construction of a separate world 'as if' requires the cooperation, however, of an enabling, sympathetic other such as Achilles' Patroclus or Antony's Cleopatra. The actor cannot buy into his own 'supreme Fiction' without a willing audience. In this section, I explain more fully how the idea of the other as a 'mirror' or 'glass' that appears at the beginning of *Julius Caesar*, as well as Brutus' horror in the end at the thought of being led in triumph, becomes in Shakespeare's later Roman play, *Antony and Cleopatra*, a much more complex investigation of the ability of the other to impose moral judgment on the self, a process that I call 'interpellation', albeit in a different sense than Althusser. Human beings are not only passible physically and emotionally, but also ethically. That is to say, we are vulnerable to being shamed, despite our ability to retreat into a separate, more subjective space of imaginative freedom, the interior world Katharine Maus describes as 'inwardness.' The objective world can intrude upon that idyll in the form of the other, even given the surprising strength of psychological defences such as denial and dissociation.

In this section, I focus on the motives behind the cultural practice Cleopatra calls 'the high Roman fashion'. The simplest explanation for Roman suicide is that it is a way to turn defeat into a kind of victory. Apparent powerlessness becomes instead an opportunity for a spectacular display of agency. Once Antony dies, Cleopatra the sybarite turns against materiality itself, for example, in terms that recall Hamlet, as well as Duke Vincentio in *Measure for Measure*. Now that she is no longer in command, life as a passible human being, embedded in the 'grotesque' material world, seems to her to be subject to innumerable indignities. Suicide, by contrast, seems to offer the subjective restoration of her former sense of omnipotence. Above all, what Antony and Cleopatra both alike hope to escape by committing suicide is the possibility of being exposed to moral judgement. To be led in triumph through Rome, or to see themselves mocked on stage represents for them an intolerable instance of the process that I call 'interpellation', in which the other forces the self to revise its own self-image, despite its efforts to resist that alteration. Caesar would extend his victory from the objective world of fact inwards, into the subjective realm of self-perception.

In order to forestall this possibility, both Antony and Cleopatra turn to the expedient of suicide. As long as they do not let themselves see themselves being seen by others as defeated, they believe they can preserve their sense of themselves as finally victorious. Suicide forestalls being exposed to the critics that they know they will encounter, if they are ever taken alive to Rome. Instead, the two lovers carefully limit their audience to people whom they trust to see them as they wish to be seen. This tactic of limiting exposure to shame by recourse to what I will call here 'audience management', as opposed to 'event management', also appears in Seneca's advice to aspiring Stoic philosophers. Like Roman suicide, Roman 'philosophy' such as Brutus' is a performance for a sympathetic coterie. Cleopatra's performance of her own death, as if she were again arriving to meet Antony on the banks of the river Cydnus, illuminates this theatrical quality of Senecan Stoicism. The histrionic nature of the quintessential 'noble Roman', Brutus, appears in a more obvious, exaggerated form as the efforts of an Egyptian queen to preserve her sense of herself as akin to a goddess, Venus. Both characters want to see themselves as exemplars of glamorous autonomy: the liberty of the Roman patrician; or, in Cleopatra's case, the licence, luxury and imperious autocracy of the Eastern potentate. They can identify with these godlike ideal selves, however, if and only if they can persuade their audience that these personae are in fact who they really are.

For Shakespeare's Romans, the simplest and most immediate reason for committing suicide is to thwart an opponent. By robbing an enemy of something he desires, even if only the opportunity to gloat, the defeated protagonist demonstrates a final, contrarian agency. For instance, Plutarch reports that when Julius Caesar heard of Cato's suicide, he saw it as a blow to his glory, since it robbed him of a chance to appear magnanimous. 'O Cato, I begrudge thee thy death; for thou didst begrudge me the sparing of thy life.'[53] From this reply, St Augustine concludes that Cato's suicide, rightly understood, was an act of envy. Cato 'envied' Caesar 'the glory of pardoning him (as indeed Caesar himself is reported to have said); or if envy is too strong a word, let us say he was ashamed that this glory should be his.'[54] When Shakespeare's Cleopatra tries to kill herself, her Roman guard Proculeius protests, 'Cleopatra, / Do not abuse my master's bounty by / Th'undoing of yourself' (5.2.41–3). So also in Daniel's version, Proculeius laments:

> Ah *Cleopatra*, why shouldst thou, (said I)
> Both injurie thy selfe and *Caesar* so?
> Barre him the honour of his victorie,
> Who ever deales most mildly with his foe?
>
> (303–6)

Suicide is a kind of sabotage, like that committed by a kamikaze pilot. It prevents the antagonist from being able to display his otherwise-superior power, and that outcome is seen as desirable, at whatever cost; even if that power might have been used to pardon. ''Tis sweet to die when we are forced to live' (74), says Daniel's Cleopatra. In Shakespeare's version, Proculeius, trying to calm Cleopatra, seems not to realise that he is only exacerbating her frenzy to escape. 'Let the world see / His nobleness well acted, which your death / Will never let come forth' (5.2.43–5). To act 'his nobleness', not her own: that is what Cleopatra refuses to accept, no matter how comfortable the terms. She sets up an alternative performance of our own, one that she herself can choreograph, precisely to replace and prevent the one that Caesar has in mind.

Above all, suicide forestalls the possibility of being led in triumph. Antony takes satisfaction in the fact that 'Not Caesar's valor hath o'erthrown Antony, / But Antony's hath triumphed on itself' (4.15.15–16). When Antony asks Eros to kill him, he reassures him, 'Thou strik'st not me; 'tis Caesar thou defeat'st' (4.14.69). Likewise, Cleopatra maintains, Antony's wife, Octavia, 'with her modest eyes, / And still conclusion, shall acquire no honour / Demuring upon me': 'If knife, drugs, serpents, have / Edge, sting, or operation, I am safe' (4.15.26–30). A more thorough explanation of these characters' suicide would require some investigation, however, of the extraordinary distress that they feel at the thought of being led in triumph. The ground of such an explanation, I propose, is a feature of human existence that these characters instinctively discern and fear: the power of the other to interpellate the self.

The concept of interpellation is associated with Althusser, who uses it to explain what he sees as the relationship between 'ideology' and the individual:

> Ideology 'acts' or 'functions' in such a way that it 'recruits' subjects among the individuals (it recruits them all), or 'transforms' the individuals into subjects (it transforms them all) by that very precise operation which I have called *interpellation* or hailing, and which can be imagined along the lines of the most commonplace everyday police (or other) hailing: 'Hey, you there!'[55]

The metaphor is familiar, and for that reason useful here, although it makes more sense in this case to assign it a different tenor. What Althusser imagines an impersonal force, 'ideology', doing to individuals, Shakespeare sees individuals incessantly doing to each other. Each individual consciousness is at once active and passive, interpellating others and being interpellated in turn, like eyes reflecting other eyes. Such interpellation can be resisted, but not entirely. In the perpetual negotiation with the other over self-perception that I have described, at times a peaceful collaboration, but at other times a violent conflict, a triumph is the nuclear option, penetrating even the most hardened, wilfully solipsistic, self-enclosed self-consciousness. Only one escape seems to remain: pre-emptive suicide.

The relationship between triumph and suicide Shakespeare explores in *Antony and Cleopatra* elaborates upon a germinal version of the connection that he found in Daniel's *Cleopatra*. There, in her opening monologue, Cleopatra spends some time reflecting on the particular horror of being 'seene' as powerless, and its incompatibility with her own understanding of her 'selfe':

> Thinke *Caesar*, I that liv'd and raign'd a Queene
> Doe scorne to buy my life at such a rate,
> That I should underneath my selfe be seene,
> Basely induring to survive my state:
> That Rome should see my scepter-bearing hands
> Behind me bound, and glory in my teares,
> That I should passe whereas *Octavia* stands,
> To view my miserie that purchas'd hers.
>
> (63–70)

Shakespeare's Cleopatra replies to Proculeius:

> Know, sir, that I
> Will not wait pinioned at your master's court,
> Nor once be chastis'd with the sober eye
> Of dull Octavia. Shall they hoist me up
> And show me to the shouting varletry
> Of censuring Rome? Rather a ditch in Egypt
> Be gentle grave unto me!
>
> (5.2.51–7)

The images here of being pinioned and hoisted aptly convey the powerlessness, the sense of being transformed into object, which Cleopatra hopes to escape. As before, she emphasises the gaze: Octavia's 'sober eye' seconds the image of her 'modest eye', earlier, in Cleopatra's conversation with Antony. Cleopatra's stated preference to stay in Egypt, under whatever circumstances, further clarifies the nature of her distress. It is not simply public exposure that is the problem, but the attitude of that public, hostile or friendly. 'Rather make / My country's high pyramids my gibbet / And hang me up in chains!' (5.2.59–61). If she must perforce undergo some sort of public humiliation, Cleopatra would rather that it happen in Egypt, because she believes that she will find there a more sympathetic audience. The Egyptian peasants would be respectful, deferential, or so she seems to imagine, not 'shouting' or 'censuring' as they would be in Rome.

In more general terms, however, Cleopatra is no great admirer of the working class. She associates them with being acted upon, that is, the state of passibility matter itself represents. *Antony and Cleopatra* opens with Antony denouncing 'kingdoms' as 'clay' and the 'earth' as 'dungy', feeding alike both 'beast and man' (1.1.36–7). 'The nobleness of life', he proclaims, is in contrast 'to do thus' (1.1.37–8), presumably, embracing or kissing Cleopatra. What is 'noble' is to escape from the restrictions upon the self that matter imposes into an alternative, mutually sustained fantasy world of infinite, godlike splendor: 'new heaven, new earth.' Antony dead, Cleopatra finds herself brought back down, however, to 'this dull world', which she now sees as 'no better than a sty' (4.15.63–4): 'the dung', she calls it, which is both 'the beggar's nurse and Caesar's' (5.2.7–8). Cleopatra is often interpreted as a voluptuary, and for most the play she is. What we see here, however, is a reversal of that perspective: a marked disdain for matter, once it is no longer under her control.

Cleopatra's retreat from materiality appears later, as well, in a conversation with her chambermaid Iras, as they discuss Dolabella's report that Caesar intends to send them to Rome. 'Now, Iras, what think'st thou?' (5.2.206) she asks:

> Thou an Egyptian puppet shall be shown
> In Rome as well as I. Mechanic slaves
> With greasy aprons, rules and hammers shall
> Uplift us to the view.
>
> (5.2.207–10)

'Puppet' here recalls 'pinioned', earlier, and 'uplift', 'hoist'; the point is that Cleopatra and Iras will no longer be autonomous centres of agency, but instead acted upon from without, like blocks of wood – or like victims of a crucifixion. 'Slaves' reinforces the idea of a loss of 'liberty'. 'Rules and hammers' echoes Antony's vow to Octavia, just after their marriage: 'I have not kept my square, but that to come / Shall all be done by th' rule' (2.3.6–7). Cleopatra's reference to such 'mechanic' tools, 'rules and hammers', in so far as it recalls Antony's 'rule' and 'square', reveals her fear of being subjected to either form of constraint, the moral ('patience', 'temperance') as well as the material ('pinioned').

The other underlying strain in Cleopatra's portrait of the Roman people is disgust at the basic fact of human embodiment. The description of the plebeians' aprons as 'greasy', for example, recalls her earlier description of the entire 'world' as a 'sty'. Cleopatra continues, to Iras' horror: 'In their thick breaths, / Rank of gross diet, shall we be enclouded / And forced to drink their vapour' (5.2.210–12). Cleopatra's disdain for people of Rome, forced, as she sees them, by their poverty to do 'mechanic' labour, their breath 'thick' with the stink of 'gross diet', is itself inspired by a reaction against the nature of matter itself as acted upon, rather than agent. As imprisonment, like old age, can make all too painfully clear, the body itself is a curb upon the autonomy of the will, more often than it is its uncomplaining instrument.

Cleopatra's desire to escape the 'dung' of 'this dull world', once it is no longer hers to command, a disgust that she projects on to symbols of embodiment, is not far afield from Hamlet's wish that his 'flesh' would 'melt, / Thaw and resolve itself into a dew'

(1.2.129–30). Hamlet is not simply or solely Puritanical here; his revulsion at the flesh is the obverse of his desire to escape from what he sees as a kind of prison. The Neoplatonic, Gnostic fantasy of becoming pure soul, bodiless, is misunderstood if conceived of as mere priggery. *In extremis*, a desire to escape being 'flesh and blood' can also be interpreted as a manifestation of the aristocrat's characteristic desire for liberty at whatever price, even death: the characteristic effort of the 'noble Roman' to transcend passibility itself.

The climax of Cleopatra's speech on the horrifying indignities that await her and Iras in Rome is the prospect of being mocked on stage.

> The quick comedians
> Extemporally will stage us and present
> Our Alexandrian revels; Antony
> Will be brought drunken forth; and I shall see
> Some squeaking Cleopatra boy my greatness
> I'th' posture of a whore.
>
> (5.2.215–20)

'Extemporally': the 'quick' comedians now, not Cleopatra, will be the ones with the power to be spontaneous, to act upon a whim, independent of that 'time' (*ex tempore*) that I have described already as her enemy. Not only that, but worse, they will redefine as low, mundane and reprehensible ('drunken', 'squeaking', 'whore') those moments, 'our Alexandrian revels', which for Cleopatra were the height of her 'greatness': Antony at her beck and call, amid all the riches of Egypt. Finally, worst of all, Cleopatra will be forced to 'see' all this herself; she will be among the audience. Iras, in response, proposes a solution. 'I'll never see't, for I am sure my nails / Are stronger than mine eyes!' (5.2.222–3). The suggestion is characteristic of Cleopatra and her court. Iras' proposal to blind herself echoes Cleopatra's threat to 'spurn' the 'eyes' of the messenger who brings her news of Antony's marriage; physical mutilation is a physical analogue of Cleopatra's wilful, self-imposed blindness throughout to the limits on her own power, as well as Antony's. Her and her chambermaids' response to a loss of power is, in general, denial. If the relational process of self-perception starts to tip towards a loss of prestige, they opt out; metaphorically speaking, they rip out their own eyes, like Oedipus.

Understood as a means to an end, suicide is not inconsistent with Cleopatra's character, a sudden outbreak of unwonted Roman Stoicism, but instead the culmination of a lifelong tendency towards wilful obliviousness. Hence the subtitle of this section: 'Suicide as Audience Management'. In this play, one way of dealing with humiliation, the Roman way, is what I would call 'event management': to strive to change the external world, so that that humiliation dissipates. The quintessential Roman, once checked or slighted in some way, becomes aggressive, like Coriolanus. Taking up arms, he aims to acquire compensatory power 'out there', outside his own imagination, as Octavian does, for example, in his relentless rivalry with the other triumvirs. Another way of dealing with humiliation, however, the Egyptian way, is what I would call 'audience management': to limit exposure to the other to a carefully selected, sympathetic audience, so that the humiliation in question can be successfully denied. As I proposed earlier, Rome in this play represents the objective expression of *libido dominandi*, whereas Egypt represents its inward involution. That turn to the subjective cannot be accomplished in isolation, however. It requires collaboration, like that which can be found in a romantic relationship.

The other can conceivably serve as a catalyst for the recognition of the truth. But exposure to the other can also be finessed. Contrarian voices can be suborned; pressed into the service of some pleasing falsehood. Intransigent naysayers can be dismissed. Yes-men can be promoted. This kind of cultivation of a coterie audience is not alien to Roman Stoicism, but in fact deeply woven into its working structure. Considered as an abstraction, the Stoic wise man should, of course, be indifferent to the opinion of others. In practice, however, Stoicism, like Cleopatra's suicide, is a performance for an elite audience, a small group of fellow sages who are 'in the know'. A. D. Nuttall sees in Shakespeare's Brutus 'a conscious Stoic', performing 'an aggregate of intellectual and social postures'.[56] His behaviour is theatrical, performative, like that of Richard II; he is trying to convince an audience, and thereby, indirectly, himself, that he really is what in fact he is only pretending to be.

For whom, exactly, is Brutus performing? Who is the Stoic's audience? In his *Letters*, Seneca urges Lucilius not to seek approval from the masses, like too many of the other self-proclaimed 'philosophers' of his time. 'Hucksters', he calls them (*circulatores*, lit. 'mountebanks, travelling showmen'). 'For what is baser than philosophy courting applause?' 'Scorn the pleasure which comes from the applause of the majority.' Seneca recognises, however, that the strenuous effort involved in the actual practice of Stoicism, especially early on, cannot be sustained without some sort of audience, whose approval the Stoic hopes to win. 'While it is not yet safe to withdraw into solitude, seek out certain individuals; for everyone is better off in the company of someone or other – no matter whom – than in his own company alone.' Better anyone than no one: 'I am content only if you act, in whatever you do, as you would act if anyone at all were looking on, because solitude prompts us to all kinds of evil.' Seneca would prefer, however, that Lucilius associate with 'good men'. 'Nothing is more successful in bringing honourable influences to bear upon the mind or in straightening out the wavering spirit that is prone to evil than association with good men.'[57]

Seneca advises Lucilius, the would-be Stoic, to seek approval for his actions from what could be described as an audience of ever-increasing interiority.[58] 'Withdraw into yourself as far as you can. Associate with those who will make a better man of you.' He urges Lucilius to retreat from the population at large to the confines of a small coterie; even to the tutelage of a single mentor. 'We should . . . have a guardian to pluck us continually by the ear and dispel rumors and protest against popular enthusiasms.' It is 'indispensable', he says, 'that we have some advocate with upright mind and, amid all the uproar and jangle of falsehood, hear one voice only' (94.59). Ideally, Lucilius would live among the philosophers themselves that he admires and attempt to win their approval by imitating their day-to-day life. 'The living voice and intimacy of a common life will help you more than the written word.'[59]

Seneca then imagines Lucilius' reply. '"Whom," you say, "shall I call upon? Shall it be this man or that?" There is another choice also open to you; you may go to the ancients; for they have the time to help you. We can get assistance not only from the living, but also from those of the past.' If the Stoic tyro cannot find wise men among the living, then he should imagine that he is performing for some great man from the past. 'Choose a master whose life, conversation and soul-expressing face have satisfied you; picture

him always to yourself as your protector or your pattern.' 'Choose
... Cato, or if Cato seems too severe, choose some Laelius, a gen-
tler spirit.' 'Set as a guard over yourself the authority of some man,
whether your choice be the great Cato, or Scipio, or Laelius.'[60] For
Shakespeare's Brutus, this watchful model seems to be chiefly his
ancestor Lucius Junius Brutus. Cassius tells Cinna, for example, to
be sure to post a letter urging Brutus to oppose Caesar 'upon old
Brutus' statue' (1.3.146).

For Seneca, which master, exactly, the aspiring Stoic sage
chooses as his mentor is not terribly important: what is important
is that he imagine an audience of some sort, and that this audience
be limited to those who would approve of Stoicism. 'Live as you
would live under the eyes of some good man, always at your side.'
'Live with the Catos, with Laelius, with Tubero. Or, if you enjoy
living with the Greeks also, spend your time with Socrates and
with Zeno ... Live with Chrysippus, with Posidonius: ... they
will bid you be stout of heart and rise superior to your threats.'
The ultimate ideal, however, is one of unfettered self-sufficiency,
in which even this imaginary audience of wise men from the
past becomes unnecessary. Ideally, the Stoic *sapiens* is his own
audience; he performs for himself and needs no one's respect or
approval other than his own. 'You are engaged in making yourself
the sort of person in whose company you would not dare to sin ...
When you have progressed so far that you ... have respect for
yourself, you may send away your attendant.' 'Be your own spectator; seek your own applause.'[61]

In *Antony and Cleopatra*, Shakespeare recreates this kind of
'audience management', but divorces it from what might be called
the 'usual suspects': severe Roman Republican *optimates* such as
Cato and Brutus. Instead, we have their polar opposites, Cleopatra
and her court, performing the characteristic withdrawal from the
world Seneca so strongly advocates. Alone together in the end in
an isolated monument, Cleopatra and her court cultivate a coterie
audience, themselves, so as to protect their imperiled self-esteem.
It may seem startling to say so, but the scene recalls, in a sense,
the death of Socrates, or of Seneca himself: the philosopher facing death in the company of a few select disciples. 'Adopting high-
Stoic rhetoric of resolute suicide,' Eric Langley observes, 'Cleopatra
successfully unifies the Roman and Egyptian, bringing both models
together in a single act.'[62]

When Cleopatra appropriates buzzwords of Stoic rhetoric such as 'liberty' and 'constancy', Shakespeare drives a point home that he had already begun to make more subtly in *Julius Caesar*. The point is not that Cleopatra, posing as a Stoic, is an emblem of hypocrisy, but rather that Stoicism itself, like Cleopatra, is inherently a species of 'hypocrisy' (Greek, *hypocrisis*, literally 'play-acting, role-playing'). The Stoic is just as histrionic as the Egyptian queen; he just happens to be playing a different role, for a different audience. Cleopatra takes refuge in the thought of Antony; so also the Stoic novice, in imagining the approval of some great man from the past. So, too, St Augustine, contemplating how he will stand before God. Safe in the thought of one person's approval, they are each able, to a surprising extent, to disregard all others. Clifford Ronan sees this aspect of Stoicism as especially pronounced in early modern English depictions of Stoic suicide. 'The element of pose and display in ancient Stoicism is strongly reflected in the Renaissance stage treatment of suicidal constancy, where there is only a fine line between heroism and heroics.'[63]

Having lost Antony, facing the imminent prospect of being led in triumph, Shakespeare's Cleopatra, like Brutus before her, knows that she must take pre-emptive action. Otherwise, she will be forced to suffer an irresistible interpellation; she will find herself redefined, even to herself, as less than absolute mistress of herself. Antony faces the same predicament earlier, when he comes to believe that Cleopatra is dead. Like Cleopatra addressing Iras, imagining herself being parodied on-stage, Antony explains to his manservant, Eros, 'th'inevitable prosecution of / Disgrace and horror' (4.14.66–7) which he foresees, if he should live.

> Wouldst thou be windowed in great Rome and see
> Thy master thus with pleached arms, bending down
> His corrigible neck, his face subdued
> To penetrative shame, whilst the wheeled seat
> Of fortunate Caesar, drawn before him, branded
> His baseness that ensued?
>
> (4.14.73–8)

'I would not see't' (4.14.78), Eros replies, foreshadowing Iras' more dramatic vow that she would rather tear out her own eyes. Eros also blinds himself, in a sense, but by a different means: suicide. 'Thus', he says, 'do I escape the sorrow / Of Antony's death'

(4.14.95–6). Even in the absence of stage directions, it is fairly clear that Antony in some sense enacts the scene he describes: 'thy master thus [etc.]', he says. In 'bending down' to await the death blow that he expects from Eros, he foreshadows what it would look like if he were led in triumph; by turning from him, he shows what Eros himself is doing by committing suicide: averting his eyes. Eros' sense of himself, like Cleopatra's, is so tightly bound to Antony's that he cannot bear to live, if he must first see his master either dead or defeated; it would be an intolerable humiliation for him, as well, by association. As Ewan Fernie explains, 'the subject of shame may be ashamed of itself directly or because of others upon whom its honour depends.'[64] Suicide allows Eros to escape the shame that Enobarbus, too, finds intolerable; the ignominy of seeing the source, if only by proxy, of his own sense of self, his master, rendered powerless.

Although distraught over Antony's death, Cleopatra aims for more, however, than merely ending her own ability to perceive. She wants to change the narrative, so that she can see herself as once again the powerful queen she once was. As if to replace even the prospect in the mind of possibly being led in triumph, a kind of involuntary theatre, Cleopatra sets up her suicide as a stage-show of her own design, one in which she will be again, if only in her own imagination, as she was at the moment of her own greatest triumph, her first meeting with Mark Antony on the banks of the river Cydnus. 'Show me, my women, like a queen' (5.2.226), she says. 'Go fetch / My best attires. I am again for Cydnus / To meet Mark Antony' (5.2.226–8). 'Bring our crown and all' (5.2.231), she adds, a moment after. Then, once the asp arrives: 'Give me my robe. Put on my crown' (5.2.279). 'I have immortal longings in me,' she reveals (5.2.279–80). She is dreaming of the afterlife, one in which, she believes, such finery will be appropriate.

Immediately following Antony's death, Cleopatra's first response is to lament how empty the world seems without him. 'All's but naught' (4.15.82), she says. Now, however, she sees a way out of her 'desolation': 'a better life' (5.2.1). She will meet Antony in the afterlife, and they will live there again as lovers, as before, scoffing at their enemies; praising each other; even enjoying each other's embrace. 'Methinks I hear / Antony call' (5.2.282–3), she tells Iras. 'I see him rouse himself / To praise my noble act. I hear him mock / The luck of Caesar' (5.2.283–5). When Iras dies first, Cleopatra makes haste to join her. 'If she first meet the curled Antony, / He'll make demand of her, and spend that kiss / Which is my heaven to have' (5.2.300–2). 'Husband, I come!' she cries (5.2.286). Cleopatra's language echoes Antony's own, earlier, as he prepares to kill himself, believing that Cleopatra has already gone on ahead. 'I come, my queen,' he says. 'Stay for me' (4.14.51).

> Where souls do couch on flowers we'll hand in hand
> And with our sprightly port make the ghosts gaze,
> Dido and her Aeneas shall want troops,
> And all the haunt be ours.
>
> (4.14.52–5)

Like Cleopatra's play within a play, 'again for Cydnus', the afterlife becomes here in Antony's imagination the opposite of the triumph that he fears. In the next world, he and Cleopatra will draw all eyes upon them, as Cleopatra did upon her arrival at his camp; they will be objects of admiration, however, not scorn, as they would be now, if they arrived in Rome as captives of Octavian. They will have 'troops', as they now no longer do; they will be masters of the next world, 'all the haunt', as they now can no longer hope to be in this one. They may even enjoy the pleasures of sexual relations: 'couch' is suggestive, as are the two lovers' separate descriptions of their deaths. Cleopatra compares the asp's bite to 'a lover's pinch'. Antony compares his suicide to a wedding night: 'I will be / A bridegroom in my death and run into't / As to a lover's bed' (4.14.100–2).

Notes

1. For scholarship on Shakespeare and judgement since Adelman, see now also Curran, ed., *Shakespeare and Judgment*.
2. Adelman, *Common Liar*, 24, 31, 39.
3. Barton, '"Nature's piece 'gainst fancy"', 47; Adelman, *Common Liar*, 39.
4. Adelman, *Common Liar*, 27, 29.
5. On the relative unimportance of material or 'objective' alienation in Shakespeare's thought about political unrest, as vs. 'subjective', see Patrick Gray and Samely, 'Shakespeare and Henri Lefebvre'.
6. Bartsch, *Mirror of the Self*, 138.

7. N. K. Sugimura compares 'Shakespeare's cloud passage' in *Antony and Cleopatra* to 'an Existentialist Crisis straight out of modern literature' and Stoicism more generally to Sartre's existentialism in Sugimura, 'Two Concepts of Reality', 73 ff.

8. For more detailed discussion of the history of the philosophy of recognition, beginning with Fichte as well as Hegel and continuing to the present, see Williams' three studies *Recognition*, *Hegel's Ethics* and *Tragedy, Recognition, and the Death of God*.

9. See Ricœur, *Oneself as Another*, and Sartre, *Being and Nothingness*.

10. See Ricœur, *Course of Recognition*.

11. The words 'marketplace' and 'common' occur much more frequently in *Coriolanus* than in any other play by Shakespeare. For 'marketplace', for example, cf. 1.5.26, 2.1.231, 2.2.159, 3.1.29, 3.1.111, 3.2.93, 104, 131. On 'common', see Watson, 'Coriolanus and the "Common Part"'.

12. Patterson, *Shakespeare and the Popular Voice*, 127; cf. also Barton, 'Livy, Machiavelli, and Shakespeare's *Coriolanus*'.

13. Kuzner, *Open Subjects*, 93.

14. Fukuyama, *End of History*, 174, 177, 165.

15. Sartre's conclusion in his play *No Exit*.

16. See Fiasse, *L'Autre et l'amitié*. For Aristotle's own thought on friendship, see Pangle, *Aristotle and the Philosophy of Friendship*.

17. Cic. *Amic.* 21.80.

18. Tilmouth, 'Passion and Intersubjectivity', 19 n. 30; cf. 19–20 and Selleck, *Interpersonal Idiom*, 92–5. See also Christopher Tilmouth, *Passion's Triumph*, 151–6.

19. Engle, *Shakespearean Pragmatism*, 151.

20. Plut. *De cohibenda ira* 456b; cf. Sen., *De ira* 2.36.1–2; cited in Bartsch, *Mirror of the Self*, 22. See Bartsch, *Mirror of the Self*, 22–3, for additional, analogous examples of the mirror as moral instrument, drawn from authors such as Diogenes Laertius, Apuleius and Ovid.

21. Jean-Pierre Vernant, 'In the Mirror of Medusa', 142, in *Mortals and Immortals: Collected Essays by Jean-Pierre Vernant*, ed. Froma I. Zeitlin (Princeton: Princeton University Press, 1991), 141–50; cited in Bartsch, *Mirror of the Self*, 23, and Langley, *Suicide and Narcissism*, 144.

22. Mikhail Bahktin, 'Toward a Reworking of the Dostoyevsky Book (1961)', 287.

23. Ibid., 286; cf. 301 n. 6. 'Dostoyevsky "only projected the landscape of his own soul"': Bakhtin cites here Lettenbauer, *Russische Literaturgeschichte*, 250.

24. Coleridge, *Coleridge on Shakespeare*, 78.

25. Coleridge, *Coleridge's Criticism of Shakespeare*, 46.

26. Bakhtin, 'Reworking', 287–9.
27. For a detailed history of nineteenth- and early twentieth-century source-hunting for Shakespeare's 'strange fellow', see Baldwin, 'Strange fellow'; cf. also Richards, '*Troilus and Cressida* and Plato'.
28. First proposed by Richard Grant White, *Studies in Shakespeare* (Boston and New York: Houghton Mifflin, 1886), 298–9; cited in Baldwin, 'Strange fellow', 411.
29. Steven Forde, 'On the *Alcibiades* I', in *The Roots of Political Philosophy*, ed. Thomas L. Pangle (Ithaca, NY: Cornell University Press, 1987), 222; cited in Bartsch, *Mirror of the Self*, 41. Cf. Langley, *Narcissism and Suicide*, 143–4, as well as Bartsch, *Mirror of the Self*, 41–56, and Gill, *Structured Self*, 344–59.
30. Plato, *First Alcibiades*, sec. 133, pp. 552–3.
31. First observed by H. R. D. Anders, *Shakespeare's Books* (Berlin: Schriften der deutschen Shakespeare-Gesellschaft Band I, 1904), 276–8; cited in Baldwin, 'Strange fellow', 411. Plato, *First Alcibiades*, sec. 133, pp. 552–3.
32. Cicero, *Those fyve Questions which M. Tullye Cicero disputed in his manor of Tusculum. . .* 1561, trans. J. Dolman (sig. E6 v) [cf. 1.27.67]; cited in Baldwin, 'Strange Fellow', 412.
33. Bartsch, *Mirror of the Self*, 52.
34. William Shakespeare, *Troilus and Cressida*, ed. K. Deighton (London: Methuen, 1906); cf. commentary on 3.3.102 ff.
35. Sir John Davies, *Nosce Teipsum* (London: Richard Field, for John Standish, 1599), 5, 9; mentioned but not cited in Baldwin, 'Strange Fellow', 412.
36. James Joyce, *Ulysses* (New York: Random House, 1961), 211–12.
37. Gifford, *Ulysses Annotated*, 248; cf. Thornton, *Allusions in Ulysses*, 210.
38. Aristotle, *Nicomachean Ethics*, sec. 1.3, p. 3.
39. Elton, 'Aristotle's *Nicomachean Ethics*'.
40. Gill, *Structured Self*, 356.
41. For an overview of arguments for and against Aristotle as author of the *Magna moralia*, see Cooper, 'The *Magna Moralia*'.
42. Nussbaum, *The Fragility of Goodness*, 364; cf. Bartsch, *Mirror of the Self*, 52–3, as well as Langley, *Narcissism and Suicide*, 52.
43. Cicero takes up this debate about the possibility and desirability of self-sufficiency in *Off.* 1.153–60 and 2.39.
44. Arist. *Mag. mor.* 2.15. For further analysis of this problem and this passage in the context of Aristotle's other works, as well as Plato's *First Alcibiades*, see Sorabji, *Self*, 230–9.
45. Arist. *Mag. mor.* 7.12; cf. Arist. *Eth. Nic.* 8.4.
46. Bartsch, *Mirror of the Self*, 17.

47. Engle, *Shakespeare's Pragmatism*, 1.
48. See, for example, Beacham, *Roman Theatre*.
49. Arist. *Mag. mor.* 2.15.
50. Cic. *Off.* 1.146.
51. *Non illum Cereris, non illum cura quietis / abstrahere inde potest.* ('Concern for neither food nor rest can draw him from thence.') Ov., *Met.* 3.435–6. Cf. Golding: 'No care of meate could draw him thence, nor yet desire of rest' (3.549).
52. Bakhtin, 'Reworking', 287–8.
53. Plut. *Cat. Mi.* 72.
54. August. *De civ. D.*1.24.
55. Althusser, 'Ideology and Ideological State', 174.
56. Nuttall, *New Mimesis*, 102; cf. Nuttall, *Shakespeare the Thinker*, 178.
57. Sen. *Ep.* 52.9, 7.12, 25.7, 25.5, 94.40.
58. For further analysis of Seneca's efforts at what I call 'audience management', see Bartsch, *Mirror of the Self*, 192 ff.
59. Sen. *Ep.* 7.8, 94.55, 94.59, 6.5.
60. Ibid., 52.7–8, 11.9–10, 25.6.
61. Ibid., 25.5, 104.22, 25.6, 78.21.
62. Langley, *Narcissism and Suicide*, 188.
63. Ronan, '*Antike Roman*', 94.
64. Fernie, *Shame in Shakespeare*, 12.

CONCLUSION TO PART II: THE LAST INTERPELLATION

For Janet Adelman, Antony and Cleopatra both manage in the end to avoid any kind of definitive moral judgement. There is no 'privileged observer' who can provide a final answer; no omnipotent judge who can impose a decisive interpellation. Through metatheatrical 'framing', the audience is kept at a distance from the action, uncertain which perspective to take, as centuries of divided assessments attest. Anne Barton for her part observes that Octavian seems for a time as if he might possess the power of a final judgement. 'If only' he can manage to return to Rome with Cleopatra, leading her in triumph, then 'he will fix the qualities of the story forever in his terms, which are those of the strumpet and the gorgon, not the lass unparallel'd and the Mars'. Cleopatra will 'fade into a mere parody queen'. Through suicide, however, the two lovers seem to be able to escape even him. Shakespeare combines Robert Garnier's and Samuel Daniel's earlier versions of the story into what Barton calls a 'divided catastrophe': first Antony's death, then Cleopatra's. Antony, clearly, 'bungles his death'. Cleopatra, however, 'dies perfectly, as a tragedy queen'. She not only forces Octavian 'to become an actor in her tragedy', but also 'redeems the bungled and clumsy nature of Antony's death'.[1]

These interpretations are not so much incorrect as incomplete. Barton misses the fact that Shakespeare includes a third catastrophe, this one truly final: 'doomsday' (5.2.231). Adelman misses Shakespeare's hints that there might be, in fact, a 'privileged observer': God. Adelman recognises that the protagonists' 'vision of themselves' is 'merely one in a series of competing visions'. As she observes, 'the device of framing forcibly dissociates us from the lovers'. 'For much of the play, we live outside their immediate universe and see them with distressing clarity from perspectives which are alien to their own.'[2] What Adelman does not recognise, however, is that one of those 'perspectives' or 'visions', introduced through ironic allusion to Scripture, is that of the person Katharine Maus calls 'the hypostasized divine observer'. As Maus explains, for a Christian, each individual is 'simultaneously the object of a double scrutiny: of a human vision that is fallible, partial, and superficial, and of a divine vision that is infallible, complete, and penetrating'.[3]

Ewan Fernie, citing Maus, advises, 'If we are to reconstruct even an approximation of the experience of the persons of the early modern period, we must imagine them as more or less aware at any particular moment of existing simultaneously in society and before God.'[4] Fernie then gives an intriguing example: Shakespeare's Richard II imagining himself as this 'divine observer', confronting Bolingbroke.

> When this thief, this traitor Bolingbroke,
> Who all this while hath reveled in the night
> Whilst we were wandering with the Antipodes,
> Shall see us rising in our throne, the east,
> His treasons will sit blushing in his face,
> Not able to endure the sight of day,
> But self-affrighted, tremble at his sin.
>
> (3.2.47–53)

Maus cites the Anglican Book of Common Prayer: God is him 'unto whom all hearts be open, all desires known, and from whom no secrets are hid'.[5] So, too, Octavian seems to wish he could be, face to face with his archrival. When Antony arrives in Rome, Octavian confronts him forthwith with his 'defects of judgement' (2.2.60), only to be thwarted and made to look ridiculous by Antony's 'excuses' and unshakable disdain (2.2.61). God, by contrast, would not be so easily disregarded. Fernie writes:

> If they felt that they were acting on the stage of the world, Renaissance people also knew that the play would soon be taken over and judged by God. In fact, God is always taken to be watching, looking down on his *theatrum mundi*, his judgment necessarily more definitive than that of any earthly audience.[6]

As Jesus says in the Gospels, 'there is nothing covered, that shall not be disclosed, nor hid, that shall not be known' (Matt. 10:26).

Literary critics influenced by Romanticism, including most notably Schlegel, Hugo, Hazlitt, Swinburne and Bradley, tend to sympathise with Cleopatra and even exalt her as transcendent.[7] She is for them Shakespeare's portrait of an artist creating herself, her own persona, in defiance of a more mundane reality. Like later modernists, these critics find in art an alternative to traditional religion, a secular substitute which they seek to glorify. Art is for them what Wallace Stevens calls 'the supreme Fiction'.[8] Cleopatra as artist, staging her own glorious demise, opting without shame or qualification for 'fancy' over 'nature', seems by this light an ethical exemplum. Her effort to transmute the lead of the world into the gold of her own fantasy is not quixotic, but heroic.[9]

This problem with this vein of criticism is that it is too one-sided; too partial to Cleopatra herself. It accurately represents her point of view, but her perspective is not that of the play as a whole.[10] To read Shakespeare's *Antony and Cleopatra* from the point of view of Cleopatra is like reading *The Sorrows of Young Werther* from the perspective of Werther. It is that *rara avis* these days, a failure of due critical suspicion. In a conversation with his friend, Johann Peter Eckermann, later in life, Goethe explained that writing *The Sorrows of Young Werther* 'freed' him from a 'stormy element', including a temptation to commit suicide, much as Werther does. 'I felt, as if after a general confession, once more happy and free, and justified in beginning a new life.' To his horror, however, the book was misunderstood, prompting a wave of copy-cat suicides. 'While I felt relieved and enlightened by having turned reality into poetry, my friends were led astray by my work,' Goethe recalled.

> For they thought that poetry ought to be turned into reality, that such a moral was to be imitated, and that, at any rate, one ought to shoot oneself. What had first happened here among a few, afterwards took place among the larger public.[11]

If Antony and Cleopatra are correct about what they will experience in the afterlife, then they achieve in death a rare victory. Through the intensity of their romance, an extravagant *folie à deux*, as well as their noble resolution in committing suicide, they manage to avoid being forced to sustain any perception of themselves as less than divine. By relying on each other, they protect themselves from being interpellated by any sceptical other, ranging from Octavian, to Octavia, to Antony's own men, who denounce him and abandon him after his ignominious flight from Actium. Even Octavian finds himself forced to grant them a degree of grandeur, in the end. He weeps for Antony and consents to allow Cleopatra to be buried with him.

Their suicides are a gamble, however. An atheist and aesthete such as Swinburne can praise Cleopatra in the strongest possible terms as 'an ideal incarnation', 'the perfect and everlasting woman', because he assumes with blithe confidence that there is no afterlife, except in art, and that Shakespeare, the playwright in question, her creator, surely would agree.[12] If death is the end of our affairs, then Antony and Cleopatra do indeed win a kind of victory. They may not meet each other once more in Elysium in the way that they expect, but they still manage to preserve an admirable degree of autonomy. Even if their hope for a new life together after death, like their grandiose image of themselves in this life, is only 'fancy', a mere 'dream', it is theirs, their 'space', which they work together to create and protect. They manage to preserve their delusion safe from the designs of the conniving, ruthless Octavian, and that degree of 'liberty', that control over their own subjectivity, is itself a glorious display of agency. Moreover, they have the atheist's version of the afterlife, earthly fame. 'No grave upon the earth shall clip in it / A pair so famous,' Octavian proclaims (5.2.358–9). The dead lovers have won what Enobarbus calls 'a place i'th' story' (3.13.47).

The possibility that death is simply the end of consciousness is evoked by the recurrent comparisons between death and sleep, just as the possibility that Antony and Cleopatra will meet again after death is evoked by Cleopatra's account of her 'dream' of Antony. Another possibility remains, however, albeit one that may not be to every critic's taste. In contrast to the encomia of nineteenth-century critics such as Swinburne, Schlegel and Hugo, this off-stage, adumbrated ending runs contrary to the play's pronounced, sympathetic strain of what we would now call Romanticism: its exaltation of the idea that we can escape through the power of our imagination, as well as sheer passionate intensity of purpose, into an alternative world that we ourselves create.[13] Over the course of the play, Shakespeare includes several pointed suggestions that the afterlife might be neither annihilation, nor the Elysium of the lovers' 'fancy', but instead, as indeed, most of the theatergoers of his time would have believed, an encounter with the Christian God.

In his use of allusion in *Antony and Cleopatra*, Shakespeare capitalises on the gap between his characters' idealised imagination of what they will encounter and Christian beliefs about their more likely fate. Pagan ignorance of Christian revelation stands in sharp contrast to the Christian sense of an inevitable Day of Judgement. Cleopatra wonders aloud at one point: 'Is it sin / To rush into the secret house of death / Ere death come to us?' (4.5.84–6). As Paul Cantor notes, 'this is the only moment in all three Roman plays in which anyone regards suicide as a sin'.[14] Shakespeare introduces an anachronism here in order to signal to the audience, in Cleopatra's own voice, not to consider her a reliable narrator. Her knowledge of the 'secret house of death', like Antony's, is incomplete.

'Where souls do couch on flowers': Antony's description of what he expects to experience in the afterlife, although enchanting, gives room for pause. As the more learned in the audience would have known, 'Dido and her Aeneas' do not end up together in the underworld. When Aeneas visits Dido in Hades, she refuses to speak to him, still angry at having been betrayed, and chooses instead to remain with her husband Sychaeus.[15] T. S. Eliot describes the scene as 'perhaps the most telling snub in all of poetry'.[16] Antony has no way of knowing the true state of 'Dido and her Aeneas'; he has made no Virgilian *katabasis* himself. But the audience, so to speak, does 'know', because they have read the *Aeneid*, just as they also know about Christian revelation.

In his study of the Roman plays in early modern England, Clifford Ronan points out that their tendency towards occasional anachronism was long misunderstood or slighted by later scholars as mere ignorant error, when in fact it is often used to convey important shades of meaning. From Ronan's perspective, 'all literature employs multiple chronotypes simultaneously'. 'By its very nature,' he argues, 'a history play will reflect language, beliefs, and customs not just of the age during which it is fictively set, but also of the age when the dramatist and his audience are living.' 'The most interesting moments to analyze' are, therefore, 'those when the dramatist prompts a spectator to travel from the play's chief historical chronotope to some present-day or eternal one.' 'Ancient Judeo-Christian allusions', for example, 'make audiences confront the differences between pagan and Christian lifestyles.'[17]

More recently, Ronan notes, critics have come to appreciate and even emphasise the possibility of deliberate dramatic irony. For Phyllis Rackin, for example, anachronism serves in context as a kind of Brechtian 'alienation device'. Much like the 'framing' that Adelman sees as characteristic of the dramatic structure of *Antony and Cleopatra*, the intrusion of some obvious reference to the future introduces dramatic irony, highlighting the limitations of the characters' perspective in comparison to that of the audience. When Cleopatra imagines seeing some 'squeaking' child actor 'boy' her 'greatness' (5.2.219), or Brutus and Cassius imagine their assassination of Caesar being reenacted 'in states unborn and accents yet unknown' (3.1.113), 'the anachronistic reference to the present theatrical occasion reminds the audience of the vast gulf of time and awareness that separates them from the historical events represented on stage.'[18]

Out of all of Shakespeare's Roman plays, *Antony and Cleopatra* contains the most allusions to Christian Scripture. Christianity in this play is less anachronistic than it might be in others; the events that it describes coincide more closely in time with key events of Christian history than those of any other Roman play. Octavian's ascent as 'Augustus Caesar' corresponds very closely to the emergence of the Christian Messiah. When Cleopatra calls Antony 'Lord of lords' (4.8.22; cf. Rev. 17:14) or Caesar proclaims, 'The time of universal peace is near' (4.6.5), these statements have an irony beyond the awareness of the characters themselves.[19] They invoke the Christian sequel to their 'place i' th' story'.[20]

In an article on dramatic irony in *Antony and Cleopatra*, William Blissett points out that Shakespeare incorporates repeated references to 'Herod of Jewry'. To be fair, Herod appears in Plutarch, as well, as part of the political action.[21] Shakespeare, however, takes pains to make the allusions specifically Christian. For instance, when Charmian asks a soothsayer for a good fortune, she asks specifically, as if in jest, for 'a child at fifty, to whom Herod of Jewry may do homage' (1.2.29–30). The allusion to the 'child at fifty' is an oblique reference to Elizabeth, mother of John the Baptist, who miraculously conceived in her old age, after many decades of infertility. When Cleopatra vows in comic anger, 'That Herod's head I'll have' (3.3.4–5), Shakespeare plays again upon the story of John, Salome and Herod, reversing the power dynamic. Cleopatra will, as Hamlet warns against, 'out-Herod Herod' (3.2.14).[22] Other allusions refer, however, not to the First Coming of Christ, but to the Second. As Hannibal Hamlin points out, most of the allusions to the Bible in *Antony and Cleopatra* are drawn neither from the Gospels, nor even the Old Testament, as one might perhaps expect, given the setting in Egypt, but instead from the eschatological Book of Revelation.[23] For instance, 'Lord of Lords', as Cleopatra calls Antony, is not a title of the Christ Child, but rather, written upon the thigh of the Word of God in his glory, when he returns on horseback 'to smite the nations' (Rev. 19:16).

When Antony and the other triumvirs meet on Pompey's ship, Lepidus struggles to keep up with Antony's drinking. The servants, unimpressed, dismiss him as a mere 'name'. One of them remarks, 'To be called into a huge sphere and not to be seen to move in't, are the holes where eyes should be, which pitifully disaster the cheeks' (2.7.14–16). Lepidus becomes a hollow-eyed skull, a painter's *memento mori*, and as such a harbinger of Antony's own eventual fate.[24] The punning conceit of a 'sphere' 'dis-astered' refers to one of the spheres of the Ptolemaic universe losing one of its stars (Latin, *aster*, 'star') and foreshadows Antony's own later description of himself in defeat. Comparing himself to Caesar, Antony laments, 'my good stars that were my former guides / Have empty left their orbs and shot their fires / Into the abysm of hell' (3.13.145–7). As Cleopatra applies the asp to her breast, Charmian cries, 'O eastern star!' (5.2.306). So, too, as Antony lies dying, one of his attendants cries, 'The star is fall'n' (4.14.106). Hamlin connects these passages to recurrent images in the Book of Revelation of stars falling from the heaven, where they are figures for the fall of Satan, in keeping with the prophet Isaiah's description of Lucifer as a falling star:

How art thou fallen from heaven, O Lucifer, son of the morning? *And* cut down to the ground, which didst cast lots upon the nations? Yet thou saidest in thine heart, I will ascend into heaven, and exalt my throne above beside the stars of God: I will sit also

upon the mount of the congregation in the sides of the North. I
will ascend above the height of the clouds, *and* I will be like the
most high. But thou shalt be brought down to the grave, to the side
of the pit. They that see thee, shall look upon thee *and* consider
thee, *saying*, Is this the man that made the earth to tremble, *and*
that did shake the kingdoms? (14:12–16)

The allusions to falling stars in *Antony and Cleopatra* align the
two lovers, in effect, with the same typology of Antichrist apparent in *Julius Caesar*: the plot-structure of punctured delusion that
I described earlier as *humiliatio potentatuum*, and which I believe
reveals the influence of medieval biblical drama, even in these
ostensibly secular plays. 'There fell a great star from heaven, burning like a torch,' St John writes (8:10). And again, 'I saw a star fall
from heaven unto the earth, and to him was given the key of the
bottomless pit' (9:1).[25]

In the opening scene of *Antony and Cleopatra*, the two lovers
have a mock-debate about the extent of Antony's love, one that
recalls in some ways Lear's debate with Cordelia at the beginning
of *King Lear*:

CLEOPATRA
    If it be love indeed, tell me how much.
ANTONY
    There's beggary in the love that can be reckoned.
CLEOPATRA
    I'll set a bourn how far to be beloved.
ANTONY
    Then must thou needs find out new heaven, new earth.
                                  (1.1.14–17)

As Richard Strier points out:

in Antony's second line here, Shakespeare gives his strumpet's fool
a reference that no Biblically literate member of the audience – of
which there were no doubt many – could have missed, a reference
to one of the grandest and most resonant apocalyptic promises of
the New Testament.[26]

In the Second Epistle of Peter, as well as the Revelation of St John,
the world after the Second Coming of Christ is described as 'a
new heaven and a new earth' (2 Pet. 3:13; Rev. 21:1).[27] Moreover,

as Hannibal Hamlin points out, St Peter and St John themselves allude here to God's prophecy in the Book of Isaiah: 'I will create new heavens and a new earth' (65:17).[28] St John recalls his vision:

> They were judged every man according to their works. And death and hell were cast into the lake of fire. This is the second death. And whosoever was not found written in the book of life was cast into the lake of fire. And I saw a new heaven and a new earth: for the first heaven and the first earth were passed away; and there was no more sea. And I John saw the holy city, new Jerusalem, coming down from God out of heaven, prepared as a bride for her husband. (Rev. 20:13–21:1)

Strier finds Antony's unwitting allusion to Christian eschatology as baffling as it is remarkable. 'Why would Shakespeare give Antony such a line?' he asks. 'Perhaps the line is meant to undercut the speaker.' 'From a dramatic point of view,' however, he concedes, 'instead of the line being undercut by some sort of gross gesture, it is allowed to hang in the air, as a vision or a prophecy, for after it, the dialogue momentarily stops, and a messenger enters.'[29] I would say, by contrast, that it makes sense that Antony's ironic allusion is allowed to come across as so portentous. Antony boasts that the only way that Cleopatra will be able to 'set a bourn how far to be beloved' is if she can 'find out new heaven, new earth', a task which he implies is, of course, impossible. According to Christian revelation, however, such a 'new heaven' and 'new earth' will indeed be found; the limit to their erotic love that Antony casts as counterfactual, inconceivable, is precisely what awaits them after death. As Jesus explains in the Gospels, 'They which shall be accounted worthy to obtain that world, and the resurrection from the dead, neither marry, nor are given in marriage' (Luke 20:35).

The sense that Shakespeare has Judgement Day on his mind is supported by another, less complex allusion, as well, which Cleopatra makes in passing just before she commits suicide. 'When thou hast done this chare,' she tells Charmian, 'I'll give thee leave / To play till doomsday' (5.2.230–1). As before the Last Judgement was the limit on earthly, romantic love, so, too, here, 'doomsday' is the end of Charmian's 'play'. In *Hamlet*, Claudius acknowledges that the world is often unjust. 'Offence's gilded hand may shove by justice' (3.3.58). 'But', he adds, ''tis not so above' (3.3.60).

There is no shuffling, there the action lies
In his true nature, and we ourselves compell'd
Even to the teeth and forehead of our faults
To give in evidence.

(3.3.61–4)

God's interpellation, 'doomsday', is irresistible. In *Antony and Cleopatra*, Shakespeare evokes divine judgement, not, I think, because he is trying to be a spoilsport, but rather because here, as in his other Roman plays, he is reflecting deeply on the role of the other in self-perception. And, like many philosophers and theologians in the twentieth century, including Buber and Ricœur, as well as Lévinas, Shakespeare wants to include in his notion of the other the divine, as well as the human. Antony and Cleopatra are able to forestall Octavian's planned interpellation; they will not be forced to redefine themselves as prisoners, led in triumph through the streets of Rome. Shakespeare speculates, however, that there may be nonetheless another, more final interpellation, of a more mysterious outcome, that they cannot so easily escape.

Notes

1. Barton, '"Nature's piece 'gainst fancy"', 51, 41, 53.
2. Adelman, *Common Liar*, 40.
3. Maus, *Inwardness and Theatre*, 11.
4. Fernie, *Shame in Shakespeare*, 69.
5. *The Prayer Book of Queen Elizabeth, 1559* (London: The Ancient and Modern Library of Theological Literature, 1914), 92; cited in Maus, *Inwardness and Theater*, 11, and again in Fernie, *Shame in Shakespeare*, 69.
6. Fernie, *Shame in Shakespeare*, 69.
7. I cite selectively: 'The principal characters . . . powerfully arrest the imagination . . . Cleopatra is as remarkable for seductive charms as Antony for the splendor of his deeds. . . . We forgive them [etc.].' Schlegel, *A Course of Lectures*, 416–17. Cf. also Heraud, *Shakespeare*, 374–87. 'La fantaisie humanie ne pourra jamais rêver rien de plus merveilleux que ce drame . . . Cléopatre est . . . le plus grand triomphe de la magie feminine. . . L'intensité de la passion en est la légitimité: telle est la vérité morale qui ressort, éclatante. . .' (cf. Othello: 'Nature would not invest herself in such shadowing passion without some instruction' [4.1.39–41], or Leontes: 'Affection! Thy intention stabs the centre' [1.2.138]). Hugo, *Oeuvres complètes de*

Shakespeare, 9 ff. 'Cleopatra . . . had great and unpardonable faults, but the beauty of her death almost redeems them.' Hazlitt, *Characters*, 64–9. 'We sympathize with them in their passion; we feel in it the infinity there is in man . . . Many unpleasant things can be said about Cleopatra, and the more that are said the more wonderful she appears.' Bradley, *Oxford Lectures*, 279–305.

8. On modernist authors' characteristic pursuit of autonomy as an ethical as well as aesthetic ideal, see Goldstone, *Fictions of Autonomy*.

9. 'They are . . . great as the gods are great . . . these people are exempt of shame: as absolutely above it as Zeus, father of gods and men, who could be ridiculous enough in his amours, and yet, when all is said, remains a very grand gentleman.' Quiller-Couch, *Studies in Literature*, 168–205. G. Wilson Knight waxes lyrical about the play as 'not merely a story of a soldier's fall, but rather a spelled land of romance achieved and victorious: a paradisiacal vision expressed in terms of humanity's quest for love'; Antony and Cleopatra 'change a crown of gold for the more sparkling and ethereal diadem of love'. Wilson Knight, *Imperial Theme*, 227, 248. John Dover Wilson describes the two lovers in Antony's own terms as 'a "peerless pair" who "stand up" against the widest and most splendid panorama Shakespeare . . . ever painted, and are magnified, not dwarfed, by it because it is represented as mere clay or dung in comparison to them'. William Shakespeare, *Antony and Cleopatra*, ed. John Dover Wilson (Cambridge: Cambridge University Press, 1950), xxv. See also Sigurd Burckhardt, *Shakespeare's Meanings*, and Markels, *Pillar of the World*. For a more recent neo-Romantic account of Cleopatra's suicide, see Strier, *Unrepentant Renaissance*, 98–125.

10. For less sympathetic evaluations of Cleopatra's character, as well as her and Antony's affair in general, see Stempel, 'The Transmigration of the Crocodile', and Gervinus, *Shakespeare Commentaries*, 353–86. For the play as a whole as a tragedy, even satire, of delusion and self-aggrandisement undercut by irony and distance, see Blissett, 'Dramatic Irony', 151–66; Stirling, *Unity in Shakespearean Tragedy*, 157–92; and Chambers, *Shakespeare: A Survey*, 249–57. For example: 'Shakespeare did not "see life truly and think about it romantically" . . . there is no meretricious sublimity cast even over the ending of *Antony and Cleopatra*' (Stirling, 159). George Bernard Shaw notoriously attacks Shakespeare as too sympathetic to the two lovers' delusions of grandeur. 'Shakespeare finally strains all his huge command of rhetoric and stage pathos to give a theatrical sublimity to the wretched end of the business, and to persuade foolish spectators that the world was well lost by the twain.' Shaw, *Prefaces*, 716–17. As a contemporary reviewer wrote, however, this judgement is

'worse than false'; it is 'half true', Cf. Bennett, review, *Academy*.
Shaw's 'anti-romantic enthusiasms blind him to an example of realism that was under his very nose'; that is to say, Shakespeare himself is more critical of the delusions he presents than Shaw himself
recognises. Couchman, '*Antony and Cleopatra* and the Subjective
Convention'.

11. Eckermann, *Conversations of Goethe*, 167, 170–1.
12. Swinburne, *Shakespeare*, 76.
13. For a critique of efforts to align Shakespeare's own sensibility with
    Romanticism, see Patrick Gray, 'Seduced by Romanticism'.
14. Cantor, *Shakespeare's Roman Trilogy*, 78.
15. Verg. *Aen.* 6.467–74.
16. Eliot, 'What is a Classic?' 64.
17. Ronan, '*Antike Roman*', 31, 16, 29.
18. Phyllis Rackin, *Stages of History: Shakespeare's English Chronicles*
    (Ithaca, NY: Cornell University Press, 1990), 94; cited in Ronan,
    '*Antike Roman*', 23.
19. A Christian tradition dating back to the Middle Ages holds that the
    Pax Romana which began with Augustus corresponds to the 'univer-
    sal peace' (Is. 39:8 ff.) which Isaiah describes as a precursor to the
    birth of the Messiah. See Fichter, '*Antony and Cleopatra*: "The time
    of universal peace"'.
20. On these and other allusions to Christian Scripture in *Antony and
    Cleopatra*, see Cantor, *Shakespeare's Roman Trilogy*, 69–70, 249 n.
    147, as well as Hamlin, *Bible in Shakespeare*, 214–30.
21. *Plutarch's Lives . . . in North's Translation*, ed. R. H. Carr (Oxford,
    1938), 221, 231–2; cited in Blissett, 'Dramatic Irony', 164 n. 36.
22. Shakespeare also brings in the story of the three Magi: Antony feasts
    'three kings' (2.2.81), and Charmian asks to be married to 'three
    kings' (1.2.28).
23. Hamlin, *Bible in Shakespeare*, 217–22, 225–30.
24. For more on such *mementi mori*, see Smith, '"This great solemnity"',
    and Vance MacMullen, 'Death imagery'.
25. Hamlin, *Bible in Literature*, 217–19.
26. Strier, *Unrepentant Renaissance*, 114.
27. See also Cox, *Seeming Knowledge*, 184.
28. Hamlin, *Bible in Shakespeare*, 217 n. 95.
29. Strier, *Unrepentant Renaissance*, 114.

CONCLUSION: BETWEEN HUMANISM AND ANTIHUMANISM

In the final turn to the idea of God as other that I have called 'the last interpellation', as well as my emphasis throughout on one-to-one relationships between individuals, it may seem amiss that I do not invoke the ideas of Emmanuel Lévinas, including especially his concept of 'the face-to-face'. Lévinas might also seem to provide the kind of Via Media between humanism and antihumanism that I find instead in the work of Bakhtin. From my perspective, however, as well as that of other critics such as Buber and Ricœur, Lévinas' underestimated antihumanism presents some cause for concern. In his analysis of the relationship between the self and the other, Lévinas too thoroughly and immediately subsumes what I have called 'the horizontal' into what I have called 'the vertical'. I discuss something like Lévinas' concept of the other in the conclusion to my analysis of *Antony and Cleopatra* as what Katharine Maus calls 'the hypostasized divine observer'. By and large, however, I want to preserve the idea that the other can also refer more simply to other people: fellow human beings. God is 'an' other, just like language is 'an' other. Neither the divine nor the symbolic order, however, is 'the' other, meaning, the only other with any effective agency, the bedrock or ground of being: 'the Other' with a capital O (*L'Autre* with a capital *A*), as per Lévinas' usage, as well as Lacan's.

For Lévinas, the other is 'infinite', 'superior'. He cannot be said to be simply any other thing whatsoever, or even any other human being. Instead, for Lévinas, the other is a specific entity, albeit one which we can describe at best only apophatically: the ineffable, wholly transcendent God of Jewish Scripture. In other

words, Lévinas' other is what Derrida would call 'the transcendental signifier', except that, unlike Derrida, Lévinas believes that this
other really does exist. The God of the Hebrew Bible is not wholly
a myth, but out there, somewhere, in an objective sense. We meet
him in person constantly, albeit not directly. Instead, we encounter
him at one remove, through quotidian, 'face-to-face' exchanges
with other people which for Lévinas are the most fundamental
'given' of human experience.[1] As regards Lévinas' premises, it
is fairly transparent that the God of traditional Judaism is to be
understood as representing something radically distinct from any
given human being. That God and the self are not secretly one and
the same is the most fundamental distinction between the Abra-
hamic religious tradition as a whole, including Christianity and
Islam, as well as Judaism, and the religious traditions of South
Asia; most clearly, the Vedanta school of Hinduism found in the
Upanishads, which holds as the highest form of enlightenment the
recognition that Atman, the individual soul, is the same as Brah-
man, the world-soul. Lévinas departs from traditional Judaism,
however, in his strenuous emphasis on God's absolute transcendence. Like Maimonides, he insists that discussion of Godhead
must be radically apophatic; so much so, in fact, that the nature of
the divine begins to lose any precise content. 'The other remains
infinitely transcendent, infinitely foreign.'[2] God's personhood
blurs, dissipates; he becomes instead an inscrutable, impersonal
force, holding the self 'captive' or 'hostage'.[3]

For Lévinas, our 'face-to-face' encounters with other people
mediate and render apparent our relationship with this mysterious
God: the ultimate 'Other'. Human relatedness evokes ethical obligations ultimately anchored in the overwhelming, commanding
power of the divine. 'The dimension of the divine opens forth in
the human face,' Lévinas writes. 'It is here that the Transcendent,
infinitely other, solicits us and appeals to us. The proximity of the
Other, the proximity of the neighbor, is in being an ineluctable
moment of the revelation of an absolute presence.' At times, Lévinas even goes so far as to suggest that interpersonal exchanges are
significant only in light of this theological import. 'To recognize
the Other is to give. But it is to give to the master, the lord, to him
whom one approaches as "You" [French, *vous*] in a dimension
of height.'[4] God in his ineffable superiority uses other people as
instruments in order to make himself known to the individual self,
presenting through them his own irresistible call.[5] That is to say,

God interpellates the self, rendering it a subject, in much the same manner as one of Althusser's Ideological State Apparatuses; other people are simply his means to that end.

For much the same reasons as apply to Lévinas, Lacan's usefulness in this case is also rather sharply limited. For Lacan, the self, conceived of as Cartesian *cogito* or as Freudian 'ego', is nothing more than an effect of language: a misleading illusion, like a mirage. Language always antedates any given individual and determines everything about that supposed person: our sense of self is in fact nothing more than a delusion or dream patched together by 'the discourse of the Other'. What Lacan means by 'the Other', moreover, is not what this phrase, 'the Other', tends to designate in most academic discourse, namely, another person, real or imagined, or another culture. Instead, Lacan's 'Other with a capital O' means 'the place ['locus'] where language exists': 'a place that is essential to the structure of the symbolic'.[6] This 'Other' is for Lacan's 'language' what the *chōra* (literally, 'space') in the *Timaeus* is for Plato's unchanging 'forms' or 'ideas'.

Where does language come from, if not from us subjects, as an attempt to represent reality? Where does it reside, if not in our minds? Since Lacan undermines the very category itself of consciousness, he is obliged to posit in its place a mysterious 'locus' that he calls 'the Other'. 'The Other is ... the locus in which is constituted the I who speaks along with he who hears.' 'This Other (to be provided with a capital O) ... is invoked by anyone when he addresses an other (with a lowercase o).' The Other is 'the locus of signifying convention'. 'We must establish the Other with a capital O as being the locus of speech's deployment.' 'In my view, the subject has to arise from the given state of the signifiers that cover him [*le recouvrent*] in an Other which is their transcendental locus.' 'The Other [is] where discourse is situated.'[7]

This peculiar definition of the other is very much original to Lacan and represents his application of the so-called 'linguistic turn' in contemporary French philosophy to a much older philosophical debate about the relationship between the self and the other.[8] More so than any of his contemporaries, many of whom, like Lacan, seized upon Saussure's linguistics as a new 'key to all mythologies', Lacan saw language or something very similar to it, a structured, symbolic order that he sometimes calls 'discourse', as the fundamental, efficacious and only true cause, not only of all human activity, but indeed of the very existence of anything at all. 'Concepts . . . engender things.'⁹ Individual consciousness, especially, is post hoc. This epiphenomenon, selfhood, devoid of any real agency, is as he sees it a by-product of a vast, impersonal and intangible symbolic order, 'language', which itself resides in 'the Other' ('with a capital O'), an immaterial 'locus'. 'Language', understood in a broad sense as a network of semiotic patterns, functions, for Lacan, as a kind of Prime Mover. Signs ontologically precede and entirely generate the things that they signify, including especially the apparent self-awareness and agency of the individual self. 'Language' in this sense also determines the character of 'the other' ('with a lowercase o'), meaning any other supposed independent consciousness to whom the self might relate.

'It is the world of words that creates the world of things.' This core claim of Lacan's is wildly implausible; so implausible, I would say, that it is literally unbelievable. Like Peter Holbrook, my reaction to such a view is to find it, not merely dubious, but 'unreal': 'so remote from my own or, I suppose, anybody else's experience that I have difficulty comprehending how anyone could seriously hold it.' 'In other words,' Holbrook explains, 'I find it difficult to imagine *living as if this proposition were true.* (One wants to know how many adherents of this theoretical orientation experience themselves in this way, as "effects" of "discourses", etc.).'¹⁰ For instance, Freud invents the term 'psychoanalysis'. Yet his having done so does not mean that the process that the term 'psychoanalysis' denotes never existed theretofore, if perhaps only *ex hypothesi*, in his own mind. Freud invents it to describe something, an idea of his that until that point had been nameless. It is his desired variation on a practice that, up until his intervention, had been called something else: 'confession'.¹¹

It would be a digression, however, to dwell here on the possible truth-value of Lacan. The nature of reality itself is not in this case the subject of inquiry; the question, rather, is the nature of Shakespeare's perception of reality, even if incorrect. Even if the concept of the individual self were completely misleading, it would still be, nonetheless, an illusion he believes in and accepts, at least to some degree.¹² In her study of Roman selfhood, *Mirror of the Self*, Shadi Bartsch declines to bring in Lacan 'either as a piñata or a *deus ex machina*'. Otherwise, she explains, she would have had to 'situate the Lacanian response to psychoanalysis in a world unfamiliar with this kind of analysis'. Like Bartsch, rather than aiming for a symptomatic reading, a critique from outside the frame of the author's own conceptual framework, I have chosen here 'to apply interpretive tools that seem more or less familiar to the ancient cultures that generated them'.[13] Lévinas' conclusions Shakespeare might have understood, if only by analogy to contemporary Calvinism.[14] Lacan's preposterous claims, however, are not even useful as a foil. Lacan is, as the saying is, 'not even wrong'.

Having distinguished Shakespeare's thought about selfhood from antihumanism such as that of Althusser, as well as Lacan, I hasten to add that I by no means wish to suggest that Shakespeare believes in the idea that the self is wholly autonomous or transcendent, in the manner of what Ricœur calls the 'Cartesian cogito', as opposed to what he calls in contrast the 'shattered cogito' of antihumanism. Rather, like Ricœur, I wish to move beyond this false dichotomy altogether: 'beyond the alternative of the cogito and the anticogito'. In his Gifford Lectures, later reprinted as *Oneself as Another*, Ricœur proposes that philosophical anthropology 'move beyond' what he calls 'the quarrel over the cogito, in which the "I" is by turns in a position of strength and of weakness', 'the great oscillation that causes the "I" of the "I think" to appear, by turns, to be elevated inordinately to the heights of a first truth and then cast down to the depths of a vast illusion.'[15]

With Descartes, Ricœur argues, the self is 'reduced' to a 'point-like ahistorical identity', 'the simplest and barest act, the act of thinking', 'at the price of the loss of relation to the person who speak, to the I–you of interlocution, to the identity of a historical person, to the self of responsibility'. 'What is there left to say about this free-floating "I"?' Ricœur asks. 'It is, in truth, no one.' Nietzsche then destroys even this supposed ground of the self by 'extending the critique' Descartes begins, the doubt introduced by the idea of the 'evil deceiver', 'to so-called internal experience'. Nietzsche doubts 'better' than Descartes, that is, even more hyperbolically. Thinking itself might be no more than a 'fiction'. In the place of this oscillation between 'exalted subject, humiliated subject', Ricœur proposes a different ground of the self: its relationship to other selves. As he explains, 'there is no self alone at the start'.[16] The self is born into a state of dialogue with other selves, the condition Hannah Arendt calls 'plurality'. This web of relationships, not Descartes' *cogito*, a variation on Aristotle's 'thought thinking itself', is the proper ground of selfhood.

Habermas makes much the same point as Ricœur about the relationship between self and other, to wit, that interpersonal relationships are an essential 'given' of identity, rather than accidental, in an essay on what he calls 'individuation through socialization'. Individuation for Habermas is not 'the self-realization of an independently acting subject carried out in isolation and freedom'. Instead, 'individuality forms itself in relations of intersubjective acknowledgement and of intersubjectively mediated self-understanding'.[17] This understanding of the fundamental nature of the self is more akin to Shakespeare's own than that of Althusser, Lacan or any other antihumanist. For this reason, Lévinas' most important source, the ethics and theology of Martin Buber, as mediated in this case through the work of Mikhail Bakhtin, provides a better analogue of Shakespeare's thought about the other than Lévinas' own paradigm.[18] Another alternative is Ricœur himself, who like Shakespeare derives his understanding of the relationship between self and other in large measure from Aristotle's theory of friendship.

Buber's positing of encounter as the ground of human existence is the source of Lévinas' characteristic emphasis on what he calls 'the face-to-face'.[19] Whereas in Lévinas' thought, however, the other is infinitely more powerful, overwhelming, because the other is, in the final analysis, God, in Shakespeare's thought, like Buber's on the 'I–thou' relationship, the other can mean instead, and mean truly, another human being. We meet this other as an equal in at least one important sense, albeit one that is metaphysically refined. In so far as any human being can be seen as a 'thou', instead of an 'it', he shares something in common with any other human being: a capacity to impinge upon other people's subjectivity and, to some degree, assimilate it to his own. This equality can be obscured or attenuated by worldly disparities of power. Nonetheless, it can never be dispelled altogether from any human relationship. The possibility of this kind of intersubjective interpellation stands as a salutary check, especially, upon that drive for absolute autocracy or *imperium* that St Augustine describes as *libido dominandi*. Neither nor the self nor the other can ever entirely overwhelm and obliterate each other's subjectivity. The 'imperial self' cannot expand forever; cannot become self-sufficient and impassible. Instead, the best we can do is to make peace with the human condition as it is, 'grotesque', dependent and vulnerable.[20]

Notes

1. For Derrida's 'religious turn', see Caputo, *Prayers and Tears*. For Derrida on Lévinas, see Derrida, *Adieu*, as well as Derrida, 'Violence and Metaphysics'. For Lévinas, see Lévinas, *Totality and Infinity*, as well as Lévinas, *Entre Nous*. For a sense of Lévinas' influence, see Cohen (ed.), *Face to Face with Lévinas*.

2. Lévinas, *Totality and Infinity*, 194.

3. Lévinas departs in this respect from traditional Judaism. Gillian Rose describes Lévinas' vision as 'Buddhist Judaism' in Rose, *Mourning Becomes the Law: Philosophy and Representation* (Cambridge: Cambridge University Press, 1996), 37, and 'Judaic Manicheism', in Rose, *Judaism and Modernity: Philosophical Essays* (Oxford: Blackwell, 1993), 43; cf. 213; cited in Hart, *The Beauty of the Infinite*, 75 n. 56, q.v.: 'The foremost representative of this [sc. Kantian] "school" of the sublime would surely be Emmanuel Lévinas, whose thought is often characterized as a kind of "Jewish" postmodernism, thought it might be more accurately described as Manichaean, Orphic, or Gnostic.' For an analogous medieval critique of Maimonides, see, for example, Wolfson, 'Crescas'.

4. Lévinas, *Totality and Infinity*, 78, 75.

5. A trenchant summary and critique of Lévinas' thought on the relationship between the self and the other, as well as a discussion of Derrida's attempt to moderate its dichotomies, can be found in Hart, *Beauty of the Infinite*, 76–92. For Martin Buber's criticisms of Lévinas, see the essays and primary sources in Atterton, Calarco and Friedman, eds, *Lévinas and Buber*. For Ricœur's critique of Lévinas, see Ricœur, *Oneself as Another*, 335 ff.

6. Lacan, *Écrits*, 379; for English, cf. Lacan, *Écrits*, trans. Fink, Fink and Grigg.

7. Lacan, *Écrits*, 431, 439, 525, 628, 655–6, 678.

8. On the rise and fall of the 'linguistic turn', see Pavel, *The Feud of Language*.

9. Lacan, *Écrits*, 276.

10. Holbrook, *Shakespeare's Individualism*, 58–9. Cf. Galen Strawson on 'consciousness deniers' and what he calls 'the Great Silliness' in Strawson, *Things that Bother Me*.

11. Foucault presents 'psychiatry' as only one instance among others of a centuries-long 'dissemination' of 'procedures of confession'. Foucault, *History of Sexuality*, 63. Another example of a historical antecedent to Freudian psychoanalysis, related to confession, but distinct, is the ancient monastic practice of 'manifesting thoughts'. 'The practice of manifesting the thoughts of the heart was simple. A monk would go to a trustworthy, usually older, monk and say, for

example, "I am bothered by thoughts of envy towards someone. I wish I could see my parents. I think a lot about the happiness of the saints in heaven. I get distracted from my prayers. I wonder if I'll ever be a real monk." Sometimes the issue might be a particular sinful act, sometimes it might be something which wasn't sinful at all, but which was preoccupying. For young monks this would have been a fairly regular practice, even daily or more frequent, as they began to learn about the topography and inhabitants of their hearts.' Stewart, 'The Desert Fathers', 25–39, 143–56. For an interesting example of this practice, see, for example, Apophthegm 509 in *Sentences des pères du désert*, 184–6.

12. Cf. Mousley, *Re-humanising Shakespeare*, as well as Headlam Wells, *Shakespeare's Humanism*. Useful background can be found in Halliwell and Mousley, eds, *Critical Humanisms*. For a contrary reading of Shakespeare as an antihumanist, see Dollimore, *Radical Tragedy*.

13. Bartsch, *Mirror of the Self*, 13; cf. Nuttall, *Shakespeare the Thinker*.

14. See also William M. Hamlin's concept of the god-surrogate in Hamlin, 'Conscience and the God-Surrogate', 243 ff., and Hamlin, *Montaigne's English Journey*, 110–28.

15. Ricœur, *Oneself as Another*, 16, 4–5.

16. Ibid., 7–8, 6, 15, 38.

17. Habermas, 'Individuation through Socialization: On George Herbert Mead's Theory of Subjectivity', 152–3, in Habermas, *Postmetaphysical Thinking: Philosophical Essays*, trans. William Hohengarten (Cambridge, MA: MIT Press, 1993), 149–204; cited in Kuzner, *Open Subjects*, 47.

18. The standard overview of Buber's life and thought remains Maurice Friedman's *Martin Buber: The Life of Dialogue*, now in its fourth edition. From Buber's own work, I am especially indebted to *I and Thou* and *Between Man and Man*.

19. Lévinas freely acknowledges this influence. 'That valuation of the dialogical relation and its phenomenological irreducibility, its fitness to constitute a meaningful order that is autonomous and as legitimate as the traditional and privileged *subject–object* correlation in the operation of knowledge – that will remain the unforgettable contribution of Martin Buber's labors . . . Nothing could limit the homage due to him. Any reflection on the alterity of the other in his or her irreducibility to the objectivity of objects and the being of beings must recognize the new perspective that Buber opened – and find encouragement in it.' Lévinas, *Outside the Subject*, Chap. 3 – 'Apropos of Buber: Some Notes', 41 ff.; cited in Friedman, *Martin Buber*, 338 n. 1.

20. Cf. tragedy as a failure of 'acknowledgement' in Cavell, *Disowning Knowledge*, as well as Markell, *Bound by Recognition*.

BIBLIOGRAPHY

Adelman, Janet. *Suffocating Mothers: Fantasies of Maternal Origin in Shakespeare's Plays*, Hamlet *to* The Tempest. New York and London: Routledge, 1992.

Adler, Alfred. 'On the Origin of the Striving for Superiority and the Social Interest'. In Adler, *Superiority and Social Interest: A Collection of Later Writings*, edited by Heinz L. Ansbacher and Rowena R. Ansbacher, 29–40. London: Routledge and Kegan Paul, 1964.

Aggeler, Geoffrey. '"Sparkes of Holy Things": Neostoicism and the English Protestant Conscience'. *Renaissance and Reformation/ Renaissance et Réforme* 26 (1990): 223–40.

Alexander, Jennifer. *The Early Art of Coventry, Stratford-upon-Avon, Warwick, and Lesser Sites in Warwickshire: A Subject List of Extant and Lost Art Including Items Relevant to Early Drama*. Kalamazoo, MI: Medieval Institute Publications, 1985.

Althusser, Louis. 'Ideology and Ideological State Apparatuses (Notes towards an Investigation)'. In Althusser, *Lenin and Philosophy and Other Essays*, 127–86. Translated by Ben Brewster. New York: Monthly Review Press, 1971.

——. 'The "Piccolo Teatro": Bertolazzi and Brecht (Notes on a Materialist Theatre)'. In Althusser, *For Marx*, 129–51. Translated by Ben Brewster. London and New York: Verso, 2005.

Anders, H. R. D. *Shakespeare's Books*. Berlin: Schriften der deutschen Shakespeare-Gesellschaft Band I, 1904.

Anderson, Miranda. *The Renaissance Extended Mind*. New York: Palgrave Macmillan, 2015.

Anson, John. '*Julius Caesar*: The Politics of the Hardened Heart'. *Shakespeare Studies* 2 (1966): 11–33.

Appiah, Kwame Anthony. *The Ethics of Identity*. Princeton and Oxford: Princeton University Press, 2005.

Arendt, Hannah. *The Human Condition*. Chicago: University of Chicago Press, 1958.

——. *The Life of the Mind.* New York: Grove, 1978.

Aristotle. *Magna Moralia.* Translated by St George Stock. In Aristotle, *The Works of Aristotle Translated into English.* Edited by W. D. Ross. Vol. 9. Oxford: Oxford University Press, 1968.

——. *Nicomachean Ethics.* Translated by David Ross, J. L. Ackrill and J. O. Urmson. Oxford: Oxford University Press, 1998.

Armitage, David, Conal Condren and Andrew Fitzmaurice, 'Introduction'. In Armitage, Condren and Fitzmaurice, eds, *Shakespeare and Early Modern Political Thought*, 1–24. Cambridge: Cambridge University Press, 2009.

Atterton, Peter, Matthew Calarco and Maurice Friedman, eds. *Lévinas and Buber: Dialogue and Difference.* Pittsburgh: Duquesne University Press, 2004.

Auerbach, Erich. *Mimesis: The Representation of Reality in Western Literature.* Princeton and Oxford: Princeton University Press, 2003.

Ayres, Harry Morgan. 'Shakespeare's *Julius Caesar* in Light of Some Other Versions'. *Proceedings of the Modern Language Association* 25 (1910): 183–227.

Babcock, Barbara, ed. *The Reversible World: Symbolic Inversion in Art and Society.* Ithaca, NY: Cornell University Press, 1978.

Bacon, Francis. *The Works of Francis Bacon.* Edited by James Spedding, Robert L. Ellis and Douglas Heath. London: Houghton Mifflin, 1878.

Bakhtin, Mikhail. *Rabelais and His World.* Translated by Hélène Iswolsky. Bloomington, IN: Indiana University Press, 1984.

——. 'Toward a Reworking of the Dostoyevsky Book (1961)'. In Bakhtin, *Problems of Dostoyevsky's Poetics*, 283–304 (Appendix II). Edited and translated by Caryl Emerson. Minneapolis and London: University of Minnesota Press, 2006.

Baldwin, T. W. 'Strange fellow, iii.iii.102 ff'. In William Shakespeare, *New Variorum Troilus and Cressida*, 411–15. Edited by Harold N. Hillebrand and T. W. Baldwin. Philadelphia: J. B. Lippincott, 1953.

Barton, Anne. 'Livy, Machiavelli, and Shakespeare's *Coriolanus*'. *Shakespeare Survey* 38 (1985): 115–29.

——. '"Nature's piece 'gainst fancy": The Divided Catastrophe in *Antony and Cleopatra*'. *Inaugural Lecture* (to the Hildred Carlile Chair of English Literature in the University of London tenable at Bedford College, October 1972). Reprinted in *William Shakespeare's* Antony and Cleopatra: *Modern Critical Interpretations*, 35–56. Edited by Harold Bloom. New York, New Haven, and Philadelphia: Chelsea House, 1988.

Barton, Carlin. *Roman Honor: The Fire in the Bones.* Berkeley, CA: University of California Press, 2001.

Bartsch, Shadi. *The Mirror of the Self: Sexuality, Self-Knowledge, and the Gaze in the Early Roman Empire*. Chicago and London: University of Chicago Press, 2006.

Beacham, Richard C. *The Roman Theatre and Its Audience*. Cambridge, MA: Harvard University Press, 1991.

Beadle, Richard, ed. *The York Plays*. London: E. Arnold, 1982.

Bell, Andrew J. E. 'Cicero and the Spectacle of Power'. *Journal of Roman Studies* 87 (1997): 1–22.

Bell, Arthur H. 'Time and Convention in *Antony and Cleopatra*'. *Shakespeare Quarterly* 24 (1973): 253–64.

Bennett, Arnold. Review, *Academy* (1901), 94. In *George Bernard Shaw: The Critical Heritage.*, 92–6. Edited by T. F. Evans. London and New York: Routledge, 1976.

Berlin, Isaiah. 'The Apotheosis of the Romantic Will: The Revolt against the Myth of an Ideal World'. In Berlin, *The Proper Study of Mankind: An Anthology of Essays*, 553–80. Edited by Henry Hardy and Roger Hausheer. New York: Farrar, Straus, and Giroux, 1998.

——. *The Roots of Romanticism*. Edited by Henry Hardy. Princeton: Princeton University Press, 2001.

Billington, Sandra. *Mock Kings in Medieval Society and Renaissance Drama*. Oxford: Oxford University Press, 1991.

Blissett, William. 'Dramatic Irony in *Antony and Cleopatra*'. *Shakespeare Quarterly* 18 (1967): 151–66.

Bloom, Harold. *Falstaff: Give Me Life*. New York: Simon and Schuster, 2017.

——. *The Invention of the Human*. New York: Riverhead, 1998.

Boswell, James, ed. *The Plays and Poems of William Shakespeare, with the corrections and illustrations of various commentators, comprehending a life of the poet and an enlarged history of the stage, by the late Edmond Malone, with a new glossarial index*, 3rd variorum edition. London: Baldwin, 1821.

Bouwsma, William J. 'The Two Faces of Humanism: Stoicism and Augustinianism in Renaissance Thought'. In Bouwsma, *A Usable Past: Essays in European Cultural History*, 19–73. Berkeley and Los Angeles: University of California Press, 1990.

Bowers, Fredson. 'The Copy for Shakespeare's *Julius Caesar*'. *South Atlantic Bulletin* 43 (1977–8): 23–36.

Braden, Gordon. 'Fame, Eternity, and Shakespeare's Romans'. In *Shakespeare and Renaissance Ethics*, 37–55. Edited by Patrick Gray and John D. Cox. Cambridge: Cambridge University Press, 2014.

——. 'Plutarch, Shakespeare, and the Alpha Males'. In *Shakespeare and the Classics*, 188–208. Edited by Charles Martindale and A. B. Taylor. Cambridge: Cambridge University Press, 2004.

——. *Renaissance Tragedy and the Senecan Tradition: Anger's Privilege.* New Haven and London: Yale University Press, 1985.

Bradley, A. C. *Oxford Lectures on Poetry.* London: Macmillan, 1909.

Bradley, Marshall. 'Caska [*sic*]: Stoic, Cynic, "Christian"'. *Literature and Theology* 8 (1994): 140–56.

Brandes, Georg. *William Shakespeare: A Critical Study.* New York: William Heinemann, 1900.

Brooks, Cleanth. *The Well-Wrought Urn: Studies in the Structure of Poetry.* New York: Reynal, 1947.

Buber, Martin. *Between Man and Man.* Translated by Ronald Gregor Smith. New York: Routledge Classics, 2002.

——. *I and Thou.* Translated by Ronald Gregor Smith. New York: Scribner Classics, 2000.

Bullinger, Heinrich. *The Decades of Henry Bullinger.* Translated by H. I. Edited by Thomas Harding. 4 vols. Cambridge: Parker Society, 1849–1852.

Bullough, Geoffrey, ed. *Narrative and Dramatic Sources of Shakespeare.* London: Routledge and Kegan Paul; New York: Columbia University Press, 1964.

Burckhardt, Jacob. *The Civilization of the Renaissance in Italy.* New York: Penguin, 1990.

Burckhardt, Sigurd. *Shakespeare's Meanings.* Princeton: Princeton University Press, 1968.

Burton, Henry. 'Seneca's Idea of God'. *American Journal of Theology* 13 (1990): 350–69.

Calvin, Jean. *Calvin's Commentary on Seneca's* De clementia. Edited by Ford Lewis Battles and André Malan Hugo. Leiden: E. J. Brill, 1969.

——. *A commentarie of Iohn Calvine, vpon the first booke of Moses called Genesis: translated out of Latine into English by Thomas Tymme, minister.* Translated by Thomas Tymme. London: Henry Middleton for Iohn Harison and George Bishop, 1578.

——. *Commentaries of the First Book of Moses Called Genesis.* Translated by John King. Grand Rapids, MI: William B. Eerdman, 1948.

——. *Commentary on the Epistle of Paul the Apostle to the Romans.* Translated by John Owen. Grand Rapids, MI: William B. Eerdman, 1947.

——. *Institutes of the Christian Religion.* Edited by John T. McNeill. Translated by Ford Lewis Battles. Philadelphia: John Knox Westminster Press, 1960.

Cantor, Paul A. *Shakespeare's Roman Trilogy: Twilight of the Ancient World* (Chicago and London: University of Chicago Press, 2017).

———. *Shakespeare's Rome: Republic and Empire.* Chicago and London: University of Chicago Press, 2017; 1ˢᵗ edn 1976.

Caputo, John. *The Prayers and Tears of Jacques Derrida: Religion without Religion.* Bloomington and Indianapolis: Indiana University Press, 1997.

Carroll, Willliam C. *The Great Feast of Language in* Love's Labour's Lost. Princeton: Princeton University Press, 1976.

Cavell, Stanley. *Disowning Knowledge in Seven Plays of Shakespeare,* updated edition. Cambridge: Cambridge University Press, 2003.

Chambers, E. K. *Shakespeare: A Survey.* London: Sidgwick and Jackson, 1925.

Charney, Maurice. *Shakespeare's Roman Plays: The Function of Imagery in the Drama.* Cambridge, MA: Harvard University Press, 1961.

Chernaik, Warren. *The Myth of Rome in Shakespeare and His Contemporaries.* Cambridge: Cambridge University Press, 2011.

Chua, Amy. *Political Tribes: Group Instinct and the Fate of Nations.* London and Oxford: Bloomsbury Academic, 2018.

Cicero. *On Duties.* Translated and edited by M. T. Griffin and E. M. Atkins. Cambridge: Cambridge University Press, 1991.

———. *On the Good Life: Selected Writings from Cicero.* Translated by Michael Grant. London and New York: Penguin, 1971.

———. *On Moral Ends.* Translated by Raphael Wolf. Edited by Julia Annas. Cambridge: Cambridge University Press, 2001.

———. *Those fyve Questions which M. Tullye Cicero disputed in his manor of Tusculum . . .* Translated by J. Dolman. London: T. Marsh, 1561.

Clayton, Thomas. "'Should Brutus never taste of Portia's death but once?'": Text and Performance in *Julius Caesar'. Studies in English Literature* 23 (1983): 237–55.

Cocking, J. M. *Imagination: A Study in the History of Ideas.* Edited by Penelope Murray. London and New York: Routledge, 1991.

Codevilla, Angelo. 'America's Ruling Class – and the Perils of Revolution'. *American Spectator* (July–August 2010).

———. 'The Rise of Political Correctness'. *Claremont Review of Books* 16 (2016).

Cohen, Richard A., ed. *Face to Face with Lévinas.* Albany: State University of New York, 1986.

Colclough, David. 'Talking to the Animals: Persuasion, Counsel, and Their Discontents'. In Armitage, Condren, and Fitzmaurice, eds, *Shakespeare and Early Modern Political Thought,* 217–33. Cambridge: Cambridge University Press, 2009.

Coleridge, S. T. *Coleridge's Criticism of Shakespeare: A Selection.* Edited by R. A. Foakes. London: Athlone, 1989.

——. *Coleridge on Shakespeare: The Text of the Lectures of 1811–12*. Edited by R. A. Foakes. London and New York: Routledge, 1971.

——. *Opus Maximum*. Edited by Thomas McFarland and Nick Halmi. Princeton: Princeton University Press, 2002.

Coletti, Theresa and Gail McMurray Gibson. 'The Tudor Origins of Medieval Drama'. In *A Companion to Tudor Literature*, 228–45. Edited by Kent Cartwright. Oxford: Wiley–Blackwell, 2010.

Colish, Marcia L. *The Stoic Tradition from Antiquity to the Early Middle Ages*. Studies in the History of Christian Thought 34. Leiden: Brill, 1985.

Connolly, Joy. 'The Promise of the Classical Canon: Hannah Arendt and the Romans'. *Classical Philology* 113 (2018): 6–19.

——. *The State of Speech: Rhetoric and Political Thought in Ancient Rome*. Princeton and Oxford: Princeton University Press, 2007.

Cooper, Helen. 'Shakespeare and the Mystery Plays'. In *Shakespeare and Elizabethan Popular Culture*, 18–41. Edited by Stuart Gillespie and Neil Rhodes. Arden Shakespeare. London: Thomson Learning, 2006.

Cooper, John M. 'The *Magna Moralia* and Aristotle's Moral Philosophy'. In Cooper, *Reason and Emotion: Essays on Ancient Moral Psychology and Ethical Theory*, 195–211. Princeton: Princeton University Press, 1999.

Corbeill, Anthony. *Controlling Laughter: Political Humor in the Late Roman Republic*. Princeton: Princeton University Press, 1996.

Couchman, Gordon W. '*Antony and Cleopatra* and the Subjective Convention'. *Proceedings of the Modern Language Association* 76 (1961): 420–5.

Cox, John D. *The Devil and the Sacred in English Drama, 1350–1642*. Cambridge: Cambridge University Press, 2000.

——. *Seeming Knowledge: Shakespeare and Skeptical Faith*. Waco, TX: Baylor University Press, 2007.

——. *Shakespeare and the Dramaturgy of Power*. Princeton: Princeton University Press, 1989.

Craig, Hardin, ed. *Two Coventry Corpus Christi Plays*. London: Oxford University Press, 1957.

Curran, Kevin, ed. *Shakespeare and Judgment*. Edinburgh: Edinburgh University Press, 2017.

Daniell, David. '*Julius Caesar* in London in 1599'. In William Shakespeare, *Julius Caesar*, 7–37. Edited by Daniell. Arden Shakespeare. London: Thomas Learning, 2000.

Davidson, Clifford. 'Sacred Blood and the Late Medieval Stage'. *Comparative Drama* 31 (1997): 436–58.

Davidson, Herbert. *Alfarabi, Avicenna, and Averroes on the Active Intellect: Their Cosmologies, Theories of the Active Intellect, and Theories of the Human Intellect.* Oxford: Oxford University Press, 1992.

Davies, Sir John. *Nosce Teipsum.* London: Richard Field for John Standish, 1599.

Deneen, Patrick J. 'The Ignoble Lie: How the New Aristocracy Masks Its Privilege'. *First Things* (April 2018).

——. *Why Liberalism Failed.* New Haven: Yale University Press, 2018.

Derrida, Jacques. *Adieu: To Emmanuel Lévinas.* Translated by Pascale-Anne Brault and Michael Naas. Stanford: Stanford University Press, 1999.

——. *Of Grammatology.* Translated by Gayatri Chakravorty Spivak. Baltimore: Johns Hopkins University Press, 1976.

——. 'Violence and Metaphysics: An Essay on the Thought of Emmanuel Lévinas'. In Derrida, *Writing and Difference*, 79–153. Translated by Alan Bass. Chicago: University of Chicago Press, 1978.

Dollimore, Jonathan. *Radical Tragedy: Religion, Ideology, and Power in the Drama of Shakespeare.* Durham, NC: Duke University Press, 2004.

Donne, John. *The Sermons of John Donne.* Edited by George R. Potter and Evelyn M. Simpson. 10 vols. Berkeley and Los Angeles: University of California Press, 1953–62.

Dostoevsky, Fyodor. *The Adolescent.* Translated by Andrew MacAndrew. New York: W. W. Norton, 1981.

Dowden, Edward. *Shakespeare: A Critical Study of His Mind and Art.* London: Henry S. King and Co., 1875.

Eagleton, Terry. *Shakespeare and Society.* New York: Schocken Books, 1967.

Eliot, T. S. 'Shakespeare and the Stoicism of Seneca'. In Eliot, *Selected Essays*, 107–20. New York: Harcourt Brace and World, 1960.

——. 'What is a Classic?' In Eliot, *On Poetry and Poets*, 52–74. London: Faber & Faber, 2009.

Elton, W. R. 'Aristotle's *Nicomachean Ethics* and Shakespeare's *Troilus and Cressida*'. *Journal of the History of Ideas* 58 (1997): 331–7.

Engle, Lars. *Shakespearean Pragmatism: Market of His Time.* Chicago and London: University of Chicago Press, 1993.

Erasmus, Desiderius. *The Adages of Erasmus.* Translated by Margaret Mann Phillips. Edited by M. A. B. Mynors and William Barker. Toronto: University of Toronto Press, 2001.

——. *The Praise of Folly.* Translated by Clarence H. Miller. New Haven: Yale University Press, 2003.

Esler, Anthony. *The Aspiring Mind of the Elizabethan Younger Generation.* Durham, NC: Duke University Press, 1966.

Fagan, Madeleine, Ludovic Glorieux, Indira Hasimbegovic and Marie Suetsugu, eds. *Derrida: Negotiating the Legacy*. Edinburgh: Edinburgh University Press, 2007.

Feeney, Denis. *Literature and Religion at Rome: Cultures, Contexts, and Beliefs*. Cambridge: Cambridge University Press, 1998.

Felman, Shoshana. 'Re-reading Femininity'. *Yale French Studies* 62 (1981): 19–44.

Fernie, Ewan. *Shakespeare for Freedom: Why the Plays Matter*. Cambridge: Cambridge University Press, 2017.

——. *Shame in Shakespeare*. New York and London: Routledge, 2002.

Fiasse, Gaëlle. *L'Autre et l'amitié chez Aristote et Paul Ricoeur: analyses éthiques et ontologiques*. Louvain: Peeters, 2006.

Fichter, Andrew. '*Antony and Cleopatra*: "The time of universal peace"'. *Shakespeare Survey* 33 (1980): 99–111.

Fine, Arthur. 'Fictionalism'. *Midwest Studies in Philosophy* 18 (1993): 1–18.

Fisch, Harold. *The Biblical Presence in Shakespeare, Milton, and Blake: A Comparative Study*. Oxford: Oxford University Press, 1999.

Flaubert, Gustave. *Correspondance*. Edited by Jean Bruneau. Paris: Gallimard, 1973.

Fleissner, R. F. 'That Philosophy in *Julius Caesar* Again'. *Archiv für das Studium der neueren Sprachen und Literaturen* 222 (1985): 344–5.

Fletcher, Angus. *Allegory: The Theory of a Symbolic Mode*. Ithaca, NY: Cornell University Press, 1964.

Forde, Steven. 'On the *Alcibiades* I'. In *The Roots of Political Philosophy*, 222–39. Edited by Thomas L. Pangle. Ithaca, NY: Cornell University Press, 1987

Foucault, Michel. *Discipline and Punish: The Birth of the Prison*. Translated by Alan Sheridan. New York: Vintage, 1979.

——. *The History of Sexuality: An Introduction*. Translated by Robert Hurley. New York: Vintage, 1990.

Freud, Sigmund. *Civilization and Its Discontents*. Translated by James Strachey. New York: W. W. Norton, 1961.

Friedman, Maurice, ed. *Martin Buber and the Human Sciences*. Albany: State University of New York Press, 1996.

——. *Martin Buber: The Life of Dialogue*. London and New York: Routledge, 2002.

——. 'Martin Buber and Mikhail Bakhtin: The Dialogue of Voices and the Word That Is Spoken'. *Religion and Literature* 33 (2001): 25–36.

Fueurbach, Ludwig. *The Essence of Christianity*. Translated by Marian Evans [AKA George Eliot]. London: John Chapman, 1854.

Fukuyama, Francis. *The End of History and the Last Man*. New York: Free Press, 2006.

——. 'Identity, Immigration, and Liberal Democracy'. *Journal of Democracy* 17 (2006): 5–20.

Gavriluyk, Paul. *The Suffering of the Impassible God: The Dialectics of Patristic Thought*. Oxford: Oxford University Press, 2004.

Gerenday, Lynn de. 'Play, Ritualization, and Ambivalence in *Julius Caesar*'. *Literature and Psychology* 24 (1974): 24–33.

Gervinus, G. G. *Shakespeare Commentaries*. Translated by F. E. Burnett. 2 vols. London: Smith Elder, 1863.

Gibbon, Edward. *The Decline and Fall of the Roman Empire*. Edited by Hans-Friedrich Mueller. New York: Modern Library, 2003.

Gifford, Don, with Robert J. Seidman. *Ulysses Annotated: Notes for James Joyce's* Ulysses. Berkeley and Los Angeles: University of California Press, 2008.

Gill, Christopher. *Personality in Greek Epic, Tragedy, and Philosophy: The Self in Dialogue*. Oxford: Clarendon Press, 1996.

——. *The Structured Self in Hellenistic and Roman Thought*. Oxford: Oxford University Press, 2006.

Gillies, John. 'The Question of Original Sin in *Hamlet*'. *Shakespeare Quarterly* 64 (2013): 396–424.

Goldstone, Andrew. *Fictions of Autonomy: Modernism from Wilde to de Man*. Oxford: Oxford University Press, 2013.

Gray, John. 'The Problem of Hyper-Liberalism'. *Times Literary Supplement* (27 March 2018): 3–5.

Gray, Patrick. 'Caesar as Comic Antichrist: Shakespeare's Julius Caesar and the Medieval English Stage Tyrant'. *Comparative Drama* 50 (2016): 1–31.

——. 'Choosing between Shame and Guilt: Macbeth, Othello, Hamlet, and Lear'. In *Shakespeare and the Soliloquy in Early Modern English Drama*, 105–18. Edited by A. D. Cousins and Daniel Derrin. Cambridge: Cambridge University Press, 2018.

——. 'The Compassionate Stoic: Brutus as Accidental Hero'. *Shakespeare Jahrbuch* 152 (2016): 30–44.

——. '"HIDE THY SELFE": Hamlet, Montaigne, and Epicurean Ethics'. In Gray and Cox, eds, *Shakespeare and Renaissance Ethics*, 213–36.

——. 'Seduced by Romanticism: Re-imagining Shakespearean Catharsis'. In *The Routledge Companion to Shakespeare and Philosophy*. Edited by Craig Bourne and Emily Caddick Bourne. London and New York: Routledge, in press.

——. 'Shakespeare et la reconnaissance: l'*Anerkennung* comme interpellation intersubjective'. In *Shakespeare au risque de la philosophie*, 159–82. Edited by Pascale Drouet and Philippe Grosos. Paris: Éditions Hermann, 2017.

——. 'Shakespeare and the Other Virgil: Pity and *Imperium* in *Titus Andronicus*'. *Shakespeare Survey* 68 (2016): 46–57.

——. 'Shakespeare versus Aristotle: *Anagnorisis*, Repentance, and Acknowledgment'. *Journal of Medieval and Early Modern Studies* 49 (2019), in press.

——. 'Shakespeare vs. Seneca: Competing Visions of Human Dignity'. In *Brill's Companion to the Reception of Senecan Tragedy: Scholarly, Theatrical, and Literary Receptions*, 203–32. Edited by Eric Dodson-Robinson. Leiden and Boston: Brill, 2016.

——. 'Shakespeare and War: Honor at the Stake'. *Critical Survey* 30 (2018): 1–25.

Gray, Patrick and John D. Cox, eds. *Shakespeare and Renaissance Ethics*. Cambridge: Cambridge University Press, 2014.

Gray, Patrick and Maurice Samely, 'Shakespeare and Henri Lefebvre's "Right to the City": Subjective Alienation and Mob Violence in *Coriolanus, Julius Caesar*, and *2 Henry VI*'. *Textual Practice*, in press.

Greenblatt, Stephen. *Shakespearean Negotiations: The Circulation of Social Energy in the Renaissance*. Berkeley and Los Angeles: University of California Press, 1988.

——. *Shakespeare's Freedom*. Chicago and London: University of Chicago Press, 2010.

Guthrie, W. K. C. *The Sophists*. Cambridge: Cambridge University Press, 1971.

Habermas, Jürgen. 'Individuation through Socialization: On George Herbert Mead's Theory of Subjectivity'. In Habermas, *Postmetaphysical Thinking: Philosophical Essays*, 149–204. Translated by William Hohengarten. Cambridge, MA: MIT Press, 1993.

Hadfield, Andrew. *Shakespeare and Republicanism*. Cambridge: Cambridge University Press, 2005.

Halliwell, Martin and Andy Mousley. *Critical Humanisms: Humanist/Anti-Humanist Dialogues*. Edinburgh: Edinburgh University Press, 2003.

Hamlin, Hannibal. *The Bible in Shakespeare*. Oxford: Oxford University Press, 2013.

Hamlin, William M. 'Conscience and the God-Surrogate in Montaigne and *Measure for Measure*'. In Gray and Cox, eds, *Shakespeare and Renaissance Ethics*, 237–60.

——. *Montaigne's English Journey: Reading the Essays in Shakespeare's Day*. Oxford: Oxford University Press, 2013.

Hampton, Timothy. *Writing from History: The Rhetoric of Exemplarity in Renaissance Literature*. Ithaca, NY, and London: Cornell University Press, 1990.

Hart, David Bentley. *The Beauty of the Infinite: The Aesthetics of Christian Truth*. Grand Rapids, MI, and Cambridge, UK: Eerdmans, 2003.

——. *In the Aftermath: Provocations and Laments* (Grand Rapids, MI, and Cambridge: William B. Eerdmans, 2009).

Hazlitt, William, *Characters of Shakespeare's Plays*. New York: Wiley and Putnam, 1846.

Headlam Wells, Robin. *Shakespeare's Humanism*. Cambridge: Cambridge University Press, 2005.

Heffner, Ray L., Jr. 'The Messengers in *Antony and Cleopatra*'. *English Literary History* 43 (1976): 154–62.

Hegel, G. W. F. 'A Conversation of Three: A Scene from *Julius Caesar*'. Translated by Christiane Seile. *Clio* 7 (1978): 247–50.

——. *Documente zu Hegels Entwicklung*. Edited by Johannes Hoffmeister. Stuttgart: Frommann, 1936.

——. *The Phenomenology of Mind*. Translated by J. B. Baillie. New York: Cosimo, 2006.

Henry, Denis and Elisabeth Walker. 'The Futility of Action: A Study of Seneca's *Hercules furens*'. *Classical Philology* 60 (1965): 11–22.

Heraud, John A. *Shakespeare: His Inner Life as Intimate in His Works*. London: Maxwell, 1865.

Hillier, Russell M. '"Valour Will Weep": The Ethics of Valor, Anger, and Pity in Shakespeare's *Coriolanus*'. *Studies in Philology* 113 (2016): 358–96.

Holbrook, Peter. *Shakespeare's Individualism*. Cambridge: Cambridge University Press, 2010.

Holquist, Michael. *Dialogism: Bakhtin and His World*. London and New York: Routledge and Kegan Paul, 1990.

Huber, Jack. 'In Search of Social Interest'. In *Readings in the Theory of Individual Psychology*, 113–22. Edited by Steve Slavik and Jon Carlson. Routledge: New York and Oxford, 2006.

Hudson, H. N. *Shakespeare: His Life, Art, and Characters*. Boston: Ginn and Company, 1872.

Hughes, G. '"A World Elsewhere": *Romanitas* and Its Limitations in Shakespeare'. *English in Africa* 28 (1985): 1–20.

Hugo, François-Victor. *Oeuvres complètes de Shakespeare*. Paris: Pagnerre, 1868.

Hunt, Maurice. 'Cobbling Souls in Shakespeare's *Julius Caesar*'. In *Shakespeare's Christianity: The Protestant and Catholic Poetics of Julius Caesar, Macbeth, and Hamlet*, 111–30. Edited by Beatrice Batson. Waco, TX: Baylor University Press, 2006.

Hunter, G. K. 'A Roman Thought: Renaissance Attitudes to History Exemplified in Shakespeare and Jonson'. In *An English Miscellany: Presented to W. S. Mackie*, 93–115. Edited by B. S. Lee. Capetown and New York: Oxford University Press, 1977.

Jagendorf, Zvi. '*Coriolanus:* Body Politic and Private Parts'. *Shakespeare Quarterly* 41 (1990): 455–69.

James, D. G. *The Dream of Learning.* Oxford: Clarendon, 1965.

Jameson, Fredric. *The Political Unconscious: Narrative as Socially Symbolic Act.* New York and London: Routledge, 2001.

Jones, Emrys. *The Origins of Shakespeare.* Oxford: Clarendon, 1977.

Joyce, James. *Ulysses.* New York: Random House, 1961.

Kahn, Coppélia. *Man's Estate: Masculine Identity in Shakespeare.* Berkeley and Los Angeles: University of California Press, 1981.

——. *Roman Shakespeare: Warriors, Wounds, and Women.* New York and London: Routledge, 1997.

Kant, Immanuel. 'Idea for a Universal History from a Cosmopolitan Point of View'. Translated by Lewis White Beck. In Kant, *On History,* 11–27. Edited by Lewis White Beck. New York: Macmillan, 1963.

Kaufmann, R. J. and Clifford Ronan. 'Shakespeare's *Julius Caesar:* An Apollonian and Comparative Reading'. *Comparative Drama* 4 (1970): 18–51.

Kaula, David. '"Let us be sacrificers": Religious Motifs in *Julius Caesar'. Shakespeare Studies* 14 (1981): 197–214.

——. 'The Time Sense of *Antony and Cleopatra'. Shakespeare Quarterly* 15 (1964): 211–23.

Kayser, John R. and Ronald J. Lettieri. '"The last of all the Romans": Shakespeare's Commentary on Classical Republicanism'. *Clio* 9 (1979–80): 197–227.

Keating, James F. and Thomas Joseph White, O. P. *Divine Impassibility and the Mystery of Human Suffering.* Cambridge and Grand Rapids: William B. Eerdmans, 2009.

King, Pamela M. 'The Early English Passion Play'. *Yearbook of English Studies* 43 (2013): 69–86.

King, Pamela M. and Clifford Davidson, eds. *The Coventry Corpus Christi Plays.* Kalamazoo, MI: Medieval Institute Publications, 2000.

Kirschbaum, Leo. 'Shakespeare's Stage Blood and Its Significance'. *PMLA* 64 (1949): 517–29.

Knight, G. Wilson. *The Imperial Theme.* Oxford: Oxford University Press, 1931.

Koeppel, Ernst, 'Bottoms "Ercles" und Studleys Übersetzung von Senecas *Hercules Oetaeus'. Jahrbuch der deutschen Shakespeare-Gesellschaft* 47 (1911): 190–1.

Kotkin, Joel. *The New Class Conflict.* Candor, NY: Telos Press, 2014.

Kuzner, James. *Open Subjects: English Renaissance Republicans, Modern Selfhoods, and the Virtue of Vulnerability.* Edinburgh Critical Studies in Renaissance Culture. Edinburgh: Edinburgh University Press, 2011.

Lacan, Jacques. *Écrits*. Paris: Le Seuil, 1966.

——. *Écrits*. Translated by Bruce Fink, Héloïse Fink and Russell Grigg. New York and London: W. W. Norton, 2006.

Lake, Peter. *How Shakespeare Put Politics on the Stage: Power and Succession in the History Plays*. New Haven and London: Yale University Press, 2016.

——. 'Shakespeare's *Julius Caesar* and the Search for a Usable (Christian?) Past'. In *Shakespeare and Early Modern Religion*, 121–30. Edited by David Loewenstein and Michael Witmore. Cambridge: Cambridge University Press, 2015.

Langley, Eric. *Narcissism and Suicide in Shakespeare and His Contemporaries*. Oxford: Oxford University Press, 2009.

La Primaudaye, Pierre de. *The French Academie*. Translated by T. Bowes. London: Edmund Bollifant for G. Bishop and Ralph Newbery, 1586. Facsimile reprint, New York and Hildesheim: Georg Olms, 1972.

Lettenbauer, Wilhelm. *Russische Literaturgeschichte* (Frankfurt am Main: Humboldt-Verlag, 1955.

Levin, Harry. *The Overreacher: A Study of Christopher Marlowe*. Cambridge, MA: Harvard University Press, 1952.

Lévinas, Emmanuel. *Entre Nous: Thinking-of-the-Other*. Translated by Michael B. Smith and Barbara Harshav. New York: Columbia University Press, 1998.

——. *Outside the Subject*. Translated by Michael B. Smith. Stanford: Stanford University Press, 1994.

——. *Totality and Infinity: An Essay on Exteriority*. Translated by Alphonso Lingis. Pittsburgh: Dusquesne University Press, 1969.

Levitsky, Ruth M. 'The elements were so mix'd . . .'. *PMLA* 88 (1973): 240–5.

Lilla, Mark. *The Once and Future Liberal*. New York: Harper Collins, 2017.

Lind, Michael. 'Classless Utopia versus Class Compromise'. *American Affairs* 2 (2018): 17–34.

——. 'The New Class War'. *American Affairs* 1 (2017): 19–44.

Lipsius, Justus. *Of Constancy*. Translated by John Stradling. Edited by John Sellars. Exeter: Bristol Phoenix Press, 2006.

Long, A. A. *Stoic Studies*. Cambridge: Cambridge University Press, 1996.

Long, A. A., and D. N. Sedley, eds. *The Hellenistic Philosophers*. Translated by Long and Sedley. Cambridge: Cambridge University Press, 1987.

Lumiansky, R. M., and David Mills, eds. *The Chester Mystery Cycle*. London, New York, and Toronto: Oxford University Press for the Early English Text Society, 1974.

Lyons, John D. *Exemplum: The Rhetoric of Example in Early Modern France and Italy*. Princeton: Princeton University Press, 1990.

MacCallum, M. W. *Shakespeare's Roman Plays and Their Background*. London: St. Martin's, 1967.

Macdonald, Ronald R. 'Playing till Doomsday: Interpreting *Antony and Cleopatra*'. *English Literary Renaissance* 15 (1985): 78–99.

Machiavelli, Niccolò. *Discourses on Livy*. Translated by Harvey Mansfield and Nathan Tarcov. Chicago: University of Chicago Press, 1996.

MacIntyre, Alistair. *After Virtue: A Study in Moral Theory*. Notre Dame, IN: University of Notre Dame Press, 1984.

Mack, Maynard. *Everybody's Shakespeare: Reflections Chiefly on the Tragedies*. Lincoln, NE, and London: University of Nebraska Press, 1993.

MacMullen, Katherine Vance. 'Death Imagery in *Antony and Cleopatra*'. *Shakespeare Quarterly* 14 (1963): 399–410.

Mallin, Eric. 'Emulous Factions and the Collapse of Chivalry: *Troilus and Cressida*'. *Representations* 29 (1990): 145–79.

Marion, Jean-Luc. *Being Given: Toward a Phenomenology of Givenness*. Stanford: Stanford University Press, 2002.

Markell, Patchen. *Bound by Recognition*. Princeton and Oxford: Princeton University Press, 2003.

Markels, Julian. *The Pillar of the World:* Antony and Cleopatra *in Shakespeare's Development*. Columbus: Ohio State University Press, 1968.

Marshall, Cynthia. 'Man of Steel Done Got the Blues: Melancholic Subversion of Presence in *Antony and Cleopatra*'. *Shakespeare Quarterly* 44 (1993): 385–408.

Maus, Katharine Eisaman. *Inwardness and Theatre in the English Renaissance*. Chicago: University of Chicago Press, 1995.

Maxwell, J. C. 'Brutus's Philosophy'. *Notes and Queries* n.s. 17 (1970): 128.

Melehy, Hassan. Review of *Mirages of the Selfe: Patterns of Personhood in Ancient and Early Modern Europe* by Timothy J. Reiss. *Biography* 26 (2003): 722–5.

Meyer, A. O. *England and the Catholic Church under Queen Elizabeth*. Translated by J. R. McKee. London: Routledge, 1967.

Miles, Geoffrey. *Shakespeare and the Constant Romans*. Oxford: Oxford University Press, 1996.

Miola, Robert S. *Shakespeare's Rome*. Cambridge: Cambridge University Press, 1983.

Mitchell, Stephen A. *Relational Concepts in Psychoanalysis: An Integration*. Cambridge, MA: Harvard University Press, 1998.

Mitchell-Buck, Heather S. 'Tyrants, Tudors, and the Digby *Mary Magdalen*'. *Comparative Drama* 48 (2014): 241–59.

Moltmann, Jürgen. *The Crucified God: The Cross of Christ as Foundation and Criticism of Christian Theology*. Translated by R. A. Wilson and John Bowden. New York: Harper & Row, 1974.

Monsarrat, Gilles. *Light from the Porch: Stoicism and English Renaissance Literature*. Paris: Didier-Érudition, 1984.

Montaigne, Michel de. *The Complete Essays of Montaigne*. Translated by Donald M. Frame. Stanford: Stanford University Press, 1958.

Motto, Anna Lydia and John R. Clark. 'Maxima Virtus in Seneca's *Hercules furens*'. *Classical Philology* 76 (1981): 101–17.

Mousley, Andy. *Re-humanising Shakespeare*. Edinburgh: Edinburgh University Press, 2007.

Nelson, Eric. 'Shakespeare and the Best State of a Commonwealth'. In Armitage, Condren and Fitzmaurice, eds, *Shakespeare and Early Modern Political Thought*, 253–70. Cambridge: Cambridge University Press, 2009.

Nichols, Stephen G. Review of *Mirages of the Selfe: Patterns of Personhood in Ancient and Early Modern Europe* by Timothy J. Reiss. *Speculum* 80 (2005): 1354–7.

Nietzsche, Friedrich. *Human, All Too Human: A Book for Free Spirits*. Translated by R. J. Hollingdale. Cambridge: Cambridge University Press, 1986.

——. *Portable Nietzsche*. Edited and translated by Walter Kaufmann. New York: Viking: 1954.

——. *The Will to Power*. Translated by Walter Kaufmann and R. J. Hollingdale. New York: Vintage, 1967.

Novick, Jack, and Anne Hurry. 'Projection and Externalization'. *Journal of Child Psychotherapy* 2 (1969): 5–20.

Nussbaum, Martha. *The Fragility of Goodness: Luck and Ethics in Greek Tragedy and Philososophy*. Cambridge: Cambridge University Press, 2001.

Nuttall, A. D. *A New Mimesis*. New Haven and London: Yale University Press, 2007.

——. *Shakespeare the Thinker*. New Haven and London: Yale University Press, 2007.

——. *Two Concepts of Allegory*. New Haven: Yale University Press, 2007.

O'Connell, Michael. 'Blood Begetting Blood: Shakespeare and the Mysteries'. In *Medieval Shakespeares: Pasts and Presents*, 177–89. Edited by Ruth Morse, Helen Cooper and Peter Holland. Cambridge: Cambridge University Press, 2013.

——. *The Idolatrous Eye: Iconoclasm and Theatre in Early Modern England*. Oxford: Oxford University Press, 2000.

——. 'Vital Cultural Practices: Shakespeare and the Mysteries'. *Journal of Medieval and Early Modern Studies* 29 (1999): 149–68.

Ogden, C. K., ed. *Bentham's Theory of Fictions*. New York: Harcourt, Brace, 1932.

Ornston, D. 'On Projection – A Study of Freud's Usage'. *The Psychoanalytic Study of the Child* 33 (1978): 117–66.

Pangle, Lorraine Smith. *Aristotle and the Philosophy of Friendship*. Cambridge: Cambridge University Press, 2003.

Parker, John. *The Aesthetics of Antichrist: From Christian Drama to Christopher Marlowe*. Ithaca, NY: Cornell University Press, 2007.

Parrott, T. M. 'The "Academic Tragedy" of *Caesar and Pompey*'. *Modern Language Review* 5 (1910): 435–44.

Partee, Charles. *Calvin and Classical Philosophy*. Leiden: Brill, 1977.

——. 'Calvin and Determinism.' *Christian Scholar's Review* 5 (1975–6): 123–8.

Paster, Gail Kern. *The Body Embarassed: Drama and the Disciplines of Shame in Early Modern England*. Ithaca, NY: Cornell University Press, 1993.

——. '"In the spirit of men there is no blood': Blood as a Trope of Gender in *Julius Caesar*'. *Shakespeare Quarterly* 40 (1989): 284–98.

Patterson, Annabel. *Shakespeare and the Popular Voice*. Oxford: Basil Blackwell, 1989.

Paulin, Roger. *The Critical Reception of Shakespeare in Germany, 1682–1914: Native Literature and Foreign Genius*. Hildesheim: Olms, 2003.

Pavel, Thomas G. *The Feud of Language: A History of Structuralist Thought*. Translated by Linda Jordan and Thomas G. Pavel. Oxford: Basil Blackwell, 1989.

Pelling, C. B. 'Introduction'. In Plutarch, *Caesar*. Translated by C. B. Pelling. Oxford: Oxford University Press, 2011.

——. 'Judging Julius Caesar'. In *Julius Caesar in Western Culture*, 1–26. Edited by M. Wyke. Malden, MA: Blackwell, 2006.

Pfau, Thomas. *Minding the Modern: Human Agency, Intellectual Traditions, and Responsible Knowledge*. Notre Dame, IN: University of Notre Dame Press, 2013.

Pinciss, Gerald M. *Forbidden Matter: Religion in the Drama of Shakespeare and His Contemporaries*. Newark, DE: University of Delaware Press, 2000.

Plato, *First Alcibiades*. In Plato, *Dialogues of Plato*, 509–58. Translated by Benjamin Jowett. Vol. 4. New York: Scribner, Armstrong, 1874.

Plutarch. *Les Vies des hommes illustres de Plutarque*. Translated by Jacques Amyot, vol. 9 (Paris: Janet et Cotelle, 1818).

——. *The liues of the noble Grecians and Romans*. Translated by Thomas North. London: Richard Field for Thomas Wright, 1595.

——. *Lives*. Translated by Bernadotte Perrin. Loeb Classical Library. 11 vols. Cambridge, MA: Harvard University Press, 1914–26.

——. *Moralia*, vol. 13, part 2. Translated Harold Cherniss. Cambridge, MA, and London: Harvard University Press, 1997.

——. *Plutarch's Lives of the Noble Grecians and Romans*. Translated by Sir Thomas North. London: AMS Press, 1967.

——. *Plutarch's Lives of the Noble Grecians and Romans Englished by Sir Thomas North*. Edited by W. E. Henley. London: David Nutt, 1895–6.

Quiller-Couch, Sir Arthur. *Studies in Literature. Second Series*. Cambridge: Cambridge University Press, 1922.

Quint, David. *Epic and Empire: Politics and Generic Form from Virgil to Milton*. Princeton: Princeton University Press, 1993.

——. 'Introduction'. In William Shakespeare, *Antony and Cleopatra*, xi–xxvi. Edited by David Quint. Longman Cultural Editions. New York: Pearson, 2008.

——. 'The Tragedy of Nobility on the Seventeenth-Century Stage'. *Modern Language Quarterly* 67 (2006): 7–30.

Rabkin, Norman. *Shakespeare and the Common Understanding*. New York: Free Press, 1967.

Rackin, Phyllis. The Pride of Shakespeare's Brutus'. *Library Chronicle* 32 (1966): 18–33.

——. *Stages of History: Shakespeare's English Chronicles*. Ithaca, NY: Cornell University Press, 1990.

Rebhorn, Wayne A. 'The Crisis of the Aristocracy in *Julius Caesar*'. *Renaissance Quarterly* 43 (1990): 75–111.

Reiss, Timothy J. *Mirages of the Selfe: Patterns of Personhood in Ancient and Early Modern Europe*. Stanford: Stanford University Press, 2003.

Richards, I. A. '*Troilus and Cressida* and Plato'. In Richards, *Speculative Instruments*, 198–213. London: Routledge and Kegan Paul, 1955.

Ricœur, Paul. *The Course of Recognition*. Translated by David Pellauer. Cambridge, MA: Harvard University Press, 2005.

——. *Oneself as Another*. Translated by Kathleen Blamey. Chicago: University of Chicago Press, 1995.

Rist, J. M. *Stoic Philosophy*. Cambridge: Cambridge University Press, 1977.

Ronan, Clifford. '*Antike Roman*': *Power Symbology and the Roman Play in Early Modern England, 1585–1635*. Athens, GA, and London: University of Georgia Press, 1995.

Rose, Gillian. *Judaism and Modernity: Philosophical Essays*. Oxford: Blackwell, 1993.

——. *Mourning Becomes the Law: Philosophy and Representation*. Cambridge: Cambridge University Press, 1996.

Rose, Mark. 'Conjuring Caesar: Ceremony, History, and Authority in 1599'. *English Literary Renaissance* 19 (1989): 291–304.

Rossiter, A. P. *Angel with Horns: Fifteen Lectures on Shakespeare*. Harlow: Longman, 1989; 1st edn 1961.

Rossky, William. 'Imagination in the English Renaissance: Psychology and Poetic'. *Studies in the Renaissance* 5 (1958): 49–73.

Rousseau, Jean-Jacques. *Émile*. Translated by Barbara Foxley. London: Dent, 1982; 1st edn 1911.

Russell, Daniel C. 'Virtue as "Likeness to God" in Plato and Seneca'. *Journal of the History of Philosophy* 42 (2004): 241–60.

Sacharoff, M. 'Suicide and Brutus' Philosophy in *Julius Caesar*'. *Journal of the History of Ideas* 33 (1972): 115–22.

Sallust. *Sallust*. Translated by J. C. Rolfe. Loeb Classical Library. Cambridge, MA: Harvard University Press, 1999.

Salmon, J. H. M. 'Stoicism and Roman Example: Seneca and Tacitus in Jacobean England'. *Journal of the History of Ideas* 50 (1989): 199–225.

Sams, Henry W. 'Anti-Stoicism in Seventeenth- and Eighteenth-Century England'. *Studies in Philology* 41 (1944): 65–78.

Sandel, Michael J. *Democracy's Discontent: America in Search of a Public Philosophy*. Cambridge, MA, and London: Harvard University Press, 1998.

Sandler, J., A. Holder and D. Meers. 'The Ego Ideal and the Ideal Self'. *Psychoanalytic Study of the Child* 18 (1963): 139–58.

Sartre, Jean-Paul. *Being and Nothingness*. Translated by Hazel Barnes. London and New York: Routledge, 2003.

Scheingorn, Pamela. 'The Moment of the Resurrection in the Corpus Christi Plays'. *Medievalia et Humanistica* n.s. 11 (1982): 111–29.

Schlegel, A. W. von. *A Course of Lectures on Dramatic Arts and Literature*. Translated by John Black and A. J. W. Morrison. London: George Bell & Sons, 1879.

Schoenbaum, Samuel. *Shakespeare: A Documentary Life*. New York: Oxford University Press in association with Scolar Press, 1977.

Schreyer, Kurt A. *Shakespeare's Material Craft: Remnants of the Mysteries on the London Stage*. Ithaca, NY: Cornell University Press, 2014.

Sellars, John. *Stoicism*. Chesham: Acumen, 2006.

Selleck, Nancy. *The Interpersonal Idiom in Shakespeare, Donne and Early Modern Culture*. New York: Palgrave Macmillan, 2008.

Seneca. *Ad Lucilium epistulae morales*. Translated by Richard M. Gummere. Loeb Classical Library. 3 vols. London: William Heinemann; New York: G. P. Putnam's Sons, 1917.

——. *Hercules Oetaeus*. Edited and translated by John G. Fitch. Loeb Classical Library. Cambridge, MA: Harvard University Press, 2004.

——. *Hercules Oetaeus*. Translated by John Studley. In Seneca, *Seneca his tenne tragedies, translated into Englysh*, 187–218. Edited by Thomas Newton. London: Thomas Marsh, 1581.

——. *Moral Essays*. Translated by John W. Basore. Loeb Classical Library. 2 vols. Cambridge, MA: Harvard University Press; London: William Heineman, 1975.

——. *Opera omnia*. Edited by Desiderius Erasmus. Basel: Johannes Froben, 1529.

Les Sentences des pères du désert: Série des anonymes. Solesmes-Bellefontaine: Abbayes, 1985.

Sextus Empiricus. *Adversus Mathematicos*. Translated by R. G. Bury, Cambridge, MA, and London: Harvard University Press and William Heinemann, 1959.

Shaheen, Naseeb. *Biblical References in Shakespeare's Plays*. Newark, NJ: University of Delaware Press, 1999.

Shakespeare, William. *The Arden Shakespeare Complete Works*. Edited by Richard Proudfoot, Ann Thompson and David Scott Kastan. London: Cengage Learning, 2002.

Shaw, George Bernard. *Prefaces by George Bernard Shaw*. London: Constable, 1934.

Simmons, J. L. *Shakespeare's Pagan World*. Charlottesville: University Press of Virginia, 1973.

Sinfield, Alan. *Faultlines: Cultural Materialism and the Politics of Dissident Reading*. Berkeley and Los Angeles: University of California Press, 1992.

——. 'Hamlet's Special Providence'. *Shakespeare Survey* 33 (1980): 89–97.

Skinner, Quentin. *Liberty Before Liberalism* Cambridge: Cambridge University Press, 1998.

Smith, Sheila. '"This great solemnity": A Study of the Presentation of Death in *Antony and Cleopatra*'. *English Studies* 45 (1964): 163–76.

Smith, Warren D. 'The Duplicate Revelation of Portia's Death'. *Shakespeare Quarterly* 4 (1953): 153–61.

Sohmer, Steve. *Shakespeare's Mystery Play: The Opening of the Globe Theatre, 1599*. Manchester: Manchester University Press, 1999.

Sorabji, Richard. *Emotion and Peace of Mind: From Stoic Agitation to Christian Temptation*. Oxford: Oxford University Press, 2000.

——. *Self: Ancient and Modern Insights about Individuality, Life, and Death*. Oxford: Clarendon Press, 2006.

Spakowski, R. E. 'Deification and Myth-Making in the Play *Julius Caesar*'. *The University Review* 36 (1969): 135–40.

Sprengnether, Madelon. 'Annihilating Intimacy in *Coriolanus*'. In *Women in the Middle Ages and the Renaissance: Literary and Historical Perspectives*, 89–101. Edited by M. B. Rose. Syracuse: Syracuse University Press, 1986.

Spriet, Pierre. 'Amour et politique: le discourse de l'autre dans *Julius Caesar*'. In *Coriolan: Théâtre*, 227–9. Edited by Jean-Paul Debax and Yves Peyré. Toulouse: Université de Toulouse-Le Mirail, 1984.

Stempel, Daniel. 'The Transmigration of the Crocodile'. *Shakespeare Quarterly* 7 (1956): 56–72.

Stevens, Martin and A. C. Cawley. *The Towneley Plays*. London, New York and Toronto: Oxford University Press for the Early English Text Society, 1994.

Stewart, Columba, O.S.B. 'The Desert Fathers on Radical Self-Honesty', *Sobornost/ECR* 12 (1990): 25–39.

Stirling, Brents. '*Julius Caesar* in Revision'. *Shakespeare Quarterly* 13 (1962): 187–205.

——. *Unity in Shakespearean Tragedy*. New York: Columbia University Press, 1956.

Stoller, Robert J. 'The "Bedrock" of Masculinity and Femininity: Bisexuality'. In *Psychoanalysis and Women*, 273–84. Edited by Jean Baker Miller. New York: Penguin, 1973.

Stone, Lawrence. *The Crisis of the Aristocracy, 1558–1641*. Oxford: Oxford University Press, 1974.

Strawson, Galen. *Things that Bother Me: Death, Freedom, The Self, Etc.* New York: New York Review of Books, 2018.

Strier, Richard. *The Unrepentant Renaissance: From Petrarch to Shakespeare to Milton*. Chicago and London: University of Chicago Press, 2011.

Sugimura, N. K. 'Two Concepts of Reality in *Antony in Cleopatra*'. In *Thinking with Shakespeare: Comparative and Interdisciplinary Essays for A. D. Nuttall*, 73–92. Edited by William Poole and Richard Scholar. London: Legenda, 2007.

Swinburne, A. C. *Shakespeare*. Oxford: Oxford University Press, 1909.

Syme, Ronald. *The Roman Revolution*. Oxford: Oxford University Press, 1939.

Taylor, Charles. 'The Politics of Recognition'. In *Multiculturalism: Examining the Politics of Recognition*, 25–73. Edited by Amy Gutmann. Princeton: Princeton University Press, 1994.

——. *Sources of the Self: The Making of Modern Identity*. Cambridge, MA: Harvard University Press, 1989.

Taylor, Gary. 'Swounds Revisited: Theatrical, Editorial, and Literary Expurgation'. In *Shakespeare Reshaped, 1606–23*, 51–106. Edited by Taylor and John Jowett. Oxford: Oxford University Press, 1993.

Thomas, Vivian. *Shakespeare's Roman Worlds*. London and New York: Routledge, 1989.

Thornton, Weldon. *Allusions in Ulysses: An Annotated List*. Chapel Hill: University of North Carolina Press, 1982.

Thorsteinsson, Runar M. *Roman Stoicism and Roman Christianity: A Comparative Study of Ancient Morality*. Oxford: Oxford University Press, 2010.

Tilmouth, Christopher. 'Passion and Intersubjectivity in Early Modern Literature'. In *Passions and Subjectivity in Early Modern Culture*, 13–32. Edited by Brian Cummings and Freya Sierhuis. Farnham: Ashgate, 2013.

——. *Passion's Triumph over Reason: A History of the Moral Imagination from Spenser to Rochester*. Oxford: Oxford University Press, 2007.

Trinkaus, Charles. *The Poet as Philosopher*. New Haven: Yale University Press, 1979.

Vaihinger, Hans. *The Philosophy of 'As If'*. Translated by C. K. Ogden. London: Routledge and Kegan Paul, 1924.

du Vair, Guillaume. *The Moral Philosophie of the Stoicks*. Translated by Thomas James. Edited by Rudolf Kirk. New Brunswick, NJ: Rutgers University Press, 1951.

Vawter, Marvin L. '"After their fashion": Cicero and Brutus in *Julius Caesar*'. *Shakespeare Studies* 9 (1976): 205–19.

——. '"Division 'tween our souls": Shakespeare's Stoic Brutus'. *Shakespeare Studies* 7 (1974): 174–95.

——. '*Julius Caesar*: Rupture in the Bond'. *Journal of English and Germanic Philology* 72 (1973): 311–28.

Velz, John W. 'Caesar's Deafness'. *Shakespeare Quarterly* 22 (1971): 400–1.

Vermeule, Adrian. 'Integration from Within'. *American Affairs* 2 (2018): 202–13.

Waith, Eugene M. *The Herculean Hero in Marlowe, Chapman, Shakespeare, and Dryden*. London: Chatto & Windus, 1962.

Watson, Robert N., 'Coriolanus and the "Common Part"'. *Shakespeare Survey* 69 (2016): 181–97.

——. *The Rest is Silence: Death as Annihilation in the English Renaissance* (Berkeley and Los Angeles: University of California Press, 1994).

——. *Shakespeare and the Hazards of Ambition*. Cambridge, MA: Harvard University Press, 1984.

Weinandy, Thomas G. 'Does God Suffer?' *First Things* 117 (2001): 35–41.

White, Bob. '*Troilus and Cressida* as Brechtian Theatre'. In *Shakespearean Continuities: Essays in Honor of E. A. J. Honigmann*, 221–39. Edited by John Batchelor, Tom Cain and Claire Lamont. New York: Macmillan, 1997.

White, Richard Grant. *Studies in Shakespeare*. Boston and New York: Houghton Mifflin, 1886.

Whittington, Leah. *Renaissance Suppliants: Poetry, Antiquity, Reconciliation*. Oxford: Oxford University Press, 2016.

Wikander, Matthew. *The Play of Truth and State: Historical Drama from Shakespeare to Brecht*. Baltimore: Johns Hopkins University Press, 1986.

Williams, Robert R. *Hegel's Ethics of Recognition*. Berkeley, Los Angeles and London: University of California Press, 1997.

——. *Recognition: Fichte and Hegel on the Other*. Albany: State University of New York Press, 1992.

——. *Tragedy, Recognition, and the Death of God: Studies in Hegel and Nietzsche*. Oxford: Oxford University Press, 2012.

Wilson, Edwin, ed. *Shaw on Shakespeare: An Anthology of Bernard Shaw's Writings on the Plays and Productions of Shakespeare*. London: Cassell, 1962.

Wolfson, Harry Austryn. 'Crescas on the Problem of Divine Attributes'. *Jewish Quarterly Review* 7 (1916): 1–44.

Wuthnow, Robert. *The Left Behind: Decline and Rage in Rural America*. Princeton: Princeton University Press, 2018.

Xenophanes of Colophon. *Fragments*. Translated and edited by J. H. Lesher. Toronto: University of Toronto Press, 1992.

Zander, Horst, ed. *Julius Caesar: New Critical Essays*. New York: Routledge, 2005.

INDEX

References to notes are indicated by n. References to *Julius Caesar* and *Antony and Cleopatra* refer to the Introduction text only.